CONTEMPORARY SOCIAL AND SOCIOLOGICAL THEORY

SECOND EDITION

To Carla Freeman for going above and beyond—you made
the impossible task of four books in a year possible and, more importantly, fun.

CONTEMPORARY SOCIAL AND SOCIOLOGICAL THEORY

Visualizing Social Worlds

SECOND EDITION

Kenneth Allan

*University of North Carolina
at Greensboro*

Los Angeles | London | New Delhi
Singapore | Washington DC

For information:

Pine Forge Press
An Imprint of SAGE Publications, Inc.
2455 Teller Road
Thousand Oaks, California 91320
E-mail: order@sagepub.com

SAGE Publications India Pvt. Ltd.
B 1/I 1 Mohan Cooperative
  Industrial Area
Mathura Road, New Delhi 110 044
India

SAGE Publications Ltd.
1 Oliver's Yard
55 City Road
London EC1Y 1SP
United Kingdom

SAGE Publications Asia-Pacific Pte. Ltd.
33 Pekin Street #02-01
Far East Square
Singapore 048763

Printed in the United States of America

Library of Congress Cataloging-in-Publication Data

Allan, Kenneth, 1951-
Contemporary social and sociological theory : visualizing social worlds / Kenneth Allan.—2nd ed.
       p. cm.
Includes bibliographical references and index.
ISBN 978-1-4129-7820-0 (pbk.)
    1. Sociology. 2. Sociology—Philosophy. 3. Sociologists. I. Title.

HM585.A52 2011
301.01—dc22   2010005108

This book is printed on acid-free paper.

10   11   12   13   14   10 9 8 7 6 5 4 3 2

Acquisitions Editor:	David Repetto
Editorial Assistants:	Nancy Scrofano and Maggie Stanley
Production Editor:	Carla Freeman
Typesetter:	C&M (P) Digitals Ltd.
Proofreader:	Cheryl Rivard
Indexer:	Molly Hall
Cover Designer:	Bryan Fishman
Marketing Manager:	Erica DeLuca

Contents

Introduction (to be read):
The Real You

This book is about you and society. When I say it's about you, I'm not necessarily talking about the personal you. I'm primarily talking about the social, theoretical you, about you as a specific kind of person living in the beginning decades of the twenty-first century. That person has changed dramatically since the start of modernity. As Stuart Hall (1996) explains, in the history of the modern world we've experienced three different kinds of persons: "The Enlightenment subject was based on a conception of the human person as a fully centered, unified individual, endowed with the capacities of reason, consciousness, and action" (p. 597). The next type of person, the sociological subject, came about in the latter half of the nineteenth and beginning years of the twentieth centuries. With it came the realization that "this inner core of the subject was not autonomous and self-sufficient, but was formed in relation to 'significant others'" (p. 597). This is the self that people like Sigmund Freud and George Herbert Mead explained. This person was no longer completely autonomous, but formed in dynamic relation with society: "Identity thus stitches . . . the subject into the structures [of society]" (p. 598). Things changed again for the person beginning in the 1980s; and these changes continue to inform our possibilities today. Of this person Hall says, "The subject, previously experienced as having a unified and stable identity, is becoming fragmented; composed, not of a single, but of several sometimes contradictory or unresolved, identities" (p. 598).

As you'll see as we journey through this book, there are many factors that have led theorists to think this way about you and society. One reason is globalization, which "brings into question foundational concepts—'society' and the 'nation state'" (McGrew, 1996, p. 468). The reason globalization is important for understanding you and society is that modernity rendered "national just about all crucial features of society: authority, identity, territory, security, law, and market" (Sassen, 2007, p. 15). As we'll see in Chapter 1, modern society was defined in direct reference to nation-states. If globalization entails processes and creates social connections that transcend national borders, then the modern idea of society may no longer hold. And if that idea no longer holds, then all of the important identities that you hold—like race, gender, sexuality, family, class, and religion—have changed as well. Each and every one of those is/was defined with reference to modern states.

Clearly I'm still talking about the theoretical you. But, what are the implications of these changes for the real you, the personal you, the one you directly experience? The implications are profound precisely because what we're talking about is theory. Theory isn't opinion; nor is theory the opposite of facts, as in "It's only a theory." Theory explains how things work or came into existence; and theories are constantly being held up to scrutiny by experts, researchers, and scholars. Thus theories give us eyes to see and understand what's happening in the world. So, in a very real way the theoretical you and the personal you are intimately connected, because these theories explain the social context wherein you experience the real you. The *theoretical you* explains the context of personhood wherein you experience the *real you.*

This book, however, isn't a social psychology text; thus most of the chapters aren't directly about identities, selves, or you. But the person, and the way he or she thinks, feels, and acts, is unavoidably implied in theories about society. This relationship between you and society has been important since the dawn of modernity. The political and economic philosophies of the Enlightenment were centered on a particular kind of person. One way to see this is to remember that under a premodern monarchy the main political person available was "subject," one who is under the dominion of another. In modernity the main political person that's available is "citizen," one who holds the power to govern. And the experiences and self-concept of a citizen are vastly different than that of a subject. Science, too, was founded on the idea of a specific kind of person: a reasoning individual capable of discovering the fundamental laws of the empirical universe. The theories in this book, then, are vitally important for you because they explain the social world in which you live, move, and have your being. Most significantly, they can help you understand what you experience as "freedom," and they can explain the possibilities of democracy and politics in the twenty-first century.

Plan of the Book

The book falls into four main sections. *Part I: Introductions* sets the general dialogue of the book. In Chapter 1, we'll look at how the time we call modernity began. We will see that modern times began with intentional purpose. And, more importantly, modernity brought with it a way of knowing that is valued above all others: science. Understanding these issues is important for grasping the critiques that feminism and others bring, for understanding theories that speak of globalization and democracy, and for understanding why you and education are important parts of the projects of modernity. This section also explains what theory is and does. You must understand theory in order to think and write theoretically (which might be a handy thing to know for a test or paper). "Chapter 2: Defining Moments in Twentieth-Century Theory" explains the impact that Talcott Parsons and the Frankfurt School of critical theory have had on social thought. Parsons gives us the primary question of sociology (social order), he gives us a way of answering that question that is undoubtedly part of your cultural capital as a student of society; and, more importantly, he crystallized the social scientific approach to theory and canonized the classics (Marx, Weber, and Durkheim), at least for American sociology. And, as we'll see, Parsons significantly set the theoretical agendas of many of the other theorists in this book. The second defining moment, the Frankfurt School and the advent of critical theory, will set the stage for us to understand the critique of positivism and culture that we'll find scattered throughout the book. And it sets the stage for our theorist who most directly addresses modern democracy, Jürgen Habermas.

Part II: The Social Situation and Its People introduces us to four theories that explain what happens when you and I are in face-to-face social encounters. This section will be the one most explicitly concerned with you—it should provide you with ideas to carry with you through the other chapters, ideas that will help you situate yourself in the social context. We'll also see that most of these theories are formed at least in part as responses to Parsons.

In *Part III: Social Structures and Systems,* each theorist talks about structure differently—there are different kinds of social structures that pattern our relationships and actions. The structures we'll be talking about here are the ones that have been central in sociological discourse and social life: race, gender, and class. *Part III* also has two systems theories. Parsons' work is probably the best-known systems approach to understanding society in the twentieth century. But Parsons' understanding of society and systems was contained within national boundaries. The systems theories in Chapters 9 and 10 are quite different: Both are cast at the world level rather than national, and one of the theories gives us a completely new understanding about how social connections (i.e., society) are made.

In *Part IV: Modernity and Postmodernity,* we'll consider the possibilities that we are no longer modern, or if we are, the projects of modernity are either disabled or out of control. Here we'll also talk about the possibility that culture has lost meaning. The theories in Chapters 13 and 14 are perhaps the most provocative and disturbing of the book: They question the very foundations of human reality. And in *Part V: Identity Politics,* we look at how race, gender, and sexuality are formed and expressed in a society infused with capitalism, mass media, advertising, social science, and dark Freudian ideas of sex.

Do Yourself a Favor: Use This Book!

Let me start this section with a story. This past semester, I was using the first edition of this text in my theory course. I employ discussion rather than lecture to teach the course, and I emphasize questions. So, every time we started a new theorist I would ask, "What are the theorist's central questions? What is the theory meant to explain?" A 20- to 30-minute lively discussion would follow with the students arguing back and forth about several possibilities. About eight weeks into the semester, one student stopped the discussion and gave two questions for the theorist we were talking about. He then looked up at me and said, "It's in the book." There's a lot in this book that will help you, but you need to look for and use them. (You'll find theorist's questions under the *Theorist's Digest.*)

First, notice that every chapter begins with an outline; use it as a guide to the rest of the chapter. The *Concepts and Theory* portions of the chapter usually correspond to specific theories. For example, in Chapter 3 you'll see three different *Concepts and Theory* sections: emergent meanings, self and action, and society and sociology. So, if you want to know what Blumer says about how the self is formed, you know where to look. The *Theorist's Digest* section provides you with a brief biography of the theorist, his or her central questions, a list of key terms, and "Simply Stated," which is an explanation of the theory in as few words as possible. Use these sections well. If you get lost in the chapter, remind yourself what the theorist is explaining (his or her questions), and look again at the simple statement of the theory; it can help orient you through the complexities. And look for the key terms throughout the text. You'll find them either *italicized* or placed in **bold**. The terms in **bold** are defined in the Glossary, which you'll find in the back of the book. (I have a story about definitions that's similar to the one about questions; except that class didn't ever find the Glossary.)

You'll also see a *Summary* section, which can be used as review or to orient your thoughts before reading the chapter. But you must read the entire chapter, and I recommend you read it at least three or four times. This is probably the easiest theory book to read that's on the market; but, even so, you should read the chapters in their entirety several times. Please believe me—theory isn't like any other material. It's abstract and systematic. You really can't understand one part of the theory by itself—all theoretical ideas are ideas within a context of an argument, so you need to be able to grasp the theory all together. (This is one reason why I focus on theorists rather than topics in the book.)

Another feature you'll find is *Taking the Perspective*. This feature is new in this edition, and it gives you an overview of the theorist's perspective, along with historical developments. All theories are written from specific perspectives; and different theories come out of different ways of seeing the world (it's why sociology and psychology usually see different things when looking at a person). You are undoubtedly familiar with three of them: structural-functionalism, conflict, and symbolic interaction; they're the ones usually given in introductory texts. But as you'll find, there are many more perspectives in sociology. Understanding the perspective will help you understand the theory as a whole, and it is what allows a theorist to do work that's similar but different from a well-known scholar (like "Marxian" or "Durkheimian" theories). Some of the theorists won't have a *Perspective* section. That's usually because I've already explained the perspective elsewhere. For example, Dorothy Smith (Chapter 16) is a feminist, and I explain that perspective in Chapter 7.

And, finally, the *Building Your Theory Toolbox* section has a number of resources to help you go beyond what's presented in the book. In "Learning More," I list the more important primary and secondary works for an author. "Check It Out" highlights some of the more important or interesting topics from the chapter and points you to resources. "Seeing the World" is pretty important as it contains what I think of as student learning goals. This section provides excellent reviews for tests and papers. In fact, if you take a course from me, you'll see that I take test and paper questions directly from this section. "Engaging the World" is focused on you using the theories to engage and or understand your world theoretically. Sometimes the engagement is scholastic, sometimes it's just interesting, but it can also be strategic. For example, after I discovered Blau's exchange theory (Chapter 6) in graduate school I used it to reduce the amount of power my professors had over me. The last is "Weaving the Threads" and in that section I ask you to begin thinking about ways the different theories can complement or critique one another.

I'd like to close this introduction and open the rest of the book with a quote from Angela Davis, a political activist from the 1960s and now retired professor, University of California, Santa Cruz. Speaking to the graduating class of Grinnell College, Professor Davis (2007) captures my hope for you:

> I hope that you will treasure the approaches and ways of thinking that you have learned more than the facts you have accumulated. For you will never discover a scarcity of facts, and these facts will be presented in such a way as to veil the ways of thinking embedded in them. And so to reveal these hidden ways of thinking, to suggest alternate frameworks, to imagine better ways of living in evolving worlds, to imagine new human relations that are freed from persisting hierarchics, whether they be racial or sexual or geopolitical—yes, I think this is the work of educated beings. I might then ask you to think about education as the practice of freedom. Freedom, then, becomes not a state for which one yearns, but rather an incessant struggle to remake our lives, our relations, our communities, and our futures.

Acknowledgments

I'm fortunate to work with what must be the best publishing team in the business. I cannot imagine a more creative, supportive, and patient group. You guys make all this seem like fun (it must be magic). I am and always will be thankful to my first editing team at Pine Forge: Jerry Westby and Ben Penner—without you none of this would exist. And my continuing respect and gratitude to Teresa Herlinger: You are still present in every word. I've also had the privilege of working closely with Carla Freeman on these editions —here's to chocolate and surf always. My thanks to David Repetto for getting it done; to Leah Mori for focusing our attention on the important things; to Karen Ehrmann for picking up the pieces; to Laureen Gleason for getting me the right stuff; and my thanks to Nancy Scrofano, you will be missed. I also want to especially acknowledge the students who have provided support and comments about the first edition. You guys make it all worthwhile. Finally, my thanks to the reviewers who took time out from busy schedules to provide valuable feedback and insights:

John Bartkowski
University of Texas at San Antonio

Mary Ellen Batiuk
Wilmington College

Lisa New Freeland
Eastern Illinois University

Stan Knapp
Brigham Young University

Michael A. Long
Colorado State University

David G. Wagner
University at Albany– SUNY

Photo Credits

Thanks to all of the rights holders of the following photographs:

Chapter 2: Talcott Parsons. © The Granger Collection.

Chapter 3: Herbert Blumer. Reprinted with permission of the American Sociological Association.

Chapter 4: Harold Garfinkel. Reprinted with permission of Bernard Leach, Manchester Metropolitan University.

Chapter 5: Erving Goffman. Collections of the University of Pennsylvania Archives.

Chapter 6: George C. Homans. Copyright © American Sociological Association.

Peter Blau. Courtesy of Judith Blau.

Randall Collins. Courtesy of Randall Collins.

Chapter 7: William Julius Wilson. Reprinted with permission of the American Sociological Association.

Janet Saltzman Chafetz. Courtesy of Henry Chafetz.

Chapter 8: Pierre Bourdieu. © Alain Nogues/Sygma/Corbis.

Chapter 9: Immanuel Wallerstein. Courtesy of Immanuel Wallerstein.

Chapter 10: Manuel Castells. Photograph by Maggie Smith (2005).

Chapter 11: Jürgen Habermas. © Ralph Orlowski/Reuters/Corbis.

Chapter 12: Anthony Giddens. Courtesy of Anthony Giddens.

Chapter 13: Michel Foucault. © Bettmann/Corbis.

Chapter 14: Jean Baudrillard. Copyright © Res Stolkiner. European Graduate School EGS, Saas-Fee, Switzerland, 2002.

Chapter 15: Cornel West. © Richard Howard/Time Life Pictures/Getty Images.

Chapter 16: Dorothy E. Smith. Courtesy of Dorothy E. Smith.

Chapter 17: Judith Butler. Courtesy of Judith Butler.

Part I

Introductions

In the Beginning There Was Modernity

This is, of course, a text about contemporary social and sociological theory. However, it is extremely difficult, if not impossible, to understand contemporary theory without first understanding modernity and the conditions under which the social disciplines were founded. The words *modern* and *modernity* are used in a number of different ways. Sometimes *modern* is used in the same way as *contemporary* or *up-to-date*. Other times it's used as an adjective, as in modern art or modern architecture. In the social disciplines, there has been a good bit of debate about the idea of modernity. Some argue that we are no longer modern, others that we never were, and still others that we are living in some different form of modernity, like liquid modernity. We're not going to enter into this debate directly; but the existence of the debate is important for us. The reason it's important is that this debate has implications for the kind of person we can be and the kind of society we can have. Whether we realize it or not, those are the very issues that sociology addresses.

In this book, we're going to begin thinking about society and our place in it using a specific view of modernity, one that assumes a rational actor and an ordered world that can be directed. It's important to note that this approach to understanding modernity and knowledge is just one of many possibilities. So, this story of modernity is simply our beginning; it's our touchstone, the place from which to organize our thinking. As you move through the book, you'll find that many contemporary theorists point to social factors and processes that make it difficult to be a reasoned social actor. There are also theories that indicate that the social world may not be ordered, but rather, is a kind of chaotic system. And, more fundamentally, the social world may not be objective, but may simply be a subjective attribution of meaning. Further, some critical theorists argue that this idea of modern knowledge is intrinsically linked to power and is thus oppressive. That's why we are starting with this view of modernity and modern knowledge: It's the ideal, and it's the one that many people assume to be alive and well in modern democracy.

The Making of Modernity

As a historical period, *modernity* began in the seventeenth century and was marked by significant social changes, such as massive movements of populations from small local communities to large urban settings, a high division of labor, high commodification and use of rational markets, the widespread use of bureaucracy, and large-scale integration through national identities—such as "American"—to unite differences like gender, race, religion, and so forth. In general, the defining institutions of modernity are nation-states and mass democracy, capitalism, science, and mass media; the historical moments that set the stage for modernity are the Renaissance, Enlightenment, Reformation, the American and French Revolutions, and the Industrial Revolution.

But modernity is more than a period of time; it's a way of knowing that is rooted in the Enlightenment and positivism. The Enlightenment was a European intellectual movement that began around the time Sir Isaac Newton published *Principia Mathematica* in 1686, though the beginnings go back to Bacon, Hobbes, and Descartes. The people creating this intellectual revolution felt that the use of reason and logic would enlighten the world in ways that fate and faith could not. The principal targets of this movement were the Church and the monarchy, and the ideas central to the Enlightenment were progress, empiricism, freedom, and tolerance.

The ideas of *progress* and *empiricism* are especially significant. Prior to the Enlightenment, the idea of progress wasn't important. The reason for this is that the dominant worldview had its basis in tradition and religion. Traditional knowledge is by definition embedded in long periods of time and thus resists change and progress. Religion is based upon revelation, which, again by definition, makes our learning about the world dependent upon God's disclosure and not upon us developing or advancing it. In order for the modern idea of progress to make sense, the universe had to be seen in a specific light. Rather than the world being a mix of the physical and the spiritual, as with religion or magic, it had to be understood as simply empirical, and our knowing of this world dependent upon our own efforts, our own observations using our five senses, and our own gathering of evidence. Traditional knowledge is valid if it stands the test of time; religious knowledge is valid if it is revealed by God; but modern knowledge is valid if and only if it is empirically tested and works.

The idea of progress is also tied up with what's called *positivism*. The basic tenet of positivism is that theology and metaphysics are imperfect ways of knowing and that positive knowledge is based upon facts and universal laws. The ideal model for positivistic knowledge is science: *Science* assumes the universe is empirical, that it operates according to law-like principles, and that human beings can discover these laws. Further, the reasons to discover these laws are to explain, predict, and control phenomena for the benefit of humankind. Scientific knowledge is built up or accumulated as theories are tested and the untenable parts discarded. New theories are built up from the previous and those in turn are tested, and so on. It's essential for you to note that this business of testing is one characteristic that separates positivistic knowledge from all previous forms: *The basis of accepting knowledge isn't faith but doubt.* It's this characteristic of positivistic knowledge that gives progress its modern meaning.

Modernity's Two Projects

Progress in modernity—and thus the intent of modern knowledge—is focused on two main arenas: technical and social. The *technical project* of modernity is generally the domain of science. In science, knowledge is used to control the universe through technology. While we've come to see science as the bastion for the technical project of modernity, the responsibility for the *social project* is seemingly less focused, at least in our minds today. Generally speaking, the institutional responsibility for the social project rests with the democratic state. Prior to Western modernity, the primary form of government in Europe was feudalism, which was based on land tenure and personal relationships. These relationships, and thus the land, were organized around the monarchy with clear social, hereditary divisions between royalty and peasants. Therefore, the experience of the everyday person in feudal Europe was one where personal obligations and one's relationship to the land were paramount. Every person was keenly aware of his or her obligations to the lord of the land. These were seen as a kind of familial relationship, with fidelity as its chief goal. The main type of political identity available in feudalism was the subject—subjects are placed under the authority, control, or dominion of the monarchy.

Modern democracy began with the American and French Revolutions. The U.S. Declaration of Independence captures this new type of government: "We hold these truths to be self-evident, that all men are created equal, that they are endowed by their Creator with certain unalienable Rights, that among these are Life, Liberty and the pursuit of Happiness." The social project of modernity, then, was founded on the belief in natural, human rights—rights that cannot be given to people by a government because they belong to every person by birth. A necessary implication of this belief is that government can rule only by consent of the governed; that is, modern government can rule only through democracy.

While the main identity available in feudalism was the subject, in a modern democracy it is the citizen. It's important for you to see the connection between modern knowledge and citizenship. Both science and citizenship are based on the idea of a new kind of person—the supreme individual with the power to use his or her own mind to determine truth and to use reason to discover the world as it exists and make rational decisions. This belief gave the Enlightenment its other name: the Age of Reason. This new idea, this reasoning person, obviously formed the basis of scientific inquiry; more importantly, for our purposes, it also formed the basis for the social project. Democracy is not only possible because of belief in the rational individual; this new person also necessitates democracy. The only way of governing a group of individuals, each of whom is capable of rational inquiry and reasonable action, is through their consent.

America and the First Sociologists

Sociology was and continues to be one of the best disciplines for inquiry into modernity's social goals, precisely because it is the study of society. The first sociologists did not hold PhD's, nor did they go to school to study sociology. They were generally found among the "thousands of 'travelers,' . . . who came to [the United States] to observe how the new revolutionary system worked" (Lipset, 1962, p. 5). In the beginning phases of modernity, the United States was seen as the first and purest experiment in democracy. Unlike Europe, where modern government had to contend with and emerge from feudalism, America was born in democracy. People thus came to the United States not only to experience freedom, but also to observe how modern democracy worked.

Three of these early sociologists were Alexis de Tocqueville, Harriet Martineau, and Jane Addams. Tocqueville was French and lived from 1805 to 1859. His best-known work is *Democracy in America,* a two-volume investigation of the United States published in 1835 and 1840. Harriet Martineau was British, lived from 1802 to 1876, and is well-known for several works. The first is her translation of Auguste Comte's *Positive Philosophy,* one of the foundation stones of science in general and sociology specifically—Comte is usually seen as the founder of sociology. Another of Martineau's important works is *How to Observe Morals and Manners,* published in 1838. The work was quite probably the first methodology book for the social sciences. It's important to note that this book is addressed to "travelers" and "tourists." Remember, modernity brought rapid increases in transportation and communication technologies; people were thus able to move about the globe in a way that was never before possible. Moreover, they were challenged and excited by the new idea of knowledge that modernity brought. Many thus set out to discover society, just as the founders of science did with the physical world.

Martineau wrote her methodology book because she was concerned: People were making observations of society haphazardly and were reaching conclusions with bias and with too little research. To make her point, Martineau (1838/2003) asks the traveler if he or she would feel confident to answer if someone were to ask about the "geology of Corsica, or the public buildings of Palermo" (p. 14). She then takes the part of the traveler and answers this rhetorical question herself with, "'Oh, I can tell you nothing about that—I never studied geology; I know nothing about architecture'" (p. 14).

Please notice clearly what Martineau is saying: People can and should observe, investigate, and discover society. But we cannot and should not take this endeavor lightly. Yes, everybody can observe, but everybody needs to be prepared: "Of all the sciences . . . [the study of society is] the most difficult in its application" (p. 15). Martineau wrote *How to Observe Morals and Manners* on her voyage to the United States, where she collected data for her subsequent three-volume work, *Society in America,* published in 1837. These two books obviously go hand in hand: *Morals and Manners* contains the methodology Martineau used to study American democracy. Martineau's basic method was to compare what America said it was going to do (morals) with what it was actually doing (manners). Today, the title might be *Ethics and Practices.* Thus, Martineau very clearly saw the American experiment as an ethical, moral issue. In her mind, then, the ethics of democracy are the most important causal—practices should flow from ethics.

Martineau isn't alone among early sociologists in seeing this connection. Jane Addams (1860–1935), the first American woman to win the Nobel Peace Prize (1931), also understood this central issue. In the introduction to her book *Democracy and Social Ethics,* Addams (1902/2002) says, "It is well to remind ourselves . . . that 'Ethics' is but another word for 'righteousness,' that for which many men and women of every generation have hungered and thirsted, and without which life becomes meaningless" (p. 5). Further, Addams sees democracy not "merely as a sentiment which desires the well-being of all men, nor yet as a creed which believes in the essential dignity and equality of all men, but as that which affords a rule of living as well as a test of faith" (p. 7).

As these early sociologists saw it, there are certain assumed practices that come with democracy. Two of the most important practices and ideas involve the association of the individual with the collective and emergent ethics. Something is said to emerge if it rises from or comes out of something else, as steam emerges out of water and heat. In this case, the ethical practices of democracy arise from specific kinds of associations between the individual and the living collective. In this way, democracy is intrinsically open-ended. It's an emergent, ongoing project. American democracy as it is set forth in the Declaration of Independence, the U.S. Constitution, and the Bill of Rights explicitly structures the system in this way. That's the reason why freedom of the press, freedom of speech, and the freedom to gather are among the rights of citizens.

Ethics and morality are thus social rather than individual and come out of experience, experimentation, and diversity. Addams (1902/2002) specifically argues that democratic citizens are morally obligated to seek out interactions with people *unlike themselves,* because truly democratic ideals and practices cannot come out of interactions within a homogeneous group. This is a law of people and culture: Patterned and repeated interactions among individuals will create and sustain similar and particularized cultural beliefs. Democracy, which is fundamentally concerned with bringing freedom and equality to all humankind, must then seek diverse people and diverse interactions, out of which will come what Tocqueville calls the moral majority.

Tocqueville's emphasis is on the morality inherent in the democratic process of the majority. The belief in back of this is the idea that "there is more enlightenment and wisdom in a numerous assembly than in a single man" (Tocqueville, 1835/1969, p. 247). The emphasis here is on diversity of thought. It is, as Tocqueville says, "the theory of equality applied to brains" (p. 247). The morality of the majority isn't found in a homogeneous belief system—quite the opposite. The moral majority is found when the greater part of the citizenry come together for political discourse where diverse ideas can clash and where reason can create consensus. Modern morality, then, isn't a static belief system; modern morality is the ongoing and public meeting of the minds of the majority of people. As Jane Addams (1902/2002) puts it, "Unless all men and all classes contribute to a good, we cannot even be sure it is worth having" (p. 97).

Democratic Institutions

Modernity also brought with it new institutions and new institutional arrangements. In premodern society, social institutions overlapped quite a bit. One of the most important overlaps was between religion and government. In feudalistic Europe, for example, the right of kings to rule was legitimized by religion, and second and third sons of royalty were often trained clergymen. If we look back further in history, we can see that in almost every society, religion and government overlapped and legitimated one another.

Modernity, then, is unique in that it intentionally separates church and state. This separation is necessary because democracy cannot function under absolute truth and **legitimation.** Theocracy is the polar opposite of democracy. In a theocracy, the power to rule comes from the top (God) down; in a democracy, the power to rule goes from the bottom (citizens) up. However, it's also clear by looking at early social thinkers and sociologists that this separation did not necessarily mean that religion wasn't important or would go away.

Another important institution for modernity is capitalism. Prior to modern capitalism social position was determined by and large by birth. One could not, for example, aspire to be king if born a commoner—political position was determined by family. The economy was just as fixed as the political system. Generally speaking, the only time one could move up to a craft position was if there were no children born to the master craftsman. And while there was buying and selling, there was no structural mechanism for entrepreneurship as there is today. Capitalism was meant to be a way through which every man (and it was only men) could stand upon their own talents and effort. We'll consider this institution in later in the book. But because of its relationship to modern knowledge and modernity, I want to turn to the place education was to hold.

Education

One of the central institutions in both the technical and social projects is education (which just so happens to be the institution you're in right now). Martineau (1838/2003) argues that in the history of humankind there are two great social powers—force and knowledge—and the story of human progress is the movement away from one and toward the other. Social relations began through physical force and domination and the idea that might makes right. Knowledge, as we understand it today, was of little worth. Rather, what was important in terms of knowledge was tradition. In such societies, the past is everything. Thus, by definition traditional authority isn't critically examined and maintains the status quo; it "falls back upon precedent, and reposes there" (p. 45).

Modern knowledge, as we've seen, is clearly different. It values reason, progress, and change. The important point here is that Martineau sees a clear link between modern knowledge and government. Power in a modern state rests upon the people. The method through which democratic citizens are to exercise their power is through knowledge, which is why education is a keystone for modernity. Tocqueville (1835/1969) likewise sees education as the foundation of democracy: "The first duty imposed on those who now direct society is to educate democracy" (p. 12). And Jane Addams (1902/2002) tells us that democracy is based on belief in the power residing in each one of us and that it is education that will unlock that potential: "We are impatient to use the dynamic power residing in the mass of men, and demand that the educator free that power" (p. 80).

Martineau (1838/2003) argues that two of the most important indicators of the relationship between education and freedom are the extent of free education and the position of the university. The extent of free education is an unmistakable measure of its support of the ideas of equality and democracy. In modern countries, education is perceived as the legitimate way to get ahead. In other words, the kind of job and pay you get is initially based on your level of education. Martineau is saying that to understand the level of equality that society supports, one need only look at the kinds of job opportunities that free, public education provides. For example, if a society supports public education only through high school, it indicates that the level of equality the state is interested in supporting is only equal to the jobs that require a high school education.

On this point, Martineau's indictment of America is clear. While our moral says that we believe in equality of opportunity for all people, our manners (practices) say different. While Tocqueville's (1835/1969) focus isn't the same as Martineau's, his criticism is identical:

> I think there is no other country in the world where, proportionately to population, there are so few ignorant and so few learned individuals as in America. Primary education is within reach of all; higher education is hardly available to anybody. (p. 55)

The second indicator of the place of education in society is the regard given the university. Martineau (1838/2003) claims that "in countries where there is any popular Idea of Liberty, the universities are considered its stronghold" (p. 203). The reason for this link between liberty and universities is precisely the connection that was made earlier: Democratic citizens are morally obligated to continually examine the state in terms of its progress in fulfilling the social goals of modernity. And this examination is to be insistent, assertive, and uncompromising. As Martineau puts it, "It would be an interesting inquiry how many revolutions warlike and bloodless, have issued from seats of learning" (p. 203).

Not only are the purpose, content, and environment of the university important, but so are its students, in particular their motivation for study. To the degree that students are motivated to obtain a university education for a job, to that degree is education for freedom compromised. Martineau (1838/2003) makes a comparison between students in Germany and those in the United States. German students are noted for their quest for knowledge: The German student may "remain within the walls of his college till time silvers his hairs." The young American student, on the other hand, "satisfied at the end of three years that he knows as much as his neighbors . . . plunges into what alone he considers the business of life" (p. 205). Obviously, in advanced capitalist society, getting a college education is important for economic success. But seeing and using education *primarily* as a method of credentialing and job placement sounds the death knell for democracy.

Theory and Its Place in Modernity

Theory is at the heart of modern knowledge and science—theory is the basis of modern control—and, most of your classes, whether it was explicit or not, are based on theoretical understandings. Yet there's a line in pop culture that says, "It's only a theory." The truth of the matter is that apart from tradition and religion, theory is all we have. All scientific work is based on theory—science and technology in all its forms would not exist if it wasn't for theory. Theories aren't accepted on faith, nor are they time honored. In fact, the business of science is the continual attempt to disprove theories! Theories are accepted because they have stood up to the constant doubt and battering of scientists. Furthermore, "facts" are actually a function of theory: Scientific data are produced through testing and using theoretical perspectives and hypotheses. So, having "just a theory" is a powerful thing.

The first and most important function of theory is that it explains how something works or comes into existence—*theory* is a logically formed argument that explains an empirical phenomenon in general terms. I came across two statements that help illustrate this point. A recent issue of *Discover* magazine contained the following statement: "Iron deficiency, in particular, can induce strange tastes, though it's not known why" (Kagan, 2008, p. 16). There are many of these empirical observations in science and medicine. For example, it's not known why some people get motion sickness and others don't, nor is it known why more women than men get Raynaud's disease. Observations like these that simply link two empirical variables together are not theoretical.

The second statement appeared in an article about how exercise improves memory and may delay the onset of Alzheimer's. In linking these variables, the article says, "It works like this: aerobic exercise increases blood flow to the brain, which nourishes brain cells and allows them to function more effectively"

(Redford & Kinosian, 2008, p. 26). Unlike the first statement, this one offers an explanation of how things work. This, then, is a theoretical statement. It describes how the empirical association between exercise and improved memory works. This function of theory is extremely important, especially for civic sociology. So in studying theory, always look for factors that, when connected, explain how something works or exists.

Theory is built out of assumptions, perspectives, concepts, definitions, and relationships. Our word *perspective* comes from the Latin *perspectus* and it literally means "to look through." Perspectives act like glasses—they bring certain things into focus and blur our vision to others. *Perspectives* thus determine what we see. Joel Charon (2001) explains it this way:

> Perspectives sensitize the individual to see parts of reality, they desensitize the individual to other parts, and they guide the individual to make sense of the reality to which he or she is sensitized. Seen in this light, a perspective is an absolutely basic part of everyone's existence, and it acts as a filter through which everything around us is perceived and interpreted. There is no possible way that the individual can encounter reality "in the raw," directly, as it really is, for whatever is seen can be only part of the real situation. (p. 3)

In other words, we never directly experience the world; we encounter it through our perspectives. For a trained sociologist, every theory is based on a perspective, it is a way of seeing and not seeing the world.

All perspectives are built upon *assumptions*—things that we suppose to be true without testing them. There's an old saying that goes like this: When you assume, you make an Ass out of U and Me. That saying is dead wrong. Human beings can't begin to think, let alone act, without making assumptions. What makes an ass out of you and me is when we don't acknowledge and critically examine the assumptions underlying our knowledge and actions.

There are three basic assumptions used in social theory: assumptions about human nature, the existence of society, and the purposes and goals of knowledge. Human nature may be seen as utterly social or egoistic, symbolic and flexible or genetically determined, rational or emotional, freely acting or determined, and so on. While there are a number of variations, the basic assumption about society is whether or not it exists objectively—as something that can act independently of the individuals that make it up. At one end of this continuum are those who assume that social structures are objective and strongly influence (or cause) human behavior. Theory that is based on this assumption seeks to explain and predict the effects of social processes using law-like principles. At the other end of the continuum are those who argue that society does not exist objectively outside of human interpretation and action. These kinds of theories don't try to predict human action at all; instead, they seek to understand and explain contextual social action. The assumption about purpose involves the value or ethics of theory and sociological work. At one end of this continuum are those who believe sociology should be value-free and only explain what exists. This is the ideal of science—knowledge for knowledge's sake. At the other end of the spectrum are those who believe the purpose of theory and sociological work is to critique society and bring about change.

The *concepts* that theory uses are abstract. The reason for this is that abstract concepts give us explanatory power. For example, in one of Karl Marx's writings he talks about "the discovery of America" and how it gave impetus to the world market. That idea of Marx's can only be used to explain one empirical event. However, if we can see what happened in more abstract terms, we can explain more than one situation. In this case we could substitute "geographic expansion" and the theory would have more explanatory power. The problem with abstract concepts is that they are indefinite, which is why definitions are so important.

Let's use a common table as an example. Any specific table is there for everyone to see and touch. We can assess it using a standard of measurement. So, we can say, "That table is 48 by 24 inches." (Of course, it changes to 121.92 by 60.96 centimeters if we use the metric system.) But a definition of *table* must be general enough to be used to classify all tables, not just this one. Definitions describe ideas and concepts. How, then, do we know where the idea or category of table begins and ends? The only way to limit the idea of table is to specify it through a definition.

If I ask you to give me a definition for table, you might say something like, "A table is a wooden structure that has four legs." But is that general enough? No. Don't we call some metal things tables as well? And some things that count as tables have three rather than four legs. So, you might then say, "A table is a structure made out of any material that has three or more legs that has a flat surface upon which we can place objects." That's better, but is it good enough? Maybe, but this definition could also apply to chairs as well as tables. Obviously, we aren't usually that concerned about the definition of table. We all know what a table is, at least within practical limits, which is all we're really concerned with in everyday life. But I hope you can see the issue for critical thinking and theory: If all we have to build arguments and theory out of are concepts, then definitions become extremely important. They are the basic fodder for critical thinking and are the fundamental building blocks of theory and arguments.

Strong definitions will go beyond a simple description and will explain the conditions necessary for belonging to the concept/class being defined. We were working toward this kind of stipulative definition in our discussion of table. In our definitions, we want to fully explain the qualities that make something what it is and not something else. *Merriam-Webster's* (2002) defines table as "a piece of furniture consisting of a smooth flat slab fixed on legs or other support and variously used (as for eating, writing, working, or playing games)." That strikes me as a fairly good definition. It's general enough to include tables with three, four, six, or eight legs, yet specific enough to exclude other similar objects like chairs (tables are used for "eating, writing, working, or playing games")—the definition *stipulates* the necessary conditions for a thing to be considered a table.

Theories also need to explain the relationships among the concepts. Keep this in mind: Theoretical concepts do work and it's the relationships that explain how they work. There are at least two concerns in spelling out theoretical relationships.

The first is the direction of the relationship. There are two basic possibilities, positive and negative. A relationship is positive if the concepts vary in the same direction (either both increase or both decrease); relationships are negative if they vary in opposite directions (if one increases, the other decreases). Let's use a simple example—education and occupation. The relationship between these two concepts is positive (at least, that's your working hypothesis for being in school): Increasing years of education will produce higher-rated jobs for the individual. Notice that because the relationship is positive, it works the same in reverse: Lower years of education produce lower-rated jobs.

The second concern with relationships is more difficult: We need to explain the relationship. More years of education might equate to a better job, but how does that work? If you think about this a moment, you'll see that the theoretical task just grew tremendously. What is it about education that would affect jobs in that way? How does this relationship work? Historically, it wasn't always true that formal education and occupation were related. Why are they now? Many people in our society know that higher levels of education lead to better jobs, but most can't explain how that works. When you can do that, you're beginning to form authoritative opinions.

But theory can and should do more. Theory should inspire and give insight; it should make us see things we wouldn't otherwise. For example, when Marx says that capitalism breeds its own gravediggers, we see something that isn't possible when giving a technical explanation of the material dialectic. Or, when Durkheim says that the collective consciousness is so independent that it will often do things for its own amusement, our mind is captured in such a way that a technical explanation of social facts can't match. The same is true with Habermas' colonization of the lifeworld, or the idea that money is a pimp, or the notion of plastic sexuality, and many others. It's important to see that this function of theory isn't simply a matter of "turning a phrase." These kinds of theoretical statements get at the essence—they help us see into the core of a social factor or process. Both functions of theory are important, but they can easily overshadow one another. Theory should thus explain how something works or came about as well as inspire us to insight.

One of the things I hope you take from this discussion is that your education in social and sociological theory isn't insignificant. It is an intrinsic part of what we mean when we talk about modernity and democracy. Yet at the same time I've set up an ideal modernity. Through our journey together we'll see that some of the ideals are substantiated in the theories we consider, but we'll also see that many are challenged. There are problems with the ideal of equality, and in Chapters 7 and 8 we specifically look at the challenges of race, gender, and class. There are also challenges to the ideals of scientific knowledge; we'll specifically see those in Chapters 13, 14, and 16. But we'll also see that some reaffirm the ideals and hold great hope for our future. Others find our future tenuous, but filled with possibilities yet unknown. The journey through contemporary theory is exciting—a roller coaster, to use Anthony Giddens (Chapter 12) imagery. But to take this journey we have to start here, firmly grounded in modernity, its vision, and most importantly its way of knowing.

BUILDING YOUR THEORY TOOLBOX

At the end of every chapter, I will be giving you exercises and projects. These activities are designed to help you understand and use the theories you've learned. The intent of these first two chapters is to provide you with a background for the rest of the book. I am thus keeping these toolboxes brief. The most important things I want you to take away from these two chapters are ideas that you can use to think through and analyze the theories that follow.

- Please define the following terms. Make your definitions as theoretically robust as possible (don't be afraid to consult other sources). You want these definitions to work for you throughout the book: *modernity, progress, empiricism, positivism, science, technical project, social project, democracy, perspectives, theoretical definitions*

- Please answer the following questions:
  - o Explain the projects of modernity and how science as a knowledge system fits in.
  - o Describe the work of the first sociologists. What were their concerns? How do you think sociology fits into the projects of modernity?
  - o Explain the institutional arrangements that are supposed to be most conducive to democracy.
  - o Define theory. In your definition be certain to explain the purpose, building blocks, and goals of theory.
  - o What are the three assumptions sociologists usually make? Describe each assumption and why it is important in the work of theory.

CHAPTER 2

Defining Moments in Twentieth-Century Theory:

Talcott Parsons and The Frankfurt School

I n Chapter 1, we saw that understanding modernity is vital for understanding contemporary theory and sociology. It's equally important for us to also understand a couple of the developments in the mid-twentieth century that formed contemporary theory, especially in the United States. For our purpose, the two most significant are Talcott Parsons and the **Frankfurt School.** In many ways these two forces took the social disciplines in opposite directions: Parsons saw himself building on the ideals of modern knowledge—the Frankfurt School did just the opposite and argued that rather than leading to social justice, social science destroys the possibility of freedom and equality. Both were centrally concerned with culture: Parsons saw culture as the most important factor leading to social cohesion and harmony—the Frankfurt School saw culture, especially popular culture, as producing false consciousness. And both have influenced contemporary theory beyond their specific ideas.

Historically, the Frankfurt School developed first. However, I'm going to start with Parsons because he extends and systematizes the things we learned about modern knowledge and society in Chapter 1. Additionally, as you'll see through this book, Parsons' influence is more central as many contemporary theorists continue to see themselves arguing for or against his work. There are good reasons for giving this much influence to Parsons, but there's also a sense in which I'm making him an ideal type, similar to what I did with modernity. Both Parsons and modernity exist and are clearly important; but I'm not presenting a well-reasoned and documented case for either. I'm using them as heuristics for our discussion throughout the book—they represent ways for us to discover questions, ideas, and theories that come with each of our theorists.

Talcott Parsons: Defining Sociology

Talcott Parsons (1902–1979) was born in Colorado Springs, Colorado. Parsons began his university studies at Amherst (Massachusetts), planning on becoming a physician but later changed his major to economics. After receiving his BA in 1924, Parsons studied in Europe, completing his PhD work in sociology and economics at the University of Heidelberg, Germany. After teaching a short while at Amherst, Parsons obtained a lecturing position in 1931 at Harvard and was one of the first instructors in the new sociology department.

Parsons' Vision for the Social Sciences

Parsons was a man with a grand vision. He wanted to unite the social and behavioral disciplines into a single social science and to create a single theoretical perspective. Parsons worked at this not only theoretically but also organizationally. In 1942, Parsons became department chair of sociology at Harvard University. One of the first things he did was to combine sociology, anthropology, and psychology into one department, the Department of Social Relations. The reason he did this was to break down the barriers between disciplines in order to create a general science of human action. His desire, then, wasn't simply to understand a portion of human action (as in sociology); he wanted, rather, to comprehend the totality of the human context and to offer a full and complete explanation of social action. The department existed from 1945 to 1972 and formed the basis of other interdisciplinary programs across the United States.

After 10 years of work, Parsons' first book was published in 1937: *The Structure of Social Action*. This book is characterized by Lewis Coser (1977) as a "watershed in the development of American sociology in general and sociological theory in particular . . . [which] set a new course—the course of functional analysis—that was to dominate theoretical developments from the early 1940s until the middle of the 1960s" (p. 562). More than any other single book, it introduced European thinkers to American sociologists and gave birth to structural functionalism, which Desmond Ellis characterized in 1971 as "the major theoretical orientation in sociology today" (p. 692). His other prominent works include *The Social System, Toward a General Theory of Action, Economy and Society, Structure and Process in Modern Societies,* and *The American University.* For much of the twentieth century, Parsons was "the major theoretical figure in English-speaking sociology, if not in world sociology" (Marshall, 1998, p. 480). As Victor Lidz (2000) notes, "Talcott Parsons . . . was, and remains, the pre-eminent American sociologist" (p. 388).

Parsons' Theoretical Project

There are at least three ways in which Parsons helped shape the center of sociological discourse in the twentieth century: the way he theorized, the problem he addressed, and the theory itself. We'll start with his theorizing. Recall that science is built upon positivism and empiricism. As such, science assumes that the universe is empirical, it operates according to law-like principles, and humans can discover those laws through rigorous investigation. Science also has very specific goals, as do most knowledge systems. Through discovery, scientists want to explain, predict, and control phenomena. Additionally, there are two other important issues in positivistic theory, which we find in the following quotes from prominent contemporary theorists:

> The essence of science is precisely theory . . . as a *generalized* and coherent body of ideas, which explain the range of variations in the empirical world in terms of general principles. . . . [I]t is explicitly *cumulative and integrating.* (Collins, 1986, p. 1345, emphasis added)

> A true science *incorporates the ideas* of its early founders in introductory texts and moves on, giving over the analysis of its founders to history and philosophy. (Turner, 1993, p. ix, emphasis added)

The first thing I want us to glean from the above quotes is that scientific theory is *generalized.* To make an idea or concept general means to make it applicable to an entire group of similar things. As you'll see when we consider Parsons' theory, his concepts are very general (and thus fairly dry—but, then, all scientific theory is that way). Scientific knowledge also involves both theory synthesis and cumulation. Synthesis involves bringing together two or more elements in order to form a new whole. For example, water is the synthesis of hydrogen and oxygen. *Theoretical synthesis,* then, involves bringing together elements from diverse theorists so as to form a theory that robustly explains a broader range of phenomena. Cumulation refers to the gradual building up of something, such as the cumulative effects of drinking alcohol. *Theory cumulation* specifically involves the building up of explanations over time. This incremental building is captured by Isaac Newton's famous dictum, "If I have seen further it is by standing on the shoulders of giants." Yet, what isn't clear in Newton's quote is that the ultimate goal of theory cumulation is to forget its predecessors.

To make this clear, let's compare the writings of two authors, Edgar Allan Poe and Albert Einstein. Here's one of Poe's famous stanzas:

> Once upon a midnight dreary, while I pondered, weak and weary,
>
> over many a quaint and curious volume of forgotten lore,
>
> While I nodded, nearly napping, suddenly there came a tapping,
>
> As of someone gently rapping, rapping at my chamber door.
>
> "Tis some visitor," I muttered, "tapping at my chamber door;
>
> Only this, and nothing more."

Here's one of Einstein's famous quotes:

$$E = mc^2$$

There are some obvious differences between these two quotes: One is poetry and the other a mathematical equation. But I want you to see a bit more. Does it matter who wrote "Once upon a midnight dreary"? Yes, it does. A large part of understanding poetry is knowing who wrote it—who they were, how they lived, what their other works are like, what style they wrote in, and so on. These issues are part of what makes reading Poe different from reading Emily Dickinson. Now, does it matter who wrote $E = mc^2$? Not really. You can understand everything you need to know about $E = mc^2$ simply by understanding the equation. The author in this sense is immaterial.

One of the above quotes is from Jonathan H. Turner's book *Classical Sociological Theory: A Positivist's Perspective*. Turner's (1993) goal in that book is "to codify the wisdom of the masters so that we can move on and *make books on classical theory unnecessary*" (p. ix, emphasis added). That last highlighted section is the heart of theory cumulation: Cumulating theory implies that we do away with the individual authors and historic contexts and keep only the theoretical ideas that explain, predict, and control the social world. In that spirit, here's a theoretical statement from Turner's (1993) book:

> The degree of differentiation among a population of actors is a gradual s-function of the level of competition among these actors, with the latter variable being an additive function of:
>
> A. the size of this population of actors,
>
> B. the rate of growth in this population,
>
> C. the extent of economical concentration of this population, and
>
> D. the rate of mobility of actors in this population. (p. 80)

First notice how general the statement is; it can be applied to any group of people, living anywhere, at any time. Notice also that there's no mention of from whom these ideas originally came. Now, you and I might know from whom this proposition comes (Durkheim), but does it matter? No. Like Einstein's formula, it's immaterial. If we are doing social science, what matters is whether or not we can show this statement to be false through scientific testing. If we can't, then we can have a certain level of confidence that the proposition accurately reflects a general process in the social world. In science, authorship is superfluous; *it's the explanatory power of the theory that matters*. The cumulation of these general statements is one of the main goals of scientific theory.

Of his groundbreaking work, Parsons (1949) says, "*The Structure of Social Action was intended to be primarily a contribution to systematic social science and not to history*" (pp. A–B). His work is actually a synthesis of three theorists. Parsons (1961) notes how he used each one:

> for the conception of the social system and the bases of its integration, the work of Durkheim; for the comparative analysis of social structure and for the analysis of the borderline between social systems and culture, that of Max Weber; and for the articulation between social systems and personality, that of Freud. (p. 31)

Yet Parsons clearly wants us to forget the historical and personal origins of the theories—for science, it's the power of the synthesized theory to illuminate and delineate social factors and processes that matters. This approach to theory is also what led to the three sociological perspectives or paradigms you were taught in your introduction to sociology courses: structural-functionalism, conflict theory, and interactionism. To say that someone is a functionalist, for example, is to pay more attention to the general features of the theory than what he or she contributes originally.

The Problem of Social Order

Parsons saw himself responding to *the problem of social order* posed by the philosopher Thomas Hobbes (1588–1679). Parsons' understanding of this Hobbesian problem of social order begins with the fact that all humans are ruled by passions. And, all people are motivated to fulfill these passions; and, more importantly, they have the right to fulfill them because "there is 'no common rule of good and evil to be taken from the nature of the objects themselves'" (Hobbes, as quoted in Parsons, 1949, p. 89). In other words, things aren't good or bad in themselves and people have different desires for diverse things—thus there is no basis for rule. In the absence of any rule, people will use the most efficient means possible to acquire their goals. "These means are found in the last analysis to be force and fraud" (Parsons, 1949, p. 90). Thus the most natural state of humanity is war of all against all. The question, then, is how is social order achieved? Parsons' basic response is the normative order—social order achieved through norms. While some of the language might be new to you, most of Parsons' response will probably feel familiar. The reason that's probably the case is that Parsons' answer to the problem of social order has become for many sociologists the basic answer given in introduction to sociology classes.

Voluntaristic Action

In thinking about humans, it's sometimes convenient to make the distinction between behavior and action: All living things behave; only humans have the potential to act. Action implies choice and decision, whereas behavior occurs without thought, as when a plant's leaves reach for the sun. Of course, humans behave as well as act; there are a lot of things we do on autopilot, but we have the potential for action. Theory that focuses on this issue is referred to as *action theory,* which has been an interest of philosophy since the time of Aristotle. Parsons' work on action theory draws from Max Weber, who argued that action takes place when a person's behavior is meaningfully oriented toward other social actors, usually in terms of meaningful values or rational exchange. *Voluntaristic action,* then, is never purely individualistic: People choose to act voluntarily within a context of culture and social situations in order to meet individual goals. And because human needs are met socially, people develop shortcuts to action by creating norms and by patterning action through sets of ends and means.

Parsons calls this context of action *the unit act.* There are a variety of factors in the unit act. The first, and in some ways the most important, are the conditions of action. There are of course occasions when we have some control over the initial context—for example, you may decide to go to the movies on Saturday or study for a test. But once the choice is made, the actor has little immediate agency or choice over the conditions under which action takes place. Parsons has in mind such things as the presence of social institutions or organizations, as well as elements that might be specific to the situation, such as the social influence of particular people or physical constraints of the environment.

The second set of factors under which people act concerns the means and ends of action. Here we can see a fundamental difference between action and reaction: Action is goal oriented and involves choice. But for people to make choices among goals and means, the choices themselves must have different meanings. According to Parsons, the meanings and relationships between means and ends are formed though shared value hierarchy. Cultural *values* are shared ideas and emotions regarding the worth of something, and values are always understood within a hierarchy, with some goals and means more highly valued than others; otherwise it would be difficult to choose between one thing and another because you wouldn't care. Choices among means and ends are also guided by norms. *Norms* are actions that have sanctions (rewards or punishments) attached to them. Taken together Parsons is arguing that human action is distinctly cultural and thus meaningful action.

Patterning Voluntaristic Action

While Parsons has now outlined the context wherein action takes place, the problem of social order isn't adequately answered. Two things need to be specifically addressed: First, Hobbes talked about a person's inner passions driving him or her; second, social order needs patterned behavior. Parsons argues that patterning action occurs on two levels: the structuring of patterned behaviors and individual internalization or *socialization.* Parsons understands internalization in Freudian terms. Freud's theory works like this: People are motivated by internal energies surrounding different need dispositions. As these different psychic motives encounter the social world, they have to conform in order to be satisfied. Conformity may be successful (well-adjusted) or unsuccessful (repressed), but the point to notice here is that the structure of the individual's personality changes as a result of this encounter between psychic energy and the social world. The superego is formed through these encounters. For Parsons, the important point is that cultural traditions become meaningful to and part of the need dispositions of individuals. The way we sense and fulfill our needs is structured internally by culture—notice how Parsons reconceptualized Hobbes' concern for passions; in Parsons' scheme they are social rather than individual. For Parsons, then, the motivation to conform comes principally from within the individual through Freudian internalization patterns of value orientation and meaning.

Action is also structured socially through modes of orientation and types of action that have become institutionalized. Modes of orientation simply refer to the way we come into a social situation with specific motives and values. These motives and values come together and form three *types of action:* instrumental, expressive, and moral. Instrumental action is composed of the need for information and evaluation by objective criteria. Expressive action is motivated by the need for emotional attachment and the desire to be evaluated by artistic standards. Moral action is motivated by the need for assessment by ultimate notions of right and wrong. People will tend to be in contact with others who are interested in the same type of action.

As we interact over time with people who are likewise oriented, we produce patterns of interaction and a corresponding system of status positions, roles, and norms. Status positions tell us where we fit in the social hierarchy of esteem or honor; roles are sets of expected behaviors that generally correspond to a given status position (for example, a professor is expected to teach); and norms are expected behaviors that have positive and/or negative sanctions attached to them. Generally these cluster together in institutions. For functionalists such as Parsons, institutions are enduring sets of roles, norms, status positions, and value patterns that are recognized as collectively meeting some societal need. In this context, then, **institutionalization** refers to the process through which behaviors, cognitions, and emotions become part of the taken-for-granted way of doing things in a society ("the way things are").

These clusters of institutions meet certain needs that society has—the institutions *function* to meet those needs. The most important set of institutions for Parsons are the ones that produce *latent pattern maintenance.* If something is latent, it's hidden and not noticed. Social patterns are maintained, then, through indirect management. For this task, society uses culture and socialization. The chief socializing agents in society are the structures that meet the requirement of latent pattern maintenance—structures such as religion, education, and family.

In addition to latent pattern maintenance, Parsons gives us three other requisite functions for a system: adaptation, goal attainment, and integration. The *adaptation* function is fulfilled by those structures that help a system to adapt to its environment. Adaptation draws in resources from the environment, converts them to usable elements, and distributes them throughout the system (the economy). *Goal attainment* is the subsystem that activates and guides all the other elements toward a specific goal (government). In Parsons' scheme, *integration* refers to the subsystems and structures that work to blend together and coordinate the various actions of other structures. In society, the structure most responsible for this overt coordination is the legal system. Together, these four functions are referred to as AGIL: Adaptation, Goal attainment, Integration, and Latent pattern maintenance. All of these functions are embedded within one another and form a bounded system that tends toward equilibrium or balance; in other words, they form society.

The Frankfurt School: The Problem With Sociology

Karl Marx spawned two distinct theoretical approaches. One approach focuses on conflict and class as general features of society. The intent with this more sociological approach is to analytically describe and explain conflict. Conflict and power here are understood as fundamental to society. And, again, this approach is based on the same question as Parsons: How is social order possible? The short version of Parsons' theory is that social order is achieved through commonly held norms, values, and beliefs. A norm, as you'll recall, "is a cultural rule that associates people's behavior or appearance with rewards or punishments" (Johnson, 2000, p. 209). This approach to understanding social order is sometimes called the "equilibrium model" because it's based on people internalizing and believing in the collective conscious. People do have selfish motivations, but they are offset by the collective conscious, thus creating a balance between individual desires and social needs.

Conflict theorists, however, would point out that there is an element of power underlying norms. Notice in the above definition that norms are founded upon an ability to reward or punish behavior, both of which are based on power. Conflict theorists also point out that the values and beliefs commonly held in society can be explained in terms of the interests of the elite. Thus, for conflict theorists, social order is the result of constraint rather than consensus and power is thus an essential element of society. Conflict theorists take the same basic scientific approach as Parsons, seeking generalizable processes and building theory cumulatively.

The other theoretical approach that is inspired by and draws from Marx is critical theory. In general, *critical theory* "aims to dig beneath the surface of social life and uncover the assumptions and masks that keep us from a full and true understanding of how the world works" (Johnson, 2000, p. 67). Critical theory doesn't simply explain how society operates. Rather, it uncovers the unseen or misrecognized ways in which society operates to oppress certain groups while maintaining the interests of others. Critical theory has one more defining feature: It is decidedly anti-positivistic. Thus, critical theory has a very clear agenda that stands in opposition to scientific sociology. This perspective was brought together by the Frankfurt School.

Historical Roots

Briefly, the Frankfurt School (also known as the Institute of Social Research) began in the early 1920s at the University of Frankfurt in Germany. It was formed by a tight group of radical intellectuals and, ironically, financed by Felix Weil, the son of a wealthy German merchant. Weil's goal was to create "an institutionalization of

Marxist discussion beyond the confines both of middle-class academia and the ideological narrow-mindedness of the Communist Party" (Wiggershaus, 1986/1995, p. 16). As the Nazis gained control in Germany, the Frankfurt School was forced into exile in 1933, first to Switzerland, then New York, and eventually California. In 1953, the school was able to move back to its home university in Frankfurt. The various leaders and scholars associated with the school include Theodor Adorno, Max Horkheimer, Herbert Marcuse, Eric Fromm, and Jürgen Habermas.

Though there were many reasons why the School and its critical theory approach came into existence, one of the early problems that these theorists dealt with was the influence of Nazism in Germany. The two decades surrounding World War II were watershed moments for many disciplines. The propaganda machine in back of Nazism and the subsequent human atrocities left a world stunned at the capacity of humanity's inhumanity. The actions of the holocaust and the beliefs that lay at their foundation spurred a large cross-disciplinary movement to understand human behavior and beliefs. One of the best-known attempts at understanding these issues is Stanley Milgram's (1974) psychological experiments in authority.

The sociological attempt at understanding this horror demanded that culture be studied as an independent entity, something Marx didn't do. It was clear that what happened in Germany was rooted in culture that was used to intentionally control people's attitudes and actions—this use of culture was formalized in 1933 with the Reich Ministry for Popular Enlightenment and Propaganda. Additionally, ideology became seen as something different, something more insidious, than perhaps Marx first suspected. The Frankfurt School asks us to see ideology as more diffuse, as not simply a direct tool of the elite, but, rather, as a part of the cultural atmosphere that we breathe.

In general, the Frankfurt School elaborates and synthesizes ideas from Karl Marx, Max Weber, and Sigmund Freud, and focuses on the social production of knowledge and its relationship to human consciousness. This kind of Marxism focuses on Marx's indebtedness to Georg Wilhelm Hegel. Marx basically inverted Hegel's argument from an emphasis on ideas to material relations in the economy. The Frankfurt School reintroduced Hegel's concern with ideas and culture but kept Marx's critical evaluation of capitalism and the state. Thus, like Marx, the Frankfurt School focuses on ideology; but, unlike Marx, critical theory sees ideological production as linked to culture and knowledge rather than simply class and the material relations of production. Ideology, according to critical theorists, is more broadly based and insidious than Marx supposed.

The Problem With Positivism:
Max Horkheimer and Theodor Adorno

The clearest expression of early critical theory is found in Theodor Adorno and Max Horkheimer's (1972) book *Dialectic of Enlightenment*, first published in 1944. Adorno was born in Germany September 11, 1903. His father was a well-to-do wine merchant and musician. Adorno himself studied music composition in Vienna for 3 years beginning in 1925, after studying sociology and philosophy at the University of Frankfurt. He finished his advanced degree in philosophy under

Paul Tillich (Christian socialist) in 1931, and started an informal association with the Institute. In 2 short years, Adorno was removed by the Nazis due to his Jewish heritage. He moved to Merton College, Oxford, in 1934 and to New York City in 1938, where he fully affiliated with the Frankfurt School in exile. When the school returned to Germany, Adorno became assistant director under Max Horkheimer, who had served as director since 1930. Horkheimer was German, also Jewish, and born into a wealthy family on February 14, 1895. After World War I, Horkheimer studied psychology and philosophy, finishing his doctorate in philosophy in 1925 at Frankfurt University, where he became a lecturer and eventually met Adorno. Horkheimer became the second director of the Institute of Social Research in 1930 and continued in that position until 1958, when Adorno took the directorship.

In the *Dialectic of Enlightenment,* Horkheimer and Adorno argue that the contradictions Marx saw in capitalism are eclipsed by the ones found in the Enlightenment. The Enlightenment promises freedom through the use of reason, rationality, and scientific method. But in the end it brings a new kind of oppression, not one that is linked to the externalities of life (such as class) but one that extinguishes the spirit and breath of human nature. As we've seen, positivism is based on reason and assumes the universe is empirical. Reason is employed to discover the laws of nature in order to predict and control it. Horkheimer and Adorno argue that the very definition of scientific knowledge devalues the human questions of ethics, aesthetics, beauty, emotion, and the good life; all of which are written off by science as concerns only for literature, which under positivism isn't valued as knowledge at all.

Science is based on the Cartesian dichotomy of subject and object, but the human sciences (sociology, psychology, psychiatry, anthropology, history, and the like) have in applying the scientific method objectified the human being through and through. In objectifying, controlling, and opposing nature, the scientific method opposes human nature—human nature is treated like physical nature, objectified and controlled. It results in such things as seeing all human sensualities and sensibilities as evil forces that must be controlled (the Freudian id); and the human psyche, emotions, sensualities, and body must all be managed and brought under the regime of science. People in positivistic social sciences become statistics in a population that must be controlled for the interests of the state (current examples include sexual practices, emotion management, bodily weight, child rearing, smoking, drinking, and so on—all of which are seen as weakness or problems within the individual).

Through the Enlightenment and science, rationality has been enthroned as the supreme human trait. Yet Horkheimer and Adorno trace this ascendency back to fear of the unknown. Rationality began in religion, as magicians, shamans, and priests began to organize and write doctrine; and this impetus toward safety and control accelerated as society relieved such people from the burden of daily work; spirit guides became professional. Their work systematized and provided control over rituals and capricious spirits. Eventually, God was rendered predictable through the ideas of sin and ritualized redemption; and the idea of direct cause and effect was established. Religious issues became universal, with one version of reality, one explanation of the cosmos and humankind's place in it. The hierarchy of gods and individual responses were thus replaced by instrumental reason. The same fear of uncertainty was the motive behind science as well. The technical control of the physical world promised to relieve threats from disease, hunger, and pestilence. And to one degree or another it has done that. Yet science, like religion before it, takes on myth form and reifies its own method: There is only one form of knowledge, only one way of knowing that is valid.

This unstoppable engine of rationality also extends to the control of everyday life (and we can see how much we've "progressed" in this since the time of Horkheimer and Adorno). The modern life is an *administered life.* Every aspect is open to experts and analysis and is cut off from real social contact and dependency. People are isolated through technology, whether it's the technologies of travel (cars and planes), technologies of communication (such as phones and computers), or the technology of management (bureaucracies). People rationally manage time, space, and relationships, as well as their own self. Self-help is the prescription of the day, guided by experts of every kind. But what's lost is self-actualization—there are only remnants of a self that hasn't been administered, only small portions to self-actualize, and even those are squashed in the name of the administered life.

Originally, the Enlightenment had an element of critical thought, where the process of thinking was examined. But it soon became as mechanical as the technologies that it creates; and it denies other ways of knowing and being. Horkheimer and Adorno's story of the Enlightenment is, then, "an account of how humankind, it its efforts to free itself from subjugation to nature, has created new and more all-encompassing forms of domination and repression" (Alway, 1995, p. 33).

The irony and problem is that the Enlightenment was to free humankind. Yet it has created a new kind of *unfreedom,* a binding of the mind that prevents it from perceiving its own chains of bondage. This of course is what Marx meant when he spoke of **false consciousness**, but for Horkheimer and Adorno the blindness is ever more insidious. The very tools of thought that were to bring enlightenment instead bring the administered life. How is it possible to get out of this conundrum? This is precisely where critical theory comes in.

First, it's important to understand that there isn't a specific goal or program. Gone are the lofty goals of the Enlightenment and the method of reason and rationality are useless as well. In back of this negation is a caution and realization. The caution is about being derailed again by believing that we've found *the way*—unlike the capitalists in Marx's scheme, the philosophers of the Enlightenment may be seen as having the best of intentions. We should, then, be cautious of any single answer. The realization is that human beings are social beings; we reflect and express the spirit of the age and the position we hold in society. Knowledge is therefore never pure.

Knowing this implies a second feature of critical theory: The way to freedom is through continual process and critical thinking, the goal of which is to unearth. In his introduction to Adorno's *Culture Industry,* Bernstein (1991) notes,

> In reading Adorno, especially his writings on the culture industry, it is important to keep firmly in mind the thought that he is not attempting an objective, sociological analysis of the phenomena in question. Rather, the *question* of the culture industry is raised from the perspective of its relation to the possibilities for social transformation. The culture industry is to be understood from the perspective of its potentialities for promoting or blockings "integral freedom." (p. 2, emphasis original)

Notice that Adorno's reading of the culture industry is not intended as a systematic, objective, sociological study. Rather, it is an act of interrogation. But it is questioning with a purpose: In Adorno's case, to assess the potentials for integral freedom that pop culture provides. The image of integral freedom calls up many images, but among the most important are that freedom must be understood with reference to the whole being of human—including social relations, economic achievement, spirituality, sensuality, aesthetics, and so on—and that its chief value is the dignity of the person. "Reason can realize its reasonableness only through reflecting on the disease of the world as produced and reproduced by man" (Horkheimer, 2004, p. 120).

BUILDING YOUR THEORY TOOLBOX

Most of the chapters in this book are in dialogue with Parsons and critical theory in one way or another. In Chapters 3 and 4, we'll see Herbert Blumer and Harold Garfinkel take Parsons to task on his solution to the problem of social order. As you'll see, a good part of their disagreement comes down to one of the basic assumptions that sociological theorists have to make, the way in which society exists. However, Parsons' ideas about structure and social systems will come back to us in Chapters 7 through 10. Though different structures and systems are referenced, these concepts first gained currency through the work of Parsons. In Chapter 11, we'll take a look at Jürgen Habermas' extension of critical theory. In Chapters 13 and 14, Michel Foucault and Jean Baudrillard will introduce us to some new theoretical perspectives, poststructuralism and postmodernism, respectively. Even though they are not directly in the line of Frankfurt critical theory, you'll see glimmers of the same issues that sparked Horkheimer and Adorno. So, again, what I'd like for you to do here is to build a basic understanding of the issues and conceptual ideas we've talked about; they will help you think your way through the rest of the theories.

- Please define the following terms. Make your definitions as theoretically robust as possible (don't be afraid to consult other sources). You want these definitions to work for you throughout the book: *generalized theory, theoretical synthesis, theory cumulation, the problem of social order, voluntaristic action, the unit act, values, norms, socialization, types of action, status positions, latent pattern maintenance, adaptation, goal attainment, integration, conflict theory, critical theory, administered life, unfreedom*

- Please answer the following questions:

  o Explain Parsons' vision for the social sciences.

  o Describe the way in which Parsons theorized. Here I want you to write what we might think of as the ideal definition for social science.

  o Explain how Parsons solves the problem of social order. In other words, according to Parsons, how are social actions patterned across time and space?

  o Describe how and why the Frankfurt School came into existence.

  o Explain critical theory's assessment of positivistic theory.

Part II

The Social Situation and Its People

Symbolic Interaction:

Herbert Blumer

(1900–1987)

O ne of the ideas of democracy that is either overstated or undervalued is the ethical foundation upon which it is built. People seem to either be dogmatic about a particular form of religion that should form the base; or, they seem to believe that any ethical or moral basis for democracy is dangerous. But as we saw in Chapter 1, many of the first sociologists would disagree with either extreme—a discourse of ethics was simply assumed by Martineau, Tocqueville, and Addams. Martineau even had a type of religion she felt best encouraged democracy: Moderate religions emphasize the overall well-being of humanity through self-actualization and education, rather than doctrine and dogma. Martineau argued that a society with a high level of this type of religion will have a culture that stresses freedom and true equality and broadmindedness. All three agree that democracy is an ethical enterprise.

It's clear, then, that American democracy is founded on an ethical base—yet at the same time there is to be a separation between church and state. This separation wasn't intended to keep religion, ethics, and morals out of public life; it was intended to allow religion's contribution to public discussions to be democratic. In a democracy, power to govern flows from the people up. Religion, on the other hand, generally creates a theocracy, where power flows from the top down. Thus, if left alone or given a privileged voice, religion will tend to destroy democracy. We are left with the question, then, about the source of democratic ethics and morals.

One answer to that issue comes from pragmatism, the only philosophy born in the United States. After the Civil War the nation was left bereft of a public philosophy: "The ideals that had served to buttress stable group life before 1861 became a casualty of that war" (Lyman & Vidich, 2000, p. 5). Out of a search to fill this gap, pragmatism was born. **Pragmatism** rejects the notion that there are any fundamental truths and instead proposes that *truth* is relative to time, place, and purpose. Pragmatism is thus "an idea about ideas" and a way of relativizing ideology (Menand, 2001, p. xi), but this relativizing doesn't result in relativism. In fact, pragmatism is founded upon clear and strong ethical beliefs. However, rather than these ethics being based in some outside, preexisting force or system, *the ethical basis of pragmatism* is the belief in human reason and consensus. Thus, truth, ethics, and morality in pragmatism are specific to community: Human action and decisions aren't determined or forced by society, ideology, or preexisting truths. Rather, decisions and ethics emerge out of a consensus that develops through interaction.

Rooted in pragmatism, "Blumer's sociology encapsulates a public philosophy that is neither shrouded in the metaphysical mysteries of historical process nor place beyond the capacity of individuals—or their elected and appointed officials— to determine and direct" (Lyman & Vidich, 2000, p. 6). Blumer lived and worked during a time in which major shifts occurred in the fabric of American society. As a result of the Great Depression of the 1930s, the government ended laissez-faire capitalism and began a program of state intervention in the economy (Keynesian economics) and a social safety net for its citizens (the welfare state). His theoretical concerns were also informed by the newly established mass media and the crystallization of the mass society. While certainly not as drastic as the Civil War, the United States experienced a time of upheaval and reassessment. And, as you would expect, sociology responded to these massive changes with a number of theoretical explanations and intense data collection and analyses; all designed to increase our understanding of what was going on. However, in his search for answers, Blumer became an "ardent critic of all the major traditions of sociological reasoning" (Plummer, 1998, p. 84). His critique was twofold: He argued that sociology had reified its concepts and reduced the lived experiences of people to objective measurements. In order to formulate this critique, Blumer (1969) relies "chiefly on the thought of George Herbert Mead" (p. 1).

THEORIST'S DIGEST

Brief Biography

Herbert Blumer was born on March 7, 1900, in St. Louis, Missouri. He completed his PhD at the University of Chicago in 1928; his dissertation was titled "Methods in Social Psychology." Blumer was on the faculty at Chicago from 1927 to 1952, during which time he also played professional football, interviewed gang members, and mediated labor disputes. In 1952, Blumer moved to the University of California at Berkeley to chair its new department of sociology. Blumer edited one of sociology's premier journals, the *American Journal of Sociology,* from 1940 to 1952, and was president of the American Sociological Society (ASA) in 1955. He is best known for his book *Symbolic Interactionism: Perspective and Method* (1969), which systematized sociology's main school of social psychology; Blumer received the ASA's Career of Distinguished Scholarship award in 1983. He passed away April 13, 1987.

Central Sociological Questions

Blumer's primary concern was to ground sociology in the real, empirical world of human action. Thus, his main question is a simple yet powerful one: What is the most empirically real thing that people do? As Lyman and Vidich (2000) argue, there was a deeper concern that motivated this question: "Blumer presents us with the problem of finding the locus of civic virtue in the modern state" (p. 101). Behind his question about sociological theory and methods was this more significant issue: What is the basis of a democratic public philosophy?

Simply Stated

The human world is utterly symbolic, meaningful, and thus an emergent quality of the interaction. People interpret meaning through the mind and self in order to control behavior pragmatically. Both the mind and self are created through language acquisition and three stages of role-taking: play, game, and generalized other. Because human reality is symbolic, the most empirically available site for sociological investigation is the interaction—thus the sense of society people have is built up through joint actions.

Key Ideas

Pragmatism, meaning, interaction, social objects, self, role-taking, generalized other, joint action, problem of reification

Concepts and Theory: Emergent Meanings

In systematizing symbolic interaction, Blumer (1969) gives us three premises upon which it is built:

Humans act toward things on the basis of the meanings . . . the meaning of such things is derived from, or arises out of, the social interaction that one has . . . these meanings are handled in, and modified through, an interpretative process used by the person in dealing with the things he encounters. (p. 2)

You'll notice that the central concept in these three tenants is meaning. In focusing on meaning, Blumer is actually basing his argument on an idea about human nature. As Snow and Anderson (1993) explain, "All animals are confronted with the challenge of material subsistence, but only humans are straddled with the vexing question of its meaning" (p. 230).

Meaning and Human Nature

But what is the meaning of *meaning?* It's an odd question, isn't it? At first glance, it looks like a play on words, kind of like "how much wood could a woodchuck chuck?" But it isn't a play on words; it's a serious question that has an answer. Asking it in the form that I did helps to point out something significant about the answer. *Webster's* (1983) defines meaning as "1. that which exists in the mind . . . 2. that which is intended to be, or in fact is, conveyed, denoted, signified, or understood by acts or language" (p. 1115). We're going to put the first definition aside for the moment and concentrate on the second. Meaning is something that is conveyed, denoted, or signified by acts, words, or objects. Notice what meaning isn't. Meaning isn't the act, word, experience, or object. By definition, meaning isn't the thing itself, whatever that thing might be.

Let's use a powerful example to see this: Think about one person killing another person. The important thing for our purposes isn't the actual act or the fact that a person's life has ended; it's the context in which the killing takes place. Killing can be war, or terrorism, or accidental homicide, or suicide, or religious sacrifice, or first-degree murder, or execution as a punishment for first-degree murder—killing can be legitimate or morally wrong, depending on its meaning context. Human life doesn't matter, in and of itself; it's the context that matters. Remember the movie or the actual events surrounding Apollo 13? The eyes of the entire world were on the three men trapped in that spacecraft. America watched the catastrophe in horror and had heartfelt concern for the lives of those three Americans—while at the same time hundreds if not thousands of people were being killed or maimed in Vietnam by American servicemen. Life itself doesn't matter; what matters is the meaning we give it.

But why do we place such importance on meaning? Ah, that's a very good question. Why can't human beings get away from meaning? Why is it fundamental to our nature? The first part of the answer is that humans are utterly and completely social. Being social is how we as a species exist. Every species is defined by its method of survival or existence. Why are whales, lions, and hummingbirds all different? They are different because they have different ways of existing in the world. What makes human beings different from whales, lions, and hummingbirds? Humans have a different mode of existence.

But being social is only part of the answer. There are a number of species that exist socially, like ants and bees, so what makes humans different? It is the magnitude of our sociability, and, more importantly, the way in which we create our social bonds. Most other social species instinctually create social bonds through a variety of things such as scent, physical spacing, and so on. Humans use symbols to create meaningful social bonds. Granted, there are some species that have a kind and degree of culture, but no other animal uses culture to the extent that humans do—and no other species uses symbols.

We are primarily built for and oriented toward using signs and symbols. Culture and language are the reasons we have the brain structure that we do; culture is the reason we have the kind of vocal structures that we do; culture is why we have the kind of hands that we do—culture is the defining feature of humanity. Meaning lifts out the object from its rooted existence in time and space. This move of abstraction or transcendence is necessary for us to be conscious, to interact, to have a self, and to have society. We will visit this notion of meaning throughout the book (after all, it is basic to human nature and society). So, keep this idea on the front burner so you can add to it as we go along.

Interactions and Emergent Meanings

This brings us to Blumer's second premise: If meaning isn't in the object, word, language, or event, then where is it? The quote above from *Webster's* says that meaning exists in the mind. However, as with most everything in a society infatuated with the individual, that definition is only partially correct. The individualized definition also lines up with an important philosophical school of thought: idealism. Idealism and realism are two sides in the philosophical debate about reality (ontology or metaphysics) and knowledge (epistemology). To even begin to scratch the surface of this debate would take much more time and text than we have (philosophers have been debating these issues for over 2,000 years), but we really don't need to. Symbolic interaction teaches us that in our day-to-day life, we are not at all interested in ontology or epistemology. Meaning for humans is a pragmatic issue.

In pragmatism, ideas and meanings are organizational instruments. That is, humans organize their behaviors based on ideas. Meaning, then, is a tool for action and it has value to us only insofar as it facilitates behavior. Pragmatism argues that people hold on to what works, and what works is the only truth that endures for humans. In true pragmatic form, symbolic interactionism argues that meaning is found only in people's behaviors and that meaning emerges out of social interaction in response to adaptive concerns. Thus, the meaning of any idea, moral, word, symbol, or object is pragmatically determined, or determined by its practical use. Thus, while meaning comes to be in the mind, it is produced and exists within pragmatically emergent social interactions—that which is in the mind is only a residue of these social interactions. In fact, this move from social to the individual is the only basis upon which we can share meanings.

Seeing meaning in pragmatic terms implies that meaning is defined and redefined in an ongoing manner as we interact with one another. As we would assume, symbolic interactionism has a very specific definition of **interaction:** It is the ongoing negotiation and melding together of individual actions. There are three distinct steps that must occur before we can say that there is interaction. First, an initial cue is given. But the cue itself doesn't carry any specific meaning. Let's say you see a person crying in the halls at school. What does it mean? It could mean lots of things. In order to determine—or, more properly, achieve—meaning there has to be a response to the cue, "Is everything all right?" Yet we still don't have meaning. There must be a response to the response. After the three phases (cue, response, and response to the response), a meaning emerges: "Nothing's wrong, my boyfriend just asked me to marry him."

We probably still aren't done, because her response has become yet another cue. What does that cue mean? We can't tell until you respond to her cue and she responds to your response. This process is how meaning emerges from the interaction. Meaning results from the back-and-forth negotiation over a symbolic object. Thus we cannot tell until after the interaction is completed what the different social objects meant to the people involved. And we may not even be done then. Quite often we take the meaning of one interaction and make it a cue in another interaction.

Symbols and Social Objects

While meanings are negotiated through interaction, the negotiation takes place around known social objects that are indicated in an interaction; you probably wouldn't have noticed the person crying if "crying" wasn't a social object. These social objects and their symbolic meanings provide initial stimulus and orientation for interaction. In fact, social objects are our primary stimulus for action. Of course it is possible for a physical object to provide motivation, like when a rock falls on your hand. But something truly amazing happens not long after the rock hits you—you turn both it and the pain into social objects.

To really understand the issue behind symbols and social objects, let's consider natural signs. A sign is something that stands for something else, like smoke stands for fire. So, if we see smoke coming out of a room, we will call and report a fire, even though we may never actually see the fire. It appears that many animals can use signs. My dog, Gypsy, for example, gets very excited and begins to salivate at the sound of her treat box being opened or the tone of my voice when I ask, "Wanna treat?" But the ability of animals to use signs varies. For instance, a dog and a chicken will respond differently to the presence of a feed bowl on the other side of a fence. The chicken will simply pace back and forth in front of the fence in aggravation, but the dog will seek a break in the fence, go through the break, and run back to the bowl and eat. The chicken appears to be able to respond directly to only one stimulus, where the dog is able to hold his response to the food at bay while he seeks an alternative. This ability to hold responses at bay is important for higher-level-thinking animals.

These signs that we've been talking about may be called natural signs. They are private and learned through the individual experience of each animal. So, if your dog also gets excited at the sound of the treat box, it is because of the dog's individual experience with it—Gypsy didn't tell your dog about the treat box. There also tends to be a natural relationship between the sign and its object, and these signs occur apart from the agency of the animal. In other words, Gypsy did not make the association between the sound of the box and her treats, I did. So, in the absolute sense, the relationship between the sound and the treat isn't a true natural sign. Natural signs come out of the natural experiences of the animal, and the meaning of these signs is determined by a structured relationship between the sign and its object.

Humans, on the other hand, have the ability to use what symbolic interactionists call significant gestures, symbols, or social objects. In contrast to natural signs, **social objects** can be abstract and arbitrary. With natural signs, the relationship between the sign and its referent is natural (as with smoke and fire). But symbolic meaning can be quite abstract and completely arbitrary (in terms of naturally given relations). For example, the year 2010 doesn't exist in the physical world. What year it is depends on what calendar is used, and the different calendars are associated with political and religious issues, not nature (for examples, look up the Chinese and Muslim calendars on the Internet). Social objects are also reflexive, calling out the same response in the person speaking and listening. For example, I may call you up and say, "Tomorrow is Monday." Chances are that neither one of us will be happy about that situation. But while Monday is a social object and thus reflexive, it is also subject to interaction. Thus Monday becomes something totally different when I say, "and all classes are cancelled." Symbols, then, are verbal and nonverbal signals that convey meaning, require interpretation, and are reciprocal.

According to symbolic interactionists, the meaning that a symbol or social object cues is its set of organized sets of responses. In other words, symbolic meaning is not the image of a thing seen at a distance, nor does it exactly correspond to the dictionary, but the meaning of a word is the action that it calls out. For example, the meaning of a chair is the different kinds of things we can do with it. Picture a wooden object with four legs, a seat, and a slatted back. If I sit down on this object, then the meaning of it is "chair." On the other hand, if I take that same object and break it into small pieces and use it to start a fire, it's no longer a chair—it's firewood. So the meaning of an object is defined in terms of its uses, or legitimated lines of behavior. This definition of action is created through social interaction, both past and present.

Because the meaning, legitimated actions, and objective availability (they are objects because we can point them out as foci for interaction) of symbols are produced in social interactions, they are social objects. Any idea or thing can be a social object. Natural features such as the Smoky Mountains, invisible things like ghosts, and ideas like freedom can all be social objects. There is nothing about the thing itself that makes it a social object; an entity becomes a social object to us through our interactions around it. Through interaction we call attention to it, name it, and attach legitimate lines of behavior to it.

If you look around the room you are sitting in, everything you notice is a social object. In fact, there is a profound way in which people only see and relate to social objects. Human reality is constituted symbolically; it's a symbolic world, not a physical one, filled with social objects rather than physical objects. But can we notice things that aren't social objects? Yes, we can, but if we do, the object will be a problem for us to respond to because we won't know the meaning of the thing—note that the response itself becomes a social object (running from an unknown danger, investigating an unidentified entity, and so on).

Concepts and Theory: Self and Action

We now come to Blumer's (1969) third premise of symbolic interaction: "Meanings are handled in, and modified through, an interpretative process used by the person in dealing with the things he encounters" (p. 2). Chances are good that the first two premises contained some ideas that you found surprising—most people don't consider the meaning of meaning. Chances are also good that the subject of this third premise is something you feel comfortable with—most people have a commonsense understanding of what a "person" or "individual" is. However, you might be surprised at Blumer's understanding of the person. We just finished talking about how meanings are created and interpreted socially, through the ongoing, three-phase process of social interaction. According to Blumer's school of symbolic interaction, the individual does it in the exact same way. In other words, the person—or, more properly, the self—engages in an internal symbolic interaction through which meaning emerges. Now think about this. A conversation takes place between two or more people. So, who are these people in your head and where did they come from?

The Self

Have you ever watched someone doing something? Of course you have. Maybe you watched a worker planting a tree on campus, or maybe you watched a band last Friday night. And while you watched, you understood people and their behaviors in terms of the identity they claimed and roles they played. In short, when you watch someone you understand him or her as a social object. After watching someone, have you ever called someone else's attention to that actor? Undoubtedly you have, and it's easy to do. All you have to say is something like, "Whoa, check her/him/it out." And the other person will look and usually understand immediately what it is you are pointing out, because we understand one another in terms of being a social object. Sometimes we will notice someone and be embarrassed for that person, sometimes we laugh at or with him or her, and other times we might feel a sense of admiration. When we point out the other person to our friend, she will probably feel the same way—because the fact that the person observed is a social object calls out the same responses in both of us.

People-watching is a pretty common experience, and most of us do it. We can do it because we understand the other individual in terms of being a social object. Let me ask you another couple of questions. Have you ever watched yourself? Have you ever felt embarrassed or laughed at yourself? Of course you have. How is that different than watching other people? It isn't. Here is a fundamental feature of symbolic interaction: We relate to and understand others because they are social objects, and we relate to and understand the self because it too is a social object.

But there is something decidedly odd about this statement. It's easy to watch someone else. And it is easy to understand how we watch someone else. If I am watching a band play, I can watch the band because they are onstage and I am in the audience. We can observe the other because we are standing outside of them. We can point to them because they are there in the world around us. But how can we point to our self, call our own attention to our self, and understand our self as a social object? Do you see the problem? We must somehow divorce our self from our self so that we can call attention to our self, so that we can understand our self as meaningfully relevant as a social object. That sounds convoluted, but it is exactly what we do.

Think about this idea of the **self** for a moment. What is it and where does it exist? There is a way in which the self doesn't live in the here and now; that is, the self is a transcendent thing that does not exist in the immediacy of experience. By definition the self must exist outside of our direct experience. It is this ability to not be in the moment that allows us to monitor our behaviors and produce society. The mind considers immediate behaviors with reference to a mental object (the self) that is made up of selected images from the past and hoped-for images from the future. Thus our conscious experience is predicated upon our being able to achieve a perspective divorced from the constraints of time. What this implies is that the self is a perspective—it is a symbolic platform on which to stand and view our own behaviors as if someone else were performing them.

The question, then, is where does this other self come from? How can part of us not be fixed in time, living in the moment? How can we get outside and watch ourselves? The self is a social achievement that comes through language, interaction, and most specifically through role-taking. **Role-taking** has a very specific definition: It is the process through which we place our self in the position (or role) of another in order to see our own self. Students often confuse role-taking with what might be called role-making. In every social situation, we make a role for ourselves. Erving Goffman (Chapter 4) wrote at length about this process and called it impression management. Role-taking is a precursor to effective role-making—we put ourselves in the position of the other in order to see how they want us to act. But role-taking is distinct from impression management and it is the main mechanism through which we are able to form a perspective outside of ourselves.

As children, we role-take through three successive stages: play, game, and generalized other. The first stage in the process of self-formation is the play stage. During this stage, the child can take the role, or assume the perspective, of certain significant others. Significant others are those upon whom we depend for emotional and often material support. These are the people with whom we have long-term relations and intimate (self-revealing) ties. This is called the play stage because children must literally play at being some significant other in order to see themselves. At this point, they haven't progressed much in terms of being able to think abstractly, so they must act out the role to get the perspective. Here is the important point: In order to play like this, a child must literally get outside of himself or herself.

Children play at being mommy or being teacher. The child will hold a doll or stuffed bear and talk to it as if she were the parent. Ask any parent; it can be a frightening experience because what you are faced with is an almost exact imitation of your own behaviors, words, and even tone of voice. It might be unnerving for the parent, but this is serious play. The child is learning to see him or her own self. So, as the child is playing mommy or daddy with a teddy bear, who is the bear? The child herself. She is seeing herself from the point of view of the parent, literally. This act is the origin of the divorced perspective that we call self. This is the genesis of the objective stance—being able to get outside of ourselves so that we can watch ourselves as if onstage.

The next stage in the development of self is the game stage. During this stage, the child can take the perspective of several others and can take into account the rules (sets of responses that different attitudes bring out) of society. But the role-taking at this stage is still not very abstract. In the play stage, the child could only take the perspective of a single significant other; in the game stage, the child can take on several others, but they all remain individuals. Take the example of a baseball game. The batter can role-take with each individual player in the field and determine how to bat based on their behaviors. The batter is also aware of all the rules of the game. Children at this stage can role-take with several people, and they are very concerned with social rules. But they still don't have a fully formed self. That doesn't happen until they can take the perspective of the generalized other.

The **generalized other** refers to sets of attitudes that an individual may take toward himself or herself—it is the general attitude or perspective of a community. The generalized other allows the individual to have a more nonsegmented self as the perspectives of many others are generalized into a single view. It is through the generalized other that the community exercises control over the conduct of its individual members. Up until this point, the child has only been able to role-take with specific others. As the individual progresses in her ability to use abstract language and concepts, she is also able to think about general or abstract others. So, for example, a man in the privacy of his home may think, "If the guys at the gym could see what a couch potato I am at home, they'd die." Or a woman may look in the mirror and judge the reflection by the general image given to her by the media about how a woman should look. There are no specific people involved, but we are able to see our self through the eyes of some generalized other, and we talk to ourselves about it.

Part of what we mean by the self is this internalized conversation. We carry on an internal dialogue about who we are, what we are doing, where we are going, what the world means, and so on. This conversation is between the two parts of the self (the observer and the actor). Symbolic interactionism calls these two interactive facets of the self the "I" and the "Me." The Me is the self that results from the progressive stages of role-taking and is treated as a social object—it is that part of our self that observes our behaviors. The Me doesn't fully come into existence until we are able to role-take with the generalized other. The Me, then, is the perspective that we assume in order to view and analyze our own behaviors; the I is that part of the self that is unsocialized and spontaneous.

Notice what we just said, the self is an internalized conversation between the I and the Me. And what do we already know about conversations and interactions? They are emergent. You and I may have a good idea of what we are going to talk about when we get together at the bar, but there's also a good chance that we'll end up talking about things we couldn't have imagined. Conversations shift and change, and meanings emerge through this negotiated interaction. And the same is true for the self. The self doesn't exist in any one place. It is a social object (something we give meaning to) that emerges through ongoing, internalized conversations and social interactions (role-taking). During the internalized interaction, it is specifically the I that makes the process emergent. The I is the actor, and it can act apart from the Me, apart from the perspective given by the generalized other.

Social Action

So, why do you have a self? Symbolic interactionism teaches us that the self is created; it isn't something we're born with. In fact, there isn't anything within us as individuals that makes it natural or imperative that we have a self. Don't get me wrong, obviously there are internal preconditions that make the self possible and that predispose us toward having a self. But if it were possible for a human baby to grow to adulthood apart from society, that person wouldn't have, nor would he or she need, a self. In fact, in such a state the self would be a liability. Why? Because the self is not an intrinsic characteristic of the individual; it is a social entity. What we see from symbolic interactionism is that the self functions to control our behaviors— it allows us to act rather than react. A person who had lived alone for his or her entire existence would need to react instinctually to situations, rather than respond to their social meaning. Thinking about the social ramifications of some action would slow the beast down and make it vulnerable. Thus, the self is mandated socially, not individually, so that we can act rather than react.

Blumer's symbolic interactionism argues that the act contains four distinct elements: impulse, perception, manipulation, and consummation (behavior). We feel an impulse to behave: We are hungry, tired, or angry. For most animals, the route from impulse to behavior is rather direct—they react to the stimulus using instincts or behavioristically imprinted patterns. But for humans, it is a circuitous route. After we feel the initial impulse to act, we perceive our environment. This perception entails the recognition of the pertinent symbolic elements (including other people, absent reference groups, and so on) as well as alternatives to satisfying the impulse. Perception is the all-important pause before action; this is where society becomes possible. After we symbolically take in our environment, we manipulate the different elements. This manipulation takes place in the mind and considers the possible ramifications of using different behaviors to satisfy the impulse. We role-take with significant present and generalized others, and we think about the elements available to complete the task. After we manipulate the situation symbolically, we are in a position to act.

Notice how much of human action takes place in the mind. In fact, we could say that all the action that is distinctly human takes place in the mind. What I mean by that is that all animals have impulses and all animals behave. Those are the first and last stages of the act. What makes action distinctly human are the middle two stages, both of which take place in the mind. And, guess what? The mind is social too. According to symbolic interactionists, the *mind* is a kind of behavior that involves at least five different abilities:

- To use symbols to denote objects
- To use symbols as its own stimulus (it can talk to itself)

- To read and interpret another's gestures and use them as further stimuli
- To suspend response (not act out of impulse)
- To imaginatively rehearse one's own behaviors before actually behaving

Let me give you an example that encompasses all these behaviors. A few years ago, our school paper ran a cartoon. In it was a picture of three people: a man and a woman arm-in-arm, and another man. The woman was introducing the men to one another. Both men were reaching out to shake one another's hands. But above the single man was a balloon of his thoughts. In it, he was picturing himself violently punching the other man. He wanted to hit the man, but he shook his hand instead and said, "Glad to meet you."

There are a lot of things we can pull out of this cartoon, but the issue we want to focus on is the disparity between what the man felt and what the man did. He had an impulse to hit the other man, perhaps because he was jealous. But he didn't. Why didn't he? Actually, that isn't a good theoretical question. Theoretically we would ask, how was he able to stop his initial impulse? He was able to not hit the other man because of his mind. His mind was able to block his initial impulse, to understand the situation symbolically, to point out to his self the symbols and possible meanings, to entertain alternative lines of behavior, and choose the behavior that best fit the situation. The man used social objects to stimulate his own behavior rather than going with his impulse or the actual world.

The mind is something that we acquire; or, more correctly, it is a set of behaviors that we learn. Infant dependency, language, and interactions are the preconditions for the formation of the mind. Human babies are completely dependent upon their parents for survival, more so and for longer periods of time than other species. They are thus forced to interact with others in already organized social environments. When babies are hungry or tired or wet, they send out what are called "unconventional gestures," gestures that do not mean the same to the sender and hearer. In other words, they cry. The caregivers must figure out what the baby needs. After they have discovered what the baby needs, parents tend to vocalize their behaviors ("Oh, did Susie need a ba-ba?"). Babies eventually discover that if they mimic the parents and send out a significant gesture ("ba-ba"), they get their needs met sooner. This is the beginning of language acquisition; babies begin to understand that their environment is symbolic—the object that satisfies hunger is "ba-ba" and the object that brings it is "da-da." Eventually, a baby will understand that she has a symbol as well: "Susie." Thus language acquisition allows the child to symbolize and eventually to symbolically manipulate her environment, including self and others. Notice, the mind is social through and through.

Concepts and Theory: Society and Sociology

Generally speaking, sociologists see society as a macro-level entity that operates according to its own laws. One of the clearest explanations of this approach was given to us by Émile Durkheim. Durkheim argues that society exists *sui generis*—a Latin term meaning "of its own kind." Durkheim (1912/1995) uses the term to say that society exists in and of itself, not as a "mere epiphenomenon of its morphological base" (p. 426). When Durkheim uses that term "morphological base," he's referring to the people that live in society. In other words, society is more than simply the sum of all the individuals within it. Society exists as its own kind of entity, obeying its own rules and creating its own effects: "*The determining cause of a social fact should be sought among the social facts preceding it and not among the states of the individual consciousness*" (Durkheim, 1895/1938, p. 110, emphasis Durkheim's). Further, this view of society also argues that society is "endowed with a power of coercion, by reason of which they control [the person]" (p. 3).

Joint Actions

A good portion of sociology, then, is concerned with these macro-level structures that control or influence human action. And this is precisely the kind of sociology of which Blumer is critical. Blumer gives us another way to see how society works and is formed—the **joint action**: interactions that are woven together as a whole. Let's take my graduate theory class for example. I'm writing this paragraph in November. In about 6 weeks I'll be standing in front of my graduate students. Between now and then, I will have written out my syllabus, sent it to the enrolled students, and given them their first reading assignment. They will perform whatever interactions necessary to obtain the books ("talk to Mom and Dad"; "get financial aid"; "drive to the bookstore"; "buy the books"; and so on). We'll have 15 class meetings, each of which is a separate joint action during which several unexpected ideas, conflicts, and relationships will emerge.

We will then link these class meetings together through the use of tests, papers, and discussions about theses, classes, ideas, and graduation. Those linkages will themselves be linked to other courses at the university (prerequisites and the like). All of these will be linked together through various kinds of interactions, like theses defenses and graduation ceremonies. All of those joint actions will be linked to the history of interactions and joint actions that have occurred at the place where one of the students will apply for a job or for further graduate work; and on and on, ad infinitum. For Blumer, most of what we mean by "society," then, exists in recurring patterns of joint action, all of which emerge and are not determined by an external social structure.

At every point of interaction or joint action, there is uncertainty. All human action has to be purposefully initiated; and we may or may not act. Once begun, actions, interactions, and joint actions can be interrupted, changed, or abandoned. Even during the course of an interaction, participants may have different definitions of what is going on. If there is a common definition, there still may be differences in the way each interaction is carried out: An individual may perform his lines of action differently; changes can impose themselves on the interaction in such a way as to make people define and lean upon one another differently. And, new situations may arise that call into question the ways things have been done in the past.

Symbolic interactionism thus shifts the question of patterned behaviors from the structure to the interaction. It entertains the possibility that each interaction and joint action could be different, and it grants freedom of choice to the participants.

There are a few things we want to note about joint actions. First, joint actions are created as we link together various interactions. The nature of interactions lies in the way in which we intertwine the many actions that create the interaction (I hear my friend introduce you, you look at me and I look at you, I give my "nice to meet you" smile and extend my hand, you see my hand as it is extending and you extend your hand, our hands meet and we judge the firmness of the grip and carefully match what we are given, and so forth—or, we do something totally different so that it becomes a contest). The same is true of joint actions, except there we link together multiple interactions.

Second, joint actions may be spoken of as such. They stand as identifiable units to us, which is why I put quotation marks in my description of obtaining class books. We see them as distinct yet joined together—"driving to the bookstore" and "buying books" are separate actions and interactions, yet we link them together into the joint action of getting ready for school. And, third, each of the interactions and joint actions must be created anew each time they are produced. For example, weddings are not simply expressions of a causal social structure called marriage. The structure of norms, values, and beliefs doesn't determine the wedding; you do, which is why your elaborate ceremony and my barefoot event at the beach can both happen and qualify as weddings. A wedding is a repetitive and stable form of joint action, yet it is as fresh and creative each time it is achieved.

Sociology

The question of whether or not society is empirical is an issue we will visit again and again in this book. The issue is important because the possibility of sociology being a science is determined by it. Many sociologists assume that society exists empirically in its structures and institutions. Not so for symbolic interactionism: Blumer (1969) argues that "the essence of society lies in an ongoing process of action—not in a posited structure of relations" (p. 71). In what way, then, does symbolic interactionism see sociology as empirical and scientific? To begin our discussion, Blumer lists six characteristics of empirical, scientific inquiry:

- Scientific inquiry uses theory. Scientific theory is a formal and logically sound argument explaining some empirical phenomenon in general or abstract terms.
- Theory is used to decide the kinds of questions that are asked.
- Theory shapes what data are relevant, how the data will be collected and tested.
- Propositions are born out of theory: Theory informs the kinds of relationships among and between the variables that are to be tested.
- The data are interpreted and brought back to change, modify, or confirm theory.

- All theory and scientific research are based on concepts. Concepts are the basic building blocks of theory. They inform the way questions are asked; they are the source of data categories (sought and grouped); they form the relationships among and between the data; and they are the chief way in which the data are interpreted.

Blumer's main point is that each part of this procedure, particularly the concepts that are used, must be scrutinized to make certain it conforms to the empirical world that is being studied. Blumer contends that this examination doesn't usually occur in the social and psychological sciences. More often than not, what sociologists and psychologists study are reified concepts of the world rather than the social world itself. Here the word *reified* means to convert an idea into something concrete or objective. The **problem of reification** is rampant in the social and behavioral sciences, according to Blumer. The two most notable examples are "attitudes" in psychology and "structures or institutions" in sociology. Neither of these concepts has a "clear and fixed empirical reference" (Blumer, 1969, p. 91), yet both are seen as having some causal force in determining human behavior.

Obviously, the issue of most concern for us is the critique that social structures are not empirical. Many sociologists see social structures as connections among sets of positions that form a network. The interrelated sets of positions in society are generally defined in terms of status positions, roles, and norms. These social and cultural elements create and manage the connections among people, and it is the connections that form the structure. Social structures are used to explain patterned behaviors. Patterned behavior in most other animals is seen as the result of instincts or naturally embedded mechanisms, like seasonal change. On the other hand, a social structure is generally seen as that which "accounts for much of the . . . patterns of human experience and behavior" (Johnson, 2000, p. 295).

Yet Blumer says there's a problem in attributing causal influence to social structures: Social structures aren't empirical. The only empirical social thing we can point to are real people interacting with one another. According to Blumer (1969), anytime we appeal to psychological or social structures as the impetus behind human behavior, "the human being becomes a mere medium through which such initiating factors operate to produce given actions" (p. 73). According to Blumer, then, most social and behavioral scientists do not investigate empirical objects. And if most of what they are looking at isn't empirical, then they aren't doing science. Thus, focusing on the interaction is the only possible way to create a social or behavioral science.

There are at least four methodological ramifications of Blumer's argument. First, to state the obvious, an empirical science needs to investigate empirical phenomena. Blumer argues that most of what passes as social or behavioral science is not empirical because most "social scientists" have not critiqued the reified concepts they are using to create theory, propose relationships, gather and analyze data, and interpret findings. As Blumer (1969) says, "Reality exists in the empirical world and not in the methods used to study that world" (p. 27).

Second, we need to understand social interaction as a moving process. Many sociological perspectives understand society in terms of one central form, such as conflict theory, structural functionalism, exchange theory, and so on. Blumer's point is that real people in real interactions will sometimes be in conflict, sometimes be functional, or sometimes be engaged in exchange. We need to see that human behavior is meaningful behavior and that humans can interpret meanings in multiple ways: Society is a moving process, not a static object.

Third, we need to understand social action in terms of the social actor. Here Blumer is emphasizing the agency of interactants. The person and the interaction are not simply modes through which social structure is expressed; rather, they are the true acting units of society. And, fourth, we need to be careful about using reified concepts to understand social life. The concepts of "institution," "structure," and "organizations" all fall short of the direct examination of the empirical world. Macro-level issues need to be understood in terms of the career or history of joint actions.

Notice the overall intent of Blumer's argument here: Be careful of using and attributing causation to reified concepts. Blumer isn't discrediting quantitative, statistical data analysis; nor is he saying that sociologists can't analyze or think about large-scale social processes. In fact, one of Blumer's (1990) last publications is an analysis of industrialization as an agent of social change. For many sociologists, industrialization is a causal factor, but for Blumer, it is neutral or indeterminate. However, saying that industrialization is neutral doesn't imply that the process doesn't exist—Blumer is simply making a question or problem out of what many sociologists take for granted. He defines industrialization in a way that most sociologists would, but he then identifies nine "points of contact with group life" (p. 42). Each of these points of contact constitutes a research site for the symbolic interactionist, because "it is the definition that determines the response" (p. 121), not industrialization. And this definition is a quality that emerges from what people bring to the situation and the ongoing process of interaction.

Blumer isn't trying to do away with quantitative analysis either. His point is actually much more powerful. Quantitative data and statistical analysis can be used to great benefit in sociology, but sociologists need to be careful about what we think is actually influencing or producing an effect. Let's say we find a statistical association between gender and salary. For the symbolic interactionist, that association isn't the end of the study; it's just the beginning. If you were the researcher, you would then have to look for the empirical actions, interactions, and joint actions in back of the association between variables. In this sense, symbolic interactionism doesn't have a specific methodology. Almost all methodological approaches can be used if human agency and social interaction are given their proper place. (See Ulmer & Wilson, 2003, for a more complete introduction to SI and quantitative analysis.)

However, Blumer does give us two methodological recommendations: exploration and inspection.

> Exploration is by definition a flexible procedure in which the scholar shifts from one to another line of inquiry, adopts new points of observation as his study progresses, moves in new direction previously unthought of, and changes his recognition of what are relevant data as he acquires more information and better understanding. (Blumer, 1969, p. 40)

Exploration is grounded in the daily life of the real social group the investigator wants to study. Rarely does a researcher have firsthand knowledge of the social world she wants to study. Thus, rather than entering another's world with preconceptions, as much as is possible the researcher naively enters the other's world and searches for the social objects that the group regularly employs in producing their meanings through interactions. The records of such social objects and interactions become comprehensive and intimate accounts of what takes place in the real world. These accounts are in turn analyzed. The researcher seeks to sharpen the concepts she is using to describe the social world, to discover generic relationships (those that appear to hold true in various settings), and to form theoretical propositions.

Summary

- Blumer gives us a way of understanding the kind of public philosophy needed in a democracy. Drawing on pragmatism Blumer argues that human action is based on meaning; meaning isn't an attribute of any object, event, or person—it is, rather, an emergent quality of interaction; and that individuals interpret meanings through an internal interactive process between the I and the Me. These tenants of SI are the basis for not only emergent group ethics but also individual responsibility, as the individual makes decisions for action and is not heavily influenced by supposed social structures.

- Human beings survive because of meaning, and meaning is something other than the thing or experience itself. Meaning is always symbolic and pragmatically oriented, and it emerges out of social interaction, a three-step interface of action: sending a symbolic cue, responding to the cue, and responding to the response. Generally speaking, social interactions do not stop at this point but continue on through many, many iterations of these three phases. Because interactions are ongoing, meaning is constantly emerging.

- The human world is made up of various social objects. Social objects come to exist as they are indicated by the interactants, and as particular kinds of actions are intended toward the thing. Social objects may be actual things, symbolic meanings, selves, or others.

- The self is a social object that is constructed through three stages of role-taking: the play, game, and generalized other. By symbolically seeing the self from the role of the other, the person learns to divorce himself or herself from his or her own behaviors. A perspective is thus created—a place from which to view and attribute meaning to one's own behaviors. This perspective is referred to as the "Me," and the acting or impulsive side is called the "I." What we mean by the self only exists in the conversation between the I and the Me.

- The social object quality of the self allows people to consider and control their behavior. The self is what allows humans to act rather than react. A single act has four stages: impulse, perception, manipulation, and consumption. All animals have impulses—thus the distinctly human elements are found in the final three stages.

- Society thus does not determine our actions; action is a choice. There are two ways in which society exists and has influence: through the generalized other (institutions) and as constructions of joint action. Generalized others are sets of attitudes with which interactants may role-take; these sets of attitudes constitute the relevant generalized others. Joint actions are various discrete interactions that are laced together.

- The only empirical and acting part of society is the interaction, and Blumer cautions us against the danger of reifying concepts such as institutions or social structures. In analyzing society, then, we need to focus on the interaction, realizing that it is an ongoing and moving process wherein individual actors exercise agency. This analysis should be in two phases. The first is exploration: Because of the emergent nature of society and self, researchers must divest themselves as much as possible from preconceived notions of what might be happening in any given situation. Theory ought to be grounded in the actual behaviors and negotiations in real interactions. Second, as theoretical concepts suggest themselves from the experience of the researcher in the field, these should be inspected to see if they might hold in other settings as well.

TAKING THE PERSPECTIVE

Symbolic interaction (SI) is a primary perspective in sociology; and there are several types of SI. The one explained in this chapter is sometimes referred to as the Chicago School, because the University of Chicago was its first institutional home. This branch of SI gained force in the 1960s as a critique of Talcott Parsons' structural functionalism. Blumer (1969) specifically takes on Parsons' notion of the unit act as "the quaint notion that social interaction is a process of developing 'complimentary expectations'" (p. 53). Approaches like Parsons' cast theoretical concepts at a high level of abstraction and rely heavily on quantitative data, both of which may lead to the problem of reification that Blumer points out. Symbolic interactionism, then, as Blumer conceptualized it is an approach that points to the necessity of interpretation and moving theory from the ground up (often referred to as "grounded theory"). More generally and historically, Blumer's work follows that of George Herbert Mead and pragmatism in emphasizing the political responsibility for choices and the emergent property of democratic ethics.

In brief, Blumer's school of symbolic interaction is a theoretical perspective in sociology that assumes that human beings are fundamentally oriented toward meaning, that meaning is not a characteristic of a word or object, and that meaning emerges from the interaction. Central issues and questions for symbolic interaction include: the production and use of the self in interaction, how meaning is achieved, and how actions and interactions are woven together.

Work developed from this perspective has taken a variety of paths, such as Howard Becker's labeling theory, *Outsiders: Studies in the Sociology of Deviance* (1963); Norman Denzin's cultural studies, *Symbolic Interactionism and Cultural Studies: The Politics of Interpretation* (1992); and R. S. Perinbanayagam's theory of dialogic acts, *The Presence of Self* (2000). An outstanding resource containing primary works is Ken Plummer's *Symbolic Interactionism,* Volumes 1 and 2 (1991).

Another school of SI that gained force in the 1970s is often called the Iowa School, best exemplified by Manford Kuhn's work (see Kuhn & McPartland, "An Empirical Investigation of Self-Attitudes," *American Sociological Review,* 1951, Vol. 19, pp. 68–76; and Kuhn, "Major Trends in Symbolic Interaction Theory in the Past Twenty-Five Years," *Sociological Quarterly,* 1964, Vol. 5, pp. 61–84). Simply put, the major difference between the two approaches is that Kuhn's work emphasizes structure whereas Blumer stresses emergence. Kuhn argues that people develop a core self, one that is stable across situations and interactions, and that social structures, which include norms and expectations, are relatively stable and heavily influence the interaction, as does one's sense of self. In contrast to Blumer's situational approach, sociological methods in this school use structured measurements. The one that Kuhn created that has had the greatest impact on the field is the Twenty Statements Test, which asks people to write twenty responses to "Who am I?" Kuhn took the responses as indicators of a person's internalized objective social statuses; that is, the parts of a social structure to which a person most relates. Kuhn argues that these form personal expectations, which, in turn, structures an individual's behavior in any situation.

BUILDING YOUR THEORY TOOLBOX

Learning More—Primary Sources

- The foundational works for symbolic interaction are
  - George Herbert Mead, *Mind, Self, and Society: From the Standpoint of a Social Behaviorist,* University of Chicago Press, 1934.
  - Herbert Blumer, *Symbolic Interactionism: Perspective and Method,* University of California Press, 1969.

Learning More—Secondary Sources

- For a good introduction to structural symbolic interactionism, look in the following:
  - Sheldon Stryker, *Symbolic Interactionism: A Social Structural Version,* Blackburn Press, 2003.
- Three important extensions of symbolic interactionism are
  - *Affect control theory:* David Heise, "Understanding Social Interaction With Affect Control Theory," in *New Directions in Contemporary Sociological Theory* (J. Berger and M. Zelditch Jr., Eds.), Rowman & Littlefield, 2002.
  - *Expectation states theory:* David. G. Wagner and Joseph Berger, "Expectation States Theory: An Evolving Research Program," in *New Directions in Contemporary Sociological Theory* (J. Berger and M. Zelditch Jr., Eds.), Rowman & Littlefield, 2002.
  - *Cultural studies:* Norman K. Denzin, *Symbolic Interactionism and Cultural Studies: The Politics of Interpretation,* Blackwell, 1992.
- For a synthesized and general theory of interaction, see
  - Turner, J. H., *A theory of Social Interaction,* Stanford University Press, 1988.

(Continued)

(Continued)

Check It Out

- The Society for the Study of Symbolic Interaction: http://sun.soci.niu.edu/~sssi/

- The Self: For further reading, I would suggest that you read a standard approach: Morris Rosenberg, *Conceiving the Self*, Basic Books, 1979, and a more postmodern reading: James A. Holstein and Jaber F. Gubrium, *The Self We Live By: Narrative Identity in a Postmodern World*, Oxford, 2000.

Seeing the World

- Write a 250-word synopsis of the theoretical perspective symbolic interactionism.

- Define the following terms—your definitions must minimally stipulate the essential characteristics: *pragmatism, meaning, interaction, social objects, self, role-taking, generalized other, joint action, problem of reification*

- After reading and understanding this chapter, you should be able to answer the following questions (remember to answer them *theoretically*):

  o What is pragmatism and what is its unique association with America? How does pragmatism inform symbolic interactionist theory?

  o What is the importance of meaning and how is it achieved?

  o How are social objects defined? What can be a social object? How are social objects used in interaction?

  o What are the mind and self and why are they functionally necessary for society? What kind of behaviors do the mind and self engage in?

  o How are the mind and self formed?

  o What is the generalized other and what role does it play in self and society?

  o What is society and how is it formed?

Engaging the World

- How would symbolic interactionists talk about and understand racial and gender inequality?

- Knowing what you know now about how the self is constructed, how do you think sociological counseling would look? Using your favorite Internet search engine, enter "clinical sociology." What is clinical sociology? What is the current state of clinical sociology?

- SI very clearly claims that our self is dependent upon the social groups with which we affiliate. Using SI theory, explain how the self of a person in a disenfranchised group might be different than one associated with a majority position.

Weaving the Threads

- At this point, all I can do is point out some ideas for you to be aware of as we work our way through this book. Begin thinking about the ideas of structure, symbols, language, meaning, self, and identity.

CHAPTER 4

Organizing Ordinary Life:

Harold Garfinkel

(1917–)

As we've seen in Chapters 2 and 3, Talcott Parsons formulated sociology's problem as that of action: How can human action be a result of individual choice and yet display the continuing patterns that make society possible? Parsons' response was to conceptualize the unit act as being constrained by cultural factors such as norms and values. Cultural values create the goals that we can choose from and norms delineate the acceptable methods through which we can obtain those goals. Both values and norms exist outside the situation and thus structure and pattern human action. Further, Parsons argued that these social norms and values also structure our innermost self. Through socialization we internalize these cultural elements to the degree that they feel natural. Our sense of self, the needs we experience, and the values we hold are in truth social structures. Thus our very motivations—the reasons we want to act in the first place—are actually expressions of culture.

Harold Garfinkel was a student of Parsons, and like Parsons is concerned with human action. However, like symbolic interactionism, Garfinkel has problems with the discrepancy between what Parsons' voluntaristic action proposes and what is empirically available. Following Freud, Parsons (1951) argued that the "need disposition in the actor's own personality structure" operates unconsciously so that people don't really know why they are doing what they're doing (p. 37). Yet empirically people can give an explanation of what they are doing and why they are doing it. A potential problem, then, "arises between the . . . analyses of action developed by sociologists and the accounts of action developed . . . by the participants" (Heritage, 1984, pp. 22–23). Thus, like Blumer, Garfinkel argues that standard sociological methods miss the mark of empirical science: True sociological knowledge is provided in the immediate experiences of our day-to-day life. Unlike Blumer, who is caught up in Mead's question of meaning, Garfinkel, like his mentor, Parsons, is concerned with the problem of social order.

Garfinkel draws inspiration from the work of Alfred Schutz. More than any other, Schutz (1967) is responsible for bringing phenomenology into the social disciplines. As a philosophy, **phenomenology** is concerned with consciousness and seeks to discover it in its purest form, apart from language and any preconceptions. The idea is to get at the essential structures of the human experience. Arguing that humans are defined socially, Schutz takes this basic idea of primary experience and argues that it is found in social things rather than the individual consciousness. Schutz tells us that the purest form of human experience is found in the natural attitude that people have in their lifeworlds. The **lifeworld** refers to the world as it is immediately experienced by each person. This lifeworld is by definition shared with others. Within this lifeworld people have a natural attitude. The natural attitude is characterized by being wide awake, suspending doubt, being engaged in work, and assuming intersubjectivity (a shared inner world). Using Schutz's work, Garfinkel is telling us that *everything we need to understand the social order can be found in the lifeworld and people's natural attitude toward it.* Sounds pretty simple, doesn't it? In principle it may be, but I think in practice and understanding it might be one of the more difficult sociological perspectives. If you get lost in our discussion of Garfinkel's theory, come back to this tenant of phenomenology.

THEORIST'S DIGEST

Brief Biography

Harold Garfinkel was born on October 29, 1917, in Newark, New Jersey. He grew up during the Depression and was discouraged from attending the university. While attending business classes at a local school, Garfinkel was exposed to the idea of "accounting practices," which he later saw as the primary feature of interaction, as well as a group of sociology students. Those experiences, along with a summer spent at a work camp building a dam, prompted Garfinkel to hitchhike to the University of North Carolina, Chapel Hill (UNCCH), where he was admitted to graduate school. He completed his master's at UNCCH, after which he was drafted into the army during WWII. After the war, Garfinkel went to Harvard to study for his PhD under Talcott Parsons. In 1954, Garfinkel joined the faculty at the University of California, Los Angeles, where he stayed until his retirement in 1987. Garfinkel's most important work is *Studies in Ethnomethodology*, which was published in 1967.

Central Sociological Questions

Social order and meaning are age-old questions for sociologists. But Garfinkel's gaze penetrates beneath the usual sociological answers. For one, he isn't so much interested in whether or not social order and meaning are actually present. That kind of concern about order and meaning always implies questions of reality, which for Garfinkel are philosophic concerns. He's interested in how we *achieve a sense* that there is order and meaning. This phrases the question empirically because whether or not there is really such a thing as society or meaning, it is empirically true that people have a sense that social order exists. He is also disturbed by how quickly sociologists explain order and meaning by referring to outside forces, like norms and social structures. This critique is also driven by an emphasis on what empirically exists: Garfinkel wants to know how a sense of social order and meaning are produced in just this way and at just this time.

Simply Stated

Social orders are identical to the commonsense methods fully aware actors use to render the situation accountable and sensible. Social situations are thus reflexive and ordered by the accounts offered and enacted by participants. Accounts are indexical; that is, they reference what is commonly understood by participants; and accounts proceed using a documentary method.

Key Ideas

Lifeworld, phenomenology, ethnomethodology, accounts, documentary method, reciprocity of perspectives, reflexivity, indexical expressions, incorrigible assumptions, secondary elaborations of belief, ad hocing

Concepts and Theory: Everyday Social Order as an Accomplishment

I think that one of the reasons that ethnomethodology can seem difficult is that it relies on what we do in unremarkable interactions to explain social order. Rather than looking for big issues like norms and structures, Garfinkel calls our attention to such small things we do unthinkingly in every social situation. The taken-for-grantedness of these behaviors is both the power and problem of the ethnomethodological account. It's powerful because it helps us see what else is going on just beneath the surface—it lets us see that you and I are more responsible for social reality than we might imagine; the ethnomethodological account is problematic for us precisely because we do these things without thinking and they seem so mundane.

Understanding Sociology

My initial exposure to Garfinkel's work came in my first semester of graduate school. I was a teaching assistant in an introduction to sociology class. The teacher was a visiting professor by the name of Eric Livingston. As is customary, on the first day of class the professor explained what the course was about. He told us that we were taking an ethnomethodological approach to sociology. At the time, nobody knew what that meant, but he did tell us one thing that struck us all as odd: We had a textbook and we were going to read it, but not in the usual fashion. You know, we usually read textbooks to understand the topic. We approach the text as an authoritative source: Geography books teach us about the earth and sociology texts teach us about society. It sounds pretty straightforward, right? Well, not in this case. Dr. Livingston told us that we were going to use the textbook as an example of how sociology organizes itself to be sociology. We were to read the book not to learn about society, but, rather, we were to study the text to see how members of sociology render situations knowable as sociology.

If you're like me, that last part was really confusing when Dr. Livingston said it. But there's something going on beneath the surface in the statement, "Sociology texts teach us about society." There's an assumption there that we rarely think about: In order to study society *one must first assume that society exists.* And while that seems commonsensical to us today, our understanding of "society" is historically specific. The word *society* came into the English language from the French and has a Latin base. The Latin root for *society* means companion or fellowship, and up until the middle of the eighteenth century it kept this basic meaning (Williams, 1983, pp. 291–292). Society thus initially referred to a group of friends or associates, like a legal or scientific society. But toward the end of the seventeenth and through the middle of the eighteenth centuries, the idea of society was seen in more abstract ways, to refer to something not only bigger than face-to-face social interactions, but also an objective entity that could act independently. This is what Durkheim (1895/1938) means when he refers to society as a *social fact,* which "consists of ways of acting, thinking, and feeling, external to the individual, and endowed with a power of coercion, by reason of which they control him" (p. 3). These ideas concerning society began to give people a language they could use to talk about such things as religion, education, family, economy, and so on as separate parts of a larger entity called society.

Not only is the idea of society as a reality in and of itself historically specific, it is also highly contested. As Charles Lemert (2005) tells us, "The status of these social things has ever since [Durkheim] been a topic of debate among professional sociologists" (p. 7). We saw part of that debate in Chapter 3. Blumer argues that society as a social fact doesn't exist; but, rather, what we mean by society is found in the symbolic interactions and joint actions of real people in social situations. Once we call into question the empirical basis of society, what question can we ask about a sociology course and its textbook? In other words, once we put aside assumptions about things existing outside the empirically real situation, what are we left with? The answer is simple and straightforward but it goes against what we usually think. Garfinkel explains what Livingston wanted us to see. There are three points to Garfinkel's (1967) argument:

1. every reference to the "real world," even where the reference is to physical or biological events, is a reference to the organized activities of everyday life. . . .

2. in contrast to certain versions of Durkheim that teach that the objective reality of social facts is sociology's fundamental principle . . .

3. the objective reality of social facts as an ongoing accomplishment of the concerted activities of daily life, with the ordinary, artful ways of that accomplishment being by members known, used, and taken for granted, is, for members doing sociology, a fundamental phenomenon. (p. vii)

Let's start with the second point. Durkheim argues that the things we refer to as social structures and institutions are social facts—they have a facticity about them that is comparable to empirical facts. Durkheim (1895/1938) also argues that the "determining cause" of any social fact is other social facts, not individual people (p. 110). This kind of argument is typical of a structuralist approach and sociology in general. Garfinkel's point is that when most sociologists come into a situation, they search for variables outside the immediate situation to explain what's happening inside it; they look for the social facts that strongly influence the observed phenomenon.

Consider the following quote from John J. Macionis's (2005) introduction to sociology textbook (one of the best-selling introductory texts ever):

Why do industrial societies keep castelike qualities (such as letting wealth pass from generation to generation) rather than become complete meritocracies? The reason is that a pure meritocracy diminishes the importance of families and other social groupings. (p. 251)

Turn a few pages in Macionis's book and you'll find the heading, "WHO ARE THE POOR?" That heading is followed by a series of subheadings: Age, Race, Ethnicity, Gender and Family Patterns, and Urban and Rural Poverty. Macionis is doing two things here: He is offering an explanation of poverty in industrialized societies, and he is listing the standard variables that describe poverty. Notice that in good Durkheimian sociological fashion, the cause of structural inequality is explained in terms of other social facts or structures: In Macionis's statement above, structural inequality persists because of the family structure. Also notice that the structure is differentiated by variables that are themselves seen as social facts: The structure of inequality varies by age, race, ethnicity, gender, family, and urban versus rural settings.

Garfinkel wouldn't challenge whether family influences the continuation of structured inequality; nor would he question whether or not inequality varies by age, race, gender, and so on. And he wouldn't provide a competing theory to explain structural inequality. Garfinkel leaves the question of the theoretical explanation untouched—because to ask such questions or to provide different theoretical explanations of the same thing would require him to assume that society exists objectively outside situations in the form of social structures that guide and pattern human action. In other words, you can give structural explanations only in response to questions posed from a structuralist point of view. In this sense, the institutional order is sociology's achievement, without question, and ethnomethodology can't claim to know better. (See Garfinkel, 1996, p. 6n.)

Let me give you another example of why Garfinkel would say that the institutional order is sociology's achievement and ethnomethodology can't claim to know better. Generally speaking, when a psychologist looks at an individual, he or she sees personality, and when a sociologist looks at the person, he or she sees the self. The self and personality are two different ideas and thus two different entities. However, the self and personality don't exist within the individual waiting to be discovered; they are produced by the differing perspectives of sociology and psychology. So in a very real way, the self is sociology's achievement and the personality is psychology's achievement. Sociology can't really claim to know better about personality because the existence of personality is wrapped up in the language, values, and ideas of psychology. It is a psychological entity; that is, it is an entity created from the point of view of psychology.

Thus, ethnomethodology can't say anything about Durkheimian social structures. The claim that ethnomethodology does want to make is found in Garfinkel's third statement: *Ethnomethodology sees social facts as an accomplishment of people within social situations.* In this case, ethnomethodology is interested in discovering the methods through which sociologists make what they do appear as sociology. Let's use the Macionis example again. What does the textbook actually do? According to Garfinkel, it doesn't teach us about society; rather, it is an example of how sociologists make what they do appear as sociology.

Garfinkel's focus is more profound than it might first appear. In adhering to the so-called rules of sociological explanation, what do sociologists do? Sociologists simultaneously create an explanation that appears to be a sociological one and they create sociology itself. This issue is why Eric Livingston (whom I later found out is one of only a handful of people who have ever published with Harold Garfinkel) asked the intro class to take the textbook as an example of how members of the sociology field render situations knowable as sociology. But, you might say, doesn't sociology discover and explain what is really happening in society? Maybe it does, but how would you know? How can you tell if sociology is really explaining the real world? What proof is given that sociology's explanation is correct? How is that proof produced and who produces it? The only people who ever try to substantiate sociology are sociologists using sociological methodologies. Sounds odd, doesn't it? It may sound odd, but it's a powerful insight, which we will return to in a few moments.

Doing Ethnomethodology

Garfinkel's interest, then, is in the everyday procedures or methods people use to account for their behaviors. In fact, the term *ethnomethodology* means the study of folk methods. Garfinkel (1974) began using the term as a result of a study he did on jury deliberations. He noticed that there were distinct methods used to render the conversations, deliberations, decisions, and judgments "jury-like," rather than sounding like the mundane opinions of the person on the street. In the process of "becoming a juror," these people drew on multiple sources for information, but the people themselves did not change much. In fact, according to Garfinkel (1967), "A person is 95 percent juror before he comes near the court" (p. 110). The process of becoming a juror didn't change the people that Garfinkel observed. They basically acquired knowledge and made decisions in the same way they always did. What did change were the accounts that the jurors offered for the way in which they came to their decisions. Juries and jury decisions are produced by the accounts that people tell about what they did.

Accounting

Social order, then, isn't the result of institutionalized types of social action; rather, Garfinkel argues, social order is the result of members making settings "account-able." Garfinkel is using the term *account* in the sense of to regard or classify, such as she was accounted to be a powerful senator. To make something **account-able,** then, is to make it capable of being regarded or classified as a certain kind of object or event. As we render a situation accountable, we simultaneously produce social order and reality. For example, a few years ago I was visiting my sister in San Diego and we went to Balboa Park, a gorgeous recreational area with museums, fountains, restaurants, street musicians, art exhibits, and so forth. While we were walking through some of the gardens, my sister said, "Oh, look, a wedding." How could my sister recognize what was happening as a wedding? That sounds like a simple and maybe silly question, but the implications are important for Garfinkel. We were all able to recognize the event before us as a wedding because the people who organized the setting did it in such a way that it would appear as a wedding, not only to others but specifically to themselves.

When we as a group organize ourselves to do something, whether it is forming a queue or waging war, there are "requirements of recognizability" (Rawls, 2003, p. 129) that must be met. In meeting those requirements, the situation is rendered accountable as a recognizable social achievement. This work of accounting is the primary job of the members. For example, if we had gone up to the people at the wedding at any time during the event (while preparing, setting up, performing, or celebrating) and asked them, "What are you doing?" their response would be something like, "We're having a wedding." This is Garfinkel's point: The members of any situation are cognitively aware of what they are doing—they are knowingly organizing their actions in just such a way as to create a sense of social order (a wedding). Because members are knowingly producing social order within a scene, and because answerability is the simplest explanation, it follows that accounting is the primary force behind social organization.

Garfinkel thus sees social order as the result of members' practical actions that are oriented toward making the setting accountable. Notice that social order is the result of members' practical actions—not the result of people conforming to external norms, values, and beliefs that guide and guard behaviors; and not the result of social structures determining people's behaviors; and not the result of self-centered actors who cooperate only to obtain gain in a battle of profit and loss. We can see accountability practices in the story of jury selection mentioned earlier. Though the way in which they actually made decisions didn't change much, the way in which the jurors accounted for their decision making did change—the accounting practices rendered them jurors doing the business of the jury.

Garfinkel (1967, pp. 18–24) tells a story of a research project he worked on at the UCLA Outpatient Clinic. The research was to determine the criteria by which applicants were selected for treatment. Two graduate students examined 1,582 clinic files. As is usually the case, the student coders were provided with a coding sheet and instructions for its use. And, as is usually the case, the findings were subjected to inter-coder reliability tests, which are used to determine the extent to which the coders agree with one another. It's generally thought that the higher the statistic, the greater the reliability. In other words, if I'm doing a study of television commercials and I have five different coders working from the same coding sheet and their inter-coder reliability is 85%, then I can be fairly certain that what they are coding actually exists in the commercials.

However, Garfinkel found that in order to code the contents of the folders, the coders actually assumed knowledge of the way in which the clinic was organized. This assumed knowledge base "was most deliberately consulted whenever, for whatever reasons, the coders needed to be satisfied that they had coded 'what really happened'" (Garfinkel, 1967, p. 20). Notice something important here: The coders were to find out how the clinic was organized, yet in order to fill out the coding sheet, the coders assumed knowledge about the way the clinic was organized. Thus, the coders' reliability rate wasn't due to their reliable use of the coding sheet to document what happened in the clinic; the reliability rate was due to something the coders themselves were doing, apart from the coding sheet or the folders.

Most researchers in Garfinkel's position would regard such issues as problems with the measurement instrument and as threats to the research. Garfinkel (1967) likens these responses to "complaining that if the walls of a building were only gotten out of the way one could see better what was keeping the roof on" (p. 22). Garfinkel is saying that most social scientists miss the boat: They don't see what's really going on because they are preoccupied in producing "sociology" or "psychology" rather than seeing the social world as it is. For Garfinkel, the graduate students' task as they saw it was to "follow the coding instructions." What the graduate students produced, then, was just that: a setting or scene that could be understood and accountable as "following the coding instructions." Garfinkel's (1967) ethnomethodological question in this case became, "What actual activities made up those coders' practices called 'following coding instruction'?" (p. 20).

This change in Garfinkel's question implies that we must attend to the practical, planned actions right here, right now, in just this way. Members continually demonstrate their accountability to the social scene. Their practical actions are intended to be seen and reported. When Garfinkel went back to the coders, he looked for precisely how, in just this way, at just this time, the coders' practices simultaneously (reflexively) produced and made accountable the action of "following the coding instructions."

Getting back to my experience with Eric Livingston, while he didn't use the textbook to teach us about social things, he did teach us about "society." Professor Livingston used everyday occurrences—he pointed us to the simple ways we make something social. One of the students' assignments was to learn how to dance; another assignment involved standing in a line; another was going out to lunch. On one occasion, he didn't come to class until 15 minutes after the period started. He had me come in and set a boom box on a stool in the center of the stage. I had been instructed to turn the tape player on at the beginning of class. I didn't know what was on the tape and I wasn't to give any sort of preamble—just walk over and turn it on. I expected a taped lecture; what I got was a ringing telephone. The boom box played the sound of a ringing phone to 300 students for 15 minutes.

But, you say, dancing, lunch, lining up, and a ringing phone are no way to teach sociology! It is, if what you mean by sociology is the study of the methods people use in everyday life to render situations accountably organized as specific kinds of social events. How is it that we organize our behaviors in just such a way as to make them understandable as a dance? How do we in just this way and at just this time organize our behaviors to make the situation appear as "lunch"? What are the methods we use to produce a queue? Livingston's point, and Garfinkel's too, is that this kind of methodology—the methods used by the actual people in the actual situation—is found in every setting, large or small. The powerful implication of this point is that everything we need to understand how society works is present in the observable situation.

Seen But Unnoticed

There is something unusual about the common or mundane situations that ethnomethodologists study: They are all *moral affairs in a knowable and observable sense.* As with Parsons, when a sociologist talks about morals or values, he or she is usually referring to something that exists outside the immediate situation. Ethnomethodologists, however, argue that the morality of social order exists in the situation itself and you can see them. You don't have to reference some outside source. Garfinkel gives us an everyday example.

It seems true that humans can't actually experience the world from another's point of view. We all "know" this: Just ask anybody what happens at a party when you start a secret story with one person and tell him or her to pass it on; or "everybody knows" that if five people witness an accident, there will be five different stories about the accident. Yet, even though we all know this, we don't act like it. In fact, in every situation we act as if everybody knows exactly (or close enough) what we are talking about and doing. In order to successfully accomplish an interaction, we have to assume *reciprocity of perspectives;* we act as if our perspectives are shared, despite whatever evidence there might be to the contrary. We assume that our standpoints are interchangeable with those around us. We assume that the world that has meaning for me also has the same meaning for you; the only difference is our particular relationship to the world. Thus, while there may be differences, I believe that you would interpret the world as I do if you stood in my place and had my experiences. We also assume that whatever differences may exist in our positions in the lifeworld are irrelevant for the purposes at hand.

In order to point out this assumption, Garfinkel (1967) had his students perform breaching demonstrations in order to discover "the socially standardized and standardizing, 'seen but unnoticed,' expected, background features of everyday scenes" (p. 36). In other words, Garfinkel wanted his students to notice the always seen but never noticed scaffolding around which daily life is built. Let me quote a few of the cases so we can get a sense of what Garfinkel (1967) is talking about (in the following dialogue, S = Subject and E = Experimenter):

CASE 2

(S) Hi, Ray. How is your girlfriend feeling?

(E) What do you mean, "How is your girlfriend feeling?" Do you mean physical or mental?

(S) I mean how is she feeling? What's the matter with you? [He looked peeved.]

(E) Nothing. Just explain a little clearer what do you mean?

(S) Skip it. How are your Med School applications coming?

(E) What do you mean, "How are they?"

(S) You know what I mean.

(E) I really don't.

(S) What's the matter with you? Are you sick?

CASE 3

"On Friday night my husband and I were watching television. My husband remarked that he was tired. I asked, 'How are you tired? Physically, mentally, or just bored?'"

(S) I don't know, I guess physically, mainly.

(E) You mean that your muscles ache or your bones?

(S) I guess so. Don't be so technical.

[After more watching]

(S) All these old movies have the same kind of old iron bedstead in them.

(E) What do you mean? Do you mean all old movies, or some of them, or just the ones you have seen?

(S) What's the matter with you? You know what I mean.

(E) I wish you would be more specific.

(S) You know what I mean! Drop dead!

CASE 4

During a conversation (with E's fiancée) the E questioned the meaning of various words used by the subject. . . .

> For the first minute and a half the subject responded to the questions as if they were legitimate inquiries. Then she responded with "Why are you asking me those questions?" and repeated this two or three times after each question. She became nervous and jittery, her face and hand movements . . . uncontrolled. She appeared bewildered and complained that I was making her nervous and demanded that I "Stop it." . . . The subject picked up a magazine and covered her face. She put down the magazine and pretended to be engrossed. When asked why she was looking at the magazine she closed her mouth and refused any further remarks. (pp. 42–43)

There are a few things that we can pick up from such tests. First, there is a great deal of "seen but unnoticed" work that goes on in organizing a setting. Second, many conversations are organized around the denial of strict rational discourse. In a rational discussion, asking for clarification would be permitted and expected (though, in the end, such clarifications are also glossed-over assumptions of shared worlds). When I bought my truck, for example, the salesperson and manager expected and cooperated with my questions that were designed to extract specific information. On the other hand, conversations organized around what Georg Simmel (1971) called "sociability," the kind of conversations that we mostly have, are specifically not organized around the sharing of specific information.

In sociability, we must not push for additional information, we must wait for clarification (that may never come), we must suspend any doubt that might come to mind as the conversation takes shape, and we must understand all statements as being of the indexical kind (referencing unseen worlds or understandings that may never materialize)—all done to give us the sense that what we are having is a "normal conversation." When we see the work that goes into making a dialogue appear to everybody as a simple conversation, we can appreciate why Garfinkel sees everything we do as an "achievement." Taken-for-granted, everyday conversations don't simply happen; they are achieved.

The third thing we can glean from these stories is that there are "sanctioned properties of common discourse" (Garfinkel, 1967, p. 41). As you probably know from your other sociology courses, sanctions are positive or negative behavioral reinforcements. For example, if in a crowded elevator you face the rear instead of looking straight ahead, you will be sanctioned. People may roll their eyes, or say "excuse me" in such a way as to convey "turn around, idiot," or "get off the elevator," or they may simply get out of your field of vision. Sociologists generally link sanctions with norms, and norms are part of the moral fabric of society.

So, we can see that there are some pretty strong norms at work in mundane conversations and surmise that there is a moral order at work. However, from the point of view of ethnomethodology, the moral basis isn't part of some cultural structure that exists outside the situation. No—in fact, we can see that there are strong norms at work. What do we see? We see sanctioning behavior. This is a very important point for understanding ethnomethodology. Such things as sanctions, norms, values, and beliefs are not preexisting social facts that tell us how to behave. "They are rather constitutive of the 'sense' of the circumstances, of 'what the circumstances are' in the first place" (Heritage, 1984, p. 98).

Garfinkel wants us to see that each and every social occasion and object is accomplished. They are accomplished through the very ways members make the situation accountable as a certain kind of gathering. We use methods that we all know and that we can all see but never pay attention to. Garfinkel wants us to notice those methods by asking, "How is (fill in the blank) made to seem as organized and real as (fill in the blank)?" We could put sociology in those blanks, or gender, or even your classroom. These methods are well-known and people are held accountable to them. We can see the accountability in the activities of the members. Garfinkel wants us to see that accountability and not attribute it to normative structures or abstract moral systems. These methods are observable in the activities of the members.

Documentary Method

To understand the practices through which we claim to be competent to offer accounts, Garfinkel (1967) uses Karl Mannheim's idea of the *documentary method:* "The method consists of treating an actual appearance as 'the document of,' as 'pointing to,' as 'standing on behalf of' a presupposed underlying pattern" (p. 78). Anytime we interpret something, we make a kind of identity statement: "This is that." We do this when we interpret conversations or when we recognize the person standing outside our door as the mail carrier. Thus, the documentary method is the work we do when we take an object or event and set it in correspondence with a structure of meaning. We do this all the time, but how do we do it?

In order to put the documentary method in sharp relief, Garfinkel did an experiment. He brought in 10 undergraduates and told them that they were part of an experiment to explore a new, alternative method of psychotherapy. The students were given the opportunity to ask the "therapist" about anything they desired. The students needed to first provide the background to the problem and then phrase their questions in such a way that they could be answered yes or no. The therapist and students were in different rooms and communicated via an intercom. The students were instructed to give the background to the problem, ask their question, listen to the therapist's answer (yes or no), and then turn the intercom off and give their reactions. The procedure was repeated for as many questions as the students wanted to ask. Of course, the hitch in the experiment was that there was no new therapy and the "therapist's" answers were given randomly. Thus, there was no real "sense" to the answers; the issue, then, was exactly how (using what methods) the students made sense out of the answers—how the students understood the answers as "standing on behalf of a presupposed underlying pattern."

Garfinkel (1967) gleaned several insights from this experiment; I'll list but a few:

The students perceived the experimenter's responses as "answers- to-questions."

After the first question, the questions the students asked were motivated by the experimenter's response—in other words, the students framed their questions by looking back at "answers" and anticipated future "helpful answers."

When the meaning of the experimenter's response wasn't apparent, the student "waited for clarification" or engaged in an "active search" for the meaning.

Incongruent answers were interpreted by imputing knowledge and motivation to the therapist.

Contradictory answers prompted an "active search" for meaning in order to rid the answer of disagreement or meaninglessness.

There was a constant search for a pattern.

The subjects made specific references to normatively valued social structures that were treated as if shared by both and as setting the conditions of meaningful decisions—for example, what "everyone knows" about family (pp. 89–94).

Garfinkel's point is that the students rendered meaningful something that was not. The work of documenting—searching for and assigning a pattern—is performed by us all in every situation. A common culture or cognitive scheme isn't so much shared as the sense of commonality in documenting is achieved. The students give us a clear case where there were no cultures or cognitive schemes shared. Nonetheless, in most cases a correspondence was achieved between the event and a meaningful structure. The students' descriptions of the events were given in such a way as to assure their "rights to manage and communicate decisions of meaning" (Garfinkel, 1967, p. 77). Further, notice that even though the individual students were doing all the work, it was perceived and reported by the students as group work, as work between the student and therapist.

Concepts and Theory: Doing Society Reflexively and Indexically

The notion of *reflexivity* is at the heart of Garfinkel's work and ethnomethodology in general. Something is reflexive if it can turn back on itself. For example, circles are created through reflexive movement: The beginning and end points are the same, and the line that connects them constitutes everything that is contained within the circle. The word *reflexive* is also sometimes used to describe the introspective action of the mind. Remember that symbolic interaction defines the mind as an internalized conversation. A conversation always entails at least two interactants; so, with whom is your mind speaking? Itself, of course. The mind turns its own abilities back on its self. The mind is reflexive; the self is part of the reflexive act.

Garfinkel isn't really concerned with these issues; he is concerned with how the situation, and everything within the situation, is organized. Remember, Garfinkel is interested in "the objective reality of social facts as an ongoing accomplishment of the concerted activities of daily life." So, how are situations and social facts organized in just such a way as to be accountable as a socially organized setting and reality? The answer is that they are organized reflexively. Ethnomethodology's "central recommendation is that the activities whereby members produce and manage settings of organized everyday affairs are identical with members' procedures for making those settings 'account-able.' The 'reflexive,' or 'incarnate' character of accounting practices and accounts makes up the crux of that recommendation" (Garfinkel, 1967, p. 1).

One of the primary ways in which scenes are reflexively organized is through **indexical expressions**. To index something is to make reference to it or to point to it. Think of your index finger: It's the finger you use to point with. This book has an index. In this case, the index points to all the important issues that may be found in the book. This last example is very important. An indexical expression is like an index entry in a book: It points to itself. The only way a book index makes any sense at all is within the context of the book. Sometime try using the index from one book to find important items in a different book; it won't work. Indexical expressions, then, are situated verbal utterances that point to and are understood within the situation.

This is a very different notion than what is commonly held. Most of us, including many social scientists, believe that language, including verbal language, is representative. If I say "tree," then I am using that word to point to the physical object. One of the difficulties associated with this idea is that language doesn't represent very well. This problem is exemplified by color (Heritage, 1984, pp. 144–145): The human eye can distinguish about 7,500,000 colors. Yet the language with the most color names (English) only has 4,500 words that denote color, and of those 4,500 words, just 8 are commonly used.

It's plain, then, that in our everyday language we are not very concerned with representation. Part of what Garfinkel is talking about with indexical expressions is similar to symbolic interaction (Chapter 3), except what Garfinkel notes isn't the emergent quality of meaning; it is the reflexive character of meaning. For Garfinkel, the meanings of such phrases as "How's it going?" "That's a nice one," "He's a novice," and "What's up?" aren't negotiated through interaction. The meanings of indexical expressions don't emerge; they are found in the context itself. In fact, as we saw in the examples of breaching demonstrations, if you try to explicitly negotiate the meanings of indexical expressions, the chances are good that you'll be sanctioned or the setting will break up. The "one among many" in "that's a nice one" is assumed to be contextually given, as is the meaning of "nice." For example, if I am showing you the new guitar I just bought and you say, "That's a nice one," we both assume the meaning is given in the context or situation. Thus, indexical expressions are reflexive because they appear in and reference the unique context in which they occur.

Situationally Constructing Reality

However, indexical expressions are reflexive for another reason. They not only appear in and reference the situation; they also bring the situation into existence. Mehan and Wood (1975) give us the example of "hello." Let's say you see me in the hall at school. You say, "Hello." What have you done? You have initiated or created a social situation through the use of a greeting. When you said "Hello," you immediately drew a circle around the two of us, identifying us as a social group distinct from the other people around us. That social situation, which we can call an encounter, interaction, or situated activity system, didn't exist until you said "Hello." But notice something very important about "hello": It can only exist as a social greeting within social situations. Every time "hello" is used, a social situation is created. Yet "hello" is only found in social situations, either real ones or imaginary ones (like with our example). Thus, "hello" is utterly reflexive: It simultaneously creates, exists, and finds meaning within the social situation.

It isn't just "hello" that exists reflexively. Let's take the phrase "You're beautiful." Its meaning is obviously contextual. You might say "You're beautiful" to a queen, to your partner after making love, to your friend who just made a particularly ironic comment, or to your friend dressed up to go to a Halloween party. But notice also that saying "You're beautiful" also creates the situation wherein beautiful is understood. The beauty of the ironic comment didn't exist until you said it; once said, it can be understood within the context that it created. Further, indexical expressions aren't limited to these sorts of catch phrases. At one point, Garfinkel asked his students to go home and record a conversation. They were to also report on the complete meaning of what was said. The following is a small snippet of one such report (Garfinkel, 1967, pp. 25–26).

	What was said:	*What was meant:*
Husband:	Dana succeeded in putting a penny in a parking meter today without being picked up.	This afternoon as I was bringing Dana, our 4-year-old son, home from the nursery school, he succeeded in reaching high enough to put a penny in a parking meter when we parked in a metered parking zone, whereas before he has always had to be picked up to reach that high.
Wife:	Did you take him to the record store?	Since he put a penny in a meter, that means that you stopped while he was with you. I know that you stopped at the record store either on the way to get him or on the way back. Was it on the way back, so that he was with you, or did you stop there on the way to get him and somewhere else on the way back?

The first thing to point out, of course, is that what was actually said is incomprehensible apart from what the members could assume the other knew. There is an entire world of experience that the husband and wife share in the first statement about Dana that gives the statement a meaning that any observer would not be able to access. So, the first point is apparent: Vocal utterances reference or index presumed shared worlds.

The second point may not be quite so obvious. The students had a difficult time filling out the far-right column. It was hard to put down in print what was actually being said and indexically understood. However, it became a whole lot tougher when Garfinkel asked them to indexically explain what was said in the far-right column. Garfinkel wanted them to explain the explanation because the explanation itself assumed indexical worlds of meaning. Garfinkel (1967) reports that "they gave up with the complaint that the task was impossible" (p. 26). The task of explaining every explanation is impossible because all our talk is indexical. Many of us come up against this issue in the course of raising a 2-year-old. All 2-year-olds are infamous for asking the same insistent question: "Why?" And every parent knows that once started, that line of questioning never ends—every answer is just another reason to ask why. It never ends because our culture is indexical and reflexive.

Mehan and Wood (1975) further point out just how fundamentally reflexive our world really is. Every social world is founded upon incorrigible assumptions and secondary elaborations of belief. *Incorrigible assumptions* are things that we believe to be true but never question. These assumptions are incorrigible because they are incapable of being changed or amended. And these assumptions form the base of our social world. *Secondary elaborations* of belief are prescribed legitimating accounts that function to protect the incorrigible assumptions. In other words, secondary elaborations of belief are ready-made stories that we use to explain why some empirical finding doesn't line up with our incorrigible assumptions. The really interesting thing about incorrigible assumptions is that the empirical world doesn't always line up with the cultural assumptions that guide and create our reality.

Mehan and Wood (1975) give us the illustration of a lost pen. Our search for the lost pen is based on the assumption of object consistency—physical objects maintain their consistency through time and space. "Say, for example, you find your missing pen in a place you know you searched before. Although the evidence indicates that the pen was first absent and then present, that conclusion is not reached" (p. 12). To do so would challenge the incorrigible assumption upon which that reality system is based—we never consider the possibility that a poltergeist took the pen or that a black hole swallowed it up. Our assumption of object consistency is protected through secondary elaborations of belief. When we find the pen where we had already looked, we say, "I must have missed it."

I want us to take one further step into this issue of reflexivity. Not only are cultures reflexively created and protected, evidence for any reality system is always reflexively provided as well. Let us take the incident of two automobiles colliding. What would you call it? Most of us would call it an "accident." But what is implied in calling this collision an accident? Accidents can exist only if humans assume that there are no other, outside forces in back of events. But what if one of the drivers is a fundamentalist Christian? Then the episode, from the point of view of that driver, may well be defined as "God's will."

Let's ask the obvious question first: What is the incident really? According to ethnomethodology, it isn't anything really; it becomes something meaningfully as we make assumptions about the world and how it works. But once we make our assumptions, what can happen to the events around us? Think about the two cars colliding. In this example, the event becomes either an accident or God's will. Then, through a neat little trick, the event becomes proof of the system that defined it in the first place. The person who has had an "accident" is confirmed in her belief that "shit happens." The person who has experienced "God's will" is confirmed in her belief in an omnipotent and merciful God. Either way, the collision is used to legitimate an existing reality system—proof of the event's definition is provided by the self-same meaning system. The same is true for science (and sociology): What counts as "proof" for the validity of science is defined by science.

Ad Hocing

Garfinkel (1967) says something that on the surface sounds pretty amazing: "For the purposes of conducting their everyday affairs persons refuse to permit each other to understand 'what they are really talking about' in this way" (p. 41). How can people refuse to let others know what they are really talking about? At first, that doesn't make much sense, until you remember Garfinkel's breaching experiments: "How's it going?" "What do you mean? How's what going?" People tend to get very upset when we break the assumed patterns of conversation, even in what we might think of as important, strategic conversations. Most people in most situations have very little tolerance when someone wants to know exactly what is being said. In that sense, they refuse to allow someone to know what they are really saying. Of course, the main reason for this refusal is that lying beneath every conversation are endlessly indexical worlds, and our conversations depend on a sense of shared worlds.

Yet most conversations go on without a hitch. How is that done? In general, Garfinkel says that we engage in *ad hocing*. *Ad hoc* comes from New Latin and literally means "for this." We say something is ad hoc when it is made for just this occasion or with a particular end or purpose in mind. Garfinkel uses the term to talk about the minute ways in which we gloss over potential problems in conversations. We can think of ad hocing, then, as the practices or methods used by members to sustain a sense and appearance of social organization and shared worlds.

We can see some of these ad hoc measures in the story of the students and therapist. This was a situation where the students were deliberately kept in the dark about the meanings of what was being said. In the face of such ignorance and with an assumed context (psychotherapy experiment), students "ad hoced": They used methods that allowed the conversation and social order to continue in the face of contrary or ambiguous dialogue. Read this carefully: They used their retrospective–prospective sense to place what was said in an ongoing context with a biographical past and future; they waited for clarification when they first heard something that seemed senseless; and they continually performed an active search for a meaning index. Notice that all this was done without calling anything into question and for the purpose of not interrupting the flow of events.

Ad hocing occurs anytime we assume the position of "a socially competent member of the arrangement." Socially competent members are compelled to present and maintain an accountable event, whether a conversation, wedding, funeral, the construction of a building, the teaching of a class, and so on. As such, we must refuse to permit each other to understand what we are really talking about. It isn't that we are being intentionally deceitful; it is simply that behind every social activity lie endless fields of indexical worlds. So we use ad hoc measures to preserve a sense of shared social worlds. We let things pass and wait for clarification of statements that never comes. And we say things like "you know" (known as the et cetera principle) to indicate that we could explain if need be, but "you know" (even though what we all "know" never appears).

Summary

- Garfinkel's perspective is unique among sociologists. He sees social order and meaning as achievements that are produced in situ. That is, Garfinkel sees social order and meaning as achieved within its natural setting—face-to-face interactions—and not through such things as institutions that exist outside the natural setting.

- The principal way this is done is through accounting. A basic requirement of every social setting is that it be recognizable or accountable as a specific kind of setting. Thus, the practical behaviors that create a setting just as it is are seen but not noticed for what they are; they are the very behaviors that achieve the setting in the first place.

- All settings and talk are therefore indexical; they index or reference themselves. The actions that create the situation of a wedding or a class are simultaneously understood as meaningful, social activities within the situation. Human activity always references itself; it is thoroughly reflexive, based upon incorrigible assumptions, discovered through the documentary method, proven through indexical methods, and protected by secondary elaborations of belief.

TAKING THE PERSPECTIVE

Generally speaking, ethnomethodology came into existence as Harold Garfinkel worked through Parsons' action theory and his answer to the Hobbesian problem of social order. Garfinkel was particularly bothered by the way Parsons discounted actors' knowledge of the situation (see Heritage, 1984, p. 9). Garfinkel saw that the simple empirical truth is that people are aware of what they're doing and why they are doing it; and that any empirically based social discipline must begin there. Garfinkel drew on Alfred Schutz's (1967) understanding of phenomenology as a way to bracket preconceptions and take the social world of empirically sit-uated actors at face value. Simply said, "Ethnomethodology...is the study of the methods people use for producing recognizable social orders" (Rawls, 2003, p. 123). It's based on the theoretical ideas that everything needed to understand social things is located in the situation and that "to be human is to know, virtually all of the time...both what one is doing and why one is doing it" (Giddens, 1991, p. 35).

In brief, ethnomethodology is a theoretical perspective that studies the commonsense proce-dures people use to reflexively achieve social order and render it sensible. Ethnomethodology assumes that social orders and the methods through which they are created are identical; in every situation people are aware of what they are doing and why they are doing it; and that social order is an ongoing endogenous achievement in which the procedures used are recog-nizable and commonsensical. While general sociology takes facticity (the existence of facts) for granted, ethnomethodology takes the way people develop a sense of facticity as a subject of study. The implication of this is that ethnomethodology literally opens up every aspect of human doings and situations for study. The general form of an ethnomethodological question is: What are the local methods used whereby people organize and make sensible _____?

Because the ethnomethodological question is open-ended, there are innumerable applications and extensions of Garfinkel's work. Perhaps the most explored and/or well-known applications are in the areas of conversation analysis and science studies. Probably more than any other, Harvey Sacks (1995) is responsible for the ethnomethodological study of conversation. Sacks basically asked what else, besides words, is being communicated when people talk with each other. He discovered that people use certain conversational devices to accomplish specific social orders. Candace West and Don Zimmerman (1987) show us an example of Sacks' approach in studying gender. West and Zimmerman ask, what conversational mechanisms are used to order gender inequality?

Ethnomethodological studies of science look at the ways scientists create a sense of doing science and producing scientific data (see Lynch, 1997). In a recent and fascinating study Linda Derksen (2010) looks at DNA measurement. While there are some distinctions from eth-nomethodology, her approach is clearly ethnomethodological. In the article she details the moment when what were subjective decisions of the operator became invisible and were ren-dered objective.

However, generally speaking, Garfinkel's work has also been hotly contested because it offers such a unique approach, one that can and does take general sociology as a topic of study. Yet Garfinkel's influence extends to many prominent general theories in sociology. One example found in this book is the work of Anthony Giddens (Chapter 14), especially in his work on self-identity. Another interesting example where Garfinkel's influence may be seen is in Jonathan H. Turner's *A Theory of Social Interaction* (1988, Stanford University Press). Turner's goal in the book, like Garfinkel, is to critique Parsons' analysis of the act, yet Turner's work itself could not be classified as ethnomethodological. Turner weaves Garfinkel's theory into a more positivistic and comprehensive explanation of the motiva-tions and actions within social interaction.

BUILDING YOUR THEORY TOOLBOX

Learning More—Primary Sources

- For someone who has founded a school in sociology, Garfinkel has written very little. However, his two primary works are essential reading:

    o *Studies in Ethnomethodology,* Prentice Hall, 1967.

    o *Ethnomethodology's Program: Working Out Durkheim's Aphorism,* edited and introduced by Anne Warfield Rawls, Rowman & Littlefield, 2002.

- However, one of the interesting things about ethnomethodology is that there are a number of primary works. Among them are these:

    o Harvey Sacks, "Sociological Description," *Berkeley Journal of Sociology, 8,* 1–16, 1963.

    o Don H. Zimmerman and Melvin Pollner, "The Everyday World as a Phenomenon," in Jack Douglas (Ed.), *Understanding Everyday Life: Toward the Reconstruction of Sociological Knowledge,* Aldine, 1970.

    o Melvin Pollner, "Mundane Reasoning," *Philosophy of the Social Sciences, 4,* 35–54, 1974.

    o Hugh Mehan and Houston Wood, *The Reality of Ethnomethodology,* Wiley, 1975.

Learning More—Secondary Sources

- For a good review of Garfinkel's life, see "Harold Garfinkel," by Anne Rawls, in George Ritzer (Ed.), *The Blackwell Companion to Major Contemporary Social Theorists,* Blackwell, 2003, pp. 131–136.

- The standard text for ethnomethodology is John Heritage's *Garfinkel and Ethnomethodology,* Polity Press, 1984.

- I would, of course, be remiss if I didn't recommend Eric Livingston's books. His *Making Sense of Ethnomethodology* (Routledge & Kegan Paul Books, 1987) is a good, clear, and short introduction to the field), and his *The Ethnomethodological Foundations of Mathematics* (Routledge & Kegan Paul Books, 1986) is an interesting look at the social order foundations of the most abstract of all languages.

- Conversation is one of the more important areas of ethnomethodological research. See Deidre Boden and Don H. Zimmerman (Eds.), *Talk and Social Structure: Studies in Ethnomethodology and Conversation Analysis,* University of California Press, 1991.

- Another important area is the study of science. See Michael Lynch, *Scientific Practice and Ordinary Action: Ethnomethodology and Social Studies of Science,* Cambridge University Press, 1997.

Check It Out

- *Phenomenology:* This philosophical tradition is one of the roots of ethnomethodological thinking, as well as a number of other theories (we'll see it again). A good and fairly accessible book is *Introduction to Phenomenology*, by Robert Sokolowski (Cambridge University Press, 1999).

- *Social order:* This is a fundamental issue for sociology. An excellent introduction is Michael Hechter and Christine Horne's (Eds.) *Theories of Social Order: A Reader* (Stanford Social Sciences, 2003).

- *Accounts:* Once you begin to grasp the idea of social accounting, you will start to see it everywhere. Read Scott and Lyman's 1968 article titled "Accounts," *American Sociological Review, 33*, 46–62.

Seeing the World

- Write a 250-word synopsis of the theoretical perspective ethnomethodology.

- After reading and understanding this chapter, you should be able to define the following terms theoretically and explain their theoretical importance to ethnomethodology: *lifeworld, phenomenology, ethnomethodology, accounts, documentary method, reciprocity of perspectives, reflexivity, indexical expressions, incorrigible assumptions, secondary elaborations of belief, ad hocing*

- After reading and understanding this chapter, you should be able to answer the following questions (remember to answer them *theoretically*):

  o What does it mean that Garfinkel is interesting in analyzing events "in just this way and at just this time"? What does his approach imply about social order and social structures?

  o How are situations reflexively organized? Specifically, how do accountability, indexicality, and the documentary method function to reflexively organize social events?

  o What are incorrigible assumptions and secondary elaborations of belief? How do they work to produce a sense of reality? Use an example from the newspaper to illustrate your answer.

Engaging the World

- Asking you to engage your world using ethnomethodology is both easy and difficult. It's easy because almost everything in your life, from saying hello, to science, to relations between nations, is organized ethnomethodologically. The difficult part is that it is hard

(Continued)

(Continued)

to observe seen but unnoticed reflexive behaviors. But once you get it, it's difficult *not* to see ethnomethods. Let me give you two tasks to get you started:

- o Describe how the textbook you have in your hands is an example of reflexively constructing sociology. Remember, get specific in your descriptions—"in just this way and at just this time."

- o Write an ethnomethodological description of the social organization of grocery store checkout lines.

Weaving the Threads

- • How would symbolic interactionism and ethnomethodology each account for social order or patterned behaviors? Can these perspectives be brought together?

- • Evaluate each of the perspectives that we've looked at so far in terms of freedom of action. In which perspective is the actor the most free? Least free?

- • Ethnomethodology is the first perspective that we've come across that didn't have a specific kind of actor. What kind of self or actor is present in symbolic interactionism and what is gained or lost by Garfinkel not including such an actor? Which of the types of actor would fit best in Garfinkel's theory and why?

CHAPTER 5

Performing the Self:

Erving Goffman

(1922–1982)

Like ethnomethodology, Goffman invites us to pay attention to things that are seen but unnoticed. Goffman's focus, however, isn't on folk methods of social organization. Rather, he wants us to notice the self. He wants us to notice what we wear, how we walk or sit, how we use the space around us, and so on. You might be thinking that you already notice those things. Yeah, you probably do. But like ethnomethodology, Goffman asks, "What else is going on?" Goffman's answer might surprise you.

The significance of Goffman's work for us lies in his emphasis on the presentation of self or what we would today call image. Goffman's work was published from the 1950s through the early 1980s. This period of time is culturally marked by the emergence and then dominance of television. Prior to this period, words, whether written (books and newspapers) or spoken (radio), defined mass media. Words give importance to story, and story emphasizes coherence and meaning. Television, however, shifted the power of mass media from word to image. What became important in news, for example, is not whether the story was complete and meaningful, but, rather, whether or not there was film or video. This emphasis on image that television conveyed was bolstered by technical advances in movie and magazine production. Movies became spectacles and magazines filled with glossy pictures. These shifts in the cultural context impacted the way people understood themselves. Self image became increasingly important and at the same time became less tied to real social groups and more informed by images seen in television, commercials, movies, and advertisement. The importance of meaning and coherence gave way to the power of an image to gain attention, to be attractive. What Goffman gives us, then, is a theory that explains how we manage our images and the impression we make on others.

THEORIST'S DIGEST

Brief Biography

Goffman was born on June 11, 1922, in Alberta, Canada. He earned his PhD from the University of Chicago. For his dissertation, he studied daily life on one of the Scottish islands (Unst). The dissertation from this study became his first book, *The Presentation of Self in Everyday Life*, which is now available in 10 different languages. In 1958, Herbert Blumer invited Goffman to teach at the University of California, Berkeley. He stayed there for 10 years, moving to the University of Pennsylvania in 1968, where he taught for the remainder of his career. Goffman also served as president of the American Sociological Association in 1981 and 1982. Goffman died of cancer on November 19, 1982.

Central Sociological Questions

Goffman (1983) was inquisitive about everything people did in face-to-face interactions: "For myself I believe that human social life is ours to study naturalistically. . . . From the perspective of the physical and biological sciences, human social life is only a small irregular scab on the face of nature, not particularly amenable to deep systematic analysis. And so it is. But it's ours" (p. 17). Goffman probed this social life incessantly. He watched people continually and asked, what are people doing? What's going on just beneath the surface of what we see? What is required for a social encounter to occur? How do these requirements influence everything that people do when they meet? Specifically, how do the constraints of presenting a self create social order?

Simply Stated

Goffman argues that for any social encounter to take place, people need to present a self. This presentation, however, isn't something that people take for granted. Impression management is serious business and people manipulate specific cues in the setting and in their appearance and manner in order to present a specific kind of self to others. These cues are prepared in the backstage and presented in a front stage wherein the audience reads the cues and in response demands a certain kind of performance from the actor. This performance may be team based; and it entails deference and demeanor rituals, face-work, and may result in stigma, if not properly executed. This fundamental need to present a self for an encounter to occur results in social order, though that is not the intent of the actors.

Key Ideas

Dramaturgy, social, personal, and ego identities, impression management, front, setting, appearance, manner, ritual states, backstage, performance teams, roles, role distance, stigma, face, deference and demeanor rituals, face-work, unfocused encounters, frames, keys, interaction order, biographies, cognitive relations

Concepts and Theory: Impression Management

Goffman's perspective has become known as dramaturgy. **Dramaturgy** is a way of understanding social encounters using the analogy of the dramatic stage. In this perspective, people are seen as performers who are vitally concerned with the presentation of their character (the self) to an audience. There are three major premises to dramaturgy. First, all we can know about a person's self is what the person shows us. The self isn't something that we can literally take out and show people. The self is perceived indirectly through the cues we offer others. Because of this limitation, people are constantly and actively involved in the second premise of dramaturgy: impression management. *Impression management* refers to the manipulation of cues in order to organize and control the impression we give to others. We use staging, fronts, props, and so on to communicate to others our "self" in the situation, and they do the same for us.

Taken alone, impression management sounds at best strategic and at worst deceitful. If everybody around us is manipulating cues in order to present a specific self, then how can we believe that it is their "true self" that we see? The short answer is that we can never be sure that we see an authentic self; we always have to assume that the self we see is real. But notice something here: For the interaction, it does not matter if the self we see is genuine or false—whether authentic or fake, all selves are communicated in the exact same way, through signs that are specifically given or inadvertently given off.

The third premise of dramaturgy is that there are particular features of face-to-face encounters that tend to bring order to interactions. The presentation of self places moral imperatives on interactions. Selves are delicate things and are easily discredited. If you have ever felt embarrassed, you know the painful reality of this truth. Selves depend upon not only our skill in presenting and maintaining cues, but also the willingness and support of others. Thus, the simple act of presenting a self creates a cooperative order. We'll address this issue specifically in the "The Interaction Order" section.

Goffman's idea of the self is clearly different than symbolic interaction. Goffman's (1959) main concern is with the self that is the subject of impression management:

> The self . . . is not an organic thing that has a specific location, whose fundamental fate is to be born, to mature, and to die: it is a dramatic effect arising diffusely from a scene that is presented. (pp. 252–253)

However, it would be incorrect to conclude that he doesn't have a concept of the core self. In *Stigma*, Goffman (1963a) proposes a three-fold typology of self identity: the social identity, the personal identity, and the ego identity. Each of these is like a story that is built up through social encounters. The *social identity* is the story that distant others can tell about us; for example, most of my students hold a social identity of me. The social identity is composed of social categories imputed to the individual by the self and others in defined situations. Each category has a complement of attributes felt to be ordinary and natural for members of a particular category. The category and the attributes form anticipations in given social settings. People in an encounter lean on these anticipations, transform them into normative expectations and righteously presented demands.

That last bit about demands is very important. One of the most interesting things about humans is that they are capable of anything. Our behaviors aren't predetermined by instincts, and we have freedom of choice. However, the only way we can function around other humans is by having some way to predict their behaviors. According to Goffman, we use social categories and their accompanying attitudes to accomplish this. We use the category to presume something about how the person works inside. Further, our expectations come to have a moral or righteous feel to them. Again, the reason for this comes back to the unpredictability of humans. Since all we have are cultural expectations, then we must make sure that people live up to them. So, when someone doesn't live up to those expectations—like a professor dating a student or not caring about education—we become morally offended.

A *personal identity* is held by people who are close to us. These are the people that have known us the longest, have interacted with us in multiple situations, and to whom we have cued more of our idea of who we see ourselves to be. Personal identities have more or less abiding characteristics that are a combination of life history events that are unique to the person. The personal identity plays a "structured, routine, standardized role in social organization just because of its one-of-a-kind quality"

(Goffman, 1963a, p. 57). What Goffman means is that the more you know about me (the more I present a self to you in different kinds of situations over long periods of time), the less free I am to organize my presentation of self in any old way. I am held accountable to the self image that I have presented.

Thus far, the selves we've talked about are within the range of the situational self; it is in the ego identity that Goffman hints at something else. The *ego identity* is "first of all a subjective, reflexive matter that necessarily must be felt by the individual whose identity is at issue" (Goffman, 1963a, p. 106). This identity is of the individual's own construction; it is the story we tell ourselves about who we are to which we get emotionally attached. The ego identity is thus "the subjective sense of his own situation and his own continuity and character that an individual comes to obtain as a result of his various social experiences" (p. 105). Note that according to Goffman, the ego identity is made out of the same materials that others use to construct our personal and social identities. Our ego identity isn't something that comes from inside us, from innate personality characteristics. Rather, we construct the story through which we see our self using the same cues and categorical expectations that others use.

Performing the Self

The basic concept Goffman uses to explain the presentation of self is that of a front. A **front** is the expression of a particular self or identity that is formed by the individual and read by others. The front is like a building façade. *Merriam-Webster's* (2002) first definition of façade is remarkably like Goffman's idea of a front: a façade is "a face (as a flank or rear facing on a street or court) of a building that is given emphasis by special architectural treatment." Like a façade, a front is constructed by emphasizing and de-emphasizing certain sign vehicles. In every interaction, we hold things back, things that aren't appropriate for the situation or that we don't want those in the situation to attribute to our self; we accentuate other aspects in order to present a particular kind of self with respect to the social role. A social front is constructed using three main elements: the setting, appearance, and manner.

The idea of the *setting* is taken directly from the theater: It consists of all the physical scenery and props that we use to create the stage and background within which we present our performance. The clearest example for us is probably the classroom. The chalkboard, the room layout with all the desks facing the front, the media equipment, and so on are all used by the professor to make claim to the role of teacher. All this is obvious, but notice that the way the setting is used cues different kinds of professorial performances. I may choose to "de-center" the role of teacher and instead claim the role of facilitator by simply rearranging the desks in a circle and using multiple, mobile chalkboards placed all around the room.

Settings tend to ground roles by making definitions of the situations consistent. For example, it would be more difficult (but not impossible) for me to use the classroom as a setting for the definition of "bar." This "groundedness" of settings is part of what makes us think that roles, identities, and selves are consistent across time and space. There is a taken-for-grantedness about the definition of the situation when we are in a geographic location that becomes more pronounced the more "institutionalized" the location is. When I say that a location is institutionalized, I mean that the use of a specific place appears restricted: The front of the classroom looks as if students are restricted, yet it is available to many professors; the office of the CEO of Microsoft, on the other hand, is even more institutionalized and restricted. However, there is still a great deal of flexibility and creativity available to those who use the space.

However, there is one specific setting wherein there is little or no flexibility: total institutions. Total institutions are organizations that control all of an individual's behaviors, from the time the person gets up until he or she is fast asleep (and even then, behaviors are regulated). Clear examples of these institutional settings include psychiatric hospitals and military boot camps. Goffman (1961) uses the idea of the total institution to demonstrate the clear association between the setting and the self: "This special kind of institutional arrangement does not so much support the self as constitute it" (p. 168).

In addition to the physical setting, a front is produced by using appearance and manner. *Appearance* cues consist of clothing, hairstyle, makeup, jewelry, cologne, backpacks, attaché cases, piercings, tattoos, and so on—in short, anything that we can place upon our bodies. While appearance refers to those things that we do to our bodies, *manner* refers to what we do with our bodies. Manner consists of the way we walk, our posture, our voice inflection, how we use our eyes, what we do with our hands, what we do with our arms, our stride, the way we sit, how we physically respond to stimuli, and so on. Both appearance and manner function to signify the performer's social statuses and temporary ritual state. What we mean by social statuses should be fairly clear. Bankers and bikers have different social statuses, and they dress differently. They don't dress differently because they have dissimilar tastes; they dress differently because different appearance cues are associated with different status positions.

Ritual states refer to at least two things. The most apparent is the ritual state associated with different life phases. We have fewer of these than do traditional societies, but we still mark some life transitions with rituals, like birthdays (particularly when they signify a change in social standing, like the 21st birthday in the United States), graduations, promotions, and retirement. The second idea that the notion of ritual state conveys is our readiness to perform a particular role. Our appearance tells others how serious we are about the role we claim. For example, if you see two people riding bicycles and they are dressed differently, one in normal street clothes and the other in matching nylon/lycra jersey and shorts along with cycling shoes and helmet, then you can surmise that one is really serious about riding and the other is less so.

As in the theater, fronts are prepared backstage and presented on the front stage. Most of what is implied in these concepts is fairly intuitive. For example, every day before you go to school, you prepare your student-self in the backstage. You pick clothes, shower, do your hair, put on makeup, or whatever it is that corresponds to the self that you want others to see and respond to. Your work in the backstage for school is different from your work in the backstage of a date (unless someone you're dating will see your performance at school). You then present the student-self that you've prepared in the front stages of class, lunchroom, hallway, and so forth. But the backstage of school extends further back than your morning preparations. All students will study, read, and write to a certain degree in preparation for class. This too is part of the backstage for class. Even if you don't read or study, you are preparing to perform as a certain kind of student. As I said, most of this is intuitive. However, we need to realize that there are multiple front- and backstages and that they can occur at almost any time and place.

Often it is *performance teams* that move from front- to backstage. Just as in the theater, most performances are carried off by a troupe of actors. There are, of course, such things as one-person shows, but by and large actors cooperate with one another to present a show to the audience. And the same is true in social encounters. We can think of teamwork as being tacit or contrived. Members of like social categories generally, though not always, assume that others within the category will cooperate in preserving the group face. For example, perhaps you and a friend went to the beach for the weekend. Monday you are both talking to a professor. Your friend, who feels she didn't do well on that morning's test, tells the professor, "I don't think I did well on the test this morning. I was sick all weekend and didn't have a chance to study." You say nothing. You're a team.

Performance teams can also be much more deliberate. Let's say you are married and are having another couple over for dinner. In the middle of dinner, your spouse asks you to help her in the kitchen. In the kitchen, you find out that what she wants your help with isn't the food, but, rather, the team performance. She tells you, in no uncertain terms, that you are not to talk about the fact that she, your wife, is looking for a new job. It turns out that the couple you are having over for dinner is friends with her current boss and she hasn't told her boss that she is leaving. You both go back to the table, then, and smoothly change the topic.

The work of Arlie Russell Hochschild takes us into an area of impression management that Goffman rarely considered. As a professor, I occasionally have students come into my office crying. They may have lost a loved one or simply want to tell me about how this has been the week from hell and they can't get their paper in on time. The thing that strikes me about this experience is that I know the student didn't start out at his or her dorm room or classroom and walk across campus crying all the way. The student not only managed his or her impression, but the emotions as well, in a way that was suitable for public display. And then, somewhere between the elevator and my office, the student had a backstage moment in which he or she accessed those emotions and allowed crying to be part of the front. This story about crying implies something important about impression management: Part of it involves emotion. Hochschild takes impression management inside the very center of the individual and invites us to consider the managed heart.

Relating to Roles

Every definition of a social situation contains roles that are normal and regularly expected. Goffman considers *roles* as bundles of activities that are effectively laced together into a situated activity system. Some of these role-specific activities we will be pleased to perform and others we perhaps will not. We can thus distance ourselves from a role or we can fully embrace it. *Role distancing* is a way of enacting the role that simultaneously allows the actor to lay claim to the role and to say that he or she is so much more than the role. Let's take the role of student, for example. There are certain kinds of behaviors that are expected of students: They should read the material through several times before class, they should sit in the front row and diligently take notes, they should ask questions in class and consistently make eye contact with the professor, they should systematize and rewrite their notes at least every week, they should make it a point to introduce themselves to the professor and stop by during office hours to go over the material, and so forth. You already know the list, though you probably haven't taken the time to write it out.

But how many of you actually perform the role in its entirety? Why don't you? It isn't a matter of ignorance or ability; you know and can perform everything we've listed and more. So, why don't you? You don't perform the role to its fullest because you want to express to people, mostly your peers, that there is more to you than simply being a student. When presenting the role of student, it is difficult to simultaneously perform another role. In this situation you are a student. Thus, in order to convey to others that you might be more than a student, you leave gaps in the presentation. These gaps leave possibilities and questions in the minds of others—who else is this person? Sometimes we fill the gaps with hints of other selves (like "athletic female" or "sensitive male") that aren't necessarily part of the definition of the situation.

Contained within the idea of role distance is role embracement. In role embracement, we adhere to all that the role demands. We effectively become one with the role; the role becomes our self. We see and judge our self mainly through this role. We tend to embrace a role when we are new to a situation or when we feel ourselves to be institutional representatives (like a parent or teacher). When we do embrace a role like this, we idealize the situation and its roles. That is, we "incorporate and exemplify the officially accredited values of the society" (Goffman, 1959, p. 35). When we manage our front in such a way, we place claims upon the audience—first, to recognize the self that we are presenting as one that embodies society, and second, to present our self in such a way as to represent society as well.

Some of the decision to distance or embrace a role is personal, but most of it is situational. For example, we expect university students to experiment and try out different things. It's a time between highly institutionalized spaces. This kind of time is sometimes referred to as "liminal space" (Turner, 1969). You are no longer a child fully under the demands of your parents, nor are you working at a job that fully demands your time, effort, and impression management. However, when you do become a full member of the economy, you won't have the time or occasion to experience different situations and the selves they entail. Your daily rounds will be more restricted and managed by others. And you will be expected to more fully embrace the self that work requires. Of course, role distancing is still possible, but we have to work harder at it and it is circum-scribed by our situations.

Sacred and Stigmatized Selves

Charles Horton Cooley recognized as early as 1902 that society rests on felt pride and shame (see Cooley, 1998, pp. 155–178). Both are emotions that are distinctly social in origin, and both help monitor human behaviors. Goffman also sees pride and shame at work in social interactions. In every interaction, we present a front, and every time we present a front, we put the self at risk. People read our cues, cat-egorize us, attribute attitudes, and then expect us to live up to the normal traits and behaviors. We are held accountable to the role.

Often we are unaware that we are making moral demands of someone's role per-formance until they are violated. These demands constitute the individual's virtual self in the situation. Participants compare the virtual self to the actual self, the actual role-related behaviors. The differences between the virtual and actual selves—and there are always differences—create the possibility of stigma. The word *stigma* comes from the Greek and originally meant a brand or tattoo. Today, *stigma* is used to denote a mark of shame or discredit. There are well-known and apparent stigmas, though if we are going to be politically correct, we don't usually talk about them as such today. Among the ones that Goffman mentions are disabilities and deformities. People with such apparent stigmas are discredited by those who Goffman calls "normals." Having someone with an obvious stigma creates tension in encounters. Normals practice careful "disattention," and the discredited use var-ious devices to manage the tension, such as joking or downplaying.

There are also well-known but not so apparent stigmas. People in this category are discreditable: They live daily and in every situation with the potential of being stigmatized. One such category that is prominent today in the United States is that of homosexuals. Being homosexual in this society is a stigmatized identity—the homosexual is viewed as having failed to live up to the expectations associated with being a sexual person. Many homosexuals practice information management (as compared to tension management); they work to pass as a normal. Passing is a concerted and well-organized effort to appear normal based on the knowledge of possible discrediting; this impression management entails a directedness that isn't usual for normals.

All of us pass. We engage in information management: We know what cues to avoid in order to successfully pull off a performance. Remember when we listed the cues associated with the perfect student? Well, we could just as easily record the sig-nals associated with being a poor student. If we think back to the issue of role dis-tance, we can see that role distancing requires a delicate balance between claiming enough cues to still be considered a student without being discredited as a poor student. Since we all pass, we are constantly in danger of being stigmatized: "The issue becomes not whether a person has experience with a stigma of his own, because he has, but rather how many varieties he has had his own experience with" (Goffman, 1963a, p. 129).

The reason that stigmas can exist and are an issue is that identities are "collective representations" in the true Durkheimian sense of the word (see Durkheim, 1912/1995, pp. 436–440). Identities belong to and represent society's values and beliefs. The representational, symbolic character of identities and the way in which we interact around those identities indicate that identities and selves are sacred objects. Durkheim (1912/1995) defines sacred things as those objects "protected and isolated by prohibitions . . . things set apart and forbidden" (pp. 38, 44). Sacred things, then, represent society, are reserved for special use, and are protected from misuse by clear symbolic boundaries. The sacred self, like all sacred objects, has boundaries that are guarded against encroachment. The sacred quality of identities and selves is the source of shame: "As sacred objects, men are subject to slights and profanation" (Goffman, 1967, p. 31). The flip side of stigma and shame is equally related to this collective feature of identities: a sense of pride in the sacred self.

Goffman uses the idea of *face* to express the dynamics of the sacred self. Face refers to the positive social value that a person claims in an interaction. As we've seen, when we present cues and we lay claim to a social identity, others grant us the identity and attribute to us a host of internal characteristics. Through role distancing we can negotiate some of these attributions, but in order to make an effective claim on the situated self, we must keep our performance within a given set of parameters—otherwise we could not be identified. Every established identity has positive social values attached to it, and over time we can become emotionally involved with those values. As individuals, we experience these emotions as our ego identity. And every time we present an identity, we expose our face, our ego identity, to risk. We risk embarrassment, but the risk is necessary in order to feel pride and a strong sense of self.

Concepts and Theory: The Encounter

This idea of putting our face at risk implies that the encounter or interaction is a ritual order. Goffman (1967) argues that interactions are ritualized insofar as they represent "a way in which the individual must guard and design the symbolic implications of his acts while in the immediate presence of an object that has a special value to him" (p. 57). Encounters are highly ritualized social interactions, particularly around the issues of self and respect. Goffman refers to the behaviors oriented around respect as *deference and demeanor rituals*.

Deference is the amount of respect we give others. We may defer to or prefer another's wishes or opinions. Deference also refers to courteous, polite, or formal behavior. All of this deference is granted in different ways. For example, we can know how much or what kind of respect to give others based on known status positions. When introduced to our physician for the first time, most of us call him or her by the title that normally goes along with the position: Doctor. This seems like a function of the status structure—we're just reflecting what the structure says. However, according to Goffman's way of seeing the world, acts of deference are prompted by someone's demeanor.

Demeanor refers most directly to the way someone holds himself or herself, as in manner. But it also entails the entire spectrum of expressive equipment we use to present a front. As such, we can see it isn't so much the structure that tells us to call our physician "Doctor," as it is the way the doctor presents herself. If the physician you visit has her office in a professional building, has the usual waiting room with glass dividers between you and the staff, has examination rooms full of medical equipment and decorated with framed college diplomas on the walls, and the doctor comes into the room wearing a white uniform and other appearance cues (like a stethoscope), then the entire atmosphere surrounding the situation screams to you to grant respect, not only in title, but in all your behaviors. On the other hand, if the office is in a remodeled home with no glass dividers, and if the exam rooms have pictures and comfortable chairs, and if the physician comes in wearing jeans and a T-shirt, and if she introduces herself as "Samantha Stevens" (rather than "Doctor Stevens"), then you will feel less concerned about exhibiting such ostentatious signs of respect.

Much of Goffman's concern with ritual has to do with *face-work:* actions oriented toward maintaining or modifying face. We tend to preserve our face not only because we are emotionally attached to it (we can experience pride or shame), but also because our face is bound up with the face of others in the situation. For example, if I see you once and only once, then I can present any self I desire. However, if we interact on a regular basis, then we tend to become attached to faces and we maintain consistency of behaviors. You tend to rely on my face in order to consistently present your face. Roles and faces do not come individually prepackaged; they come in sets: My being a teacher would be impossible without the role of student. And my face as a good teacher would be equally impossible without your face as a good student. Once we present an identity, we and others build later responses on it so that our faces are intrinsically bound up one with another. We thus sustain a ritualized equilibrium in interactions through accommodating one another's lines.

The most basic kind of face-work is avoidance: We avoid contacts and requests where threats are likely to occur. For example, a student might avoid encounters where the two women he is dating might meet, or where he might see the professor to whom he owes a paper. This kind of avoidance is rather obvious, but there are other less obvious avoidance procedures. I might, for example, change the topic of conversation because it is getting too near a place where my face might be threatened. Or, when I make a claim about myself, I can do it with belittling modesty. Let's say you see me walking from my truck carrying a guitar. The guitar cues the identity of musician and creates a certain level of expectations. First you ask to see the guitar and then you ask me to play something. But before I do, I say, "Sure, but I haven't practiced for a long time." With such an account, I am simultaneously laying claim to the identity of musician and creating space where I might fail the normal expectations. Such a move not only allows me to avoid embarrassment, it also opens up the possibility of my meeting the normal expectations but being seen as exceptional for doing so. I set the performance expectations low so that when I play average, it will seem like I am playing well.

All of these avoidance procedures create a safe space within the interaction: We are able to make mistakes or not meet the expectations of the identity and still maintain our self, identity, and face. Sometimes, however, things happen that would disqualify us from making positive claims to identity, face, and self. When this occurs, the encounter suffers "ritual disequilibrium" and we normally engage in a corrective process that has four moves: the challenge—participants take on responsibility of pointing out action; the offering—the offender either renders the problem understandable by redefining the action or encounter ("I thought we were teasing.") or offers compensations or penance; the acceptance—the interactants believe the offering; the appreciation—the offender expresses gratitude, and the interaction is repaired.

All of this necessary face-work implies the possibility of aggressive face-work. In aggressive face-work, we depend on others' reactions by intentionally introducing a threat to equilibrium: Knowing the rules of ritualized interaction, we can manipulate the encounter to our own benefit. If we know that others will respond to self-effacing comments by praising us, then we can "fish for compliments." If we know that they will accept our account or apology for an offense, then we can safely offend them. And if we are particularly good at face-work, then we can arrange for others to offend us so that they will be emotionally indebted to us.

All of what I've been describing is part of what Goffman calls *focused encounters*. Focused encounters occur when two or more individuals extend to one another "a special communication license and sustain a special type of mutual activity that can exclude others who are present in the situation" (Goffman, 1963b, p. 83). The last part of the definition is a clue to understanding what Goffman is talking about. Focused encounters can obviously happen when the group engaged in mutual activity is alone, but its particular qualities stand out when we consider it around others. All focused encounters have a membrane that includes some people and excludes others. It's an invisible line that marks the gathering as an encounter of social beings belonging to just those people.

The most defining feature of a focused encounter is face engagement. We engage one another's faces through a single visual and cognitive focus of attention, a sense of mutual relevance in our actions, and by granting preferential communication rights. This is easy to illustrate. Picture yourself walking down the hallway at school. You see someone you know and speak a ritualized opening—"Hi, Tom." Once Tom responds, you visually and cognitively focus on one another to the exclusion of all others in the hall. You see Tom's subsequent behaviors as mutually relevant to yours in a way those of the others in the hall are not. And you grant communication rights to Tom that you don't give to those surrounding you. Out of this comes an emergent "we" feeling (versus everybody else in the hall). The invisible wall surrounding you and Tom is also apparent in the use of ritualized openings, closings, entrances, exits, transformations, and so on.

One of the main values of Goffman's conceptualization of focused encounters is that he can call our attention to how we manage *unfocused encounters*. We encounter people all the time, but often we are required to keep the encounter unfocused. Goffman shows us that when we are walking down the hall at school, or through the mall, or any other public place, we are working hard to maintain the unfocused nature of our encounters. While it is our job in focused interactions to call attention to the self we are presenting, there are norms in unfocused encounters that prohibit bringing attention to our self. If for some reason we do, we must repair the encounter. For example, when a person is walking in public and stumbles, it is common practice for the person to look back at the walkway where the trip occurred. Whatever this action does for us personally, socially it conveys to everyone around us that we are in control of our actions and we were tripped by some object in our path.

Another benefit from using Goffman's idea of focused encounters is the notion of rounds. We can think about rounds in terms of a doctor making her rounds at the hospital: She moves from one area of the hospital to the next, checking in on her patients, the lab, the nurses' stations, and so on. The important thing in this analogy is that there is a route that is habitually covered. In our everyday lives, we tend to make our rounds as well. There are given places that we habitually frequent, like home, school, work, and the gym. These rounds of focused interactions tend to give us a sense of permanence about the self.

Concepts and Theory: Frames and Keys

In one of his last works, Goffman took on the social construction of reality, but with a twist. Generally, concern has focused on human reality itself. In contrast, Goffman begins with the individual and asks the question, "Under what conditions do we think things are real?" As such, Goffman (1974) is interested in the internal organization of individual experience: "I am not addressing the structure of social life but the structure of experience individuals have at any moment of their social lives" (p. 13). Specifically, this means that Goffman is not interested in the reality or ontological status of the world itself, but, rather, in the process through which an individual might experience a portion of the world as being more real than another.

In taking this perspective, Goffman is intentionally distancing himself from Garfinkel's ethnomethodology. Garfinkel is similarly concerned with the reality status of the world, but he approaches it more in terms of the rules and methods people use in interactions to create a sense of taken-for-grantedness about a shared reality. In other words, Garfinkel is interested in the folk methods people use in social interaction to gloss over the subjective and reflexive nature of reality. To present his answer to the reality question, Goffman shifts his analytical focus and changes his analogy. Up to this point, Goffman has been focused on the encounter. However, to analyze the reality experience, Goffman focuses on the individual, not the situation. Goffman also changes his analogy from the stage to photography. Goffman uses the notion of a film strip (this was before digital photography) to talk about the stream of human activity: Apart from the categories, or in this case, frames, that we use, our experience of the world through time is an undifferentiated stream of intimately linked events—it's like a film strip that never ends.

If we look closely at a strip of film, what we see are individual frames wherein activity is stopped or freeze-framed. This notion of "frame" is Goffman's chief concept for understanding how people have real or less real experiences. **Frames** are principles of organization that govern social events and our subjective involvement in them. We use frames to pick out certain elements of a situation to pay attention to and others to ignore. Just like literal picture or film-strip frames, frames of organization include and exclude certain things from the picture. For example, picture frames tell us where art ends and the mundane wall begins.

One of the things that Goffman does with his notion of frames is to expand the idea of the definition of the situation. The various definitions that a situation may have are built up from the principles of organization that are found in frames. Frames thus tell us not only what to see but also how to be involved actively and emotionally in any occasion. Notice that we are now talking about many definitions of a situation rather than the definition. Goffman argues that multiple frames can be used in any setting. They can be built up and layered in almost endless ways. Thus, the human experience can be complex and layered. And since roles and selves are attached to definitions of the situation, we can play multiple roles in any location.

Structuring the experience of multiple realities are two primary frames. Primary frames are seen by the people using them as not based upon or requiring a previous interpretation; primary frames initially organize activity into something that is meaningful. Primary frames divide the world into two spheres: natural and social. A natural frame tells people that whatever is occurring is not due to some intentional act or human agency; it is simply and purely physical. The rising of the sun is generally understood as a natural event. Social frames, on the other hand, imply that a human agent or willful intention is involved or necessary. Economic or political activities are two clear examples.

Primary frames can be keyed. Goffman has in mind the keying of music, where music written in one key may be transposed into a different key: The music is basically the same, but it sounds different. Keying thus refers to sets of conventions through which a strip of activity that has already been given meaning by a primary frame is experienced by the participants as something else. That definition sounds pretty academic, but I think it will become clear once we consider the various ways we key things.

Goffman lists five basic keys employed in our society: make-believe, contests, ceremonies, technical redoings, and regroupings. Make-believe is activity that looks real but the participants don't expect any real outcomes. One of the things that Goffman finds interesting about make-believe is that it requires our full attention and we tend to become engrossed in the process, even though everyone acknowledges that what is happening isn't real. Play, fantasy, and dramatic scripting are three examples of make-believe keying. One of the most common examples of play is when we "joke around." The very label we use—joking around—is designed to bracket off some behaviors from reality and key them into a different meaning. Make-believe fantasy keys are very common today, particularly with the widespread use of computers and the Internet. Obviously, a lot of what we do with computers is seen as real, but the territory itself—virtual reality—leads us to key action strips to the fantastic: We can maintain multiple virtual identities associated with a variety of avatars (or incarnations) interacting with manifold groups in imaginary rooms of our choosing.

In addition to make-believe, we also use the contest key. For example, the army regularly participates in war games. These are contests that looks like the real thing and that demand full attention, yet aren't really wars, though there are always winners. Sports are another example of contest keying. Sports like boxing, football and soccer, lacrosse, hockey, and especially the Olympic Games can be seen as ritualized violence. Another interesting type of keying is ceremonial. A ceremonial key references an event, such as the opening ceremony of the Olympic Games, wherein the event and people represent some significant social meaning. Ceremonies thus take events and social positions and idealize them and link them to a symbolic meaning that transcends the activity strip itself.

We have two more kinds of keys to consider: technical redoings and regroupings. Regroupings are, as Goffman (1974) notes, "the most troublesome of the lot" (p. 74). The idea of regrouping references the participants' motives—some motives in performing a strip of activity are in keeping with those that are normally expected and others are outside the normal expectations. An example of regrouping is an upper-class woman working as a salesperson at a church yard sale. In technical redoings, we take ordinary activities out of their context and perform them for reasons completely different from those that are normally understood. A male might, for example, practice different pickup lines with a close female friend; a music group might rehearse the show they will perform in a week; we watch demonstrations of laying carpet at the local Home Depot; or in therapy we might be asked to act out our feelings or talk to a dead father. Goffman notes that people can conceptualize (key) almost anything as an experiment.

By now it should be clear that our experience of life can be pretty complex. That is part of Goffman's point. People are playing with and moving in and out of keys almost continually. To top things off, keys and frames can be fabricated. There is an assumption of authenticity with any of the keyings that we've looked at. Even with such things as make-believe, we assume that it is authentically make-believe, that there is no other hidden agenda behind the play or fantasy. But sometimes there is something else going on and the keyed frame that we are asked to accept is a fabrication. Under a keyed frame, all the participants have the same point of view. But under a keyed frame that is fabricated, there are different perspectives. All con games work using fabricated frames. A less dramatic example might be a high school girl who joins the school production of a play in order to be close to someone she is interested in. At rehearsal, the play is keyed (note that the play itself is the result of a keying), and everybody at rehearsal understands the key, including the young woman. However, she has a different perspective than the rest: For her, the key enables her to meet and interact with her love interest.

This multi-contextual game is probably more prominent today, in technically advanced societies, than in previous ages. The reasons for this change are extensive and complex, but they are not our concern at the moment. Our cultural life is extremely complex and will probably become more so. Goffman's point is that no matter how complex the keys and fabrications might become, they are generally built up from two primary frames. We can think of our experience, particularly in the beginnings of the twenty-first century, as layered from the most basic to the most abstract. We might play with virtual selves and abstract ideas like hyperreality, but the scaffolding of keys and fabrications can and will fall apart like a house of cards when reality asserts itself, as it tends to do.

Concepts and Theory: The Interaction Order

Together, impression management, all the issues of the encounter, and frames create what Goffman calls the *interaction order*. In many ways, Goffman is not so much interested in the interaction per se, as he is in the order that is demanded by interaction. This is a ritualized order; an order that is produced not because of participants' accounts about what they are doing (ethnomethodology) and not as an emergent phenomenon of negotiated meanings (symbolic interactionism). It is an order that is produced out of the simple demand that a self is needed to interact. It is ritualized—patterned in unthinking ways—because what occurs is for the express purpose of presentation, the first and primary step in a social encounter.

The content of the interaction, its meanings and motivations, isn't Goffman's concern. For us to interact there are certain rules, ways of behaving, and effects that are demanded and come about simply because a presentation is required. These have little if anything to do with our personal motives, but have significant power over the effects of the interaction. For example, when we enter an interaction, we find out what people are talking about, what kinds of roles are important, what statuses are claimed, how involved people are in the interaction, and so on. Then, once we've checked out the terrain, we gradually introduce our talk and self into the flow of interaction. The motive behind such care, Goffman tells us, is to save our self from embarrassment. The effect, however, is that the organization of the interaction is preserved: "His aim is to save face; his effect is to save the situation" (Goffman, 1967, p. 39).

Goffman, however, is quick to tell us that he is not proposing a situational reductionism, where the only thing that exists is face-to-face interactions. Goffman doesn't talk in terms of structures or institutions, but he names at least three things that exist outside of the immediate interaction. First, settings strongly inform the definition of the situation. The definition of the situation is important because it tells us what kind of selves to present, what to expect from others, how to interpret meaning, and so forth. For example, the selves, meanings, and others available in a university classroom are different than at a local bar.

Another element that exists outside the encounter is *biographies*. People come into interactions with biographies. These biographies are previously established stories about our self and others. There are two kinds of biographical stories that we use, individual and categoric. If we see someone with whom we have interacted previously, then we have an individual biography of that person and he or she of us. As we will see, these biographies or story lines are the result of impression management.

Yet, once established, you and I are both committed to maintaining that story. When a personal biography isn't available, as when you first meet someone, then categoric biographies are used—stories that go along with the type of person you are meeting. For example, when you first meet a professor, there's a categoric biography that you access, a story about that person even though you've never met before. Both individual and categoric biographies structure the encounter.

The third extra-interactional element that Goffman (1983) explicitly talks about is *cognitive relations:* "At the very center of interaction life is the cognitive relation we have with those present before us" (p. 4). As members of categoric groups, each of us has identifiable knowledge bases, and these islands of knowledge are related to other specific categoric groups. For example, let's say it's Friday after work and you've just stopped by a local bar to unwind. As you sit down at the bar, the person next to you strikes up a conversation. The small talk continues as you chat about work, the poker tournament on the television, and other bits and pieces of social life. Then one of you mentions music and you find out that one plays guitar and the other drums. Suddenly an entire horizon of shared knowledge opens up. You can almost feel the expansion from a narrow sliver of shared reality to a world of cognitive relations.

Thus, Goffman isn't arguing that more macro-level entities don't exist, or that they are any less an abstraction than the interaction order (though you might notice that the way he talks about such large-scale things is distinctly different from most structural sociologists). It's Goffman's (1983) perspective that "in all these cases [of both the macro and micro phenomena] what we get is somebody's crudely edited summaries" (p. 9). Yet Goffman is also arguing that interactions are unique in that they, more than any other social site, are "worn smooth" through constant use. People interact more in face-to-face encounters than they do in other social units, such as formal organizations (for example, Wal-Mart and Target) or nations (like the United States and England). The interaction order achieved through encounters, then, is our most stable and routine social entity, and it seems "more open to systematic analysis than are the internal or external workings of many macroscopic entities" (Goffman, 1983, p. 9).

Summary

- Goffman understands interactions through the analogy of the stage. Dramaturgy assumes that all we can know about a person's self is what we can pick up by reading cues. Individuals manipulate cues through impression management, in order to claim a certain kind of self in the interaction. If people use dramaturgy, then the encounter itself may be seen as an activity system, like a particular kind of stage or background that places its own demands upon the performers. Goffman's entire analysis, then, is focused on the presentation of self that organizes the interaction order.

- One way of understanding impression management is to see it through the notion of social, personal, and ego identities. Social identities are biographies held by distant others, personal identities are stories that intimate others hold, and the ego identity is the biography that the individual holds about the self. Each of these stories, even the ego identity, is created out of the way the individual manages a dramatic front using the expressive equipment of appearance, manner, and setting. The self must be seen to be known, and it is only seen through impression management cues. Typically, this impression management is prepared in the backstage and presented to an audience on the front stage. And while there are undoubtedly soliloquies in life as onstage, most of the presentations of self are managed by teams or troupes of actors.

- In an interaction, participants depend upon cues to attribute an identity and its attendant attitudes to the individual. The identity and its attitudinal and behavioral expectations form righteously imputed expectations. Sensing this, most people are careful in the way they manage the impression they give others. This work can be seen to vary on a continuum from role distance to role embracement. In role distance, one manages impression in such a way as to simultaneously lay effective claim to the role, its virtual self, and a yet unseen self. The purpose of such work is to claim a self that is more than the role communicates. In role embracement, the individual disappears within the virtual self. Such work idealizes the situation and its roles.

- The longer we perform a particular role or the closer we come to role embracement, the greater is the possibility of embarrassment. Goffman refers to this emotional attachment to roles as face. Every interaction represents a risk to self: We can either lose or maintain face. As such, most interactions are ritualized around face-work. Most face-work is performed through avoidance procedures. For our self, we avoid settings and topics that represent threat, we initially present a front of diffidence and composure, and we make claims about self with belittling modesty. For others, we do such things as leaving unstated "facts" that may discredit them, deliberately turning a blind eye to behaviors that might discredit them, providing accounts for them when needed, and when making "belittling demands" we may use a joking manner.

- Face is closely linked to the ideas of ego identity and sacred self. The idea of the sacred self points out the facts that the self is a social entity and that the sacredness of the self as well as our emotional attachment to the self are produced through ritualized interactions. We experience a sacred self with a sense of emotional attachment to an ego identity as a result of the nature and structure of our interactions. We experience a sense of a core, unchanging self because (a) identities and selves are grounded in geographic settings; (b) we regularly frequent a daily, weekly, or monthly round of settings; and (c) focused interactions within those settings are ritually oriented toward maintaining face.

- Settings and encounters obtain meaning through the use of frames. Frames are interpretive schemes that individuals use to section off parts of the endless stream of activities and events. There are two primary frames: natural and social. The natural frame sections off elements from the stream of life and interprets them as normal and natural—rather than due to some intentional act or human agency.

The social frame interprets activities and events in terms of a human agent or willful intention. The use of these two primary frames is how individuals experience things as real. The frames, however, may be keyed through make-believe, contests, ceremonies, technical redoings, and regroupings, and those keys may be authentic or fabricated. Keys and fabrications allow for the possibility of multiple and abstract levels of meaning, yet they are all tied to one of the two primary frames.

TAKING THE PERSPECTIVE

As Fine and Manning (2003) note, "It is difficult to trace precisely the intellectual forces that influenced Goffman's distinct creativity" (p. 41). Goffman rarely, if ever, engaged in the scholastic practice of citing sources in order to substantiate his position or to build on the work of predecessors (a distinct practice of science). What he did was to describe in minute detail the social happenings he explored. "Though Goffman was surely the sociologist he professed to be, he was every bit as much, simply, a writer" (Lemert, 1997, p. xiii). Though there's little in Goffman's writings to link him to any theoretical tradition, it is undoubtedly the case that his graduate student days at the University of Chicago affected his perspective. According to Fine and Manning, his cohort took a "skeptical stance toward the dominant functionalist and quantitative perspective of mid-century American sociology, postulating an alternative . . . of interpretive sociology" (p. 41). We also know that Goffman was invited to Berkeley by Herbert Blumer, an invitation he accepted; and both *Forms of Talk* (1981) and *Frame Analysis* (1974) were written in response to ethnomethodology.

Briefly, dramaturgy is a theoretical perspective and methodology that uses the analogy of the stage to understand and illuminate social life. In this perspective people are seen as actors who constantly manage the impression others have of self. Importantly, the need for and emphasis upon the presentation of self in every social encounter creates an underlying structuring process that produces social order. Dramaturgists are interested in the continual production of a social self, which places moral imperatives on the interaction order.

Goffman's work continues to provide inspiration for researchers who focus on image and the presence of self in social encounters—reference to his work can be found in literally thousands of books and articles. Theoretically, Goffman's biggest impact is with frame analysis and interaction ritual theory. Frames are basic cognitive structures that guide perception and attention; frames thus tell us what is real. Frame analysis extends Goffman's theory to social movements (Benford & Snow, 2000). The argument is that before a social movement can begin, certain frames must exist that call attention to specific details in society. This can be done intentionally through frame alignment, linking new frames to existing ones. Interaction ritual theory is an elaboration by Randall Collins (2004). Drawing on both Goffman and Durkheim, Collins argues that interaction rituals are chained together through emotional energy and cultural capital. These chains provide the basic fabric of society by linking together individual situations.

BUILDING YOUR THEORY TOOLBOX

Learning More—Primary Sources

- I would suggest that you begin with Goffman's last publication, "The Interaction Order" (1983), in the *American Sociological Review, 48.* Then move to his classic, *The Presentation of Self in Everyday Life* (1959). There is also a good reader: *The Goffman Reader,* edited by Charles Lemert and Ann Branaman, Blackwell, 1997.

Learning More—Secondary Sources

- Gary Alan Fine and Philip Manning's chapter on Goffman in *The Blackwell Companion to Major Contemporary Social Theorists,* edited by George Ritzer (Blackwell, 2000), is a good beginning.
- *Goffman's Legacy,* edited by A. Javier Treviño (Rowman & Littlefield, 2003), contains good chapters on Goffman's impact on or connections with other ideas and schools of thought.

Check It Out

- *Stigmatized identities:* For an insightful and disturbing account of how Goffman's theories can be used to understand homelessness, see David Snow and Leon Anderson's *Down on Their Luck: A Study of Homeless Street People,* University of California Press, 1993.
- *Frames:* The idea of frames has been creatively applied to the use of culture in social movements. See David Snow, "Frame Alignment Processes: Micromobilization and Movement Participation," in the *American Sociological Review, 51,* pp. 464–481, 1986.

Seeing the World

- Write a 250-word synopsis of the theoretical perspective dramaturgy.
- After reading and understanding this chapter, you should be able to define the following terms theoretically and explain their theoretical importance to impression management: *dramaturgy, social, personal, and ego identities, impression management, front, setting, appearance, manner, ritual states, backstage, performance teams, roles, role distance, stigma, face, deference and demeanor rituals, face-work, unfocused encounters, frames, keys, interaction order, biographies, cognitive relations*
- After reading and understanding this chapter, you should be able to answer the following questions (remember to answer them *theoretically*):
  - What produces the interaction order?
  - What is a front and how is it managed?

o What are the different ways in which we can relate to social roles? What are the effects of these different ways?

o What are the differences between focused and unfocused encounters?

o How are frames related to social reality and how do they work?

Engaging the World

- Compare and contrast at least two of your professors using Goffman's idea of impression management. How are their offices different? How about the way they dress and talk? How do they use the setting differently? How do their demeanors communicate different levels of expected deference?

- How would flirting and video games be understood as forms of keying? What other examples of keying can you think of?

- Using Goffman's theory, explain Internet interactions. How are they both different from and similar to face-to-face interactions?

- Using a sporting event, concert, or newscast, use frame analysis to explain the different frames that have probably been used in the past and are being used currently.

- How would a dramaturgical theory explaining class, race, gender, and sexual inequality be different from a symbolic interactionist theory? How would they complement one another?

Weaving the Threads

- What are the differences between the symbolic interactionist notion of "Me" and Goffman's theory of ego identity?

- Compare and contrast the ways Goffman and symbolic interactionists conceive of the way behaviors and selves become patterned and predictable.

- Compare and contrast the SI notion of emergent interactions, Garfinkel's ethnomethodology, and Goffman's idea of the interaction order. Bringing them together, answer the question: How are social encounters both emergent and patterned?

CHAPTER 6

Social Exchanges:

George Homans, Peter Blau, and Randall Collins

None of the theories that we've looked at thus far have been able to tell us much about how **power** works or how it becomes structured. After this chapter those issues become central—after all, power is a central issue in modern societies and democracies. In Chapter 7, we will be looking at how power and structure are organized around the issues of race and gender. Chapter 8 will tell us about how class inequalities are subject to symbolic violence and thus structured over time. We'll pick up the issue of power again in Chapter 13; Foucault's interest there is how knowledge systems are used to delineate what is possible and impossible and thus control populations. Chapters 16 and 17 will pick up that thread from Foucault and explain how systems of knowledge create patterns of inequality around gender and sexuality. In Chapter 15, we'll see how increased advertising and markets have damaged the psyche of black America and contributed to antidemocratic energies. And Chapters 9 and 10 will examine how power and politics are changing in the twenty-first century. But what about power in face-to-face social encounters? Is power confined to factors found only outside social encounters? Two of the theorists in this chapter, Peter Blau and Randall Collins, give us a handle on how power is produced and patterned in social exchanges. In doing so, they also provide us with a transition from the micro-level (small, face-to-face encounters) to macro-level (large, social structures) concerns.

The issue of the micro to macro link is one that is obvious in contemporary theory and virtually unknown in classical theory. For some time, sociologists have thought about macro-level phenomena and micro-level interactions separately. In some ways, the two different domains seemed to discount one another. Micro-level theorists like George Herbert Mead saw social institutions more in terms of symbols and ways of thinking and behaving, with their importance and influence emerging out of interactions. On the other hand, structuralists such as Émile Durkheim saw human consciousness and behaviors as being the result of institutional arrangements. Eventually, sociologists began to see a theoretical issue here. If there are two separate fields, face-to-face interactions and social structures, then how are they related? Both Blau and Collins use exchange theory to provide us with answers here as well. More than any other, exchange theory was given a place of prominence by George C. Homans.

Elementary Forms of Social Behavior:
George Homans (1910–1989)

Theorist's Digest
Concepts and Theory: Basic Principles of Behavioral Psychology
    Secondary Propositions
Summary

George Homans very clearly sees his theory as a corrective to Parsons. In his Presidential Address to the 1964 annual meeting of the American Sociological Association, he characterizes the question of Parsons' theory as "the most general intellectual issue in sociology" (Homans, 1964, p. 809). He characterizes structural-functionalism as making its beginning point the study of norms, its empirical interest the interrelationships of roles and institutions, and being more concerned with the consequences (functions) rather than the causes of institutions. Homans' first point is, perhaps, the most obvious and in his mind the most detrimental; and it is captured in the title of his address: "Bringing men back in" (today we would say, "bringing people back in"). If you look at the characterizations of Parsons' theory, you'll see his point—there are no people in structural-functionalism.

Homans' (1964) second point is that Parsons' theory isn't theoretical in the scientific sense: "If sociology is to be a science, it must take seriously [the job] of providing explanations for the empirical relations it discovers" (p. 818). You'll remember from Chapter 1 that positivistic theory is to explain how something works or came into existence. In order to do that, it must contain relationships between concepts. As Homans (1961) puts it, "No explanation without propositions!" (p. 10). I invite you to go back and quickly look over Parsons' theory in Chapter 2. If you do, you'll see Homans' point. Parsons gives us an analytical scheme; a set of concepts that can be used as a perspective to describe what is happening. You won't find any statements of relationship.

Homans' interest and intent, however, is very similar to Parsons'. He wants to explain how social behaviors are patterned over time. To do this he starts in a similar way as Parsons. You recall that Parsons got down to, what in his mind at least, was the most basic piece of society: action. And he proceeded to describe how action takes place within a unit of voluntaristic action. Homans wants to bring people back in and so he looks at what happens between two people in social encounters. What Homans sees is that behaviors that are rewarded are the ones that are repeated; repeated, patterned behaviors are what we're concerned with in the problem of social order. Then, in order to explain how rewards work to pattern behaviors, he turns to psychological behaviorism, which provides him with a set of propositions that explain the conditions under which a person is likely to repeat behaviors. Before we consider the theory, I want to point out one thing. Homans is usually categorized as an exchange theorist; and that isn't quite accurate. While there is a back-and-forth exchange-like movement between two people, the focus of the theory and the dynamic that produces patterns is more on the individual than the relationship. It's important in any theory to see where the driving force is located, and for Homans it's the individual. This becomes clear when Homans talks about a situation becoming a stimulus for behavior, rather than the exchange relation.

THEORIST'S DIGEST

Brief Biography

George Homans was born August 11, 1910, in Boston, Massachusetts, and was a true Bostonian, as his mother was a descendant of President John Adams. Homans graduated from Harvard University in 1932 with a degree in English Literature. Homans never earned a doctorate and came to sociology by accident, having collaborated on a sociological paper. Homans taught at Harvard between 1939 and 1971, when he retired; he served in the navy during World War II. His two most important books are the *Human Group* (1950) and *Social Behavior: Its Elementary Forms* (1961). Homans served as president of the American Sociological Association in 1964. Of Homans' work, Jonathan Turner (1991) says he was "one of the most prominent theorists of this century" (p. 303). Homans died May 29, 1989.

(Continued)

(Continued)

Central Sociological Questions

Homans (1961) was interested in what he called *elementary social behavior,* which "occurs at all times and never lacks form" (p. 4). The form that he was interested in wasn't located in social structures or rules but, rather, in the person. He was interested in social order, like Parsons, yet did not look to either institutions or even situations for understanding how it comes about. Homans defined social behavior in terms of specific relationships of one person to another; specifically, when a person acts toward another, he or she must be rewarded or punished by that person and not by a third party. So, in a manner similar to Parsons and Blumer, Homans reduced action down to what he felt were its basic elements. To phrase it as a question: What are the fundamental elements of social behavior?

Simply Stated

The basic social relationship is one through which people learn how to socially behave toward another. The drive behind this relationship is the desire to receive rewards and avoid punishments. Social behavior will tend to be patterned when it is repeatedly reinforced with high-value rewards. The situations where the behaviors and rewards occur can themselves become valuable to people, thus allowing for long chains of patterned actions. However, if a reward is given too often, it will lose value; and if an expectation of reward isn't forthcoming, the person will become angry and aggressive.

Key Ideas

Elementary social behavior, respondent behaviors, respondent conditioning, law of effect, reinforcement, matching law, stimulus proposition, value, success proposition, value proposition, deprivation-satiation proposition, frustration-aggression proposition

Concepts and Theory:
Basic Principles of Behavioral Psychology

The fundamental task in behavioral psychology is to find the conditions under which a given behavior (response) will be repeated. The basic distinction is between respondent and operant behaviors. *Respondent behaviors* are automatic and occur by simple application of a stimulus; we often talk about these as "knee-jerk" reactions. The source of such behaviors is genetic and the result of natural selection; yet it is possible to control such behaviors through respondent conditioning (see Figure 6.1). The classic example is Pavlov's dogs. Dogs salivate when presented with food, a natural association between stimulus (food) and response (salivation) (Figure 6.1.A). Pavlov created an unnatural association between the presenting of food and a ringing bell, paired stimuli (Figure 6.1.B). After Pavlov repeated this association enough times, the dogs would salivate in response to the bell alone (Figure 6.1.C). The dogs' response to the bell was conditioned—the process through which the connection was made is called *respondent conditioning* (or sometimes *classical conditioning*).

Figure 6.1   Respondent Conditioning

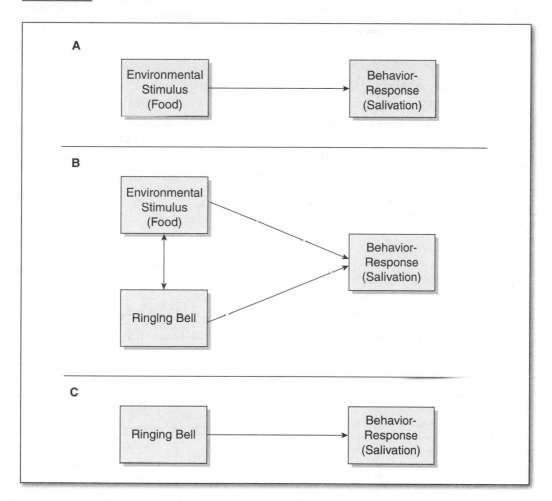

Operant behaviors, on the other hand, are those where a connection is made between stimulus and behavior that isn't there naturally. Rather than some part of the environment acting as a stimulus for behavior, as with the natural association between food and salivation, the behaviors first *operate on the environment*, hence the name *operant conditioning*. All animals, including people, have general drives or needs, such as the drive for sex or food. The strength of these drives differs by species and individuals. So, for example, one person's sex drive may be stronger than another's. When one of these drives is unfulfilled, the animal/person becomes agitated and moves about "exploring and investigating its environment" (Homans, 1987, p. 59). Eventually this

directionless activity hits upon something that satisfies a drive. The behavior has pro-
voked a response in the environment. *Reinforcement* occurs, then, as the link between
behavior and stimulus is strengthened in such a way as to increase the probability of
the behavior occurring again. Homans calls this the *stimulus proposition.*

As just described this reinforcement of the behavior is happenstance. However,
the association can also be intentional. The fundamental idea behind operant conditioning is that learning is based on consequences. Animals and people learn things
that they associate with positive rewards. The goal is to either increase or decrease
the frequency of the behavior. Positive responses increase the frequency and negative
responses decrease the frequency; and to be effective the response or reinforcer must
follow the response quickly and be clearly contingent on the response. So a professor may want you to contribute to class discussion. He or she could figure out a
reward (positive reinforcement) that would be given the first time you spoke up.
The more frequently this association is made, the more likely you are to contribute.
The trick here of course is that the reward has to offset whatever negative reinforcement you may associate with speaking up in class, like embarrassment or peer
sanctions. This relationship is depicted in "A" of Figure 6.2.

Figure 6.2 Operant Conditioning

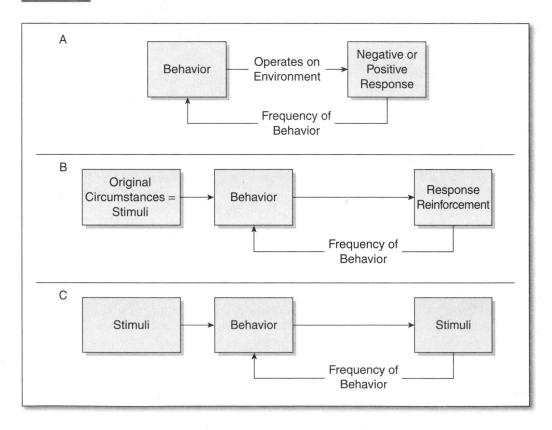

Further, the original circumstances (the "environment" in A, Figure 6.2) may become a stimulus to behavior. This is what you see in B, in Figure 6.2. Thus in our above example as you speak up in class and get rewarded repeatedly, simply being in class will act as a stimulus and prompt prompt you to speak up. The next step is that the stimulus itself can become its own reward. In our example simply being in class becomes rewarding in and of itself. This is depicted in C, in Figure 6.2.

Homans (1987) talks about this as the *matching law* and is "of the greatest importance for the understanding of human behavior" (p. 61). There are two reasons for this importance. First, humans are able to link together long chains of stimuli → response patterns. If you think about this for a moment, you'll probably see that this is yet another answer to Parsons' problem of social order. These long chains create patterns of ordered behavior, all based on operant conditioning. The second reason this law is important for understanding people is that it allows Homans to introduce a new variable: value. *Value* here is understood as the degrees of reward a stimulus provides. Adding this variable allows Homans to describe two factors that determine how often a person will perform one action over others when confronted with choices.

The first factor is the *success proposition* and is based on relative frequency of reward. If you're faced with five different sets of behaviors you have to choose from and one of them has been more consistent in giving rewards than the others, you will be more likely to choose the consistently rewarded behavior. The second factor that determines choice is value; and Homans naturally calls this the *value proposition*. The more highly valued a particular result, the more likely a person is to perform that action. Using our class example for both these, if I give you a choice between working in small groups verses a class discussion and you have consistently received rewards in class discussion but not small-group work, you will tend to choose class discussion more consistently. If, on the other hand, you still get embarrassed in class despite my best efforts and you don't in small-group work, then avoiding embarrassment has greater value for you and you will tend to choose small-group work more frequently. Note that I just introduced a new idea: *cost*. Homans (1958) calls this "adverse stimulation"—avoiding adverse stimulation is its own reward (p. 589).

Taking these together, Homans comes up with a *rationality principle*. In choosing between alternate actions, people take into account the probability of obtaining a particular reward times the value of the reward (Value × Probability = Action). Notice that the relationship is multiplicative, which basically means they reinforce one another. However, and this is a point Homans specifically wants to make, this rationality principle only holds in the moment. What this means is that you may make a decision today that in 2 years looks really dumb. So, Homans (1987) holds this idea of rationality lightly and actually sees *the idea* of rational behavior working in a way we might not expect: "'Rational' is a normative term, used to persuade people to behave in a certain way" (p. 62).

Secondary Propositions

Homans (1987) maintains that there are two secondary propositions that "a sociologist ought to keep with the main ones in his intellectual kit if he is to understand human social behavior" (p. 62). These are derived from the above and are the deprivation-satiation proposition and the frustration-aggression proposition. *Deprivation-satiation proposition* says that people have thresholds of value. Thus, if a person's action is rewarded past this threshold, subsequent rewards become less and less valuable and the frequency of behavior goes down as a result. For example, on a whim a man may bring his wife flowers Friday evening after work. She is so surprised and delighted that her face beams, she jumps in his arms and gives him a long kiss, she excitedly brings out the best vase, and then calls her best friend to brag on him. A lightbulb goes off in the guy's head: Friday night flowers = happy wife (stimulus proposition). So, he of course repeats the behavior next Friday (success proposition), brings his wife flowers and gets the same response. He figures it's a gold mine and does this weekly. Soon he notices that his wife isn't nearly as happy, he gets a slight kiss on the cheek, the flowers laid on the table, and no phone calls to the best friend (satiation). The reverse is true as well: If deprived of a thing of value, its value goes up. Homans says this principle may not hold for generalized reinforces like money, because these may be used to obtain other, more specific rewards.

The *frustration-aggression proposition* is based on expectations. It says that if a person doesn't receive the response he or she expects or receives punishment when expecting a reward, the person will become angry and tend to act out aggressively. This emotionally driven behavior can then function in place of the reward as a way of satisfying the initial desire: A person may learn to use aggressive action like any operant that is followed by a reward.

Summary

- The basic behavioral exchange propositions are (1) the success proposition: People will repeat behaviors for which they are rewarded; (2) the value proposition: The more highly valued a reward or result is to a person, the more likely he or she is to repeat behaviors associated with that reward/response; (3) the stimulus proposition: If a particular situation has been the occasion where a person's behaviors have been rewarded, then the more closely a situation mirrors the first, the more likely the person is to repeat those behaviors; (4) the rationality proposition: Given alternative choices among behaviors, a person will most likely choose the behavior that is seen to be the most rational, determined by the value of the reward times the probability of receiving it.

- From these are derived two secondary propositions: (1) the satiation proposition: The more frequently in the recent past a person has received a reward, the less valued the reward becomes and the less likely the person is to perform the behaviors associated with it; and (2) aggression proposition: When a person does not receive an expected reward (either less than expected or punishment), the more likely is the person to be angry and act aggressively, and the responses to such behavior become valued.

Social Exchanges and Power:
Peter Blau (1918–2002)

Theorist's Digest
Concepts and Theory: Social Exchanges
> *Basic Exchange Principles*

Concepts and Theory: Creating Power and Social Structures
> *Building Social Structures*

Summary

B
lau and Homans have an interesting intellectual relationship. Homans, for his part, uses the empirical data from Blau's book *The Dynamics of Bureaucracy* in forming his theory of the elementary forms of social behavior. Blau singles out Homan's book *Social Behavior: Its Elementary Forms,* as an important influence on his thinking, "despite some fundamental differences in approach" (Blau, 2003, p. xix). And I think you'll pick up on these differences right away. The most fundamental one is that while Homans is more focused on the behavioral dynamics of the individual, Blau is concerned with the social exchange relation itself. As I mentioned in the Homans section, it's important and informative to clearly understand where a theorist is focused.

Broadly speaking, Blau recognizes two main influences on human behavior: (1) the situational and personal factors that influence the preferences people have and the choices they make and (2) those external conditions that restrict or enable those choices and preferences. Blau recognizes three factors that influence choices and preferences. There are the psychological or personality aspects (individual likes and dislikes), the social-psychological factors (how social position/ class and experience influence choice and preference), and the actual properties of exchange. Blau argues that exchange is an emergent property of interaction that cannot be reduced to the psychological attributes of individuals. And, so, that's where he starts.

For Blau, exchange is an elementary process of human life and the prototype of social phenomena. By definition, exchange can take place only in social settings between two or more people. Social exchange focuses on the actions of the participants and how they are influenced by both the anticipated and past actions of others. The influence, then, is decidedly social and not based on personal achievements, such as education, or individual attitudes. However, Blau claims, not all face-to-face inter-actions are exchanges. This is a rather unique position among exchange theorists, many of whom see exchange or rational choice as universal to all human action. Blau (1968), on the other hand, sees that "the concept of exchange loses its distinc-tive meaning and becomes tautological if all behavior in interpersonal relations is subsumed under it" (p. 453). Other factors he sees as influencing people in interac-tions are morals in the form of internalized norms, irrationality (purely emotional responses), and coercion.

THEORIST'S DIGEST

Brief Biography

Peter M. Blau was born on February 7, 1918, in Vienna, Austria, the year the Austro-Hungarian Empire fell. The son of secular Jews, he watched the rise of fascism in postwar Austria with growing concern. Blau became a U.S. citizen in 1943, and he served in the U.S. Army during World War II, earning the Bronze Star for valor. After the war, Blau attended school and was awarded his PhD from Columbia University in 1952; Robert K. Merton was his dissertation chair. His dissertation was subsequently published as *The Dynamics of Bureaucracy* and has since become a classic in organizational literature. Peter Blau held pro-fessorships at Chicago, Columbia, the State University of New York at Albany, and the University of North Carolina at Chapel Hill. He also taught at the Academy of Social Sciences in Tianjin, China, and he was president of the American Sociological Association in 1973. Blau published hundreds of articles and eleven books, and he received numerous awards for his contributions to sociology and to society at large. Peter Blau passed away March 12, 2002.

Central Sociological Questions

Not all relationships are equal. But what makes them equal or unequal? How is power created in social relationships? How do these sorts of relationships provide the basis for larger social structures? These are the questions that occupy Blau.

Simply Stated

Blau uses two basic factors to understand how power and structures are created: reciprocity and imbalance. All social encounters happen because each actor hopes to gain something from it. Reciprocity, then, the give and take of some elements of value, is the fundamental ele-ment of social relations and is intimately related to balance. People will always try to balance out exchanges. If they are unable to, or if they can't find alternatives, then deference and compliance will be offered to balance the relationship. In the relation between a group and single supplier, which by definition involves power, power will be legitimated if the norms of reciprocity and fair exchange are adhered to and will be opposed if not.

Key Ideas

Social exchanges, rational motivation, power, alternatives, marginal utilities, norm of reciprocity, norm of fair exchange, secondary exchange relations

Concepts and Theory: Social Exchanges

Social exchanges are distinct from economic exchanges in at least four ways. First, they lack specificity. All economic exchanges take place under the contract model. In other words, almost all of the elements of the exchange are laid out and understood in advance, even the simple exchanges that occur at the grocery store. Social exchanges, on the other hand, cannot be stipulated in advance; to do so would be a breach of etiquette. Imagine receiving an invitation for dinner that also stipulated exactly how you would repay the person for such a dinner ("I'll give you one dinner for two lunches"). Social exchanges, then, cannot be bargained and repayment must be left to the discretion of the indebted.

This first difference implies the second: Social exchanges necessarily build trust, while economic exchanges do not. Since social exchanges suffer from lack of specificity, we must of necessity trust the other to reciprocate. This implies that relationships that include social exchange—and almost all do—build up slowly over time. We begin with small exchanges, like calling people on the phone, and see if they will reciprocate. If they do, then we perceive them as worthy of trust for exchanges that require longer periods of time for reciprocation, such as friendship.

The third difference between social and economic exchanges is that social exchanges are meaningful. The way we are using it here, meaning implies signification. In other words, an object or action has meaning if it signifies something beyond itself. What we are saying about exchange is that a purely economic exchange doesn't mean anything beyond itself; it is simply what it is: the exchange of money for some good or service. Social exchanges, on the other hand, always have meaning. For an example, let's take what might appear as a simple economic exchange: prostitution. If a married man gives a woman who is not his wife money for sex, it is a social exchange because it has meaning beyond itself: In this case, the meaning is adultery.

Finally, the fourth difference between social and economic exchanges is that social benefits are less detached from the source. We use money in economic exchanges, but the value of money is completely detached from the person using it. I may use money every time I go to the music store, but the value of that money for exchange is a function of the U.S. government and has nothing to do with me—the value of money is completely detached from me. However, the value in all social exchanges is dependent upon the participants in some way. For example, the social exchange between you and your professor requires you to fulfill the requirements of the course to get a grade. Someone else can't do the work and you can't legitimately buy the grade.

Taken together, these four unique features of social exchange create diffuse social obligations. For example, let's say you and your partner invite another couple over for dinner. You expect that the invitation will be reciprocated in some way, but exactly how the other couple is to reciprocate isn't clear—nor can it be clear; to make it clear would reduce it to an economic exchange. So you have a general, unspecified expectation that the other couple will reciprocate in some way. The reciprocation has to be in the indefinite future (the other couple can't initially respond to your invitation by scheduling their "repayment" dinner—then it would really look like a repayment in economic terms), yet it has to be repaid specifically by the couple (the other couple can't have a different couple invite you for dinner and have it count for them). The dinner is meaningful, but the meaning isn't clear as of yet (Are you all going to be friends? If so, what kind of friends?). Thus, you have to trust the other couple to provide the future unspecified meaning and reciprocation. The other couple is obligated to you, but in a very diffuse manner.

Basic Exchange Principles

There are three basic exchange principles that Blau gives us; they concern motivations, alternatives, and marginal utilities. The first principle is that people are *rationally motivated* in exchanges to weigh out costs and benefits. In this respect, the ideal type of exchange is economic, where the calculations are specific and known. As we've seen, Blau argues that social exchanges are different from economic ones, and one implication of this is that our calculations will be different. They are not as specific or concrete as economic calculations. Thus, we have to view social exchange "rationality" in limited terms. It's a general motivation in back of our actions. We don't specifically think, "If I invite Bob to the barbeque, then I can borrow his truck next Thursday." It's more of a general and diffuse motivation—a broad desire for social profits and a sense of how we stand in our exchanges.

Alternatives are extremely important in exchange relations. We'll talk more about alternatives when we get to the section on power, but for now we should simply be aware that when alternatives are present, people will gravitate toward exchanges among equals. We tend to look for someone with whom we can balance out costs and benefits in the long run. These balanced exchange relations tend to reduce uncertainty and to lessen power differences. Blau also notes that balanced relationships tend to create unbalanced relations elsewhere. In this, Blau is positing that we have limited resources and to invest resources in one relationship is to deny it to another.

Let's use the example of dating and marriage. When we get married, one of the things we are doing is committing a large amount of our personal resources to one relationship. We do so because of the anticipation of rewards, both intrinsic and extrinsic, but when we do so we simultaneously take away the possibility of using those resources in an alternative relationship. In these circumstances, friendships can only go so far. If you are married, and if one of your friends wants to exchange more than you are able due to the commitment of resources to your marriage partner, then that friendship will become an unbalanced exchange relation. Unbalanced or unequal exchange relations tend to be less strained if the differences are known, clear, and marked. We can see this easily in our marriage example: Your unbalanced relationship with your friend who wants more will be very strained if you are unclear about what you are willing and unwilling to exchange. However, the strain is lessened as the trade boundaries become clear and marked—the other person will be less likely to entertain unreal exchange expectations.

The principle of *marginal utilities* posits that people have satiation points regarding goods and services. In other words, too much of a good thing may not be a good thing. When we first enter into an exchange relationship, the profits that we glean have high value. However, repeated profits of the same kind have declining value. For example, the first time a man gives flowers to his partner, it has high value. And it probably has high value the second and third times it happens. But if the man brings flowers to his partner every Friday after work, the value of the gift declines as the partner becomes satiated. Thus, the value of any good or service is higher if there is some degree of uncertainty or a sporadic quality associated with it.

Concepts and Theory: Creating Power and Social Structures

There are two norms associated with social exchange: the *norm of reciprocity* and the norm of fair exchange. Blau sees exchange as the starting mechanism for social interaction and group structure. Before group identities and boundaries, and before status positions, roles, and norms are created, interaction is initiated in the hopes of gaining something from exchange. That we are dependent upon others for reaction implies that the idea of reciprocation is central in exchange. The word *reciprocate* comes from Latin and literally means to move back and forth. Exchange, then, always entails the give and take of some elements of value, such as money, emotion, favors, and so forth. As such, one of the first behaviors to receive normative power is reciprocity. The norm of reciprocity implies another basic feature of society, that of trust. As we've seen, social exchange requires that the reciprocated good or service be unspecified and that reciprocation is delayed to some undisclosed future. This lack of specificity obviously demands trust, which forms the basis of society and our initial social contact. Exchanges are also guided by the *norm of fair exchange*. Something is fair, of course, if it is characterized by honesty and free from fraud or favoritism. The expectation of fairness increases over the length of the exchange relation.

Because of the lack of specificity in social exchange and the norm of reciprocity, exchange creates bonds of friendship and establishes power relations. The basic difference between friendship and power relationships concerns the equity of exchange and is expressed in the amount of repayment discretion. Friendship is based on an equal exchange relationship: All parties feel that they give about as much as they take in the relationship. This equal reciprocity among friends leads to a social bond built on trust and a high level of discretion in repayment. On the other hand, inequality in exchange leads to unfulfilled obligations that, in turn, grant power over repayment to the other.

According to Blau, there are four conditions that affect the level of social power. I've diagramed these conditions in Figure 6.3. In the diagram, we have a social exchange relation between A and B. In thinking through the way the model works, you can visualize yourself as either person and get a sense of the way the power flows in the relationship. Social capital refers to the ability to participate in an exchange with goods or services that the other desires. As you can see, there is a negative relationship between social capital and power. In other words, the less ability Actor A has to control goods and services (exchange capital) that Actor B desires, the greater will be B's power over A. Alternatives are important for power as well. If I have a large number of alternatives through which I can obtain the social good or service that I desire, then others will have little power over me. However, the fewer the number of alternatives, the greater will be the power of others who control the social good. This inverse relationship is noted by the negative sign.

Figure 6.3 Exchange Principles of Power

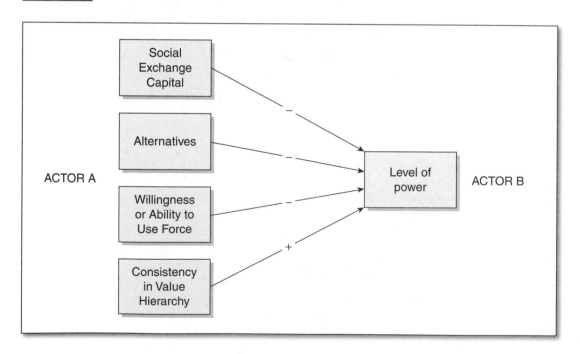

There are two other important factors in establishing social power: the actor's willingness to use force and the consistency of the value hierarchy. If Actor A has the ability and willingness to use force, then by definition there is no exchange relation and, thus, social power is impossible. This somewhat obvious condition tells us something important about social power: There is always a choice involved. With social power, "There is an element of voluntarism . . . the punishment could be chosen in preference to compliance" (Blau, 2003, p. 117). The relationship between Actor A's willingness to use force and Actor B's power is negative: The less likely Actor A is to use force to obtain social goods, the greater is the potential for social power for Actor B.

The last condition implies a consistent value hierarchy. If the value system of Actor A changes and he or she no longer values the social goods B controls, then there can be no power. If, on the other hand, Actor A consistently values the goods B has to offer, then social power will increase, if the other conditions hold as well. Try this thinking exercise: Think about the relationships that you have with various professors as exchange relations. Use each of these four variables—social capital, alternative, willingness to use force, and consistent value hierarchy—and ask the following: Who has more power and why? I believe you'll find that your professors have varying levels of power because of the different ways these factors align. At minimum, this implies that social power is not a simple function of bureaucratic position.

There are five possible responses to power. Four of the responses correspond to the four conditions of power and constitute attempts to change the balance of power. In other words, if you want to change the amount of power someone has over you, you could do one of the following:

- Increase your exchange capital by obtaining a good or service that the other person desires
- Find alternative sources to what you receive from the other person
- Get along without the good or service the other person controls
- Attempt to force the other person to give you what you need

The only other possible response is subordination and compliance. Compliance, unlike most features of social exchange, can be specified and functions like money: "Willingness to comply with another's demands is a generic social reward, since the power it gives him is a generalized means, parallel to money, which can be used to attain a variety of ends" (Blau, 2003, p. 22). The power to command is like a credit, an IOU in social exchange. It is what we give to others when we can't participate in an equal exchange yet we desire the goods they control.

Building Social Structures

Secondary exchange relations result from power and occur at the group level among those who are collectively indebted to someone or to another group. In order for secondary exchange relations to come into play, people who are individually indebted to a person or group must have physical proximity and be able to communicate with one another. For example, let's say you are tutoring a number of students in sociology without charging them money. Each of those individuals would be socially indebted to you, and each individual relationship would be subject to the dynamics of exchange (alternatives, marginal utilities, and norms). As long as you only met with each person individually and they were unaware of each other, the exchange relations would remain individual. On the other hand, if you decide that your time would be better spent tutoring them as a group, then secondary exchange relations could come into play. You've provided them with the ability to become a group through physical proximity and communication. When a group like this is brought together physically and able to communicate, two possibilities exist with regards to power: The group may either legitimate or oppose your power as the tutor.

Blau gives us a very basic process through which power is either legitimated or de-legitimated. Both possibilities are in response to the group's perception of how those in power perform with regard to the norms of fair exchange and reciprocity. If the norms of reciprocity and fair exchange are adhered to, then social power will be legitimated. Blau posits that the path looks something like this: reciprocity and fair exchange with those in power → common feelings of loyalty → norm of compliance → legitimation and authority → organization → institutionalized system of exchange values. As the group communicates with one another about the level of adherence of those in power to the norms of fair exchange and reciprocity, they collectively develop feelings of loyalty and indebtedness. Out of these feelings comes the norm of compliance: The group begins to sanction itself in terms of its relationship to those in power. This process varies in the sense that the more those in power are seen as consistently generous, that is, exceeding the norms of fairness and reciprocity, the more the group will feel loyal and the stronger will be the norm of compliance and sense of legitimation. Out of legitimation come organization and an institutionalized system of values regarding authority (see Blau & Meyer, 1987, for Blau's treatment of bureaucracy).

In his theory of secondary exchange relations, Blau is giving us an explanation of the micro–macro link. We can see this move from individual exchanges to institutions in the path of secondary relations noted above. The "glue" that holds this path together consists of generalized trust and the norm of reciprocity. As we've already seen, all social exchanges are built on trust; the element of time and lack of specificity in social exchanges demand trust. Organizations and institutions are, in Blau's scheme, long chains of indirect exchanges of rewards and costs. And, as we've seen, exchange intrinsically entails reciprocation. Every step, then, along the chain of exchanges is held together by the norm of reciprocity.

Secondary exchange relations can thus lead to legitimated authority, but they can also lead to opposition and conflict. If those in power do not meet the norms of fair exchange and reciprocity, and if those indebted are brought together physically and are able to communicate with one another, then feelings of resentment will tend to develop. These feelings of resentment obviously lead to de-legitimation of authority. This path of secondary exchange relations looks like this: lack of reciprocity and fairness from those in power → feelings of resentment → communication (a function of physical proximity and communication technologies) → de-legitimation of authority → ideology → solidarity → opposition → probability of change.

Groups experiencing a lack of fairness and reciprocity that are in close physical proximity and are able to communicate with one another will tend to develop a set of beliefs and ideas that justify both their resentment and their de-legitimation of authority. This ideology, in turn, enables group solidarity and overt opposition, thus increasing the probability of change. The last part of this path comes from the conflict theories of Marx and Weber. To this general theory of conflict and change, Blau adds the micro dimension of exchange: the beginning part of the path. Keep in mind that all of these factors function as variables and are therefore changeable.

Summary

- Social exchanges are different from economic exchanges because they lack specificity, they require and build trust, they are meaningful, and social benefits are detached from the source. These differences imply that social exchanges create diffuse obligations, which in turn form the basis of society—social relations must be maintained in order to guarantee repayment of these obligations. Population structures are made up from the distributions of a population along various continuums of difference or social position. These continuums of difference create or hinder opportunities for social contact, social mobility, and social conflict.

- There are three basic principles and two norms of exchange. The contours of all social exchanges are set by the principles of rational motivation, the presence of alternatives, and satiation. Because of the peculiar properties of social exchanges, rationality within them is limited, as compared to economic exchanges. People are rational in social exchanges to the extent that they tend to repeat those actions that they received rewards from in the past. People are also rational in the sense that they will gravitate toward exchanges that are equal, the equality of exchanges being determined by the presence of alternatives. And all social exchanges are subject to the principle of marginal utilities—a social good loses its value in exchange as people become satiated; in other words, value in exchange is determined to some extent by scarcity and uncertainty. All social exchanges are subject to the norms of reciprocity and fair exchange.

- Social actors achieve power through unequal exchanges, with inequality in exchange determined by four factors: the level of exchange capital, the number of potential source alternatives, the willingness and ability to use force, and consistency in value hierarchy. The first three are negatively related to power. That is, in an exchange relationship between Actor A and Actor B, as Actor A's capital, alternatives, and ability to use force go down, Actor B's power over Actor A increases. Consistency is a positive or at least steady relationship—continuing to value the goods that Actor B controls places Actor A in a possible subordinate position.

Ritualized Exchanges:
Randall Collins (1941–)

Theorist's Digest
Concepts and Theory: Emotion—The Generalized Media of
   Exchange
Concepts and Theory: Interaction Ritual Chains (IRCs)
   Ritualized Social Structures
Concepts and Theory: The Ritualized Production of Stratification
   The Vertical Dimension of Power
   The Horizontal Dimension of Networks
   Reproducing Class and Power
Summary

Collins (1993) brings us yet another way of seeing exchanges. Like Homans, Collins has a strong individual component to his theory. But Collins isn't interested in the psychological processes of the individual. In fact, he's doubtful about the existence of what is usually implied by the "individual." He points out that what we mean by the individual varies by the social and cultural context and is thus a poor focus for social science research. There are two ways to understand his point. The first is to understand that what we mean by "the individual" is really the social point at which various social identities meet. For example, if I were to ask you to tell me who you are, most of your answers would be in the form of social categories and would involve such things as age, gender, sexuality, friendship, marital status, and so on. The individual, from this point of view, is *a reflection of sociopolitical organization rather than essential characteristics.*

The other way to see that the individual varies by social context is much more profound. From this perspective, the entire idea of "the individual" is the product of political, religious, and social changes that have occurred in the past few centuries. More specifically, the idea of the individual came about as Western society defined civil rights (as a result of the rise of democracy) and moral responsibilities (as a result of the Protestant Reformation). The idea of the individual also became more pronounced through capitalism (consumerism) and social diversity. About the individual, Collins (2004) says,

> The human individual is a quasi-enduring, quasi-transient flux in time and space. . . . It is an ideology of how we regard it proper to think about ourselves and others . . . not the most useful analytical starting point for microsociology. (p. 4)

Like Blau, Collins is more interested in what happens between people than within the individual, but Collins focuses on broader elements of the situation than simply the exchange relation *per se*. Collins also has a different way of seeing how "society" comes about. In the end, Blau, like Parsons, falls back on the power of norms. For Collins, social structures and systems are *heuristics*—that is, they are aids to discovery. Collins (1987) is arguing that we can use the ideas of structure and social systems to "make generalizations about the workings of the world system, formal organizations, or the class structure by making the appropriate comparisons and analyses of its own data" (pp. 194–195). But the reality behind these heuristics is the pure number of face-to-face situations strung together through time and space. In other words, *social structures are built up by the aggregation of many interactions over long periods of time and large portions of geographic space*. The primary way in which they are linked together is emotion.

THEORIST'S DIGEST

Brief Biography

Randall Collins was born in Knoxville, Tennessee, on July 29, 1941. His father was part of military intelligence during WWII and then a member of the state department. Collins thus spent a good deal of his early years in Europe. As a teenager, Collins was sent to a New England prep school, afterward studying at Harvard and the University of California, Berkeley, where he encountered the work of Herbert Blumer and Erving Goffman, both professors at Berkeley at the time. Collins completed his PhD in 1969. He has spent time teaching at a number of universities, such as the University of Virginia, the Universities of California at Riverside and San Diego, and has held a number of visiting professorships at Chicago, Harvard, Cambridge, and at various universities in Europe, Japan, and China. He is currently at the University of Pennsylvania.

Central Sociological Questions

Collins has enormous breadth. Overall, his passion is to understand how societies are produced, held together, and destroyed through emotionally rather than rationally motivated behaviors. In terms of social exchange, then, his interest is to understand how emotion forms the basic motivation and outcome of an exchange. And, like Blau, he's interested in how each individual situated exchange is linked together to form macro-level structures of inequality.

Simply Stated

Collins argues that the most general goods that are exchanged among people are emotional energy and cultural capital, and that the basic social unit is the interaction ritual. The level of ritualized activities varies by co-presence, common emotional mood and focus of attention, and barrier to outsiders. As these variables go up, the group involved will create higher levels of emotion, which then creates group solidarity and group symbols; these, in turn, are carried within the individual and provide the motivation to re-create rituals. Collins argues that this process is how stratified power and class are reproduced.

(Continued)

(Continued)

Key Ideas

Emotional energy, rituals, co-presence, shared focus of attention, rhythmic entrainment, common emotional mood, barrier to outsiders, group symbols, group solidarity, standards of morality, generalized and particularized cultural capital, market opportunities, stratification, deference and demeanor, principle of order giving, principle of ritual coercion, principle of anticipatory socialization, principle of bureaucratic personality, social network, authoritarian, cosmopolitan

Concepts and Theory: Emotion—The Generalized Media of Exchange

Collins' use of emotion is based on three long-standing critiques of exchange theory. First, exchange theory has a difficult time accounting for altruistic behavior. *Merriam-Webster's* (2002) defines altruism as "uncalculated consideration of, regard for, or devotion to others' interests." If most or all of our interactions are exchange-based and if all our exchanges are based on self-motivated actors making rational calculations for profit, how can altruism be possible? Collins claims that exchange theorists are left arguing that the actor is actually selfish in altruistic behavior—he or she gains some profit from being altruistic. However, just what that profit is has generally been left unspecified.

Second, there is evidence that suggests that people in interactions are rarely rational or calculative. In support of this, Collins cites Goffman's and Garfinkel's work, the idea of bounded rationality in organizational analysis, as well as psychological experiments that indicate that when people are faced with problems that should prompt them to be rational, they use nonoptimizing heuristics instead. These heuristics function like approximate or sufficient answers to problems rather than the most rational or best answer. The third criticism of exchange theory is that there is no common metric or medium of exchange. Money, of course, is the metric and medium of trade for exchanges involving economically produced goods and services; however, money isn't general enough to embrace all exchanges, all goods, and all services.

Collins sees each of these problems solved through the idea that **emotional energy** is the common denominator of rational action. Let's note from the beginning that this approach is rather adventuresome in that it combines two things that have usually been thought of as oil and water—emotion and rationality just don't mix. At least, they didn't before Collins came along. Emotional energy does not refer to any specific emotion; it is, rather, a very general feeling of emotion and motivation that an individual senses. It is the "amount of emotional power that flows through one's actions" (Collins, 1988, p. 362). Collins (2004) conceptualizes emotional energy as running on a continuum from high levels of confidence, enthusiasm, and good self feelings to the low end of depression, lack of ambition, and negative self-feelings (p. 108). The idea of emotional energy is like that of psychological drive, but emotional energy is based in social activity.

Collins is arguing that emotional energy is general enough to embrace all exchanges. In fact, emotional energy is the underlying resource in back of every exchanged good and service, whether it's a guitar, a pet, a conversation, a car, a friend, your attendance at a show or sporting event, and so on. *More basic than money, emotional energy is the motivation behind all exchanges.* Emotional energy can also be seen in back of social exchanges that might seem counterintuitive. Why would I exchange my free time to work at a soup kitchen on Sunday mornings? This, of course, is an example of altruistic behavior. Exchange theory, apart from the idea of emotional energy, is hard-pressed to explain such behaviors in terms of exchange. Collins gives us a more general property of exchange in the form of emotional energy. People engage in altruistic behaviors because of the emotional energy they receive in exchange.

The idea of emotional energy also solves the problem of the lack of rational calculations. As Collins notes, people aren't generally observed making rational calculations during interactions. Rather than being rationally calculative, "human behavior may be characterized as emotional tropism" (Collins, 1993, p. 223). A tropism is an involuntary movement by an organism that is a negative or positive response to a stimulus. An example of tropism is the response of a plant to sunlight. The stems and leaves react positively to the sun by reaching toward it, and the roots react negatively my moving away from it and deeper in the ground. Collins is telling us that people aren't cognitively calculative in normal encounters. Instead, people emotionally feel their way to and through most interactions, much like the leaves of a plant reach toward the sun.

Concepts and Theory: Interaction Ritual Chains (IRCs)

For Collins, **rituals** are patterned sequences of behavior that bring four elements together: bodily co-presence, barrier to outsiders, mutual focus of attention, and shared emotional mood. These elements are variables—as they increase, so also will the effects of ritualized behavior. There are five main effects of interaction rituals: group solidarity, group symbols, standards and feelings of morality, individual emotional energy, and individual cultural capital. Collins' theory is diagramed in Figure 6.4.

One of the first things that the model in Figure 6.4 calls our attention to is physical *co-presence,* which describes the degree of physical closeness. Even in the same room, we can be closer or further away from one another. The closer we get, the more we can sense the other person. As Durkheim (1912/1995) says,

> The very act of congregating is an exceptionally powerful stimulant. Once the individuals are gathered together, a sort of electricity is generated from their closeness and quickly launches them to an extraordinary height of exaltation. (pp. 217–218)

Figure 6.4 The Interaction Ritual

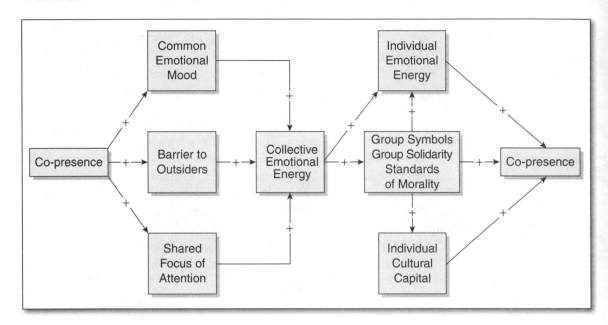

Bodily presence appears theoretically necessary because the closer people are, the more easily they can monitor one another's behaviors.

Part of what we monitor is the level of involvement or *shared focus of attention,* the degree to which participants are attending to the same behavior, event, object, symbol, or idea at the same time (a difficult task, as any teacher knows). We watch bodily cues and eye movements, and we monitor how emotions are expressed and how easily others are drawn away from an interaction. Members of similar groups have the ability to pace an interaction in terms of conversation, gestures, and cues in a like manner. Part of the success or intensity of an interaction is a function of this kind of rhythm or timing.

The key to successful rituals "is that human nervous systems become mutually attuned" (Collins, 2004, p. 64). Collins means that in intense interactions or ritual performance, we physically mimic one another's body rhythms; we become physically "entrained." *Rhythmic entrainment* refers to recurrent bodily patterns that become enmeshed during successful rituals. These bodily patterns may be large and noticeable as in hand or arm expressions, or they may be so quick and minute that they occur below the level of human consciousness.

It is estimated that human beings can perceive things down to about 0.2 second in duration. Much of this entrainment occurs below that threshold, or below the level of consciousness—which indicates that people literally feel their way through intense ritualized interactions. Collins (2004, pp. 65–78) cites evidence from conversational analysis and audience–speaker behavior to show that humans become rhythmically coordinated with one another in interactions. Some research has shown that conversations not only become rhythmic in terms of turn-taking, but the acoustical voice frequencies become entrained as well. EEG (electroencephalo-gram) recordings have indicated that even the brain waves of interactants can become synchronized. In a study of body motion and speech using 16mm film, Condon and Ogston (1971) discovered that in interaction, "a hearer's body was found to 'dance' in precise harmony with the speaker" (p. 158).

A shared focus of attention and common emotional mood tend to reinforce one another though rhythmic entrainment. *Common emotional mood* refers to the degree to which participants are emotionally oriented toward the interaction in the same way. In ritual terms, it doesn't really matter what kind of emotion we're talk-ing about. What is important is that the emotion be commonly held. Having said that, I want to point out that there is an upper and lower limit to ritual intensity. One of the things that tends to become entrained in an interaction is turn-taking. The rule for turn-taking is simple: One person speaks at a time. The speed at which turns are taken is vitally important for a ritual. The time between statements in a successful conversation will hover around 0.1 second. If the time between turns is too great, at say 1.0 second, the interaction will be experienced as dull and lifeless and no solidarity will be produced. If, on the other hand, conversational statements go in the other direction and overlap or interrupt one another, then the "conversation" breaks down and no feeling of solidarity results. These latter kinds of conversations are typically arguments, which can be brought about by a hostile common emo-tional mood. Collins (2004) points out that it is generally the case at the micro level that "solidarity processes are easier to enact than conflict processes. . . . The impli-cation is that conflict is much easier to organize at a distance" (p. 74).

Being physically co-present tends to bring about the other variables, particularly, as we've seen, the shared focus of attention. Co-presence also aids in the production of ritual barriers. *Barrier to outsiders* refers to symbolic or physical obstacles we put up to other people attempting to join our interaction. The use of barriers increases the sense of belonging to the interaction that the participants experience. The more apparent and certain that boundary, the greater will be the level of ritualized inter-action and production of group emotional energy. Sporting events and rock con-certs are good illustrations of using physical boundaries to help create intense ritual performance.

Notice that there is a total of five effects coming out of the emotional energy that is produced in rituals. Let's first talk about the interrelated group effects: group symbols, solidarity, and standards of morality. *Group symbols* are those symbols we use to anchor social emotions. The greater the level of collective effervescence that's created in rituals, the greater will be the level of emotion that the symbol comes to represent. It's this investment of group emotion that makes the symbol a collective symbol. The symbol comes to embody and represent the group. If the invested emotion is high enough, these symbols take on sacred qualities. We can think of the U.S. flag, gang insignia, and sport team emblems and colors as examples, in addi-tion to the obvious religious ones. The symbols help to create group boundaries and identities. Group symbols have an important ritual function: They are used to facilitate ritual enactment by focusing attention and creating a common emotional mood.

Group solidarity is the sense of oneness a collective can experience. This concern originated with Durkheim (1893/1984, pp. 11–29) and meant the level of integration in a society, measured by the subjective sense of "we-ness" individuals have, the constraint of individual behaviors for the group good, and the organization of social units. Collins appears to mean it in a more general way. Group solidarity is the feeling of membership with the group that an individual experiences. It's seeing oneself as part of a larger whole. One of the important things to see here is that the sense of membership is emotional. It is derived from creating high levels of collective effervescence. Of course, the higher the level of effervescence, the higher will be the sense of belonging to the group that an individual can have.

Standards of morality refer to group-specific behaviors that are important to group membership and are morally enforced. Feelings of group solidarity lead people to want to control the behaviors that denote or create that solidarity. That is, many of the behaviors, speech patterns, styles of dress, and so on that are associated with the group become issues of right and wrong. Groups with high moral boundaries have stringent entrance and exit rules (they are difficult to get in and out of). Today's street gangs and the Nazi party of World War II are good examples of groups with high moral boundaries.

One of the things to notice about our example is the use of the word *moral*. Most of us probably don't agree with the ethics of street gangs. In fact, we probably think their ethics are morally wrong and reprehensible. But when sociologists use the term *moral*, we are not referring to something that we think of as being good. A group is moral if its behaviors, beliefs, feelings, speech, styles, and so forth are controlled by strong group norms and are viewed by the members in terms of right and wrong. Because the level of standards of morality any group may have is a function of their level of interaction rituals, we could safely say that, by this definition, both gangs and World War II Nazis are probably more "moral" than we are, in this sense, unless one of us is a member of a radical fringe group.

Ritualized Social Structures

Notice the arrows coming out of individual cultural capital and emotional energy in Figure 6.4. They feed into and create another co-presence—this is how interaction rituals become linked or chained together. In Collins' theory of interaction ritual chains, the individual is the carrier of the micro–macro link. There are two components to this linkage: emotional energy and cultural capital. Emotional energy is the emotional charge that people can take away with them from an interaction. And as such, emotional energy predicts the likelihood of repeated interactions: If the individual comes away from an interaction with as high or higher emotional energy than he or she went in with, then the person will be more likely to seek out further rituals of the same kind. Emotional energy also sets the person's initial involvement within the interaction. People entering an interaction who are charged up with emotional energy will tend to be fully involved and more readily able to experience rhythmic entrainment and collective effervescence.

Cultural capital is a shorthand way of talking about the different resources we have to culturally engage with other people. The idea of cultural capital covers a full range of cultural items: It references the way we talk; what we have to talk about; how we dress, walk, and act—in short, anything that culturally references us to others. Collins lists three different kinds of cultural capitals. *Generalized cultural capital* is the individual's stock of symbols that are associated with group identity. As Figure 6.4 notes, a great deal of this generalized cultural capital comes from interaction rituals. This kind of cultural capital is group specific and can be used with strangers, somewhat the way money can. For example, the other day I was in the airport standing next to a man wearing a handmade tie-dyed T-shirt with a dancing bear on it. Another fellow who was coming off a different flight saw him and said, "Hey, man, where ya from?" These two strangers were able to strike up a conversation because the one man recognized the group symbols of Deadheads—fans of the band The Grateful Dead. They were able to engage one another in an interaction ritual because of this generalized cultural capital.

Particularized cultural capital refers to cultural items we have in common with specific people. For example, my wife and I share a number of words, terms, songs, and so forth that are specifically meaningful to us. Hearing Louis Armstrong, for instance, instantly orients us toward one another, references shared experiences and meanings, and sets us up for an interaction ritual. But if I hear an Armstrong song around my friend Steve, it will have no social effect—there are no shared experiences (past ritual performances) that will prompt us to connect. From these two examples, you get a good sense of what cultural capital does: It orients people toward one another, gives them a shared focus or attention, and creates a common focus of attention, which are most of the ingredients of an interaction ritual.

The last kind of cultural capital that Collins talks about is *reputational capital*. If somebody knows something about you, he or she is more likely to engage you in conversation than if you are a complete stranger. That makes sense, of course, but remember that this is a variable. Mel Gibson, for example, has a great deal of cultural capital. If he were seen in a public space, many people would feel almost compelled to engage him in an interaction ritual.

Thus every person comes into an interaction with stocks of emotional energy (EE) and cultural capital (CC) that have been gleaned from previous interactions. The likelihood of an individual seeking out an interaction ritual is based on his levels of emotional energy and cultural capital; the likelihood of two people interacting with one another is based on both the similarity of their stocks and the perceived probability that they might gain either emotional energy or cultural capital from the encounter. The micro–macro link for Collins, then, is created as individual carriers who are charged up with emotional energy and cultural capital seek out other interaction rituals in which to revitalize or increase their stocks.

One further point before we leave this idea: People have a good idea of their *market opportunities,* which is directly linked to cultural capital and indirectly to emotional energy. As we noted earlier, we exchange cultural capital in the hopes of receiving more cultural capital back. Part of our opportunity in the cultural capital market is structured: Our daily rounds keep us within our class, status, and power groups. However, our interpersonal markets are far more open in modern societies than they were in traditional ones. In these open markets, we are "rational" in the sense that we avoid those interactions where we will spend more cultural capital than we gain, and we will pursue those interactions where we have a good chance of increasing our level of cultural capital. We also tend to avoid those interactions where our lack of CC will be apparent. As a result, we tend to separate ourselves into symbolic or status groups.

Concepts and Theory: The Ritualized Production of Stratification

Using the idea of status from Weber, the notion of deference and demeanor from Goffman (Chapter 5), and his theory of interaction rituals, Collins forms a theory of stratification that has important cultural, social-psychological elements. *Stratification* is always an issue of replication: How is the unequal distribution of scarce resources perpetuated generationally by social groups? Collins' theory looks at how stratification is enacted empirically in the situation and how people subjectively experience their lives differently based on social stratification; in particular, he looks at deference and demeanor rituals. *Deference* refers to respect given and *demeanor* to the cues that indicate the level of respect anticipated. In that these are ritualized, Collins is telling us that these behaviors produce emotional energy and cultural capital and that they are generally part of our regular routine in interaction. For example, you probably don't even notice when you call your instructor "Professor" or "Doctor," but in doing so, you are performing a deference ritual that creates and perpetuates status inequalities.

The Vertical Dimension of Power

In the main, Collins argues that there are two dimensions of stratification: the vertical dimension of power and the horizontal dimension of social networks. As we make our way through Collins' ideas about power, notice that power is not so much seen as a property of social structure as it is enacted in ritual performance. On the vertical power dimension, there are four variables or principles: the principles of order giving, ritual coercion, anticipatory socialization, and bureaucratic personality. The *principle of order giving* says that the occupational position of people runs on a continuum of order giving and taking. At the high end are those who do not take orders from anyone but give orders to many; at the low end are those who only take orders and do not give them; and in the middle are those who take orders from some and give orders to others.

We can understand order giving and taking as types of Goffmanian front- and backstage rituals. Order givers dominate the front stage and give off cues through their demeanor that they are worthy of respect. They make themselves appear dominant and in control, and they internally link their organizational position with their own sense of self. We can also understand order givers as a type of sacred object in the rituals where power is at issue. They are the focus of the interaction and set the emotional mood. In some sense, "it is no longer a mere individual who speaks but a group incarnated and personified" (Durkheim, 1912/1995, p. 212).

Order givers dominate the front stage and develop a front stage personality; they idealize their jobs and see them as more than simple occupations. Order takers, on the other hand, are passive in the front stage and find their rewards in the backstage of organizational life, in such activities as being a sports fan, playing games, or watching television.

The *principle of ritual coercion* says that the more coercion and threat are used in order-giving rituals, the greater will be the level of deference demanded and given, and the greater will be the effects of the principle of order giving. Two obvious examples are medieval aristocracies and the U.S. military; both demand high levels of deference, noted by such terms as "your highness" and "sir" and "ma'am." The *principle of anticipatory socialization* explains that individuals who look forward to occupying an order-giving position sometime in the future tend to identity with that culture even if they are presently order takers. Thus, those in middle and non-management positions who expect promotion will begin to perform the deference and demeanor ritual in keeping with their anticipated position.

Finally, the *principle of bureaucratic personality* addresses the people in the middle, those who take orders from some and give orders to others. These people will have a rather unique cultural outlook and practice. Their place is in between: They stand between upper management and workers or between the organization and the public. As such, they tend to exhibit personal tendencies of both positions: They identify outwardly with the rules and regulations of the organization rather than inwardly believing in the overall mission of the group, and they tend to strictly enforce the rules and regulations on the front stage (in performance for the public or workers) because it is the only stage that they can control.

The Horizontal Dimension of Networks

The second dimension of stratification is the social network aspect of occupational cultures. Every one of us has a *social network*—a string or chain of interactions that form a pattern. The way in which that pattern is put together is vitally important. Social networks are particularly important because they form the way a person thinks and sees the world. Let's use the analogy of cloth to get a grasp on what we are talking about.

Cloth is made out of a network of threads. Two things about this network are especially important for the kind of cloth with which we will end up: the diversity of threads and the density of the weave. The diversity of threads is a vital issue. If the threads that are used are all of one color, what will be the result? A cloth of one color. The same is true of social networks. If the diversity of a person's network is low, if she doesn't interact with different kinds of people in different kinds of situations, then her fabric will only be of one color. This kind of individual will tend to see things concretely, with very little overlap. Her point of view will be very narrow and her number of lifestyle alternatives few. The inverse is true as well: If an individual's social network reveals diversity, then her ideas and perspectives will be more abstract and encompassing. She will tend to be more accepting of others and a diversity of lifestyles.

In cloth, the density of the weave helps determine how durable it is. With social networks, this function is fulfilled by network density. Network density varies by frequency and longevity of interactions. The more frequently a person interacts with the same people and the greater the length of time over which these interactions take place, the denser will be his or her network. Both network diversity and density correspond to elements in interaction rituals. The diversity of the network gets at the degree to which we share a common focus of attention. If the groups that you interact with share a common focus of attention, if there is little variety in what you are paying attention to, then the social objects that occupy your attention become reified.

Social density brings in another ritual element—physical co-presence. Let's think about our cloth again. If the threads of a piece of cloth are tightly wound and densely packed together, what kind of cloth is the result? The cloth would be tough, inflexible, and resilient. Dense interaction networks where people spend a great deal of time in one another's presence tend to yield people who tend to have reified ideas; that is, their ideas are seen as the only possible reality.

There's an old saying: "Birds of a feather flock together." What Collins is telling us is just the opposite: "Birds become of a feather *because* they flock together." In other words, the most prominent characteristics of people come about because of the pattern of their interactions. People tend to be narrow-minded if their interaction pattern is not diverse; people tend to be more accepting and to hold abstract rather than particularized beliefs if their interaction pattern is diverse. And socially constructed ideas tend to be seen as objectively real when the interaction network is dense. These two variables don't necessarily have to go together, but when they do, the results are impressive. Interaction rituals that take place within homogeneous, dense networks produce high levels of social conformity. Some contemporary examples where the network is both dense and uniform include religious cults such as the People's Temple and Heaven's Gate, and the group solidarity the U.S. government fosters in military boot camps.

Reproducing Class and Power

When power and network variables come together, they form predictable patterns of personalities. Remember that for Collins there isn't a self that people are born with; nor is the self a particularly individual entity—the self is social in both creation and function. Like Blumer, Collins sees the self as emerging from patterns of interaction. George Herbert Mead (1934), the philosopher from whom Blumer draws, explains that "the self is not something that exists first and then enters into relationship with others, but it is, so to speak, an eddy in the social current and so still a part of the current" (p. 26). Eddies are currents of air or water that run contrary to the stream. It isn't so much the contrariness that Mead wants us to see, but the fact that an eddy exists only in and because of its surrounding current. The same is true for selves: They exist only in and because of social interaction. The self doesn't have a continuous existence; it isn't something that we carry around inside of us. It's a mechanism that allows social interactions and action to happen.

With Collins we may find the analogy of a "junction" useful. A junction is a place or point where two or more elements are joined. Here the elements are the dimensions of power and network—the person is where these two social factors meet and are expressed. Someone who is high on both network density and power will have an *authoritarian,* upper-class-type personality; and he or she will display all the front-stage work that comes with it. They generally interact only with those with whom they share similar interests—they attend the same schools, parties, country clubs, and so forth—and they interact frequently with those people. As a result, they are quite rigid in their sense of what is right and wrong. They are authoritarian and attempt to impose their values on society at large.

An individual who is high on the power dimension but low on network/ritual density will have and display a cosmopolitan, upper-class personality. *Merriam-Webster's* (2002) defines *cosmopolitan* as "marked by interest in, familiarity with, or knowledge and appreciation of many parts of the world: not provincial, local, limited, or restricted by the attitudes, interests, or loyalties of a single region, section, or sphere of activity." The cosmopolitan upper classes, then, are those that have a broad view of the world and are very accommodating in terms of accepting people. Because their ritual density is low, they associate with many, many different kinds of groups and thus give credence to a variety of viewpoints. These are the kind of upper-class people that tend to use their influence and money to help others through political and humanitarian efforts, such as Band-Aid and the international AIDS foundations.

The same sort of personality type is located in the working class as well, but with different practices. Someone who is low on the order giver/taker dimensions and high on the social network dimension will conform to local, working-class culture. The stereotype of "redneck" is a good example. On the other hand, someone low on the power dimension and low on the network dimension will be part of the working-class party crowd. It isn't important for you to know these types, but it is important for you to see what Collins is arguing. Collins is showing us that class isn't simply an economic structure: It's a power structure that is modified by complex networks of ritual density. Collins takes us beyond Marx and Weber in our understanding of stratification by including Durkheim and Goffman. We'll see another interesting approach to understanding how class is reproduced with Pierre Bourdieu's theory of habitus (Chapter 8).

Summary

- Rituals are patterned sequences of behavior that entail four elements: bodily co-presence, barrier to outsiders, mutual focus of attention, and shared emotional mood. Each of these is a variable, with increasing levels of each leading to increasing ritual performance and effects. Rituals result in group solidarity, group symbols, feelings of morality, individual emotional energy, and individual cultural capital. The greater the level of ritual performance, the greater will be the levels of each of these outcomes. Emotional energy and cultural capital are particularly important because they create the links among chains of interaction rituals. As individuals move from one interaction to another, they carry differing levels of emotional energy and cultural capital. These differing levels strongly influence the likelihood and subsequent effects of further rituals.

• Drawing on Weber, Durkheim, and Goffman, Collins argues that there are two dimensions of class stratification: power and social networks. Collins conceptualizes power in terms of order taking and order giving. In their jobs, people regularly experience a given proportion of order giving and taking. These relatively stable positions result in predictable and repeated ritual performances around deference and demeanor. Order givers are the focus of attention in such rituals; thus, the greater the level of power a person has, the more he will be the ritual focus of attention, the more will his identity take on sacred qualities, and the more he will develop a front-stage personality. Social networks vary by their level of diversity and density. Network diversity and density are both associated with authoritarian or cosmopolitan orientations—higher density and lower diversity create an authoritarian outlook, and lower density and higher diversity produce the more flexible, cosmopolitan perspective. The two features of social networks tend to vary inversely, with low levels of diversity being associated with high levels of density, and high levels of diversity being associated with low levels of density. However, they don't necessarily vary in this way, and this feature adds a great deal of complexity to the class stratification system.

TAKING THE PERSPECTIVE

The idea of exchange as a social dynamic began with utilitarianism, an eighteenth-century philosophy that came out of the Age of Enlightenment's concern with human happiness and scientific calculation. The principles of utilitarianism were most clearly stated by Jeremy Bentham (1789/1996, pp. 11–16), who argued that happiness and unhappiness are based on the two sovereign masters of nature: pleasure and pain. The "utility" in utilitarianism refers to those things that are useful for bringing pleasure and thus happiness. Bentham developed the felicific or utility calculus, a way of calculating the amount of happiness that any specific action is likely to bring. The calculus had seven variables: intensity, duration, certainty/uncertainty, propinquity/remoteness, fecundity, purity, and extent. Thus Bentham introduced the idea of rational calculation being used to decide human behavior and the moral status of any act.

Georg Simmel (1858–1919) was the first sociologist to have a clearly articulated exchange theory. He saw exchange as a type of social form, a patterned mode of interaction through which people meet personal and group goals. For Simmel, exchange is the basic social form because it is based on reciprocity. His theoretical focus is on how value is set or achieved. Value is based on sacrifice and scarcity, both of which are most directly determined by the immediate exchange relationship. Even though value is felt subjectively, it is determined by the totality of elements in the exchange (how scarce the exchange object is and how much someone is willing to sacrifice for it).

Contemporary exchange theory has by and large gone in two different directions. First is an approach initially developed by Richard Emerson (1972) and his colleague Karen Cook (1978).

Blau takes the exchange between two people (dyad) as the archetype of exchange. In contrast, Emerson and Cook focus more on the network of exchange rather than the exchange itself. Social networks are defined by the patterns and positions of a group's interaction. For a quick example, think about an organizational chart. A person's position on that chart determines his or her general pattern of interaction. The same is true for any social group of which you are a member. Within a group there are specific patterns of interaction: Some members of the group interact more than others, and some members don't interact together at all, even though they are in the same group. Social networks, then, are another kind of structure that produces effects that don't originate with the individual, that don't come from social group membership or identity, and about which the individual may or may not be aware.

Rational choice theory shifts focus back to the individual and the outcomes of his or her rational choices. One of the problems posed is that what may be rational for a group may not be rational for the individual. For example, if a group of six people were to move a piano upstairs, it's rational for the group to work together but not rational for the individual. People rationally seek to avoid cost and pain; moving a piano involves one and perhaps both. From the point of view of the individual, then, it's rational to appear as if he or she is contributing but in fact allow the others to do the actual work. This is called the problem of the "free rider." Because of this tendency of rationality and because there are certain goods that can only be created by a group, people rationally develop norms that limit or require action. These norms are rights given to some individuals to control the actions of others; and members agree to these obligations in exchange for comparable limitations and obligations being place on others. (See James S. Coleman's [1990] *Foundations of Social Theory* for a systematic argument from this perspective.)

BUILDING YOUR THEORY TOOLBOX

Learning More—Primary Sources

- Homans' two most important works are the *Human Group,* Harcourt Brace Jovanovich, 1950, and *Social Behavior: Its Elementary Forms,* Harcourt, Brace & World, 1961.

  - For a very good, brief introduction to Homans' work, see "Behaviourism and After," in A. Giddens & J. H. Turner, *Social Theory Today,* Stanford University Press, 1987.

- Blau's most significant work in exchange theory is *Exchange and Power in Social Life,* Transaction, 2003. Blau moved on from exchange theory and became concerned with population structures. That work can be found in *Structural Contexts of Opportunities,* University of Chicago Press, 1994.

(Continued)

(Continued)

- Blau has also written two short pieces that provide an excellent overview of his ideas:
  - o Social Exchange. In David L. Sills (Ed.), *International Encyclopedia of the Social Sciences,* Macmillan, 1968.
  - o Macrostructural Theory. In Jonathan H. Turner (Ed.), *Handbook of Sociological Theory,* Kluwer Academic/Plenum, 2002.
- For an introduction to Collins' central idea of interaction ritual chains, read pages 188 to 203 in his *Theoretical Sociology,* Harcourt Brace Jovanovich, 1988. For a complete exposition of this idea, read *Interaction Ritual Chains,* Princeton University Press, 2004.
- Collins integrates a number of exchange principles in his theory. For his basic ideas on this subject, read "Emotional energy as the common denominator of rational action," *Rationality and Society, 5,* 203–230, 1993; for an interesting look at markets, see "Market Dynamics as the Engine of Historical Change," *Sociological Theory, 8,* 111–135, 1990.
- Collins is also a well-known conflict theorist. For a quick overview of his approach, read "What Does Conflict Theory Predict About America's Future?" *Sociological Perspectives, 36,* 289–313, 1993. For a complete exposition of conflict theory, see *Conflict Sociology,* Academic Press, 1975.

Learning More—Secondary Sources

- *George C. Homans: History, Theory, and Method,* by A. Javier Trevino, Paradigm Publishers, 2007.
- *Structures of Power and Constraint: Papers in Honor of Peter M. Blau,* edited by Craig J. Calhoun, Marshall W. Meyer, and W. Richard Scott, Cambridge University Press, 1990.
- Collins is one of the few contemporary theorists for whom we have a biographical statement that links his life experiences with his theorizing. See Alair Maclean and James Yocom, "Interview With Randall Collins, "2000, http://www.ssc.wisc.edu/theory@madison/papers/ivwCollins.pdf.

Check It Out

- Utilitarianism is a philosophy of morals and government that has had a strong influence on the formation of the United States. The first two are primary texts and the third is a contemporary look at the implications:
  - o *An Introduction to the Principles of Morals and Legislation,* Jeremy Bentham, Oxford University Press, 1966.
  - o *Utilitarianism,* John Stuart Mill, Hackett, 2002.
  - o *Contemporary Ethics: Taking Account of Utilitarianism,* William Shaw, Blackwell, 1998.

- Behavioral psychology: *About Behaviorism*, B. F. Skinner, Vintage, 1976.

- Micro–macro link: For a good review of the many approaches to this issue, see *The Micro–Macro Link*, J. C. Alexander, B. Giesen, R. Münch, and N. J. Smelser (Eds.), University of California Press, 1987.

- Emotion: This is a growing field in sociology. For an up-to-date review, see *The Sociology of Emotions*, by Jonathan H. Turner and Jan E. Stets, Cambridge University Press, 2005.

Seeing the World

- Write a 250-word synopsis of exchange theory.

- After reading and understanding this chapter, you should be able to define the following terms theoretically and explain their theoretical importance to Homans' theory of the elementary forms of social behavior: *elementary social behavior, respondent behaviors, respondent conditioning, law of effect, reinforcement, matching law, stimulus proposition, value, success proposition, value proposition, deprivation-satiation proposition, frustration-aggression proposition*

- After reading and understanding this chapter, you should be able to define the following terms theoretically and explain their theoretical importance to Blau's exchange theory: *social exchanges, rational motivation, power, alternatives, marginal utilities, norm of reciprocity, norm of fair exchange, secondary exchange relations*

- After reading and understanding this chapter, you should be able to define the following terms theoretically and explain their theoretical importance to Collins' theory of ritual exchanges: *emotional energy, rituals, co-presence, shared focus of attention, rhythmic entrainment, common emotional mood, barrier to outsiders, group symbols, group solidarity, standards of morality, generalized and particularized cultural capital, market opportunities, stratification, deference and demeanor, principle of order giving, principle of ritual coercion, principle of anticipatory socialization, principle of bureaucratic personality, social network, authoritarian, cosmopolitan*

- After reading and understanding this chapter, you should be able to answer the following questions (remember to answer them *theoretically*):

    o Explain how behaviors are patterned (social order is achieved) using Homans' theory of elementary behaviors.

    o Explain how power is achieved through social exchanges.

    o What are the five possible responses to power?

    o How are social structures created through social exchange?

    o Explicate the dynamics and effects of interaction rituals.

    o How do interaction rituals produce a micro–macro link?

    o How are power and status produced and reproduced through interaction rituals?

(Continued)

(Continued)

Engaging the World

- One of the enlightening aspects of exchange theory is that it helps us understand our relationships in terms of exchange. For example, what kinds of exchange dynamics are at work in your family or significant relationships? How can you understand your relationship with your professor using exchange theory? Specifically, how is power achieved and how could you reduce the level of power?

- What does Collins' theory add to understanding race, class, gender, and sexual inequalities?

- How does emotion solve the three long-standing critiques of exchange theory?

Weaving the Threads

- Assess Homans' and Blau's understanding of value. Which do you think is more useable and why?

- Explain how each of the theorist's assumptions—Homans, Blau, Collins—informed their approach to theorizing. What specifically did the assumptions lead them to focus on? Do you think these approaches are mutually exclusive? Justify your answer.

- Assess the strengths and weaknesses of Blau's and Collins' "social glue." Can these be synthesized to give us a more robust understanding of how micro processes create larger macro entities? Critique this theory using Blumer's symbolic interaction.

- Garfinkel gives us a theory of how social order is achieved at the micro level. Blau gives us a theory of how power is achieved and maintained at the micro level. How can these two theories be joined? Is power a part of social order? If so, how?

- Compare and contrast Blau's and Collins' ideas of power. What is power and how does it work in these two theories?

- Compare and contrast Blau's and Collins' theories of the micro–macro link. Put them together in such a way as to begin to form a single theory. What do you think is still missing?

- We have now examined four different ways that we can conceptualize what happens when social actors get together: symbolic interaction, ethnomethodology, dramaturgy, and exchange. Come up with a one- or two-word description for what each perspective tells us is happening. Now, under each of the descriptors, list at least five points that make that perspective unique and five insights you would get using that theory (in other words, what is the theory good for?).

- Compare and contrast Blumer's theory of the self with Collins' idea of the individual. In this analysis be certain to explore and give examples of situations where the symbolic interactionist's idea of the self is more appropriate or functional and situations where Collins' notion of the person as the carrier of ritual elements makes more sense. Which do you find more theoretically persuasive and why?

- What are the differences and similarities between Blumer's idea of joint actions and Collins' idea of chains of interaction rituals?

Part III

Social Structures and Systems

Structures of Racial and Gender Inequality:

William Julius Wilson and Janet Saltzman Chafetz

Since its beginning, modernity has been captivated by social and technical projects. The technical project, of course, is aimed at controlling the natural environment. And the social project is focused on democracy and social justice. Equally apparent is that both projects have proven to have unanticipated consequences and be more difficult to master than was first believed. We've obviously had tremendous success in the technical, such as eradicating polio and smallpox, producing more food than the world has ever seen, and so on; but we've also had our share problems, such as global warming and resistant strains of bacteria. The same is true with the social project, some resounding successes but some significant and persistent problems: In the United States, our efforts at extending social justice and equality to blacks and women have been less than successful. There has obviously been some success, but it's also true that full equality has meet with resistance.

When we think of this resistance to equality, most of us think of racist or sexist individuals. But while there's no doubt that such people have an effect, the theorists in this chapter view continued inequality as a result of *social structures*. You'll remember from Chapter 3 that our idea of structure goes back to Durkheim. He argued that social structures are entities that exist connected to but not dependent upon individual people or the micro level of social interaction. Social structures thus have their own sets of laws and dynamics. Most importantly, social structures coerce or force people to think and behave in certain ways. And we saw with Parsons that social structures or institutions work to pattern human action. From this perspective, then, social structures are the underlying cause of social order. In this chapter, the order that is persisting and influencing people's thoughts and actions is stratified racial and gender inequality.

Many of the theorists from this point on work with the notion of structure. And as we'll see, structures can be made up of different things. So I want us to have general definition with which to work: *Structures are composed of different substances that impose organization, boundaries, and behaviors.* From this definition we get three questions that we can use in working with different structures. The first question we should ask is, "Of what substance is the structure made up?" For example, the organs in your body are structured. The structure is made up of cells and tissues. Socially, we can talk about linguistic structures, economic structures, organizational structures, and so on. So, our first task is to identify its substance, and it may not always be as easy as you think. If you were to say that linguistic structures are made up of language, you wouldn't be exactly wrong but you wouldn't be right. There are actually many different kinds of linguistic structures, so always be careful to understand exactly what the structure is made of.

Then ask, "What do these structures do?" For the organs of the body the answers are fairly well-known; the lungs, for example, function to convert air into oxygen. But for a good number of the structures that matter socially, the effects aren't part of the general knowledge (most people don't know enough sociology). For example, Jeffrey Alexander (1985) argues that cultural structures are made up of binary oppositions of purity and impurity that prompt and guide our discussions of democracy. The next question is, "How do they do it?" For Alexander, binary structures define political motives, social relations, and institutions, which are then used to define in- and out-group members, civil and uncivil people. For example, the civil sphere includes people who are active and autonomous (purity) and excludes those who are passive and dependent (impurity). Keep these issues in mind as we work through a theorist's use of structure: What's it made of? What does it do? and How does it work? If you do this, you'll discover how the phenomenon in question works.

In this chapter, both William Julius Wilson and Janet Saltzman Chafetz argue that the inequalities that are associated with race and gender continue because of certain kinds of social structures. Wilson talks about how political and economic structures pattern race relations in the United States. Chafetz actually talks about a number of different types of structures; such as the division of labor, organizational structure, and intrapsychic structures. As we move through these theories, please understand and keep in mind that for these kinds of theories *individuals aren't as important as structures.* In the chapters up to this point, individuals have been significant. But they are much less so now because structures are seen as a bigger, coercive force.

The Declining Significance of Race:
William Julius Wilson (1935–)

Theorist's Digest
Concepts and Theory: American Racial History
    The Plantation Economy
    Post–Civil War to New Deal Politics
    World War II and Beyond
Concepts and Theory: Policy Implications
Summary
Taking the Perspective

While gender is more universal, the use of race as a category of distinction has historically been more destructive. Though women have been seen as less than men, in general their essential humanity wasn't denied. The modern category of race, however, is based on such a distinction. While people have obviously been aware of differences of skin tone and facial features, in premodern societies race wasn't an important way that people used to mark difference. Religion, territory, and eventually civilized versus uncivilized were much more important for most of human history. Race, as such, became important only with the dawn of modernity and specifically capitalism. Capitalism provided the motivation (accruing profit at the least possible expense) and the means (commodification) to make race the primary marker of difference in modern nations. While slavery had always existed, it wasn't until the advent of capitalism that chattel slavery—people seen as property—could exist. It was also modernity that brought to the forefront the issue of human nature as a political concern. You'll recall that political rights in modernity exist for the individual simply because of their humanity. Thus one's standing as human became an issue of concern and definition.

We are without a doubt at a significant moment of change in U.S. race relations. In 2008 the United States elected its first black president. But are we now in a "post-racial" society, one in which race no longer makes a difference? Current statistics appear to say no. The 2008 median income for white families was $55,530, while black family median income was $34,281 (Income, Poverty, and Health Insurance Coverage in the United States, 2008). The U.S. Department of

Justice (2008) reports that at midyear 2008 there were 4,777 black male inmates per 100,000 U.S. residents being held in state or federal prisons and local jails, compared to just 727 white male inmates per 100,000 U.S. residents. The National Urban League (2009) has an overall statistical measure of African American equality as compared to whites: The 2009 Equality Index is 71.1 %. However, are these discrepancies due to racism or some other factor? William Julius Wilson gives us what is perhaps an unexpected answer.

THEORIST'S DIGEST

Brief Biography

William Julius Wilson was born on December 20, 1935, in Derry Township, Pennsylvania. Wilson attended Wilberforce and Bowling Green Universities before completing his PhD in sociology at Washington State University in 1966. His first professorship was at the University of Massachusetts at Amherst, and he joined the faculty of the University of Chicago in 1972. There he held the position of professor and was the director of the Center for the Study of Urban Inequality. He moved to Harvard in 1996, where he currently holds the Lewis P. and Linda L. Geyser University Professorship. Wilson has received many top honors in his career, including the 1998 National Medal of Science (the highest such honor given in the United States), and he was named by *Time* magazine as one of America's 25 Most Influential People in 1996. He has authored several groundbreaking and significant books including *The Declining Significance of Race, The Truly Disadvantaged,* and *When Work Disappears: The World of the New Urban Poor.*

Central Sociological Questions

Wilson is driven to discover the structural causes of poverty that exist in the United States for African Americans. His interest is fueled by the question of policy—he wants to know how racial inequality works so it can be eradicated. So, his central question is, "What social policies need to be in place to improve the lives of African Americans?"

Simply Stated

Race relations in the United States have gone through three distinct phases: the plantation economy, post–Civil War to late 1930s, and World War II to present day. Because of changes in the relationships among government, capitalists, and workers, each of these phases needs to be understood using different theories: classic Marxian analysis, split labor market theory, and class-based analysis. Wilson (1980) concludes that "economic class is now a more important factor than race in determining job placement for blacks" (p. 120).

Key Ideas

Social structure, racism, exploitation, split labor market, Jim Crow, postindustrial economy

Wilson gives us a unique and complex way of seeing racial inequality. Obviously, his concern is the oppression of black people in the United States, but to simply see this inequality as a product of racism is too simplistic. There are two components to *racism:* beliefs and practices. A racist belief system assumes that physical, mental, emotional, and behavioral characteristics are genetically inherited, attributes these characteristics to race, and believes that these characteristics are hierarchically valued, privileging one race over another. Racist practices are those that in fact privilege one race over another. It's important to know that these two issues don't necessarily go together. A person may believe racist ideology but never act it out. And actions that privilege one race over another don't necessarily have to be based on racist beliefs. We'll see this distinction with Wilson. Wilson argues that racism as such, entailing both beliefs and practices, requires a particular kind of structural configuration among the state, the economy, and social relations. Conceptually, this triangle of relations comes from Marx. But Wilson recognizes that the relationship between business and government changes depending on the circumstances, which Marx never saw. Wilson's approach is to first understand the state as a relatively independent actor that can limit capitalism as well as support it. Wilson also questions whether racism is always the causal force in the oppression of blacks. In order to answer that question, Wilson analyzes black inequality in the United States from slavery to the current system.

In the end, Wilson argues that racism (entailing both beliefs and practices) as a causal factor in determining the overall condition of blacks in the United States has been declining in significance since the Civil War. To document the causal force of racism, Wilson tracks the changing relationships between the economy and the state. We'll see that to be effective, racism needs a particular kind of institutional configuration. In its absence, other factors become important for influencing the position of blacks in the United States—in particular, a split labor market and class. As we discuss Wilson's theory, keep in mind that he is not arguing that racism is no longer present or important. Racism is still a problem, but Wilson is pointing out that because of shifts in the relationship between the economy and the state, the *relative importance* of race has declined over time and has been replaced by class-based issues.

Concepts and Theory: American Racial History

Wilson divides U.S. history into three economic phases and demonstrates that different theories are best at explaining different kinds of economic, race relations. There's an important insight into theory that we can glean from Wilson's approach. Most theories contain scope conditions; there are very few claims to be a "theory of everything." Scope conditions limit the applicability of any theory; and understanding the scope conditions of a theory is a part of evaluation in critical thinking. Most students understand that scope conditions can be set by topic. So, for example, Blumer's social-psychological theory may not be the best bet for explaining globalization. But scope conditions can also include issues of time or historical change. In Wilson's case, he uses three different theories—Marx's state-capitalist collusion, split labor market theory, and his own class-state theory—to explain race relations for the three different time periods: pre–Civil War, post–Civil War through the 1930s, and post–World War II.

The Plantation Economy

Marx's theory argues that capitalists as the dominant class use their power to exploit workers and to enlist the state's active support. Modern capitalism is defined by the endless pursuit of capital for its own sake. People have always produced and sold goods; but the purpose of such selling was to earn money to live on. The goal of modern capitalism, however, isn't enough money to live on; nor is it really making enough money to be rich. Both of those goals can be achieved. But modern capitalism is insidious in the sense that its goal can never be achieved. The goal is to acquire capital in order to invest; profit from the investment is reinvested in order to make more capital. This is why modern capitalism is restless, always creating new products and markets.

The fundamental source of profit and capital is exploitation. **Exploitation** is the difference between what a worker produces and what a worker is paid. Capitalists must pay workers less than they earn, and they will always gravitate to the lowest possible wage. The key here is for you to see that the very nature of modern capitalism drives exploitation; and because the drive for capital has no natural limit, the drive for exploitation is just as limitless. Using race as a key in exploitation gave capitalists a group of workers they could exploit without limit, a group that had no power: "There is a chance for exploitation on an immense scale for inordinate profit . . . This chance lies in the exploitation of darker peoples" (Du Bois, 1920/1996b, pp. 504–505). With the invention of chattel slavery, capitalism changed blacks into commodities, and commodities have no power over their owners whatsoever. But notice that this type of exploitation is based on cooperation with the state. The state must support the capitalists' claim that certain racial groups have no civil rights.

In this model, the state and economy are in collusion to exploit the worker. Wilson argues that Marx's theory is best for explaining the racial-caste system that worked under the American plantation economy, at least in the South. This type of nonmanufacturing agrarian society is characterized by a simple division of labor and a small aristocracy. In such a society, there is very little if any job market competition. During this period in the southern United States, working whites were either craftsmen or serfs, and blacks were generally held as slaves. Additionally, in a plantation economy there is a vast distance between the upper and lower classes. Because of this distance, there is little contact between classes, and what contact does happen is highly ritualized and subject to strong social norms of manners and etiquette. These conditions result in little to no class conflict, with the white workers having "little opportunity to challenge the control of the aristocracy" (Wilson, 1980, p. 13).

In such systems of production, the aristocracy dominates both economic and political life. In the United States, the white, landed elite were able to secure laws and policies extremely favorable to their economic interests, and they were able to propagate a ruling ideology concerning the differences between the races. As in classic Marxian thought, the system of production and the state formed a mutually reinforcing cycle. As a result, "the system of slavery severely restricted black vertical and horizontal mobility" (Wilson, 1980, p. 24) and race relations with elite whites took the form of paternalism (the care and control of subordinates as a father). An important issue to notice is *who benefits from the system:* In this case, it's the capitalist class.

Post–Civil War to New Deal Politics

After the U.S. Civil War, the industrialization of the economy grew quickly and the southern economy in particular expanded rapidly. In addition, the Thirteenth and Fourteenth Amendments to the Constitution abolished slavery and granted civil rights to the black population. As a result, from the latter part of the nineteenth century through the 1930s, there were massive changes in the system of production and race relations. This period marks a shift from race relations based on a paternal racial-caste system to a more class-based labor market. In the South, economic expansion greatly increased the political power of the white working class. Blacks were freed but had very little economic or political power. White workers, then, attempted to control the newly available skilled and unskilled positions. The outcome was an elaborate system of *Jim Crow* segregation that was reinforced with a strong ideology of biological racism. The name "Jim Crow" doesn't refer to an actual person but to the stereotypical characterization of blacks in minstrel shows at the time. The idea of Jim Crow segregation references the laws that many states enacted after the Civil War in order to control blacks and preserve white privilege. Jim Crow segregation generally benefited the higher-paid white working class by keeping blacks out of the competition for jobs, especially in the South.

The North experienced a different configuration. Due to high levels of migration of blacks from the South and high immigration rates of European whites, blacks most often entered the job market as strikebreakers. White workers would strike for better wages or working conditions and management would bring in black workers to keep production going. In some cases, management would preempt a strike by hiring black workers on permanently. This move obviously created high tension between black and white workers, which culminated in a number of race riots in 1917 and 1919. The Great Depression of the 1930s shifted things considerably for both black and white workers in the North. During the Depression, there was a strong movement toward unionizing. The unions themselves began to recruit black workers. As a result, black antagonism toward the unions was reduced; black and white workers saw themselves as united in their stand for economic reforms; and the practice of employers using blacks as strikebreakers was eliminated.

Wilson argues that race relations in this time period are best explained using *split labor market theory.* This theory assumes that after slavery, business would support a free and open market where all laborers compete against one another regardless of race. This kind of competition would result in an overall higher level of exploitation because capitalists could pit blacks against whites. In addition, split labor theory proposes three key classes, rather than the two of orthodox Marxian theory: the capital business class, higher-paid labor, and cheaper labor. Understanding that there is another interest in the labor market besides capitalists, and knowing that capitalists would benefit from an open rather than restricted job market, we see that segregation benefited the white working class rather than capitalists.

The emphasis in this theory is on how the market for labor splits and who benefits. The labor market refers to any collective of workers vying for the same or similar positions within a capitalistic economy. A labor market splits when there are two or more social groups whose price for the same work is different, one being cheaper than the other. The price difference is primarily based on dissimilar resource levels, determined by economic and political resources and the availability of information. That is, if there is an ethnic or racial group within a labor market whose standard of living is significantly lower, who lacks the ability to politically organize, and who is less informed about labor market conditions, then the labor market will split. The important thing to see here is that when a market splits, it is more beneficial to higher-paid workers than to business owners. According to this theory, free and open competition would displace the higher-paid workforce and result in lower wages and higher exploitation generally.

Race, then, became a tool of the higher-paid working class to preserve their own economic interests. The white higher-paid working class promoted racist ideologies and discriminatory practices in order to monopolize skilled labor and management positions, prevent blacks from obtaining necessary skills and education, and deny blacks political resources. Thus, while race was still an issue, it originated with white workers rather than collusion between capitalists and the state. Also notice that class became increasingly important during this time. Labor markets are primarily split over class, not race. Race, then, became a marker for class antagonisms rather than for racism itself.

World War II and Beyond

Before describing this time period, I want us to be clear about Wilson's theoretical argument. It's a structural argument, which means that structural arrangements determine social relations. For Marx, the driving structure is the economy: The means of production determine the relations of production. As we've seen, Wilson adds an independent state to this theory. What this implies about Marx's notion of the means and relations of production is that it isn't just the economy that structures social relationships: The interrelations between the state and economy will structure our social relationships, in this case race relations and black inequality. Wilson argues that the role of the state is continuing to change from the classic Marxian model. World War II brought a ban on discrimination in defense and government agencies. This move also provided for on-the-job training for blacks. Black workforce participation continued to expand under the equal employment legislation of the 1950s and 1960s and growing affirmative action programs. These changes obviously didn't come as a result of the government's desire for equality, but in response to civil rights movements, which also boosted black political involvement. But regardless of the source, the state took successive steps to address black inequality.

In addition, the trend toward industrialization that began in the North prior to the Civil War expanded geographically and exponentially from the 1940s onward. This facilitated a shift in the black population toward urbanization, away from rural, agricultural settings and low-paying farm jobs and to cities and industries with better-paying jobs. A large black population thus began to develop in urban centers, which, in turn, prompted the growth of black business owners and black professionals oriented toward serving the needs of the growing black community. As a result of affirmative action and these economic and population shifts, more and more businesses were seeking black employees. For example, during the 10-year period between 1960 and 1970, the average number of corporate recruitment visits to traditionally black colleges jumped from 4 to 297; in some southern colleges, the number rose from zero to 600 corporate visits. During this time, there was also a jump in the percentage of blacks working in government jobs, rising from 13% to almost 22%, and the overall percentage of black males in white-collar positions rose from 16% to 24% (Wilson, 1980, pp. 88 109).

However, the United States began to noticeably shift toward a **postindustrial economy** beginning in the 1970s. This move away from manufacturing and toward service- and knowledge-based goods brought the decentralization of U.S. businesses, further expansion in government and corporate sectors, and demographic shifts from urban to suburban settings (sometimes referred to as "white flight"). These economic and population changes created a situation in which city tax resources either declined or increased at slower than necessary rates. At the same time, and due to the same social factors, cities experienced a sharp increase in expenditures. This situation obviously creates problems for municipal services, such as public assistance and urban schools.

The picture that Wilson gives us of the time following World War II involves two push–pull forces. On the one hand, political and economic opportunities for blacks increased dramatically. Through the 1930s, 1940s, and 1950s, the black working class experienced increasing opportunities and urbanization, which at the time was a positive move. On the other hand, from the 1970s on, there was the decentralization of American business, decreases in manufacturing and increases in government and corporate jobs, and white flight from urban to suburban settings. These overlapping yet opposing forces fragmented the black labor force and resulted in "vastly different mobility opportunities for different groups in the black population" (Wilson, 1980, p. 121).

Those African Americans who were already moving toward the middle class were poised to take advantage of the economic and political shifts. They continued to experience upward mobility and "unprecedented job opportunities in the corporate and government sectors" (Wilson, 1980, p. 121). These middle-class blacks, like their white counterparts, have been able to move to more affluent neighborhoods. The other segment of the black labor force, however, has become locked into the cycle of inner-city problems: declining city revenues in the face of increasing social needs. These are "the relatively poorly trained blacks of the inner city, including the growing number of younger blacks emerging from inferior ghetto schools" (Wilson, 1980, p. 121) who are locked into low-paying jobs with high turnover rates and little hope of advancement.

Wilson wants us to see that race, as it was used in previous times, is a declining factor in predicting the economic and political success of blacks in the United States. Again, this is a proportional evaluation. Race still matters, but class distinctions within the black population have greater impact on black opportunities than does race itself. Prior to the mid-1960s, studies indicated that "race was so much of a dominant factor that very little of black economic achievement was determined by class background" (Wilson, 1980, p. 167). Since that time, those blacks already "in the system" have continued to experience occupational and salary gains. "For those blacks who are not in the system, however, who have not entered the mainstream of the American labor market, the severe problems of low income, unemployment, underemployment, and the decline in labor-force participation remain" (Wilson, 1980, p. 171). It is thus the class positions prior to the sixties and seventies that currently oppress poor and working-class blacks rather than race itself.

In addition, Wilson argues that the character of racial strife has changed. Previous to this time period, racial tensions focused on the economy. From the Civil War through the civil rights era, racial tensions revolved around granting blacks equal access to economic opportunities. Since the segmentation of the black labor pool, racial tensions have shifted to the sociopolitical order. The actors are the same—blacks and the white working class—"but the issues now have more to do with racial control of residential areas, schools, municipal political systems, and recreational areas than with the control of jobs" (Wilson, 1980, p. 121).

Concepts and Theory: Policy Implications

Wilson's basic conclusion is that concern for racial equality needs to move from a focus on race to a focus on class. In other words, policies pointed at creating a tight labor market will go further toward improving the overall condition of blacks in the United States today than will laws aimed at ending racial discrimination. The differences between a tight and a slack labor market basically revolve around the level of employment. In a tight labor market, there are a high number of job openings relative to the labor pool. In other words, those who want to work can work. High employment/low unemployment rates mean that it is a worker's market: Workers have choices of positions; wages are high; and unemployment, when it does occur, is relatively short. On the other hand, a slack labor market means that there are more workers than positions (unemployment is high). This is a capitalist's market: Business owners have their choice of workers, wages are low, and unemployment is chronic.

Unfortunately, in recent times the United States has moved away from "using public policy as a means to fight social inequality" and instead has placed emphasis "on personal responsibility, not inequalities in the larger society" (Wilson, 1996–1997, pp. 569–570). For example, in the year 2000, low-income programs made up 21% of the federal budget but constituted 67% of the spending cuts that year. In order to combat this trend, Wilson is acting to galvanize both private and public support for creating national performance standards for schools. Wilson specifically cites other capitalist democracies that have national policies that emphasize critical and higher-order thinking skills. Along with this emphasis on national standards, Wilson argues that national policy should provide the kind of support needed by inner-city and disadvantaged neighborhood schools to meet such standards. Currently, the unequal funding of schools produces what Jonathon Kozol (1991) refers to as "savage inequalities."

Wilson also advocates improving the family support system in the United States. Currently, the United States is the only modernized country that does not provide universal preschool, child support, and parental leave programs—much-needed support structures in the face of changes in the family and the social structures surrounding it. Along with this support for the changing family structure, Wilson argues that the United States needs to do a better job at linking families, schools, and work. Currently, U.S. firms take 5 years longer than other developed nations to hire high school graduates. Whereas in Germany and Japan students are hired directly out of high school, typically the larger firms in the United States don't hire high school graduates until they have reached their mid-twenties.

Unfortunately, we don't have the space to review all of Wilson's proposals. Wilson has fully documented his policy concerns in *When Work Disappears: The World of the New Urban Poor* (1997), and I encourage you to read it. But from what was just discussed, you can see that Wilson has shifted the discourse concerning the plight of black Americans from one that focuses specifically on race to one that emphasizes class. I want to point out that Wilson's conclusions are based on his ability to use different theories in diverse contexts. Explanations of social injustice aren't as simple as most of us think, and this is becoming truer the more our society and economy become globalized. Having a number of theories at our disposal and possessing the flexibility of mind to use them creatively will go a long way in enabling us to see, explain, and impact the social world around us.

Wilson shows us that our very best efforts at ending racial inequality should be vitally concerned with and aimed at improving the class opportunities of

Americans as a whole, especially as we move into a postindustrial, globalized economy. While these efforts would alleviate the economic suffering of many people,

> Their most important contribution would be their effect on the children of the ghetto, who would be able to anticipate a future of economic mobility and share the hopes and aspirations that so many of their fellow citizens experience as part of the American way of life. (Wilson, 1997, p. 238)

Summary

- Wilson considers three different theories in explaining race relations in the United States: Marxist elite theory, which sees complicity between elite capitalists and the state; split labor market theory, which calls attention to the different resource levels of diverse class positions; and Wilson's own class–state theory. Wilson's theory argues that economic and race relations are based on changing configurations among the state, economy, and class relations. Further, Wilson argues that racism requires a specific kind of relationship between economic elite and polity that was most purely found in the plantation South.

- Using these three different theories, Wilson examines three periods of American race relations: pre– and early post–Civil War, the latter 1800s to the 1930s, and the period from World War II on. The race relations within each of these periods is best explained by different theories: Marxist elite theory best explains the racism prevalent in pre– and post–Civil War America; split labor market theory explains the class growth period up until the Great Depression of the 1930s; and Wilson's class-state theory describes current race relations. Wilson's conclusion is that over time there has been a declining significance of race in explaining the position of African Americans.

- Based on his analysis, Wilson proposes a number of policy changes aimed at improving the overall welfare of the American worker, which, in turn, will improve the conditions of African Americans.

TAKING THE PERSPECTIVE

I've found that the writings of people who study and think about race tend to be distinct and different from people writing about other sociological issues. Probably the best known of "classic" race theorists in the United States is W. E. B. Du Bois, who wrote from the 1890s through the early 1960s. Du Bois gave us a number of significant theoretical ideas, such as double consciousness, and produced some of the first social scientific studies of black Americans. Yet, reading Du Bois is more than reading theory and data, it is an *experience.* In his writing Du Bois moves back and forth among intellectual argumentation, song, prayer, poetry, irony, parable, data, riddles, analogy, and declaration. He weaves a tapestry for the reader, one that touches every part of the reader's being. He wants us to be able to understand the objective state of blackness as well as experience its soul.

This dual approach of blending theory and experience seems fairly common among African American writers. A colleague of mine who teaches African American Social Thought in our department said it this way: "When these folks write . . . they are presenting a lens of dual reality, blackness in America, America on blackness: 'How do I feel about my country and how does my country feel about me?'" (S. Cureton, personal communication, October 9, 2009). A good contemporary example of this approach is Cornel West, who we'll consider in Chapter 15. However, this issue isn't limited to sociologists—it runs deeper. Quite a few African American authors writing about race in fiction, essay, poetry, and the like tend to include what we see as social and sociological theory, because "challenging race legacy touches on everything we know to be sociological!" (S. Cureton, personal communication, October 9, 2009).

I think that a good part of the reason for this twofold nature of black writing is due to the fact that to write about blackness is to write about humanness. Frantz Fanon (1961/2004) writing about colonialism and race said, "The *ruling species* is first and foremost the outsider from elsewhere, different from the indigenous population, 'the others'" (p. 5, emphasis added). He wrote this in comparison to Marx's idea of the "ruling class." For Fanon "ruling class" does not adequately capture how this type of ruling takes place. It's not a class issue, *it is a species issue.* Racial oppression squarely stands on denying or limiting the humanness of blacks. Thus centering race in writing, either creative or scientific, can always evoke the existential cry "How does it feel to be a problem?" in response to "measuring one's soul by the tape of a world that looks on in amused contempt and pity" (Du Bois, 1903/1996a, pp. 101–102).

Additionally, this approach to doing sociology and writing chronicles and puts in the public record the very human experiences of blacks living under inhuman circumstances. This record serves two purposes. It first preserves a truer history of black experience for the African American community. The writings, both disciplinary and otherwise, contain generational knowledge that provides the building stones for a black identity that "speaks to the existential issues of what it means to be a degraded African" . . . and "involves self-respect and self-regard, realms inseparable from, yet not identical to, political power and economic status" (West, 1993/2001, p. 97). The second purpose is that these writings offer for "public consumption the 'soul of blackness' . . . in a society that addresses blackness as deviant" (S. Cureton, personal communication, November 20, 2009). They proclaim the strength of a people proven in a cauldron of suffering. This was undoubtedly the intent that Du Bois had when he penned the above words for the beginning lines of *The Souls of Black Folk.*

Note: My thanks to Dr. Steven R. Cureton, Associate Professor, UNCG Department of Sociology, for enlightening conversations and priceless insights into the writings of black Americans. All the mistakes are mine; all the pearls of wisdom are his.

The Structures of Gender Inequality:
Janet Saltzman Chafetz (1942–2006)

Throughout history, the social category of gender has been and continues to be the most fundamental way in which distinctions are made among people. As such, gender as a social category influences almost every form of discrimination. Take the obvious example of class. According to the Business and Professional Women's Foundation (2004), women generally get paid 76% of what a man makes for the same job with the same education, which means that women are underpaid by about half a million dollars over a lifetime. Interestingly, this discrepancy increases for some of the best-paying and most powerful occupations. Female physicians, for instance, earn about 68% of what comparable male doctors do.

Women also experience what is referred to as "the glass ceiling," an invisible wall that stops women from advancing up corporate and political ladders past a certain point. Thus, men hold most of the top company positions in the United States: In 2002, there were only six female chief executive officers in the *Fortune* 500. Men also hold most of the political positions: In the 108th Congress (2003–2004), women held only 14% of the seats in both the U.S. Senate and the House of Representatives.

The list of the social consequences of gender is almost endless: Women are more likely to have been sexually molested than men; women suffer far more domestic violence than men; women have less decision-making power in organizations and relationships; women typically receive less education than men; women control fewer conversations than men; women are more supportive in conversations than men; the sexual expectations for women are oppressive when compared to men; women are more likely to be hassled in public than are men; and on and on.

THEORIST'S DIGEST

Brief Biography

Janet Saltzman Chafetz was born in Montclair, New Jersey, in 1942. She received her BA in history from Cornell University and her MA in history from the University of Connecticut. While at the University of Connecticut, she began graduate studies in sociology and completed her PhD at the University of Texas at Austin. Chafetz served as president of Sociologists for Women in Society (SWS), 1984–1986, and as chairperson of the American Sociological Society (ASA) Theory Section, 1998–1999. Chafetz was also honored as the first invited lecturer for the Cheryl Allyn Miller Endowed Lectureship Series, sponsored by SWS; her book *Gender Equity* won the American Educational Studies Association Critic's Choice Panel Award (1990) and was selected by *Choice* magazine for their list, Outstanding Academic Books (1990–1991). Chafetz was currently Professor of Sociology at the University of Houston and had been working on immigrant and transnational religion. Professor Chafetz passed away July 6, 2006, after a 7-year struggle with cancer.

Central Sociological Questions

Chafetz is a positivist seeking to understand and facilitate change in the system of gender inequality. She approaches gender inequality like a scientist would approach disease. In order to eradicate a disease, the laboratory researcher must first understand how it works. Understanding how it works can lead to targeted methods of cure rather than trial-and-error shots in the dark. As Chafetz (1990) says, "In practical terms, a better understanding of how change occurs . . . could contribute to the development by activists of better strategies to produce change" (p. 100).

Simply Stated

Gender inequality is replicated by four different levels of structure: macro, meso, micro, and individual. The chief structuring agent is the gendered division of labor in the economy—proportionately there are fewer women than men in the economy; and women who do work have significantly less power, prestige, and pay associated with their jobs than do men who do the same work. This pattern of workforce participation creates organizational structures that reduce women's opportunities for advancement and their relative numbers, as well as ghettoizing women in positions with little power. These three issues work collectively to create a sense of learned helplessness, which in turn produce practices that affirm gender stereotypes.

(Continued)

(Continued)

Because women have fewer economic resources, when they marry they are in an unequal exchange relation. In order to balance the exchange, women offer compliance and deference to men; men use this power to control women's access to work and to gender the household division of labor. Boys and girls raised in such a home learn that they are rewarded when they perform according to gender stereotypes and punished when they do not. Additionally, the fact that the man is little involved in the home and parenting sets up dynamics that form gendered intrapsychic structures, which then provide the basis for women continuing to "choose" to be oppressed by believing in and replicating the very actions that produce gender inequality, most notably the choices associated with workforce participation.

Key Ideas

Feminism, social structure, levels of analysis, women's workforce participation, organizational variables (career path, organizational power, relative numbers), social exchange, micro-power, gender definitions, legitimation, intrapsychic structures, social learning, gendered impression management, unintentional and intentional forces of change

Concepts and Theory: Coercive Structures of Gender Inequality

Another theoretical issue that we need to keep in mind is *levels of analysis*. Generally speaking, sociologists talk about three different levels: macro, meso, and micro. Each of these levels is usually seen as having their own factors and dynamics. The micro level is the domain of face-to-face social encounters. This is the level with which the previous four chapters is concerned. Taken together the theorists in those chapters tell us that there are at least four different features—interaction, ethnomethods, impression management, and exchange—each with their own dynamics. Obviously there are overlaps and advanced work is being done to synthesize these theories (see Turner, 1988). The meso level is the level of organization. This level represents a significant move because in it we are considering something that exists outside of the individual and his or her immediate social situation. It's something more than a mere aggregate of individuals and it works according to processes of its own. Sociological interest in this area began with Max Weber and his ideas about bureaucracy and rationalization. A good introduction to the field is Michael Handel's (2002) reader, *Sociology of Organizations*. The macro level conceptualizes factors and dynamics that work at the highest levels of social systems. Examples include the economic structure as a whole (IBM and Ford are organizations within the economy), society (usually thought of as a nation), and global systems.

There is also another level of analysis, though it isn't usually separated from the others. However, I think it's important to do so especially with Chafetz. The fourth level that sociologists touch on is the level of the individual. Obviously, sociologists never see the individual apart from the context from which it originates and exists, as Blumer and Mead never see the self apart from social interaction (even when it's internalized). The reason it's important to make the distinction with Chafetz is that she conceptualizes elements within the individual as structures. These structures are formed socially, but they then can have individual effects and don't require interaction in order to exist (as do symbolic interaction's and dramaturgy's concepts of the self). Chafetz is one of the very few theorists whose work encompasses the usual three levels; she is particularly rare in that she theorizes at the level of the individual as well.

Macro-Level Coercive Structures

Chafetz draws from specific theories to explain how the coercive and voluntaristic features work. The coercive theories tend to correspond to the three levels of analysis, so that there is a particular theory that is used at each level. Her primary orientation for the macro-level structural features of gender stratification comes from Marxian feminist theory. The basic orientation here is that patriarchy and capitalism work together to maintain the oppression of women. And the central dynamic in the theory is *women's workforce participation*.

Marx argued that social structure sets the conditions of social intercourse. In this sense, society itself has an objective existence and it thus strongly influences human behavior. More than that, social change occurs because of structural change. In Marx's theory, the economic structure itself contains dynamics that push history along. In general, Chafetz draws from Marx's emphasis on the economy as the most important site for social stability and change. She also explores his ideas about the way capitalism works.

Capitalism requires a group who controls the means of production as well as a group that is exploited. This basic social relationship is what allows capitalists to create profit. Patriarchy provides both: men who control the means of production and profit and women who provide cheap and often free labor. That latter part is particularly important. Much of what women do in our society is done for free. No wages are paid for the wife's domestic labor—this work constitutes the unpaid labor force of capitalism. Without this labor, capitalism would crumble. Paying women for caring for children and domestic work would significantly reduce profit margins and the capitalists' ability to accumulate capital. In addition, the man's ability to fully work is dependent upon the woman's exploitation as a woman as well. When women are allowed in the workforce, they tend to be kept in menial positions or given lower wages for the same work as men.

Because of the importance of women's cheap and free labor to the capitalist system, elite males formulate and preach a patriarchic ideology that gives society a basis for believing in the rightness of women's primary call to child rearing and domestic labor. Elite men also use their structural power to disadvantage women's workforce participation. For example, in the United States, elite males have been able to systematically block most attempts at passing national comparable worth amendments or laws that would guarantee equal pay for equal work.

In brief, Chafetz argues that the greater the workforce participation of women, particularly in high-paying jobs, the less the structure of inequality is able to be maintained. The inverse is true as well: The less workforce involvement on the part of women, the greater the inequality on all levels. Thus, the type and level of their involvement in the workforce (macro) play out at both the meso and micro levels. Though we've framed our discussion in terms of capitalism, Chafetz notes that since humans began to farm and herd animals, men have disproportionately controlled the means of production and its surplus. Throughout time, men have been slow to give up their economic positions.

Meso-Level Coercive Structures

To explicate the dynamics that sustain gender inequality at the meso level, Chafetz cites Rosabeth Kanter's (1977) work on organizations. Kanter gives us a social-psychological argument where the structural position of the person influences his or her psychological states and behaviors. Kanter points to three factors related to occupational position that influence work and gender in this way: the possibility of advancement, the power to achieve goals, and the relative number of a specific type of person within the position. Each of these factors in turn influences the individual's attitudes and work performance—or what we could call his or her organizational personality.

The Possibility of Advancement

Most positions in an organization fall within a specific career path for advancement. The path for a professor, for example, goes from assistant, to associate, to full professor. The position of dean doesn't fall within that path. A professor could aspire to become dean, but she would have to change her career trajectory. Kanter argues that women typically occupy positions within an organization that have limited paths for advancement. We can think of the occupational path for women as constricted in two ways: (1) The opportunities for advancement in feminized occupations, such as administrative assistant or secretary, are limited by the nature of the position; and (2) women who are on a professional career path more often than not run into a glass ceiling that hinders their progress.

The Power to Achieve Goals

Positions also have different levels of power associated with them. Again, this is a feature of the location within the organization, not of the individual. For example, if you were in my theory class, I would have you write theory journals. Most of my students do the journals because I tell them to. But my authority to assign work doesn't have anything to do with me; it's a quality of the position. If there were another person in my position, the students would do what he or she told them. Please note that this power is different than the power that comes out of exchanges between men and women in long-term relations (see below). Again, women typically hold positions with less power attached to them than do men. Clearly, there are some women who transcend this situation. But women who are in positions of power are typically seen as "tokens," because there are no similar others in those positions within the company (Kanter's third organizational variable).

Relative Numbers

One of the things within organizations that facilitates upward mobility is the relative number of a social type within a position. Imagine being a white male and reporting to work on your first day. You're given a tour of the facilities. As you are introduced to different people in the company, you notice that almost all the positions of power are held by black men. Most of the offices are occupied by black men, and most of the important decisions are made by black men. There are whites at this place of employment, but they almost all hold menial jobs. By and large they are the secretaries and assistants and frontline workers. Being white, how would you gauge your chances for advancement at such a firm? Further, imagine that after the end of your first week, you notice that there are two or three whites who seem to hold important positions. Would the presence of a few whites in management change your perception? It isn't likely. Though we like to talk as if individuals are the only things that matter, in fact, humans respond more readily to social types than to individual figures. That's why the few minorities that do make it up the corporate ladder are seen as tokens—exceptions to the rule—rather than as any real hope that things are changing.

As I've pointed out, these qualities are attributes of the position more than the person. This issue is important for Kanter's argument because social contexts influence individuals and their attitudes and behaviors. Positions that are similar in the organization produce similar contexts for people that most importantly include power and opportunity. These contexts influence the way the incumbents—the people that occupy the position—think and act. In situations where power is available and the gates in the organizational flow lines are open, people develop a sense of efficacy. They feel empowered to control their destiny within the organization, and they behave in a "take charge" manner. The reverse is true as well. People in positions where there are few opportunities and where power is limited are much less certain about showing positively aggressive behaviors. They feel ineffectual and limited in what they can achieve within the organization.

These issues are true for any who occupy these different positions. Humans are intimately connected to their context. Our social environment always influences who we are and how we act. The problem in organizations is that women are systematically excluded from positions of power and opportunity. As a result, they experience and manifest a self that corresponds to the position, one that feels and behaves ineffectual and limited. Though these differences in behavior and attitude are linked to organizational position, people generally attribute them to the person. Thus, women who occupy positions that have little power or hope of advancement demonstrate powerlessness and passivity. These attitudes and behaviors are then used to reinforce negative stereotypes of gender and work, which, in turn, are used to reinforce gender inequality within the organization.

I've modeled the relationships we've talked about so far in Figure 7.1. Follow the arrows and think through the relationships—remember, these are theoretical

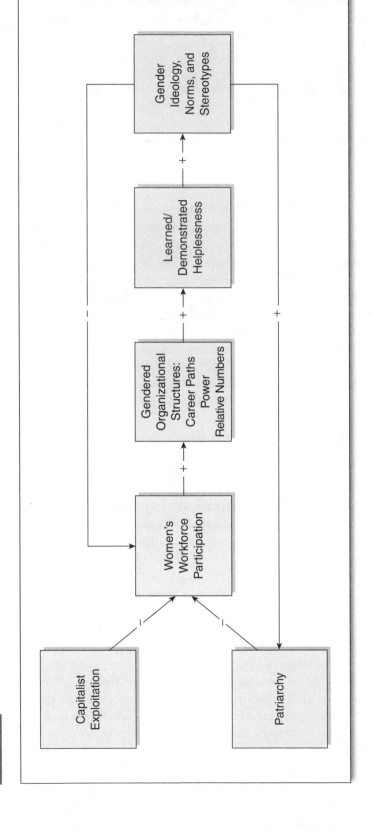

Figure 7.1 Macro–Meso Dynamics of Gender Inequality

relationships and speak of the direction of the relationships. So, signs on the arrows (paths of effects) may not mean what you think at first. The negative sign (−) means that the relationship is inverse. That is, if one variable goes up, the other will go down (and the inverse is true as well). The positive sign (+) means that the relationship is positive and both variables move in the same direction, either up or down. To get you started, let's look at part of one of the paths. The path from the level of capitalist exploitation to women's workforce participation is marked with a negative sign. This means as exploitation goes up, women's presence in the job market goes down. As women's workforce participation goes down, the three organizational variables (career path, power, relative numbers) all go down as well. Keep working through the model until you understand the relationships.

Concepts and Theory: Micro-Level Coercive Structures

Before we begin this section, I want to point out that even though we are talking about the micro level, Chafetz is talking about structures that have the power of coercion. This is important to keep in mind because many micro-level theories are oriented toward choice and agency. Chafetz talks about those issues in the section on voluntaristic gender inequality, but for now we are considering how gender inequality is a structural force at the micro level. Chafetz uses exchange theory to begin to explicate coercive processes at the micro level (see Chapter 6).

Gendered Social Exchanges

Exchange theory argues that people gravitate toward equal exchanges. Both partners in an exchange need to feel they are getting as much as they are giving. If an exchange isn't balanced, if one of the participants has more resources than the other, the person who has less will balance the exchange by offering compliance and deference. Because everyone has access to his or her own behaviors and abilities, compliance and deference are generalized goods. What that means is that they can be offered in exchange for almost anything else (because they are the one thing that everyone has). According to exchange theory, this is the source of power in social relationships.

Exchange theory also makes a distinction between economic and **social exchanges**. Economic exchanges are governed by explicit agreements, often in the form of contracts. The particulars of the exchange are well-known in advance, and there is a discernable end to the exchange. For example, if you are buying a car on credit, you know exactly how much you have to pay every month and when the payments will stop. You know when your debt is paid off. However, in social exchanges the terms of the exchange cannot be clearly stated or given in advance. Imagine a situation where a friend of yours invites you over for dinner and tells you when and how you will be expected to repay. Chances are you wouldn't go to dinner because the other individual broke the norms that make an exchange social.

Thus, social exchange is implicit rather than explicit and it is never clear when a debt has been paid in full.

Chafetz argues that these two issues together create a coercive micro structure that perpetuates gender inequality for women. Because of their systematic exclusion from specific workforce participation, women typically come into intimate relationships with fewer resources than men in terms of power, status, and class. The imbalance is offset by the woman offering deference and compliance to the man. This arrangement gives the man *micro power* within the relationship. The man's power in this exchange relationship is insidious precisely because it is based on social exchange. As we've seen, social exchanges are characterized by implicit agreements rather than explicit ones, with no clear payoff date or marker. While insidious, this micro power is variable. Generally speaking, the more the economic structure favors men in the division of labor, the greater will be a man's material resources relative to the woman's, and the greater will be his micro-level power. The inverse is also true: "The higher the ratio of women's material resource contribution to men's, the less the deference/compliance of wives to their husbands" (Chafetz, 1990, p. 48).

The greater power that men typically have is used in a variety of ways. One common way is in relation to household work. Much of the work around the home, especially in caring for the young, is dull, repetitive, and dirty. Men typically choose the kinds of tasks that they will do around the home, as well as the level of work they contribute. Thus, men usually do more of the occasional work rather than repetitive work, such as mowing the lawn or fixing the car rather than the daily tasks of doing dishes or changing diapers. Men can also use their power to decide whether or not women work out of the home and to influence what kinds of occupations their wives take. Because women in unbalanced resource relations bear the greater workload responsibility for the children and home, they are restricted to jobs that can provide flexible hours and close proximity to home and school.

I've modeled the micro-level variables in Figure 7.2. Notice that I've also taken the liberty of placing the different issues in voluntaristic gender inequality in the model as well. As you can see from the model, the micro-level variables are all driven by the level of women's workforce participation and their subsequent ability to participate in equal exchanges with their life partner. This is precisely what you would expect from a theory that begins with Marx's idea that economic relations are the things that ultimately drive everything else in society. Again, follow the direction of the relationships. The relationship between equality in exchange and men's micro power is negative, which means the more the exchange is equal, the less micro power men will have. And, obviously, the reverse is true. In an unequal exchange relation, women offer deference and compliance and men use their micro power to control gender ideologies, norms, and stereotypes, as well as the gendered household division of labor. Controlling those decreases women's workforce participation (shown by the feedback arrows) and increases the level that individuals are socialized into gender-specific practices and tend to see and experience themselves as gendered individuals.

| **Figure 7.2** | Micro-Level Dynamics of Gender Inequality |

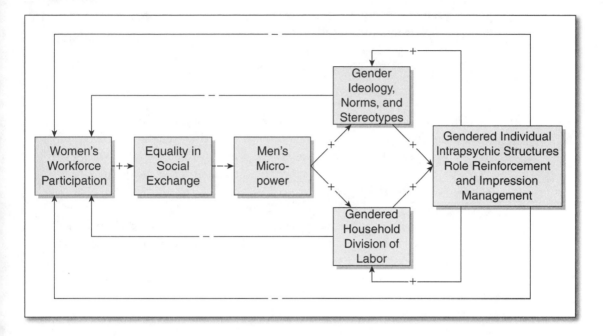

Voluntaristic Gender Inequality

As we noted before, gender inequality usually functions without coercion. This implies that women cooperate in their own oppression. More exactly, "people of both genders tend to make choices that conform to the dictates of the gender system status quo" (Chafetz, 1990, p. 64). Chafetz refers to this as voluntaristic action; but, as we'll see, some of these behaviors and attitudes are unthinkingly expressed and so aren't "voluntary" in the sense of chosen. The patterns that support gender inequality are latently maintained; they are quiet and hidden.

The reason for this kind of maintenance is simple, and it is how society works in general: We simply believe in the culture that supports our social structures. Max Weber pointed this out many years ago. Every structural system is sustained through legitimation, whether it is a system of inequality or the most egalitarian organization imaginable, and legitimation provides the moral basis for power—it gives us reasons to believe in the right to rule. Part of the way legitimation works has to do with the place culture has in human existence: Culture works for humans as instinct does for animals. Another important reason for the significance of legitimation is that coercive power is simply too expensive, in terms of costs of surveillance and enforcement, to use on anything but an occasional basis.

Thus, Chafetz argues that much of what sustains the system of gender inequality is voluntarism. Both men and women continue to freely make choices and display behaviors that are stereotypically gendered. There are three types of *gender definitions* that go into creating gendered voluntaristic action: gender ideology, norms, and stereotypes. These three types vary by the level of social consensus and the extent to which gender differences are assumed. Chafetz draws on three theoretical traditions to explain these issues: Freudian psychodynamic theory; social learning theory; and theories of everyday life, including symbolic interactionism, ethnomethodology, and dramaturgy.

Intrapsychic Structures

Nancy Chodorow's work (1978) forms the basis of Chafetz's psychodynamic theory. Chodorow argues that men's and women's psyches are structured differently due to dissimilar childhood experiences. The principal difference is that the majority of parenting is given by the mother with an absent father. Before we talk too much about Chodorow's theory, we need to make sure we understand the idea of psychic structure, or, more specifically, *intrapsychic structure*. The idea comes from Freud, who argues that the psychic energy of an individual gets divided up into three parts: the id, the ego, and the superego. These three areas exist as structures in the obdurate sense. They are hard and inflexible and produce boundaries between the different internal elements of the person. Thus, when we are talking about intrapsychic structures, we mean the parts of the inner person that are fixed and divided off from one another. It's almost like we're talking about the structure of the brain. The "intra" part of intrapsychic structures refers to how these three parts are internally related to each other. Thus, Chodorow's, and Chafetz's, argument is that the internal workings of boys and girls are structurally different—their intrapsychic structures are gendered.

Both boys and girls grow up with their chief emotional attachment being with their mother. Girls are able to learn their gender identity from their mothers, but boys have to sever their emotional attachment to their mother in order to learn their gender identity. The problem, of course, is that the father has historically been absent. His principal orientation is to work, a situation that was exacerbated through industrialization and the shift of work from the agricultural home to the factory. Girls' intrapsychic structure, then, is one that is built around consistency and relatedness—they don't have to break away to learn gender and their social network is organically based in their mother. Women, then, value relationships and are intrapyschically oriented toward feelings, caring, and nurturing. Boys have to separate from their mother in order to learn gender, but there isn't a clear model for them to attach to and emulate. More exactly, the model they have is "absence."

The male psyche, then, is one that is disconnected from others, values and understands individuality, is more comfortable with objective things than relational emotions, and has and values strong ego boundaries. According to Freud, this male psyche also develops a fear and hatred of women (misogyny)—as the boy tries to break away from his mother, she continues to parent because of the absent father. The boy unconsciously perceives her continued efforts to "mother" as attempts to smother his masculinity under an avalanche of femininity. He thus feels threatened and fights back against all that is feminine.

Remember, these differences between males and females are dissimilarities in the structure of their psyches. This is a much stronger statement than saying that boys and girls are socialized differently. Intrapsychic structures are at the core of each person, according to Freudian theory, and much of what happens at this level is unconscious. Chafetz isn't necessarily saying that men consciously fear or hate women—it's much deeper than that. It is at the core of their being. But also keep in mind that these structures vary according to the kind of parenting configuration a child has. It's very possible today for a boy to be raised principally by the father while the mother works (though our economic structure makes this unlikely), or for a single father to raise a child. The intrapsychic structure of such a boy would be dramatically different than those raised in a situation where maleness is defined by absence and separation.

These intrapsychic differences play themselves out not only in male/female relationships, but also in the kinds of jobs men and women are drawn to. Generally, then, men are drawn to the kinds of positions that demand individualism, objectification, and control. Women, on the other hand, are drawn to helping occupations where they can nurture and support. While there have certainly been changes in occupational distribution over the past 30 years, most of the stereotypically gendered fields continue to have disproportionate representation. Thus, for example, while there are more male primary school teachers and nurses today than 30 years ago, the majority continue to be women, and while there are more women who are CEOs, construction workers, and politicians today, those fields continue to be dominated by men. The important point that Chafetz is bringing out here is that the "personal preference" individuals feel to be in one kind of occupation rather than another is strongly informed by gendered intrapsychic structures. These personal choices, then, "voluntarily" perpetuate gender structures of inequality.

Gendered Social Learning

Chafetz also draws on socialization theories such as social learning to explain the voluntaristic choices men and women make. The important components of *social learning theory* come to us from Albert Bandura (1977). Bandura argues that learning through experimentation is costly and therefore people tend to learn through modeling. For example, it's much easier to learn that fire is hot by the way others act around it than by sticking your hand in it. Social learning occurs through four stages: attention, retention, motor reproduction, and motivation.

Children pay attention to those models of behavior that seem to be the most distinctive, prevalent, or emotionally invested or have functional value. And they retain those models through symbolic encoding and cognitive organization, as well as rehearsing the behaviors symbolically and physically. Motor reproduction refers to acting out the behaviors in front of others. Further motivation to repeat behaviors comes through rewards and positive reinforcement. Children are discouraged from repeating inappropriate behaviors through punishment and negative reinforcement. Eventually, children negatively or positively reinforce their own behaviors—as adults we thus self-sanction most of our gendered behaviors.

Gendered Impression Management

Theories of everyday life look at how people produce social order at the level of the interaction and manage their self-identities. Chafetz specifically draws on Erving Goffman's (1977) work on gender. Goffman argues that selves are hidden and the only way others know the kind of self we are claiming is by the cues we send out. Others read these cues, attribute the kind of self that is claimed, and then form righteously imputed expectations. People expect us to live up to the social self we claim. If we don't, that part of our self will be discredited and stigmatized.

Because gender is arguably the very first categorization that we make of people—one of the first things we "see" about someone is whether the person claims to be male or female—gender is thus an extremely important part of impression management and self-validation. As such, Goffman (1959) would see gender as a form of idealized performance in that we "incorporate and exemplify the officially accredited values of the society" (p. 35). In other words, social norms, ideologies, and stereotypes are used more strongly in gendered performances than in most others. Goffman also sees idealization as referencing a part of the "sacred center of the common values of the society" (p. 36) and this kind of performance as a ritual.

Thus, gender is an especially meaningful and risky performance that is produced in almost every situation. We tend to pay particular attention to the cues we give out about our gender and the cues others present. Goffman further points out that we look to the opposite gender to affirm our managed impression. Our gendered performances, then, are specifically targeted to the opposite sex and tend to be highly stereotypical. According to Chafetz (1990), "For men, this quest [for affirmation] entails demonstrations of strength and competence. However, for women it entails demonstrations of weakness, vulnerability, and ineptitude" (p. 26).

The Structure of Gender Inequality

In Figure 7.3, I've placed our two models together to give us a complete picture of how gender inequality is structured. It's extremely important that you think through each of the relationships keeping in mind two things. First, notice the direction of the relationship. The reason this is important is that Chafetz is going to tell us how to change gender inequality. Good theories explain how something works and in doing so they also explain how to change something. If this model depicts a good theory of gender stratification, then changing it involves working within the theoretical relationships that it gives us. The second thing I want you to think through is why or how each of the variables influences the others. Knowing that the gendered division of labor in the household has a positive relationship to gendered individuals is good; but it isn't enough. What is it about gendered household chores that impacts intrapsychic structures, role reinforcement, and impression management? So, a good theorist will know both the direction and the reasons for the relationship.

Figure 7.3 The Structure of Gender Inequality

155

Concepts and Theory: Changing Gender Inequality

To begin this section, we should note that Chafetz argues that structural rather than cultural changes are necessary to bring about gender equality. As we will see throughout this book, sociologists give different weights to culture and structure. Some argue that culture is an extremely important and independent variable within society; others claim that culture simply reinforces structure and that structure is the most important feature of society. Chafetz falls into the latter camp. While voluntaristic processes, which are associated in one way or another with culture, are the key way gender inequality is sustained, "substantial and lasting change must flow 'downward' from the macro to the micro levels" (Chafetz, 1990, p. 108).

Unintentional Change

As with her understanding of gender stability, Chafetz divides her theory of gender change into unintentional and intentional processes. Quite a bit of the change regarding the roles of women in society has been the result of unintended consequences. Another way to put this is that the bulk of changes in the gender system of inequality happen for structural reasons, not because people willingly and intentionally want to change things. For example, the moves from hunter-gatherer to horticulture to agrarian economies were motivated by advances in knowledge and technology. But these moves also produced the first forms of gender inequality, as men came to protect the land (which gave them weapons and power) and to control economic surplus through inheritance and the control of sexual reproduction (women's bodies). The intent behind technological advancement wasn't gender inequality; the intent was first survival and then to make life less burdensome. But in the end, economic developments produced gender inequality.

In explicating the unintended change processes, Chafetz is interested in what she terms the demand side. She argues that quite a bit of work on gender focuses on the supply side, which concentrates on the general attributes of women. For example, contemporary women tend to have fewer children, to be better educated, and to marry later than in previous generations. These supply-side attributes may influence what kinds of women become involved in the economy, but they "do not determine the rate of women's participation" (Chafetz, 1990, p. 122). For example, a woman may have a master's-level education, but unless there is a structural demand for this quality, she will remain unemployed. In addition, Chafetz assumes gender stability in theorizing about change. This means that males are the default to occupy a given position in the economy. The bottom line here is that "*as long as there are a sufficient number of working-age men available to meet the demand for the work they traditionally perform, no change in the gender division of labor will occur*" (p. 125, emphasis original). Thus, what we are looking for are structural demands that outrun the supply of male labor.

Chafetz lists three different kinds of processes that can unintentionally produce changes in the structure of gender inequality: population growth or decline, changes in the sex ratio of the population, and technological innovations and changes in the economic structure. The processes and their effects are listed below:

- *Population changes:* If the number of jobs that need to be filled remains constant, then the greater the growth in the working age population, the lower will be women's workforce participation. The inverse is true as well: As the size of the working population declines, women will gain greater access to traditionally male jobs, if the number of jobs remains constant.

- *Sex ratio changes:* The sex ratio of a population, the number of males relative to the number of females, tends to change under conditions of war and migration. If in the long run there is a reduction in the sex ratio (more women than men) of a population, women will gain access to higher-paying and more prestigious work roles. Conversely, if there is an increase in the sex ratio, the restrictions on women's workforce participation will tend to increase.

- *Economic and technological changes:* There are two general features of men's and women's bodies that can influence women's workforce participation: Men on average tend to be stronger than women, and women carry, deliver, and nurse babies. When technological innovations alter strength, mobility, and length of employment requirements, then there are possibilities for gender change in those jobs. Women will tend to gain employment if new technologies reduce strength, mobility, and time requirements. In addition to work requirements, technology can also change the structure of the job market. As the economy expands due to technological innovations, women will tend to achieve greater workforce participation (holding population growth constant). On the other hand, if the economy contracts for whatever reason, women will tend to lose resource-generating work roles.

Intentional Change

In addition to unintentional change processes, Chafetz argues that there are specific ways in which people can act that help to address gender inequality. But before we get into those processes, we need to note that Chafetz maintains that gender change is particularly difficult for two reasons. First, women have more cross-cutting influences than any other group. Think about it this way: Almost every social group is gendered. This means that women are black, white, Chicano, Baptist, Buddhist, Jewish, pagan, homosexual, bisexual, heterosexual, homeless, professional, and so on. Women thus "differ extensively on all social variables except gender" (Chafetz, 1990, p. 170). These cross-cutting group affiliations make it extremely difficult to form a woman's ideology that doesn't cut across or offend some of the women the ideology is trying to embrace. The second issue is that women, unlike many disenfranchised groups, do not live in segregated neighborhoods. Chafetz argues that this reduces women's political clout because they are "dispersed throughout all electoral districts" (p. 171). Because of these difficulties, gender change may occur more slowly or diffusely than other types of change.

I've placed Chafetz's addition intentional change factors into the model we've developed thus far (see Figure 7.4). Again, I want you to think through the relationships both in terms of direction and influence (What specifically does this factor accomplish?). You'll notice that the initial variables (capitalism and patriarchy) have been replaced with macro-level variables. Chafetz's approach to gender is

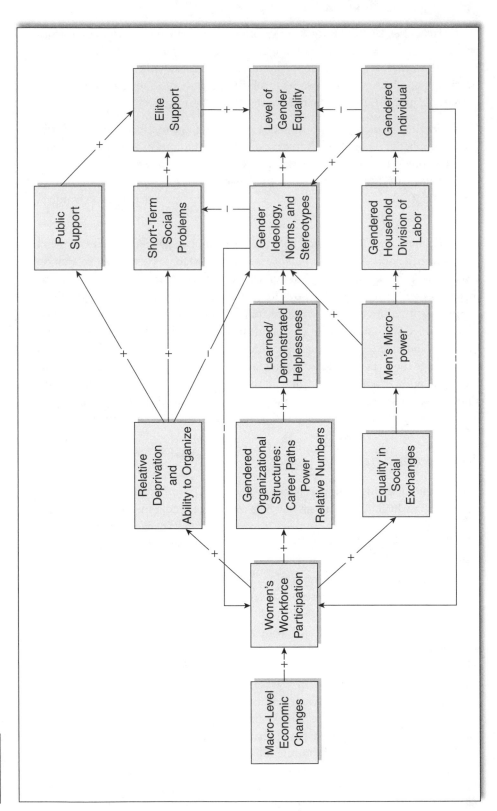

Figure 7.4 Reducing Gender Inequality

similar to the way Karl Marx saw the production of class consciousness. According to Marxian theory, structure leads social change. Class consciousness is necessary for social change but it is produced as dialectical elements of the economic structure, such as increasingly disruptive business cycles and overproduction, play themselves out. For Marx, it is the structure that pushes people together and gives them the ability to see their oppression, communicate with one another, and mount the resistance that will lead to the demise of capitalism.

The macro-structural changes that Chafetz focuses on are *industrialization, urbanization, and the size of the middle class.* Chafetz claims that historically almost all women's movements have been led by middle-class women. These women are among the first to experience gender consciousness due to the effects of industrialization and urbanization. Industrialization initiates a large number of social changes such as increases in urbanization, commodification, the use of money and markets, worker education, transportation and communication technologies, and so forth. These all work together to expand the size of the middle class. The importance of this expansion isn't simply that there are more middle-class people; it also means that there are more middle-class jobs available. Many of these are nondomestic jobs that may be filled by women.

Industrialization thus structurally creates workforce demands that women can fill. Women are more likely to be called upon to fill these roles when the number of males is kept fairly constant or at least the number doesn't increase at the same rate as the demand for labor. The more rapid the growth of industrialization and urbanization, the more likely the demand for labor will outpace the supply of men. As women increase their workforce participation, they increase their level of material and political resources as well, thus decreasing males' relative micro power and the level of gender differentiation, as well as weakening gender stereotypes, ideologies, and normative expectations (gender social definitions). In addition, as women's resources and thus their micro power increase, they are more able to influence the household division of labor and men's contribution to familial and domestic work; and, as men contribute more to domestic and familial work, women are more able to gain resources through workforce participation. So far what we've talked about all fits with the model in Figure 7.4. It's the structural changes that put into motion the possibility of successful social movements.

In addition to influencing these micro-level issues, industrialization, urbanization, and women's increased workforce participation do two other things: They increase women's experience of relative deprivation and the number of women's social contacts. While absolute deprivation implies uncertain survival, relative deprivation is a subjective, comparative sense of being disadvantaged. Social movements are extremely unlikely with groups that experience absolute deprivation. They have neither the will nor the resources to organize political movements. *Relative deprivation,* on the other hand, implies a group that has resources and experiences rising expectations. Thus, women who are newly moving into the workforce will tend to experience relative deprivation. They will begin to see that their salaries are not comparable to men's, and they will begin to accumulate resources that can potentially be used to become politically active.

Urbanization and industrialization also increase a group's ability to organize. Ralf Dahrendorf (1957/1959) talked about this ability to organize as the principal difference between quasi-groups and interest groups. Quasi-groups are those collectives that have latent identical role interests; they are people that hold the same structural position and thus have similar interests but do not experience a sense of "belongingness." Interest groups, on the other hand, "have a structure, a form of organization, a program or goal, and a personnel of members" (p. 180).

The interest group's identity and sense of belonging are produced when people have the ability to communicate, recruit members, form leadership, and create a unifying ideology. Urbanization and industrialization structurally increase the probability that these conditions of interest group membership will be met. Women living and working in technically advanced urban settings are more likely to come into contact with like others who are experiencing relative deprivation and the status and role dilemmas that come from women working a *double workday*.

As women begin to organize and as traditional gender definitions become weakened, public support for change is likely to arise. Chafetz argues that a significant portion of what women's movements have been able to achieve is related to articulated critical gender ideologies and radical feminist goals. While the public may not buy into a radical ideology or its set of goals, the ideologies and goals of women's movements will tend to justify gender change more broadly. This support, along with pressure from short-term social problems and a direct effect from women's workforce participation, places pressure upon elites to create laws, policies, and programs to help alleviate the unequal distribution of scarce resources by gender.

Let's pause a moment and talk about *short-term social problems*. Chafetz argues that as a result of women having and using greater levels of resources, short-term social problems are likely to arise. Chafetz uses the term "social problem" in a general sense to indicate the challenges that society at large have to overcome anytime significant change occurs. In other words, change to the social system brings a kind of disequilibrium that has to be solved so that actions and interactions can once again be patterned. Such social problems tend to accompany any type of social change as a society adjusts culturally and socially. In the case of gender, the short-term problems are related to women having greater levels of resources and thus higher levels of independence and power. Examples of these kinds of problems include increases in the divorce rate and women's demands for control over their own bodies. Social disruptions such as these tend to motivate elite support of women's rights in order to restore social order.

Sociologists have learned that every social movement eventually requires support from the elite. *The elite* not only pass laws and oversee their enforcement, they can also lend other material or political support, such as money and social capital (networks of people in powerful positions). The first way elites show up is in the way we have been talking about so far. Elites create new or support already established laws that help bring social order. In this case, the support comes mostly because elites perceive some form of social disorder. In other words, "they may perceive that basic problems faced by their society, which negatively affect large numbers of people and may possibly jeopardize their incumbency in elite roles, are exacerbated by a gender system that devalues and disadvantages women" (Chafetz, 1990, p. 152). This kind of change may be incremental and not specifically associated with women's movements. Elites may also support women's movements as women are perceived as a political resource.

I'm going to restate Chafetz's theory of gender change in brief propositions, since this is the discourse in which Chafetz works. Be sure to follow the elements of the propositions through the model. This way you'll be able to get a textual and visual rendering of the ideas:

- Taken together, the level of reduction in gender stratification due to intentional efforts is a positive function of the level of male domestic labor, elite support, and women's control of material resource and is a negative effect of the level of male micro power.
- Women's level of control over material resources is a positive function of industrialization, urbanization, and the size of the middle class. Elite support in general is a positive function of the level of women's control over material resources, the level of short-term social problems, the level of public support for changes advanced by women's movements, and elite competition.

Summary

- In general, Chafetz argues that workforce participation and control over material resources both stabilize and change a system of gender inequality. Gender inequality is perpetuated when women's participation in the workforce is restricted and reduced when women are allowed to work and control material resources.

- Chafetz argues that gender is stabilized more through voluntaristic actions rather than the use of coercive power. When men control the division of labor in society, they are able to exercise authority at the meso level through assuring male incumbency in elite positions and at the micro level through women's exchange of deference and compliance for material resources. Men thus control gender social definitions that set up engenderment processes: psychodynamic structuring, gender socialization, and the idealized expression of gender through impression management and interaction. Engenderment and wifely compliance work in turn to solidify women's exclusion from the workforce, to impose double duty upon those women who do work, to stabilize the unequal distribution of opportunities and resources, and to define negative worker attributes for women but positive ones for men.

- Gender inequality is reduced as women are allowed greater participation in the workforce and increased control over material resources. These factors decrease women's reliance upon men and men's authority over women. Men then contribute more to domestic and familial work, which further frees women to participate in the workforce and weakens gender stereotypes, norms, and ideologies. In addition, women's access to resource-generating work roles increases the probability of women's political movements, which along with weakened gender definitions positively impacts public opinion and elite support for women. Short-term social issues that come about because of women's increased workforce participation also impact elite support, as well as the elite's desire to consolidate or gain political power. Gender stratification is reduced as women move into the workforce and control more material resources, as elites support women's rights and legislation, and as men's micro resource power is reduced and their domestic contribution increased.

TAKING THE PERSPECTIVE

One of the delights of working with Chafetz's theory is that she brings together a number of really interesting theoretical issues. The first is the way in which she theorizes. She is one of the best examples of the positivist approach to theory cumulation. The number and diversity of theories and ideas she brings together is astounding. In explaining gender inequality, Chafetz brings together the work of Karl Marx, Rosabeth Kanter, Nancy Chodorow, Albert Bandura, Erving Goffman, and Ralf Dahrendorf, as well as elements from exchange theory and social movements theory.

Chafetz also focuses our attention on gender and feminism. Though the issue itself was decentered for much of sociology's history, the study of gender for the discipline goes back to the work of Harriet Martineau. Martineau (2005) argued that the test of any democratic nation is the "condition of that half of society over which the other half has power" (p. 291). Her assessment of the condition of gender in the United States in the beginning of the nineteenth century is that "tried by this test, the American civilization appears to be of a lower order than might have been expected" (p. 291). Karl Marx saw gender as a central social issue. Marx (Engels, 1884/1978) argued that the communist household "Implies the supremacy of women" and that the oppression of women in the home "contains within itself in *miniature* all the antagonisms which later develop on a wide scale within society and its state" (pp. 735, 737, emphasis original).

The term *feminism* was first used to refer to feminine traits. It wasn't until the First International Women's Conference of 1892 that the term took on its critical, political bent. Since then it has been associated with two principal ideas. The first is a set of ideas and beliefs about knowledge and ways of governing that are defined as distinctly feminist and are set against the masculinist ways of exercising power and knowing about the world. The second refers to a variety of perspectives that are used to understand gender inequality. These two main ideas can blend together in various ways for different theorists, but Chafetz clearly falls into the latter.

In Western European societies, inequalities of gender have been addressed through three waves of feminism. Inklings of the first wave began when ideas about the equal rights of women emerged during the Enlightenment. The first significant expression of these concerns was Mary Wollstonecraft's book *A Vindication of the Rights of Woman* (1792). But the first wave of feminism didn't become organized until the 1848 Seneca Falls Convention, which called for equal rights to vote and own property, full access to educational opportunities, and equal compensation for equal work.

The second wave of feminism grew out of the civil rights movements of the 1960s. Publication of Simone de Beauvoir's *The Second Sex* (1949) and Betty Friedan's *The Feminine Mystique* (1963) were particularly important for this second wave of feminists, as was the founding in 1966 of the National Organization for Women (NOW). Central issues for this movement were pay equity; equal access to jobs and higher education; and women's control over their own bodies, including but not limited to sexuality, reproduction, and the eradication of physical abuse and rape.

In the early 1970s, two clear divisions began to appear among second-wave feminists. One camp emphasized the more traditional concerns of women's rights groups and generally focused on the similarities between men and women. Their primary concern was structural inequality. The other group moved to more radical issues. Rather than emphasizing similarities, they focused on fundamental differences between men and women. In some ways, the concerns of this group, described in the paragraph below, are more radical than equal opportunity. This more critical group is often described as a "third wave" of feminism.

The idea of third-wave feminism began to take hold around the intersection between race and gender—there are marked distinctions between the experiences of black and white women. But more recently, it has gained currency with reference to age. It appears that the experiences of young, contemporary feminists are different from those of second-wave feminists. Young feminists grew up in a social world where feminism was part of common culture. These young women are also playing out some of the postmodern ideas of fluid identities. The result is that many young feminists can best be described through contradiction and ambiguity. As Jennifer Drake (1997) says in a review essay, "What unites the Third Wave is our negotiation of contradiction, our rejection of dogma, our need to say 'both/and'" (p. 104). For example, third wavers might claim their right to dress sexy for fun while simultaneously criticizing patriarchy for objectifying women.

In this book, there are three theorists that specifically address gender. Two of these theorists, Dorothy Smith and Judith Butler, are among those that take the more radical view of feminism. For them, the life experiences and perspectives of men and women are different, and gender equality is more fundamental than structural equality. Dorothy Smith (Chapter 18) focuses on the unique consciousness and lived experience of women. Smith argues that women have a bifurcated awareness of the world, split between the objective world of men and their own lived experiences. Judith Butler (Chapter 19) focuses first on the body and secondarily on consciousness, or more accurately, subjectivity. She argues that gender inequality presumes a more basic construction: the normative sexing of the body.

Both Smith and Butler present critical understandings that show how women are controlled through systems of knowledge and embodiment. This type of control is deeply embedded in the mind and body, and it generally functions below the level of awareness. The key to sex or gender equality for Smith and Butler seems to lie in subversion—practices that critically expose the assumptions upon which the control of women is based.

BUILDING YOUR THEORY TOOLBOX

- Write a 250-word synopsis of the theoretical perspective of race.
- Write a 250-word synopsis of the theoretical perspective of feminism.
- After reading and understanding this chapter, you should be able to define the following terms theoretically and explain their theoretical importance to structural theories of race and gender inequality: *social structure, racism, exploitation, split labor market, Jim Crow, postindustrial economy, feminism, social structure, levels of analysis, women's workforce participation, organizational variables (career path, organizational power, relative numbers), social exchange, micro power, gender definitions, legitimation, intrapsychic structures, social learning, gendered impression management, unintentional and intentional forces of change*
- After reading and understanding this chapter, you should be able to:
  - Compare and contrast Marxian elite theory, split labor market theory, and Wilson's class–state theory
  - Explain Wilson's three periods of American race relations and use Marxian elite theory, split labor market theory, and Wilson's class–state theory to analyze the different periods. In other words, you should be able to demonstrate, using Wilson's theory, that class is becoming more important in race relations than race itself.
  - Explain why the workforce of women is so important to Chafetz's theory
  - Explain how exchange processes work to produce gender inequalities. How do men use their micro power to their gendered advantage?
  - Explain the differences between the intrapsychic structures of boys and girls. Explain how they are created and how they influence gender inequality.
  - Explain how social learning theory and dramaturgy contribute to our understanding of how gender inequality is voluntaristically reproduced
  - Explain how gender inequality unintentionally changes
  - Tell which two characteristics of gender, according to Chafetz, make change difficult (Be sure to explain them fully.)
  - Explain how women's movements form and how they influence changes in gender inequality. What does this tell us about social movements in general?

Learning More: Primary Sources

- Janet Saltzman Chafetz:
  - Chafetz, J. (1990). *Gender Equity: An Integrated Theory of Stability and Change.* Newbury Park, CA: Sage, 1990.
  - Chafetz is also the editor of the excellent *Handbook of the Sociology of Gender*, New York: Kluwer/Plenum, 1999.

- William Julius Wilson:

  o Wilson, W. J. (1980). *The Declining Significance of Race* (2nd ed.). Chicago: University of Chicago Press.

  o Wilson, W. J. (1987). *The Truly Disadvantaged.* Chicago: University of Chicago Press.

  o Wilson, W. J. (1997). *When Work Disappears.* New York: Vintage.

Learning More: Secondary Sources

- In 1993, Chafetz joined Rae Lesser Blumberg, Scott Coltrane, Randall Collins, and Jonathan Turner to produce a synthesized theory of gender stratification. This is their rare and powerful effort:

  o "Toward an Integrated Theory of Gender Stratification," *Sociological Perspectives, 36,* 185–216.

Check it Out

- Check out the group Sociologists for Women: http://newmedia.colorado.edu/~socwomen/. You can become involved in starting a local chapter or in specific student concerns.

- The following are just a few of the many excellent Web sites concerning women's rights and feminism: http://feminism.eserver.org/ or http://www .amnestyusa.org/women/index.do

- Wilson served as the eightieth president of the American Sociological Association. See http://www.asanet.org/galleries/default-file/PresidentialAddress1990.pdf for his presidential address concerning inner-city social dislocations.

- As we've seen, Wilson argues that education and research are important factors in producing equality. In 2003, Wilson gave a brief talk at Amherst College addressing the place of social science: http://www.amherst.edu/news/inauguration/panel/wilson.html

- Currently, Wilson is the director of the Joblessness and Urban Poverty Research Program at the John F. Kennedy School of Government. Check out the school, its mission, and what Wilson is doing there: http://www.ksg.harvard.edu/index.shtml

Seeing the World

- Using your favorite Internet search engine, type in "African American policy." Thoroughly review at least three sites. Would you say that the information and thrust of the sites are in keeping with Wilson's analysis and policy implications? In not, why do you think that is? If so, which policies do you think will have the greatest impact on structural inequality? How can you get involved in promoting this or other policy changes?

(Continued)

(Continued)

- Consult at least four reliable Internet sources to learn about the "separation of spheres." What is it and how does it figure into Chafetz's theory? List at least six ways that this historical, structural issue influences your life.

- Using your favorite search engine, type in "global gender inequality." Based on information from at least three different societies, prepare a report on the state of gender inequality in these diverse countries. Also, compare and contrast these societies with the one you live in. How applicable do you think Chafetz's theory would be in those other three societies?

- Volunteer at a local women's shelter or resource center.

CHAPTER 8

Structuring Class:

Pierre Bourdieu

(1960–2002)

As I mentioned in Chapter 1, modernity was founded on specific ideas. One of the interesting things about this is that modernity may be the most self-aware era in human history. What I mean by that is that the ideas and social institutions of modern times are intentional. A clear example of this is the separation of church and state that we find in most modern democracies. That move was profound in that it was the first time in human history that government and religion were intentionally separated. Up until modern times religion and government were intrinsically related. Governments were always legitimated by religion. Western European monarchies, for example, were legitimated by the "divine right of kings to rule." So intrinsic was this relationship that King Henry VIII pushed for the establishment of the Anglican Church when the Catholic pope refused to grant him an annulment (though there were other factors at work as well).

This chapter isn't about religion, but it is about another social institution that was seen to have an intentional relationship with the projects of modernity—that institution is capitalism. Adam Smith is often considered the founder of free-market capitalism, the person who more than any other before him explained that modern governments should not interfere with capitalist enterprise. Smith explained that capitalism is the result of social evolution, a superior economic system that would preserve the natural rights of humanity:

> The obvious and simple system of natural liberty establishes itself of its own accord. Every man . . . is left perfectly free to pursue his own interest his own way, and to bring both his industry and capital into competition with those of any other man, or order of men. (Smith, 1776/1937, p. 247)

The reason that capitalism shouldn't be regulated is because it, like natural evolution, contains a type of natural selection dynamic that Smith called "the invisible hand." Unfettered competition would weed out weaker businesses, regulate prices, and result in the best product for the least cost. In this free market capitalism, which Smith termed "economic individualism," the differences in wealth or social standing among people would be the result of their own determination and effort. In traditional societies social standing was mostly determined by birth and there was little social mobility. But under capitalism this was to change. Class, then, was to be a reflection of one's talent and efforts.

That was the hope and the ideal. While capitalism did achieve some of its goals, the reality, especially in the beginning decades of capitalism, was quite different than the ideal. Child labor was common, with children as young as 4 forced to work in factories and mines, many of whom lost their lives or were maimed (child labor is a continuing issue in developing nations). There were no safety regulations, no minimum wage, no limit on hours worked, no health insurance, and so on. Rather than producing an even playing field, if left to itself, capitalism produces monopolies and insurmountable gaps between the rich and poor. And rather than uplifting the dignity of humankind, capitalism will push exploitation to its furthest limits. My purpose here isn't to rehash the litany of early abuses of capitalism. Rather, I want you to see the ideal of capitalism in modernity on the one hand, and, on the other, the unanticipated consequences of that system. This world of early capitalism is the one that Karl Marx spoke to.

Since the time of Marx, sociology has been concerned with capitalism and class because we've discovered that the class system is stratified. If class actually worked the way people thought it would, sociology wouldn't have an interest in it. The original idea was that capitalism would be a meritocracy—a system where people would be rewarded according to their individual merit. In our last chapter we saw that money, status, and power are actually distributed according to group affiliation, rather than individual merit. In addition to race and gender, we see in this chapter that class itself is structured: There's something at work in capitalism that continually patterns class position in one's life as well as across generations (so generally speaking, there will be little change in the class position you were born into). Since something is structuring this pattern, we need to ask our questions of structure: Of what substance is the structure made up; what do these structures do; and, how do they do it?"

THEORIST'S DIGEST

Brief Biography

Pierre Bourdieu was born August 1, 1930, in Denquin, France. Bourdieu studied philosophy under Louis Althusser at the École Normale Supérieure in Paris. After his studies, he taught for 3 years, 1955–1958, at Moulins. From 1958 to 1960, Bourdieu did empirical research in Algeria (*The Algerians,* 1962) that laid the groundwork for his sociology. In his career, he published over 25 books, one of which, *Distinction: A Social Critique of the Judgment of Taste* (1979/1984), was named one of the twentieth century's 10 most important works of sociology (International Sociological Association). He was the founder and director of the Centre for European Sociology, and he held the French senior chair in sociology at Collège de France (the same chair held by sociologist and anthropologist Marcel Mauss). Craig Calhoun (2003) writes that Bourdieu was "the most influential and original French sociologist since Durkheim" (p. 274). Bourdieu died in Paris January 23, 2002.

Central Sociological Questions

Bourdieu's passion was intellectual honesty and rigor. He of course was concerned with class, and particularly the way class is created and re-created in subtle, nonconscious ways. But above and beyond these empirical concerns was a driving intellect bent on refining critical thinking and never settling on an answer: "An invitation to think with Bourdieu is of necessity an invitation to think beyond Bourdieu, and against him whenever required" (Wacquant, 1992, p. xiv).

Simply Stated

Bourdieu tells us that class is structured in the body through cultural capital, which is made up of tastes, habits, social and linguistic skills, and so on. People thus display their class position in an unthinking ongoing manner, simply in the way they walk, sit, talk, and so forth. Every social encounter becomes, then, a market. In interactions where class positions are comparable, people will feel comfortable because everybody's tastes are similar. The disadvantage of such encounters is that no one can gain higher levels of cultural capital. In encounters where the class positions are different, people with lower cultural capital will tend to feel uncomfortable and will be likely to not participate or participate poorly. Thus when in a position to increase cultural capital, and thus class position, most people withdraw and are unable to gain profit. Class is thus structured in the body where it insidiously restricts and replicates a person's class position in all social interactions.

Key Ideas

Economic capital, social capital, symbolic capital, cultural capital, taste, habitus, distance from necessity, education, field, linguistic market, symbolic violence, constructivist structuralism, dialectic

Concepts and Theory: Structuring Class

The basic fact of capitalism is capital. Capital is different from either wealth or income. Income is generally measured by annual salary and wealth by the relationship between one's assets and debt. Both income and wealth are in a sense static; they are measurable facts about a person or group. Capital, on the other hand, is active: It's defined as accumulated goods devoted to the production of other goods. The entire purpose of capital is to produce more capital.

Four Kinds of Capital

Bourdieu actually talks about four forms of capital—economic, social, symbolic, and cultural—all of which are invested and used in the production of class. Bourdieu uses *economic capital* in its usual sense. Economic capital is generally determined by one's wealth and income. As with Marx, Bourdieu sees economic capital as fundamental. However, unlike Marx, Bourdieu argues that the importance of economic capital is that it strongly influences an individual's level of the other capitals, which, in turn, have their own independent effects. In other words, economic capital starts the ball rolling; but once things are in motion, other issues may have stronger influences on the perpetuation of class inequalities.

Social capital refers to the kind of social network an individual is set within. It refers to the people you know and how they are situated in society. The idea of social capital can be captured in the saying, "It isn't what you know but who you know that counts." The distribution of social capital is clearly associated with class. For example, if you are a member of an elite class, you will attend elite schools such as Phillips Andover Academy, Yale, and Harvard. At those schools, you would be afforded the opportunity to make social connections with powerful people—for example, in elections over the past 30 years, there has been at least one Yale graduate running for the office of President of the United States. But economic capital doesn't exclusively determine social capital. We can build our social networks intentionally, or sometimes through happenstance. For example, if you attended Hot Springs High School in Arkansas during the early 1960s, you would have had a chance to become friends with Bill Clinton.

Symbolic capital is the capacity to use symbols to create or solidify physical and social realities. With this idea, Bourdieu begins to open our eyes to the symbolic nature of class divisions. Social groups don't exist simply because people decide to gather together. Max Weber recognized that there are technical conditions that must be met for a loose collection of people to form a social group: People must be able to communicate and meet with one another; there must be recognized leadership; and a group needs clearly articulated goals to organize. Yet, even meeting those conditions doesn't alone create a social group. Groups must be symbolically recognized as well.

With the idea of symbolic capital, Bourdieu pushes us past analyzing the use of symbols in interaction (Chapter 3). Symbolic interactionism argues that human beings are oriented toward meaning and meaning is the emergent result of ongoing symbolic interactions. We're symbolic creatures, but meaning doesn't reside within the symbol itself; it must be pragmatically negotiated in face-to-face situations. We've learned a great deal about how people create meaning in different situations because of symbolic interactionism's insights. But Bourdieu's use of symbolic capital is quite different.

Bourdieu recognizes that all human relationships are created symbolically and not all people have equal symbolic power. For example, I write a good number of letters of recommendation for students each year. Every form I fill out asks the same question: "Relationship to applicant?" And I always put "professor." Now, the *meaning* of the professor–student relationship emerges out of my interactions with my students, and my student–professor relationships are probably somewhat different from some of my colleagues as a result. However, neither my students nor I created the student–professor relationship. Bourdieu (1991) tells us that objective categories and structures, such as class, race, and gender, are generated through the use of symbolic capital: "Symbolic power is a power of constructing reality" (p. 166).

Bourdieu (1989) characterizes the use of symbolic capital as both the power of constitution and the power of revelation—it is the power of "world-making . . . the power to make groups. . . . The power to impose and to inculcate a vision of divisions, that is, the power to make visible and explicit social divisions that are implicit, is political power par excellence" (p. 23). This power of world-making is based on two elements. First, there must be sufficient recognition to impose recognition. The group must be recognized and symbolically labeled by a person or group that is officially recognized as having the ability to symbolically impart identity, such as scientists, legislators, or sociologists in our society. Institutional accreditation, particularly in the form of an educational credential (school in this sense operates as a representative of the state), "frees its holder from the symbolic struggle of all against all by imposing the universally approved perspective" (p. 22).

The second element needed to world-make is some relation to a reality: "Symbolic efficacy depends on the degree to which the vision proposed is founded in reality" (p. 23). I think it's best to see this as a variable. The more social or physical reality is already present, the greater will be the effectiveness of symbolic capital. This is the sense in which symbolic capital is the power to consecrate or reveal. Symbolic power is the power to reveal the substance of an already occupied social space. But note that granting a group symbolic life "brings into existence in an instituted, constituted form . . . what existed up until then only as . . . a collection of varied persons, a purely additive series of merely juxtaposed individuals" (p. 23). Thus, because legitimated existence is dependent upon symbolic capacity, an extremely important conflict in society is the struggle over symbols and classifications. The heated debate over race classification in the U.S. 2000 census is a good example.

There is a clear relationship between symbolic and cultural capital. The use of symbolic capital creates the symbolic field wherein cultural capital exists. In general, **cultural capital** refers to the informal social skills, habits, linguistic styles, and tastes that a person garners as a result of his or her economic resources. It is the different ways we talk, act, and make distinctions that are the result of our class. Bourdieu identifies three different kinds of cultural capital: objectified, institutionalized, and embodied. *Objectified cultural* capital refers to the material goods (such as books, computers, and paintings) that are associated with cultural capital. *Institutionalized cultural capital* alludes to the certifications (like degrees and diplomas) that give official acknowledgement to the possession of knowledge and abilities. *Embodied cultural capital* is the most important in Bourdieu's scheme. It is part of what makes up an individual's habitus, and it refers to the cultural capital that lives in and is expressed through the body. This function of cultural capital manifests itself as taste.

Taste refers to an individual preference or fondness for something, such as "he has developed a taste for expensive wine." What Bourdieu is telling us is that our tastes aren't really individual; they are strongly influenced by our social class—our tastes are embodied cultural capital. Here a particular taste is legitimated, exhibited, and recognized by only those who have the proper cultural code, which is class specific. To hear a piece of music and classify it as baroque rather than elevator music implies an entire world of understandings and classification. Thus, when individuals express a preference for something or classify an object in a particular way, they are simultaneously classifying themselves. Taste may appear as an innocent and natural phenomenon, but it is an insidious revealer of position. As Bourdieu (1979/1984) says, "Taste classifies, and it classifies the classifier" (p. 6). The issue of taste is "one of the most vital stakes in the struggles fought in the field of the dominant class and the field of cultural production" (p. 11).

Habitus

Taste is part of habitus and habitus is embodied cultural capital. Class isn't simply an economic classification (one that exists because of symbolic capital), nor is it merely a set of life circumstances of which people may become aware (class consciousness)—class is inscribed in our bodies. **Habitus** is the durable organization of one's body and its deployment in the world. It is found in our posture, and our way of walking, speaking, eating, and laughing; it is found in every way we use our body. Habitus is both a system whereby people organize their own behavior and a system through which people perceive and appreciate the behavior of others.

Pay close attention: This system of organization and appreciation is *felt* in our bodies. We physically feel how we should act; we physically sense what the actions of others mean, and we approve of or censure them physically (we are comfortable or uncomfortable); we physically respond to different foods (we can become voracious or disgusted); we physically respond to certain sexual prompts and not others—the list can go on almost indefinitely. Our humanity, including our class position, is not found in just our cognitions and mental capacity; it is in our very bodies.

One way to see what Bourdieu is talking about is to use a sports analogy. I love to play sand volleyball, and I only get to play it about once every 5 years, which means I'm not very good at it. I have to constantly think about where the ball and other players are situated. I have to watch to see if the player next to me is going for the ball or if I can do so. All this watching and mental activity means that my timing is way off. I typically dive for the ball 1.5 seconds too late, and I end up with a mouthful of sand rather than the ball (but the other bunglers on my team are usually impressed with my effort). Professional volleyball players compete in a different world. They rarely have to think. They sense the ball and their teammates and they make their moves faster than they could cognitively work through all the particulars. Volleyball is inscribed in their bodies.

Explicating what he calls the Dreyfus model, Bent Flyvbjerg (2001) gives us a detailed way of seeing what is going on here. The Dreyfus model indicates that there are five levels to learning: novice, advanced beginner, competent performer, proficient performer, and expert. Novices know the rules and the objective facts of a situation; advanced beginners still have concrete knowledge but see it contextually; and the competent performer employs hierarchical decision-making skills and feels responsible for outcomes. With proficient performers and experts, we enter another level of knowledge. The first three levels are all based on cognitions, but in the final two levels knowledge becomes embodied. Here situations and problems are understood "intuitively" and require skills that go beyond analytical rationality. With experts, "their skills have become so much a part of themselves that they are not more aware of them than they are of their own bodies" (p. 19).

Habitus thus works below the level of conscious thought and outside the control of the will. It is the embodied, nonconscious enactment of cultural capital that gives habitus its specific power,

> Beyond the reach of introspective scrutiny or control by the will . . . in the most automatic gestures or the apparently most insignificant techniques of the body . . . [it engages] the most fundamental principles of construction and evaluation of the social world, those which most directly express the division of labour . . . or the division of the work of domination. (Bourdieu, 1979/1984, p. 466)

Bourdieu's point is that we are all, each one, experts in our class position. Our mannerisms, speech, tastes, and so on are written on our bodies beginning the day we are born.

There are two factors important in the production of habitus: education and distance from necessity. In *distance from necessity,* necessity speaks of sustenance, the things necessary for biological existence. Distance from the necessities of life enables the upper classes to experience a world that is free from urgency. In contrast, the poor must always worry about their daily existence. As humans move away from that essential existence, they are freed from that constant worry, and they are free to practice activities that constitute an end in themselves. For example, you probably have hobbies. Perhaps you like to paint, act, or play guitar as I do. There is a sense of intrinsic enjoyment that comes with those kinds of activities; they are ends in themselves. The poorer classes don't have that luxury. Daily life for them is a grind, a struggle just to make ends meet. This struggle for survival and the emotional toll it brings are paramount in their lives, leaving no time or resources for pursuing hobbies and "getting the most out of life."

We should think of distance from necessity as a continuum. You and I probably fall somewhere in the middle. We have to be somewhat concerned about our livelihood, but we also have time and energy to enjoy leisure activities. The elite are on the uppermost part of the continuum, and it shows in their every activity. For example, why do homeless people eat? They eat to survive. And if they are hungry enough, they might eat anything, as long as it isn't poisonous. Why do working classes or nearly poor people eat? For the same basic reason: The working classes are much better off than the homeless, but they still by and large live hand to mouth. However, because they are further removed from necessity, they can be more particular about what they eat, though the focus will still be on the basics of life, a "meat and potatoes" menu. Now, why do the elite eat? You could say they eat to survive, but they are never aware of that motivation. Food doesn't translate into the basics of survival. Eating for the elite classes is an aesthetic experience. For them, plate presentation is more important than getting enough calories.

Thus, the further removed we are from necessity, the more we can be concerned with abstract rather than essential issues. This ability to conceive of form rather than function—aesthetics—is dependent upon "a generalized capacity to neutralize ordinary urgencies and to bracket off practical ends, a durable inclination and aptitude for practice without a practical function" (Bourdieu, 1979/1984, p. 54). And this aesthetic works itself out in every area. In art, for example, the upper-class aesthetic of luxury, or what Bourdieu calls the *pure gaze*, prefers art that is abstract while the popular taste wants art to represent reality. In addition, distance from economic necessity implies that all natural and physical desires and responses are to be sublimated and dematerialized. The working class, because it is immersed in physical reality and economic necessity, interacts in more physical ways through touching, yelling, embracing, and so forth than do the distanced elite. A lifetime of exposure to worlds so constructed confers cultural pedigrees, manners of applying aesthetic competences that differ by class position.

This embodied tendency to see the world in abstract or concrete terms is reinforced and elaborated through *education*. One obvious difference between the education of the elite and the working classes is the kind of social position in which education places us. The education system channels individuals toward prestigious or devalued positions. In doing so, education manipulates subjective aspirations (self-image) and demands (self-esteem). Another essential difference in educational experience has to do with the amount of rudimentary scholastics required—the simple knowing and recognizing of facts versus more sophisticated knowledge. This factor varies by number of years of education, which in turn varies by class position. At the lower levels, the simple recitation of facts is required. At the higher levels of education, emphasis is placed on critical and creative thought. At the highest levels of education, even the idea of "fact" is understood critically and held in doubt.

Education also influences the kind of language we use to think and through which we see the world. We can conceive of language as varying from complex to simple. More complex language forms have more extensive and intricate syntactical elements. Language is made up of more than words; it also has structure. Think about the sentences that you read in a romance novel and then compare them to those in an advanced textbook. In the textbook, they are longer and more complex, and that complexity increases as you move into more scholarly books. These more complex syntactical elements allow us to construct sentences that correspond to multileveled thinking—this is true because both writing and thinking are functions of language. The more formal education we receive, the more complex are the words and syntactical elements of our language. Because we don't just think *with* language, we think *in* language, the complexity of our language affects the complexity of our thinking. And our thinking influences the way in which we see the world.

Here's a simple example: Let's say you go to the zoo, first with my dog and then with three different people. You'd have to blindfold and muzzle my dog, but if you could get her to one of the cages and then remove the blinders, she would start barking hysterically. She would be responding to the content of the beasts in front of her. All she would know is that those things in front of her smell funny, look dangerous, and are undoubtedly capable of killing her, but she's going to go down fighting. Now picture yourself going with three different people, each from a different social class and thus education level. The first person has a high school education. As you stand in front of the same cage that you showed to my dog, he says, "Man, look at all those apes." The second person you go with has had some college education. She stands in front of the cage and says, "Gorillas are so amazing." The third person has a master's-level education and says, "Wow, I've never seen *gorilla gorilla, gorilla graueri,* and *gorilla berengei* all in the same cage."

Part of our class habitus, then, is determined by education and its relationship to language. Individuals with a complex language system will tend to see objects in terms of multiple levels of meaning and to classify them abstractly. This type of linguistic system brings sensitivity to the structure of an object; it is the learned ability to respond to an object in terms of its matrix of relationships. Conversely, the less complex an individual's classification system, the more likely are the organizing syntactical elements to be of limited range. The simple classification system is characterized by a low order of abstractedness and creates more sensitivity to the content of an object, rather than its structure.

Bourdieu uses the idea of habitus to talk about the replication of class. Class, as I mentioned earlier, isn't simply a part of the social structure; it is part of our body. We are not only categorized as middle class (or working class or elite), we *act* middle class. Differing experiences in distance from necessity and education determine one's tastes, ways of seeing and experiencing the world, and "the most automatic gestures or apparently most insignificant techniques of the body—ways of walking or blowing one's nose, ways of eating or talking" (Bourdieu, 1979/1984, p. 466). We don't choose to act or not act according to class; it's the result of lifelong socialization. And, as we act in accordance with our class, we replicate our class. Thus, Bourdieu's notion of how class is replicated is much more fundamental and insidious than Marx's and more complex than Weber's.

However, we would fall short of the mark if we simply saw habitus as a structuring agent. Bourdieu intentionally uses the concept (the idea originated with Aristotle) in order to talk about the creative, active, and inventive powers of the agent. He uses the concept to get out of the structuralist paradigm without falling back into issues of consciousness and unconsciousness. In habitus, class is structured but it isn't completely objective—it doesn't merely exist outside of the individual because it's a significant part of his or her subjective experience. In habitus, class is *structured but not structuring*—because as with high-caliber athletes and experts, habitus is intuitive. The idea of habitus, then, shows us how class is replicated subjectively and in daily life, and it introduces the potential for inspired behaviors above and beyond one's class position. Indeed, the potential for exceeding one's class is much more powerful with Bourdieu's habitus than with conscious decisions—most athletes, musicians, and other experts will tell you that their highest achievements come under the inspiration of visceral intuition rather than rational processes. It is through habitus that the practices of the dialectic are performed.

Fields

Bourdieu uses the analogy of the field to explain how empirical and symbolic worlds work (see Calhoun, 2003). Bourdieu was a rugby player, which is a European game somewhat like American football, but it is considered by most to be much more grueling than football. In rugby, the play is continuous with no substitutions or time-outs (even for injury). The game can take anywhere from 60 to 90 minutes, with two halves separated by a 5-minute halftime. An important part of the game is the scrum. In a scrum, eight players from each side form a kind of inverted triangle by wrapping their arms around each other. The ball is placed in the middle and the two bound groups of men struggle head-to-head against each other until the ball is freed from the scrum. To see the struggle of the scrum gives a whole new perspective on Bourdieu's idea of social struggle.

Rugby matches take place on a field, involve strategic plays and intense struggles, and are played by individuals who have a clear physical sense of the game. Matches are of course structured by the rules of the game and the field. The field not only delineates the parameters of the play, but each field is different and thus knowledge of each field of play is important for success. The rules are there and, like in all games, come into play when they are broken, but a good player embodies the rules and the methods of the game. The best plays are those that come when the player is in the "zone," or playing without thinking. Trained musicians can also experience this zone by jamming with other musicians. Often when in such a state, the musician can play things that he or she normally would not be able to, and might have a difficult time explaining after the fact. The same is true for athletes. There is more to a good game than the rules and the field; the game is embodied in the performer. And, finally, there is the struggle, against not only the other team, but also the limitations of the field, rules, and one's own abilities.

What I just gave you is actually an explanation of Bourdieu's theory through analogy. Keep your eyes open for how it fits. Just like in rugby, fields are delineated spaces wherein "the game" is played. Obviously, in Bourdieu's theoretical use of **field**, the parameters are not laid out using fences or lines on the ground. The parameters of the theoretical field are delineated by networks or sets of connections among objective positions. The positions within a field may be filled by individuals, groups, or organizations. However, Bourdieu is adamant that we focus on the relationships among the actors and not the agents themselves. It's not the people, groups, or even interactions that are important; it's the relationships among and between the positions that sets the parameters of a field. For example, while the different culture groups (like theater groups, reading clubs, and choirs) within a region may have a lot in common, they probably do not form a field because there are no explicit objective relationships among them. On the other hand, most all the universities in the United States do form a field. They are objectively linked through accreditation, professional associations, federal guidelines, and so forth. These relationships are sites of active practices; thus, the parameters of a field are always at stake within the field itself. In other words, because fields are defined mostly through relationships and relationships are active, which positions and relationships go into making up the field is constantly changing. Therefore, what constitutes a field is always an empirical question.

Fields are directly related to capitals. The people, groups, and organizations that fill the different objective positions are hierarchically distributed in the field, initially through the overall volume of all the capitals they possess and secondly by the relative weight of the two particular kinds of capital, symbolic and cultural. More than that, each field is different because the various cultures can have dissimilar weights. For example, cultural capital is much more important in academic rather than economic fields; conversely, economic capital is more important in economic fields than in academic ones. All four capitals or powers are present in each, but they aren't all given the same weight. It is the different weightings of the cultures that define the field, and it is the field that gives validity and function to the capitals.

While the parameters of any field cannot be determined prior to empirical investigation, the important consideration for Bourdieu is the correspondence between the empirical field and its symbolic representation. The objective field corresponds to a symbolic field, which is given legitimation and reality by those with symbolic capital. Here symbolic capital works to both construct and recognize—it creates and legitimates the relations between and among positions within the field. In this sense, the empirical and symbolic fields are both constitutive of class and of social affairs in general. It is the symbolic field that people use to view, understand, and reproduce the objective.

I've pictured Bourdieu's basic theory of class structuring in Figure 8.1. When reading the model, keep in mind Bourdieu's intent with open concepts. This model is simply a heuristic device—something we can use to help us see the world. The figure starts on the far left with the objective field and the distribution of capitals. But for Bourdieu, the objective field isn't enough to account for class reality and replication, and that is where many sociologists stop. Bourdieu takes it further in that the objective field becomes real and potentially replicable through the use of symbolic capital. The use of symbolic capital creates the symbolic field, which in turn orders and makes real the objective field. The exercise of symbolic capital, along with the initial distribution of capitals, creates cultural capital that varies by distance from necessity and by education. And cultural capital produces the internal structuring of class: habitus. But notice that the model indicates that the potential of habitus to replicate is held in question—it is habitus exercised in linguistic markets and symbolic struggles that decides the question.

Figure 8.1 Habitus and the Replication of Class

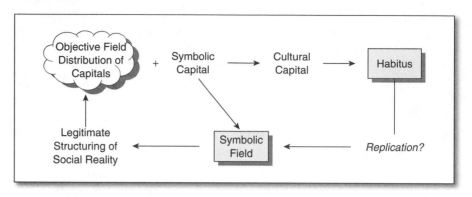

Concepts and Theory: Replicating Class

Linguistic Markets

Bourdieu (1991) says that "every speech act and, more generally, every action" is an encounter between two independent forces (p. 37). One of those forces is habitus, particularly in our tendency to speak and say things that reveal our level of cultural capital. The other force comes from the structures of the linguistic market. A **linguistic market** is "a system of relations of force which impose themselves as a system of specific sanctions and specific censorship, and thereby help fashion linguistic production by determining the 'price' of linguistic products" (Bourdieu & Wacquant, 1992, p. 145).

The linguistic market is like any other market: It's a place of exchange and a place to seek profit. Here exchange and profit are sought through linguistic elements such as symbols and discourses. The notion of a free market is like an ideal type: It's an idea against which empirical instances can be measured. All markets are structured to one degree or another, and linguistic markets have a fairly high degree of structuring. One of the principal ways they are structured is through formal language.

Every society has formalized its language. Even in the case where the nation might be bilingual, such as Canada, the languages are still formalized. Standard language comes as a result of the unification of the state, economy, and culture. The education system is used to impose restrictions on popular modes of speech and to propagate the standard language. We all remember times in grammar school when teachers would correct our speech ("there is no such word as *ain't*"). In the university, this still happens, but mostly through the application of stringent criteria for writing.

Linguistic markets are also structured through various configurations of the capitals and the empirical field. As we've seen, empirical fields are defined by the relative weights of the capitals—so, for example, religious fields give more weight to symbolic capital and artistic fields more import to cultural capital, but they both need and use economic capital. The same is true with linguistic markets. Linguistic markets are defined through the relative weights of the capitals and by the different discourses that are valued. For example, the linguistic market of sociology is heavily based on cultural capital. And in order to do well in that market, you would have to know a fair amount about Karl Marx, Émile Durkheim, Michel Foucault, Pierre Bourdieu, Dorothy Smith, and so forth. Linguistic markets are also structured by the empirical field, in particular by the gaps and asymmetries that exist between positions in the field (by their placement and position of capitals, some positions in a field are more powerful than others). These empirical inequalities help structure the exchanges that take place within a linguistic market.

When people interact with one another, they perform speech acts—meaningful kinds of behaviors that are related to language. In a speech act, habitus and linguistic markets come together. In other words, the person's embodied class position and cultural capital are given a certain standing or evaluation within the linguistic market. The linguistic market contains the requirements of formal language; the salient contour of capitals; and the objective, unequal distribution of power within the empirical field.

Let me give you three examples from my own life. When I go to a professional conference, I present papers to and meet with other academics. My habitus has a number of different sources, among them are training in etiquette by a British mother and many years spent studying scholarly texts and engaging in academic discourse. The linguistic market in academia is formed by the emphasis on cultural and symbolic capital, and by the positions in the empirical field held by everyone at the conference; some people have more powerful positions and others less so. Each encounter, each speech act, is informed by these issues. In such circumstances, I tend to "feel at home" (habitus), and I interact freely, bantering and arguing with other academics in a kind of "one-upmanship" tournament.

This weekend, I will be going to the annual Christmas party at my wife's work. Here the linguistic market is different. Economic capital and the cultural capital that goes along with it are much more highly prized. And the empirical field is made up of differing positions and relationships achieved in the struggle of American business. Because of these differences, my market position is quite different here from what it was at the professional conference. In fact, I have no market position. Worse, my habitus remains the same. The way I talk—the words I use and the way I phrase my sentences—is very different from the other people at this event. The tempo of my speech is different (it's much slower) as is the way I walk and hold myself. In this kind of situation, I try and avoid speech acts. When encounters are unavoidable, I say as little as possible because I know that what I have to say, the way I say it, and even the tempo of my speech won't fit in.

These two different examples illustrate an extremely important point in Bourdieu's theory: Individuals in a given market recognize their institutional position, have a sense of how their habitus relates to the present market, and anticipate differing profits of distinction. In my professional conference example, I anticipate high rewards and distinction; but in the office party example, I anticipate low distinction and few rewards. In situations like the office example, anticipation acts as a *self-sanctioning mechanism* through which individuals participate in their own domination. Perhaps "domination" sounds silly with reference to an office party, but it isn't silly when it comes to job interviews, promotions, legal confrontations, encounters with government officials, and so forth. I gave you an example that we can relate to so that we could more clearly understand what happens in other, more important speech acts.

These kinds of speech acts are the arena of symbolic violence. **Symbolic violence** is the exercise of violence and oppression that is not recognized as such. More specifically, "Symbolic power is that invisible power which can be exercised only with the complicity of those who do not want to know that they are subject to it or even that they themselves exercise it" (Bourdieu, 1991, p. 164). For example, for quite some time, patriarchy was seen as part of the natural order of things. Yet, in believing in her husband's right to rule, a woman participated in and blinded herself to her own oppression. Here's another example: In believing that schools should be locally controlled and funded and that education is the legitimate path to upward social mobility, we actively participate in the perpetuation of the class system in the United States (see Kozol, 1991).

More insidious for Bourdieu is the way language is used to inflict symbolic violence. Have you ever been around someone of higher social status that you wanted to talk to but didn't? Why didn't you? If you're like me, you didn't because you were afraid of making a fool out of yourself. I had a professor in graduate school that I so admired, but I never talked to him unless it was absolutely necessary. I just knew that I would misspeak and say something foolish. Every social group has specific languages. It is easily seen with such pop culture groups as hip-hop, skaters, and graffiti taggers. But it is also true with experts and people in high-status positions, including the elite class. They typically have specialized languages. And, while we don't know the language, we *know* that we don't know the language, "which condemns [us] to a more or less desperate attempt to be correct, or to *silence*" (Bourdieu, 1991, p. 97, emphasis original).

My third example is from a conversation with my wife. In most conversations among equals, formal linguistic markets have little if any power. We talk and joke around, paying no attention to the demands of proper speech. I'm certain that you can think of multitudes of such speech acts: talking with friends at a café or at the gym or in your apartment. And those kinds of speech acts will always stay that way, unless one of you has a higher education or a greater distance from necessity—that is, unless your habitus is different. Even in such cases, however, linguistic markets usually won't come into play. But they can. "Every linguistic exchange contains the *potentiality* of an act of power, and all the more so when it involves agents who occupy asymmetric positions in the distribution of the relevant capital" (Bourdieu & Wacquant, 1992, p. 145, emphasis original). Bourdieu tells us in such situations, where the market position is different or the habitus is different, the potential for power and symbolic violence is only set aside for the moment.

Symbolic Struggle

Social change for Bourdieu is rooted in symbolic struggles, which makes sense given Bourdieu's emphasis on symbolic capital and power. Part of that struggle occurs within the speech act or encounter. As we've seen, encounters are structured by markets of differing distinction, and habitus expresses itself naturally within those markets. We will feel at home or foreign in an encounter; we will speak up or silence ourselves, all without thought. However, we also have to keep in mind that habitus is embodied and expresses itself through intuitive feelings. And sometimes our intuitions can lead us to brilliant moves, whether on the sports field, the game board, the music stage, or the speech act. Just so, our habitus at times can lead us to speech acts that defy our cultural, symbolic, economic, or social standings.

This kind of symbolic struggle can bring some incremental change. Bourdieu gives us hints about how more dynamic change can occur, but keep in mind that his isn't a theory of social change or revolution. Bourdieu allows that there are two methods by which a symbolic struggle may be carried out, one objectively and the other subjectively. In both cases, symbolic disruption is the key. Objectively, individuals or groups may act in such a way as to display certain counter-realities. His example of this method is group demonstrations held to manifest the size, strength, and cohesiveness of the disenfranchised. This type of symbolic action disrupts the taken-for-grantedness that all systems of oppression must work within—it offers an objective case that things are not what they seem.

Subjectively, individuals or groups may try and transform the categories constructed by symbolic capital through which the social world is perceived. On the individual level, this may be accomplished through insults, rumors, questions, and the like. A good example of this approach is found in bell hooks' (1989) book *Talking Back: Thinking Feminist, Thinking Black:* "It is that act of speech, of 'talking back,' that is no mere gesture of empty words, that is the expression of moving from object to subject—the liberated voice" (p. 9). Groups may also operate in this way by employing more political strategies. The most typical of these strategies is the redefinition of history; that is, "retrospectively reconstructing a past fitted to the needs of the present" (Bourdieu, 1989, p. 21). But notice that with each of these kinds of struggle, a response from those with symbolic capital would be required. These disruptions could bring attention to the cause, but symbolic power would be necessary to give it life and substance within the symbolic field first and then the objective field.

Concepts and Theory: Toward a New Sociology

It would be a disservice to restrict our introduction to Bourdieu to his theory of class. Bourdieu actually gives us a different way of practicing sociology. He gives us a way of looking at social behaviors as practices that overcome a sticky issue that has faced sociology probably since the time of Max Weber. This dichotomy, and those derived from it, sets some of the basic parameters of our discipline, such as the distinction between quantitative and qualitative methods and the divergence between structuralism and interactionism. This dichotomy also sets up one of the thorniest issues sociologists address: the link between the micro and macro levels of society. The dichotomy that I am referring to is the dilemma of structure (objective) versus agency (subjective), or, as Bourdieu talks about it, social physics versus social phe-nomenology. Though we didn't address it at the time, this dichotomy is the primary difference between Chapters 3, 4, and 5 and the approach of Wilson and Chafetz in Chapter 7. It's why the approaches are so different. Bourdieu characterizes this dichotomy between objective and subjective knowledge as one of the most harmful in the social sciences. And Bourdieu (1985) sees overcoming the break between objective and subjective knowledge as the most steadfast and important factor guid-ing his work (p. 15).

Bourdieu brings the two sides of the dichotomy together in what he calls *con-structivist structuralism,* or structuralist constructivism—Bourdieu uses the term both ways—in which both structure and agency are given equal weight. Bourdieu (1989) says that within the social world, there are "objective structures independent of the consciousness and will of agents, which are capable of guiding and con-straining their practices or their representations" (p. 14). He thus keeps structures in the objective social world that Durkheim gave us (although Bourdieu thinks a little differently about how and where these structures exist).

Yet, at the same time, Bourdieu emphasizes the constructivist and subjective sides. In Bourdieu's (1989) scheme, the subjective side is also structured in terms of "schemes of perception, thought, and action" (p. 14), which is habitus. Part of what Bourdieu does is to detail the ways through which both kinds of structures are constructed; thus, there is a kind of double structuring in Bourdieu's theory and research. But Bourdieu doesn't simply give us a historical account of how structures are produced. His theory also offers an explanation of how these two structures are dialectically related and how the individual uses them strategically in linguistic markets.

Dialecticism and a Theory of Practice

In preserving both sides of the dichotomy, Bourdieu has created a unique theo-retical problem. He doesn't want to conflate the two sides as Giddens (Chapter 12) does, nor does he want to link them up. He wants to preserve the integrity of both domains and yet he characterizes the dichotomy as harmful. Bourdieu is thus left with a sticky problem: How can he keep and yet change the dichotomy between the objective and subjective moments without linking them together or blending them together? Let's take this issue out of the realm of theory and state it in terms that are a bit more approachable. The problem that Bourdieu is left with is the relation-ship between the individual and society. Do we have free choice? Bourdieu would say yes. Does society determine what we do? Again Bourdieu would say yes. How can something be determined and yet be the product of free choice? I've stated the issue a bit too simplistically for Bourdieu's theory, but I want you to see the prob-lem clearly. Structure and agency, or the objective and subjective moments, create tension because they stand in opposition to one another. And that tension is exactly how Bourdieu solves his theoretical problem.

Bourdieu argues that the objective and constructive moments stand in a dialec-tical relationship. The idea of **dialectic** was brought into sociology by Karl Marx.

A dialectic contains different elements that are naturally antagonistic or in tension to one another—this antagonism is what energizes and brings change; it's the engine. In the material world of capitalist production, the primary contradictions are found in exploitation and overproduction. For Marx, the dialectic continues until an economic system in keeping with species being comes into existence. Bourdieu's dialectic occurs between the field and the habitus. Both are structures; habitus is "incorporated history" and the field is "objectified history" (Bourdieu, 1980/1990, p. 66). The tension of the dialectic is between the subjective and objective structures, and the dialectic itself is found in the individual and collective struggles or practices that transform or preserve these structures through specific practices and linguistic markets. In other words, Bourdieu is arguing that a number of different elements in our lives are structured, and among them are the habitus of the individual (schemes of thought, feeling, and action) and the social field (structured social positions and the distribution of resources). These different structures dialectically exert force upon one another through the strategic actions and practices of people in interaction. And, as with most dialectics, the tension can produce something new and different out of the struggle; these differences can then influence the structures of habitus and field.

Reflexive Sociology

Bourdieu wants us to engage in reflexive sociology, where we move "in a spiral between theory, empirical work and back to reformulating theory again but at a different level" (Mahar, Harker, & Wilkes, 1990, p. 3). If we were to look at one of Bourdieu's books, such as *Distinction*, we would see this reflexive vision of theory and the social world graphically laid out. On any given page, there may be two or three different print fonts with lines separating the different text. What Bourdieu is doing graphically is moving back and forth between dense empirical descriptions and abstract theory. In this back-and-forth movement, Bourdieu proposes a concept, considers it in light of the empirical world, and then continually reconsiders it throughout the book. In this way, his methodological stand and writing are themselves theoretical statements of structural constructivism. Theory, like social practice, is embedded in the empirical world, and theory, like social structures and practice, moves dialectically: It's never finished, it never arrives, but it is always transformed through its intrinsic tensions.

Bourdieu never published a definitive statement of his theory—the closest he came to it is in *An Invitation to Reflexive Sociology*—and his later works don't necessarily build upon or include his earlier work. Bourdieu doesn't like "professorial definitions" but much prefers the idea of "open concepts" (Bourdieu & Wacquant, 1992, p. 95). Reflexive sociology, then, is more concerned with insight and inspiration than creed and rigor. Bourdieu gives us an inspiring way through which to bridge the gap between objective and subjective sociology. He gives us a dynamic space from which to think about the relations between structure and agency. Hopefully, at this point you can see the relations between this new perspective Bourdieu is introducing and his theory of class.

Summary

- Bourdieu is specifically concerned with the reproduction of class. In contrast to Marx, Bourdieu sees class replicated through symbolic violence rather than overt oppression. Bourdieu argues that there are four types of capital: economic, social, cultural, and symbolic. The latter two are his greatest concern. Symbolic capital has the power to create positions within the symbolic and objective fields. The objective field refers to social positions that are determined though the distributions of the four capitals. But these positions don't become real or meaningful for us unless and until someone with symbolic capital names them. This naming gives the position, and the individuals and groups that occupy it, social viability. The symbolic field has independent effects in that it can be manipulated by those with symbolic capital; people use the symbolic field to view, understand, and reproduce the objective field.

- Cultural capital refers to the social skills, habits, linguistic abilities, and tastes that individuals have as a result of their position in the symbolic and objective fields. Cultural capital is particularly important because it becomes embodied. This embodiment of cultural capital becomes the individual's habitus: the way the body exists and is used in society. Distance from necessity and level of education are two of the most important ways in which habitus is structured, both of which are related to economic capital. Class position, then, is replicated through the embodied, nonconscious behaviors and speech acts of individuals.

- Habitus is expressed in linguistic markets. Linguistic markets are structured by different weightings of the various capitals. One's position within the market is determined by different rankings on the capitals and the embodied ability to perform within the market. Linguistic markets are played out in speech acts where individuals sense how their habitus relates to the market and thus anticipate differing profits of distinction. This nonconscious sense provides the basis for symbolic violence: Anticipating few rewards in acts where they are "outclassed," individuals simultaneously sanction themselves and legitimate the hierarchical relations of class and power.

- There is, however, the possibility of symbolic struggle. The struggle involves symbolic disruption. First, individuals or groups can act in such a way as to objectively picture alternative possibilities. This is what we normally think of as social movements or demonstrations. But because Bourdieu sees the importance of symbolic power in the replication of class, he understands these demonstrations as pictures—they are objective images of symbolic issues that disrupt the taken-for-grantedness in which oppression must operate. Second, individuals and groups can challenge the subjective meanings intrinsic within the symbolic field. In daily speech acts, the individual can disrupt the normality of the symbolic field through insults, jokes, questions, rumors, and so on. Groups can also challenge "the way things are" by redefining history.

- Bourdieu's basic approach is constructivist structuralism. With this idea, Bourdieu is attempting to give us a point of view that gives full weight to structure and agency. There is tension between constructivism and structuralism, between agency and structure, and it is that tension that Bourdieu uses to understand how both can coexist. The tension is a dialectic and is played out in symbolic markets and social practices.

TAKING THE PERSPECTIVE

There are two ways we can think of Bourdieu's theoretical perspective in terms of how it is situated in the discipline. The first way is to see his theory as neo-Marxian. I have to admit that this is a very loose categorization and a number of our theorists would fall in this category, such as William Julius Wilson (Chapter 7) and Immanuel Wallerstein (Chapter 9). Generally, neo-Marxian theorists are concerned with one of Marx's central issues; they usually don't see the economy quite as dominant as did Marx; and they usually add elements from other theoretical approaches. This latter characteristic is most clearly seen in the Frankfurt School's use of psychoanalysis (Chapter 2).

There is a sense in which Bourdieu's theory may be seen as the mirror image of Marx. According to Marx, the economy and class are two of the most important structures in society. And whereas Bourdieu's theory begins with material class, he clearly moves the reproduction of class structures into the symbolic realm. In the reproduction of class, it is the symbolic field and the relations expressed by and through habitus that have the greater causal force. Like Marx, Bourdieu defines the social world as the place where the competition for scarce resources takes place. The result of this competition is an unequal distribution of economic capital. But unlike Marx, Bourdieu sees much of this competition as taking place in a symbolic realm that produces an unequal distribution of four different kinds of capital: economic, social, cultural, and symbolic. And, Bourdieu is particularly concerned with Marx's notion of misrecognition, the idea that people fail to see or recognize the relations of production within a commodity or means of production. Bourdieu expands Marx's idea by arguing that misrecognition is present within all social practices and forms of knowledge, as well as a necessary condition for symbolic violence and oppression.

Another approach to working with Marx's theory of class is demonstrated in Erik Olin Wright's (1978) work. Rather than augmenting Marx's theory, Wright's analytical Marxism seeks to theoretically explicate Marx's concepts. The main reason for doing so is to render the theory more amenable to scientific testing. During your undergraduate education, you may have heard that Marx's theory didn't work; the revolution never materialized and capitalism survived. An analytical Marxist would counter and ask, "How did you measure Marx's concepts? How did you test his theory?" The truth of the matter is that very little of Marx's theory has been scientifically tested. Analytical Marxism is trying to change that.

The other perspective in which Bourdieu figures prominently is culture. Calhoun (2003) argues that Bourdieu's theory is the "single most important theoretical approach to the sociology of culture," and, perhaps, more significantly, "he helped to bring the study of culture into a central place in sociology" (p. 303). While culture has been central to sociology since its inception, it has appeared generally as a topic of study, like you would study class, race, or gender. What Bourdieu helped accomplish was to move culture to the sociological approach in general. Rather than culture being something studied on its own, this cultural sociology sees culture as intrinsic to everything people do: "To believe in the possibility of a cultural sociology is to subscribe to the idea that every action . . . is embedded to some extent in a horizon of affect and meaning" (Alexander & Smith, 201, p. 136). An indicator of the importance culture is gaining is the 2003 annual meetings of the American Sociological Association.

BUILDING YOUR THEORY TOOLBOX

Learning More—Primary Sources

- I recommend that you begin your exploration of Bourdieu with the following:
  - o *Distinction: A Social Critique of the Judgment of Taste,* Harvard University Press, 1984.
  - o "Social Space and Symbolic Power," *Sociological Theory, 7,* 14–25, 1989.
  - o *Language and Symbolic Power,* Harvard University Press, 1991.
  - o *An Invitation to Reflexive Sociology,* University of Chicago Press, 1992.
  - o *Acts of Resistance: Against the Tyranny of the Market,* New Press, 1999.

Learning More—Secondary Sources

- There are a number of good secondary sources. The two I find most helpful are:
  - o David Swartz, *Culture and power: The Sociology of Pierre Bourdieu,* University of Chicago Press, 1998.
  - o Richard Jenkins, *Pierre Bourdieu (Key Sociologists),* Routledge, 2002.

Check It Out

- "Symbolic Differences and Identity," Michele Lamont & Marcel Fournier (Eds.), *Cultivating Differences: Symbolic Boundaries and the Making of Inequality,* University of Chicago Press, 1993.
- *Overcoming Dichotomies.* See Anthony Giddens in this book, Chapter 12.

Seeing the World

- Write a 250-word synopsis of the theoretical perspective of constructivist structuralism.
- After reading and understanding this chapter, you should be able to define the following terms theoretically and explain their theoretical importance to Bourdieu's theory: *economic capital, social capital, symbolic capital, cultural capital, taste, habitus, distance from necessity, education, field, linguistic market, symbolic violence, constructivist structuralism, dialectic*
- After reading and understanding this chapter, you should be able to answer the following questions (remember to answer them *theoretically*):
  - o Explain Bourdieu's constructivist structuralism approach.
  - o How are symbolic fields produced?
  - o What is habitus, and how is it produced?
  - o How are class inequalities replicated, and how is class contingent? In your answer, be certain to explain linguistic markets, symbolic violence, and the role that habitus plays.

Engaging the World

- Use Bourdieu's theory to describe and explain the differences between the way you talk with your best friend versus the way you talk with your theory professor.

- Using Bourdieu's take on misrecognition, analyze the following ideas: race, gender, and sexuality. What kinds of things must we misrecognize in order for these to work as part of the symbolic violence of this society? Look up Bourdieu's notion of *doxa* (1972/1993, p. 3; 1980/1990, p. 68). How do doxa and symbolic violence work together in the oppression of race, gender, and sexuality?

- Choose the structure of inequality that you know best (race, gender, sexuality, religion). Using what you already know, analyze that structure using Figure 8.1. How would approaching the study of inequality change using Bourdieu?

Weaving the Threads

- What does Bourdieu's theory of linguistic markets add to our understanding of symbolic interaction (Chapter 3)?

- How could you specifically integrate Goffman's (Chapter 5) theory of impression management with Bourdieu's theory of habitus and linguistic markets?

- Can you think of ways in which you could use Bourdieu's theory to make Chafetz's theory of gender inequality more robust, especially in her ideas of what happens at the micro level?

CHAPTER 9

Global Capitalism:

Immanuel Wallerstein
(1930–)

Theorist's Digest
Concepts and Theory: The Dialectics of Capitalism
    The Division of Labor and Exploitation
    Accumulation and Overproduction
Concepts and Theory: The End of the World as We Know It
    World-Empires and World-Economies
    Kondratieff Waves
    The Modern Crisis
    Structural and Cultural Signs of the End
Summary
Taking the Perspective
Building Your Theory Toolbox

The idea of globalization isn't new. In fact, a globally connected economy is inherent in modern capitalism. As Marx (1848/1978b) said, "The bourgeoisie has at last, since the establishment of Modern Industry and of the world-market, conquered for itself, *in the modern representative State,* exclusive political sway" (p. 475, emphasis added). One of the reasons that modern capitalism created world-markets is due to its intrinsic characteristic of expansion. People have always created products to sell in order to make a profit. What's distinct about modern capitalism is the reason for profit. In traditional capitalism the profit was used to live, to maintain a standard of living. The motivation behind modern capitalism's drive for profit is investment. In modern capitalism the reason to gain profit is to be able to reinvest it;

profit then becomes capital. Notice that in traditional capitalism there is a natural limit to profit: A standard of living is a real thing and an achievable goal. But modern capitalism has no natural limit because its driving force is simply to make money in order to make more money, in order to make more money, ad infinitum—modern capitalism is defined by capital chasing capital without end. Thus, modern capitalism must continually push for expanding markets, commodification, and exploitation. We'll see that this constant expansion is an integral part of Immanuel Wallerstein's theory.

There are three related and important ideas that come with the idea of globalization. The first is that anytime we are talking about globalization we are talking about *systems*. You remember that we spent a bit of time tending to the definition of social structure. We need to do the same here and we also need to recognize that the concept of social structures implies the idea of systems. We've used the idea of structure to consider racial, gender, and class inequalities. But those structures are always understood as existing within a system; the economic, political, and religious systems are good examples that impact inequality. A **system**, then, "is any pattern of relationships between elements, and is regarded as having emergent properties of its own, over and above the properties of its elements" (Marshall, 1998, p. 621). What's important, then, in approaching a systems analysis is to identify the elements, their relationships, and the emergent properties. The latter sounds more difficult than it is—it simply means that systems have their own laws and processes.

The second idea that comes out of the notion of systems is that systems always exist in environments. For example, animals are biological systems that exist within ecosystems. The important issue here is that systems have boundaries. Biological systems and ecosystems relate to one another but they are clearly separate. This leads me to the third important idea. Generally speaking, when modern sociologists talk about society, they are talking about a bounded system of interrelated structures. The assumption of most sociology is that society is a system with "a nation-state at its centre that organizes the rights and duties of each citizen" (Urry, 2006, p. 168). So, society is a system of interrelated structures whose boundaries are defined by a nation-state. We can thus, for example, talk about the United States as a society and Germany as a separate society.

As I said, the idea of *globalization* isn't new. However, there is something new about today's globalization: the extent of globalization. When Marx talked about world-markets he had in mind economies situated in different nations participating in global exchanges regulated by national states (notice the emphasized part in the quote above). What we are seeing today challenges that picture: "Such challenges arise out of the fact that the global . . . simultaneously transcends the exclusive framing of national states yet partly inhabits national territories and institutions" (Sassen, 2007, p. 3). Saskia Sassen further tells us that contemporary globalization involves two dynamics, both of which call into question the modern idea of society (pp. 5–6). The first is the establishment of distinctly global structures and organizations—so there are elements of the system that do not exist within any nation—the second involves processes that link various nationally based actors and processes—so, while a company may in fact be based in Japan, the way it is connected to markets, other companies, and other economic systems involves issues that transcend national boundaries. The point I want you to take away from this discussion is simple yet profound: It's possible that the idea of society as a national system may be an antiquated way to think about social processes.

In the next two chapters, we are going to look at two very different global systems. Wallerstein will tell us about the processes associated with global capitalism. If you're familiar with Marx (and I assume you are if you're taking a course in contemporary theory), then his ideas will have a familiar feel. Our next theorist, Manuel Castells (Chapter 10), will however take us in a totally different direction. Rather than systems of institutions and social relations, Castells argues that globalization is built on networks of communication, mostly structured through the Internet. These networks not only transcend the boundaries of nation, they completely redefine human connections. The globalized network society, then, can only be understood through the logics of computer networks; and in this network, social class, power, politics, meaning, and identities are radically redefined.

THEORIST'S DIGEST

Brief Biography

Immanuel Wallerstein was born in New York City on September 30, 1930. He attended Columbia University where he received his bachelor's (1951), master's (1954), and PhD (1959). Wallerstein has also formally studied at various universities around the globe, including the Université Paris 7–Denis-Diderot, Université Libre de Bruxelles, and Universidad Nacional Autónoma de México. His primary teaching post was at Binghamton University (SUNY), where he taught from 1976 to his retirement in 1999. However, he has also held visiting professor posts in Amsterdam, British Columbia, and the Chinese University of Hong Kong, as well as several other locations. In addition to many professional posts, he has served as president of the International Sociological Association and director of the Fernand Braudel Center for the Study of Economies, Historical Systems, and Civilizations.

Central Sociological Questions

Wallerstein is driven to first critically understand (through a Marxian perspective) how the nations of the world are joined together in a global system of capitalism, and second to find ways to politically act to change that system.

Simply Stated

Because of exploitation and overproduction, global capitalist economy goes through cycles of expansion and depression. Each cycle is deeper than the previous; and the cycles eventually reach a point where the economy can't rebound. During that last depression the global system will go through a chaotic period out of which a new system will be born.

Key Ideas

Modern capitalism, globalization, systems, exploitation, dialectical materialism, division of labor, externalized costs, quasi-monopolies, overproduction, world-empires, world-economies, core states, periphery states, semi-periphery states, Kondratieff waves, world-systems theory

Concepts and Theory: The Dialectics of Capitalism

Wallerstein's theory is founded on Karl Marx's theory of capitalism. According to Marx, in humanity's purest economic form people produced what they needed through collective cooperation, what Marx calls "primitive communism." It began small, but eventually we started using economic systems that were contrary to the social nature of humans. In these economies, the structures have contradictions that will eventually destroy it because the system is out of sync with the social, collective nature of people. Marx talks about these economic antagonisms or contradictions as *dialectical materialism*. The *material* in his use of materialism isn't the physical universe as it is with most philosophers; it's the world of material goods that people create. The word *dialectic* looks very much like dialogue; in fact, the two words are related. In this case, the dialogue is among the contradictions present in every economic form except communism.

Marx is saying that every economic system, other than one that is socially and collectively based, contains contradictions. These structural contradictions create tensions within the economy that push it toward change by resolving the contradictions in some way. In capitalism, for example, there are things that capitalists must do (such as expanding markets) that naturally create pressures within capitalism (such as overproduction) that will eventually lead to its downfall. Notice that the contradictions, while detrimental, are necessary for the economic system. These economic contradictions are what produce history—the contradictions are the energy that pushes for social change. As these contradictions resolve, new economies and social structures are born. In Wallerstein's hands, dialectical factors such as exploitation, accumulation, and overproduction work out in the long run to the collapse of global capitalism, out of which a new system will emerge.

The Division of Labor and Exploitation

The *division of labor* is one of the more important elements in the Marxian perspective; in some ways, it is the most important. Marx starts his theory with the idea of species being. Species being contains two ideas: First, the way the human species exists is through creative production; second, humans become conscious of their existence (or being) through the mirror effect of the product. Humanity, then, is defined and knows itself through creative production. There is, then, an intimate connection between producer and product: *The very existence of the product defines the nature of the producer.* If you think about it, we acknowledge this connection every time we meet someone new. One of the first questions we ask a new person is, "What do you do?" In doing so, we assume the connection between what people do and who they are.

For Wallerstein, the importance of the division of labor is that it is the defining characteristic of an economic world-system. Labor, of course, is an essential form of human behavior; without it we would cease to exist. By extension, the division of labor creates some of the most basic kinds of social relationships; these relationships are, by definition, relations of dependency. In our division of labor, we depend upon each other to perform the work that we do not. I depend upon the farmer for food production, and the farmer depends upon teachers to educate his or her children. These relations of dependency connect different people and other social units into a structured whole or system. Wallerstein argues that the world-system is connected by the current capitalist division of labor: World-systems are defined "quite simply as a unit with a single division of labor and multiple cultural systems" (Wallerstein, 2000, p. 75). Multiple cultural systems are included because world-systems connect different societies and cultures.

The important feature of this division of labor is that it is based on **exploitation**, which is simply the measurable difference between what a worker gets paid and the worth of the product produced. For example, you get paid $150.00 for a day's work and you produce $500.00 worth of product; the difference is the level of exploitation. That difference is also the main source of profit for the capitalists; without it capitalists couldn't exist. It's a simple thing, but it has some profound effects. First, because modern capitalism needs ever more capital, it will be driven to find the highest level of exploitation possible. Second, exploitation is a potential source of power for workers. Thus there's a general tendency for workers to use that power to increase benefits and rights, such as a 40-hour work week, overtime, minimum wage, health benefits, safety regulations, and so forth. Third, different societies can have different levels of exploitation. For example, if we compare the situation of automobile workers in the United States with those in Mexico, we will see that the level of exploitation is higher in Mexico.

What is important to see here is that profit is based on exploitation and it gives workers power that could be used to increase worker benefits and wages, thus lowering the level of exploitation in a country. Yet the drive for exploitation doesn't let up; capitalists by definition are driven to increase profits. The search for new means of exploitation, then, eventually transcends national boundaries: *Capitalists export exploitation.* Because of the limitations on the exploitation of workers in advanced capitalist countries—due primarily to the effects of worker movements, state legislation, and the natural limitations of technological innovation—firms seek other labor markets where the level of exploitation is higher. Marx had a vague notion of this, but Wallerstein's theory is based upon it. It is the exportation of exploitation that structures the division of labor upon which the world-economy is based.

Accumulation and Overproduction

As we've noted, "We are in a capitalist system only when the system gives priority to the *endless* accumulation of capital" (Wallerstein, 2004, p. 24, emphasis original); and we see the drive to make money in order to make more money all around us. But most people only think about the personal effects this kind of capitalism has (like the fact that Bill Gates is worth $46.6 billion). But what are the effects on the economy? Most Americans would probably say that the effect on the economy is a good one: continually expanding profits and higher standards of living. Perhaps, but Wallerstein wants us to see that something else is going on as well. In order to fully understand what he has in mind, we need to think about the role of government in the endless pursuit of the accumulation of capital.

It's obvious that for capitalism to work, it needs a strong state system. The state provides the centralized production and control of money; creates and enforces laws that grant private property rights; supplies the regulation of markets, national borders, interorganizational relations; and so forth. But there is something else that the state does in a capitalist system. We generally assume that the firm that pays the cost enjoys the benefits, as in the capitalist invests the money so he or she can enjoy the profit. However, the state actually decides what proportion of the costs of production will be paid by the firm. In this sense, capitalists are subsidized by the state.

There are three kinds of costs that the state subsidizes: the costs associated with transportation, toxicity, and the exhaustion of raw materials. Firms rarely if ever pay the full cost of transporting their goods; the bulk of the cost for this infrastructure is borne by the state, for such things as road systems. Almost all production produces toxicity, whether noxious gases, waste, or some kind of change to the environment. How and when these costs are incurred and who pays for them is always an issue. The least expensive methods are short-term and evasive (dumping the waste, pretending there isn't a problem), but the costs are eventually paid and usually by the state. Capitalist production also uses up raw materials; but again, firms rarely pay these costs. When resources are depleted, the state steps in to restore or re-create the materials. Economists refer to the expenses of capitalist production that are paid by the state as *externalized costs,* and we will see that in this matter not all states are created equal.

However helpful these externalized costs are to the pursuit of accumulation, states that contain the most successful capitalist enterprises do more: They provide a structure for *quasi-monopolies.* A monopoly is defined as the exclusive control of a market or the means of production; quasi-monopolies don't have exclusive control but they do have considerable control.

Wallerstein argues that totally free markets would make the endless accumulation of capital impossible. Totally free markets imply that all factors influencing the means of production are free and available to all firms, that goods and services flow without restriction, that there is a very large number of sellers and a very large number of buyers, and that all participants have complete and full knowledge. "In such a perfect market, it would always be possible for the buyers to bargain down the sellers to an absolutely minuscule level of profit," which would destroy the basic underpinnings of capitalism (Wallerstein, 2004, pp. 25–26). The converse of a totally free market is a monopoly, and monopolized processes are far more lucrative than those of the free market. Thus, the perfect situation for a capitalist firm is to have monopolistic control; it would then be able to pursue the endless accumulation of capital with the greatest efficiency and success.

The most important way in which states facilitate quasi-monopolies is through patent laws that grant exclusive production rights for an invention for a certain number of years. This state guarantee allows companies to gain high levels of profit in a monopolistic market for long enough to obtain considerable accumulation of capital. The practice of granting patents also results in a cycle of leading products. The largest and most successful firms actively market a patented product as long as the profit margin is high. As soon as the product becomes less profitable through more open competition, the product is given over to less profitable companies, with the original firm creating new leading products. Producers of the unpatented product engage in freer competition but with less profit.

We're about ready to discuss the effect of all this, but we need to throw in one more ingredient. Marx (1932/1978c) argues that "life involves before everything else eating and drinking, a habitation, clothing and many other things. . . . that the satisfaction of the first need . . . leads to new needs; and this production of new needs is the first historical act" (p. 156). In other words, human beings have the unique ability to create additional or secondary "needs." And, because people can create new needs, there is no limitation placed upon the proliferation of commodities.

Now think about what this means: Capitalists are driven to endlessly accumulate capital (it's the definition of modern capitalism). In this pursuit, they are subsidized by the state, most importantly through the support of quasi-monopolies. The state's support of quasi-monopolies means that new products are always being created, with the older ones still being produced. And, by nature, human beings create new needs and thus produce and buy new commodities endlessly. Together, the continuous expansion of commodification and production inevitably leads to *overproduction*—too much production for the current demand. Capitalists will continue to create new and produce existing commodities until the market will no longer bear it. Therefore, overproduction is a fundamental property of capitalism that inexorably leads to production cutbacks, worker layoffs, and, in due course, economic downturns.

Interestingly, the issue of overproduction has entered the mind-set of popular culture. Commenting on a slow holiday season, *Time* magazine carried an article saying,

> Karl Marx theorized that capitalism was condemned to repeated depressions because of "cycles of overproduction." . . . if Marx had hit the shopping malls last week and seen the heavy discounting—or looked on the Internet and seen the emergence of cut-rate sites like Amazon.com's new outlet store—he would no doubt have felt vindicated. (Cohen, Baumohl, Buia, Roston, Ressner, & Thompson, 2001, p. 21)

The cycles of overproduction and exploitation work in tandem, both of them driven by accumulation. Accumulation increases the demand for labor and product innovation. State protection through patent rights, tax incentives, and the like creates a state sanctioned quasi-monopoly that in and of itself increases accumulation, better enabling the firm to engage in product innovation and increasing the demand for labor. Over time, the demand for labor decreases the size of the labor pool, which drives wages up and profits down, which, in turn, precipitates an economic slowdown, the collapse of small businesses, and the search for new methods of exploitation through technological innovation in the work process or exporting exploitation. In the medium run, exporting exploitation is the more efficient of the two because technologies become diffused throughout the business sector.

Exporting exploitation implies the movement of specific goods outside the national boundaries, and product movement from most profitable to less profitable firms explicitly entails such a shift. Both processes, then, move goods and labor from advanced capitalist countries to rising capitalist countries. And both processes lead to the collapse of small businesses and the centralization of accumulation—that is, capital held in fewer and fewer hands.

Concepts and Theory:
The End of the World as We Know It

World-Empires and World-Economies

Worlds end and worlds change. Of course, very few people living in any specific world think about their world ending; but they all do. The great Mesopotamian, Greek, and Roman empires are gone; the sun has set on the British Empire; and even more recently, the USSR crumbled and is no more. Of course, just like the Phoenix, new worlds arise out of the ashes and history moves on. But what of our world? History tells us all worlds fail—when will our world fail? Generally, we live in a modern world, and more specifically, one that is defined by American capitalism. Wallerstein asks us to consider the possibility that our world is failing and that we are in a chaotic period between historical moments. Perhaps shockingly for some of us, Wallerstein argues that this shift in historical epochs will lead to the demise of the United States as we know it. So, let's take these questions seriously: In what historical epoch do we live and how is it affecting our world?

Wallerstein argues that there have been two types of world-systems throughout history, one with a common political system and one without. Systems with a common political entity are called world-empires. *World-empires* exist through military dominance and mandatory economic tribute. The political influence of one government is spread and held in place through a strong military, but this sets up a cycle that eventually leads to the demise of the empire. Maintaining a standing army that is geographically extended costs quite a bit of money. This money is raised through tribute and taxation. Heavy taxes make the system less efficient, in terms of economic production, and this increases the resistance of the populace as well. Increasing resistance means that the military presence must be increased, which, in turn, increases the cost, taxation, and resistance, and it further lowers economic efficiency. These cycles continue to worsen through structural time (see historicity above) until the empire falls. Examples of such world-empires include Rome, China, and India.

These world-empire cycles continued until about 1450, when a world-economy began to develop. Rather than a common political system, *world-economies* are defined through a common division of labor and through the endless accumulation of capital. As we saw earlier, in the absence of a political structure or common culture, the world-system is created through the structures intrinsic to capitalism. The worldwide division of labor created through the movement of products and labor from advanced capitalist nations to rising capitalist nations creates relationships of economic dependency and exploitation. These capitalist relationships are expressed through three basic types of economic states: core, semi-periphery, and periphery.

Briefly, *core states* are those that export exploitation; enjoy relatively light taxation; have a free, well-paid labor force; and constitute a large consumer market. The state systems within core states are the most powerful and are thus able to provide the strongest protection (such as trade restrictions) and capitalist inducements, such as externalizing costs, patent protection, tax incentives, and so on. *Periphery states* are those whose labor is forced (very little occupational choice and few worker protections) and underpaid. In terms of a capitalist economy and the world-system, these states are also the weakest—they are able to provide little in the way of tax and cost incentives, and they are the weakest players in the world-system. The periphery states are those to which capitalists in core states shift worker exploitation and more competitive, less profitable products. These shifts result in "a constant flow of surplus-value from the producers of peripheral products to the producers of core-like products" (Wallerstein, 2004, p. 28).

The relationship, then, between the core and the periphery is one of production processes and profitability. There is a continual shift of products and exploitation from core to periphery countries. Furthermore, there are cycles in both directions: Periphery countries are continually developing their own capitalist-state base. As we've seen, profitability is highest in quasi-monopolies and these, in turn, are dependent upon powerful states. Thus, changing positions in the capitalist world-economy is dependent upon the power of the state.

Over time, periphery economies become more robust and periphery states more powerful: Worker protection laws are passed, wages increase, and product innovation begins to occur; the states can then begin to perform much like the states in core countries—they create tax incentives and externalize costs for firms, grant product protection, and they become a more powerful player in the world-system economy. These nations move into the semi-periphery. *Semi-periphery states* are those that are in transition from being a land of exploitation to being a core player, and they both export exploitation and continue to exploit within their own country.

A good illustration of this process is the textile industry. In the 1800s, textiles were produced in very few countries and it was one of the most important core industries; by the beginning of the twenty-first century, textiles had all but moved out of the core nations. A clear and recent example of this process is Nike. Nike is the world's largest manufacturer of athletic shoes, with about $10 billion in annual revenue. In 1976, Nike began moving its manufacturing concerns from the United States to Korea and Taiwan, which at the time were considered periphery states. Within 4 years, 90% of Nike's production was located in Korea and Taiwan.

However, both Korea and Taiwan were on the cusp, and within a relatively short period of time they had moved into the semi-periphery. Other periphery states had opened up, most notably Bangladesh, China, Indonesia, and Vietnam. So, beginning in the early 1990s, Nike began moving its operations once again.

Currently, Indonesia contains Nike's largest production centers, with 17 factories and 90,000 employees. But that status could change. Just a few years ago, in 1997, the Indonesian government announced a change in the minimum wage, from $2.26 per day to $2.47 per day. Nike refused to pay the increase and in response, 10,000 workers went on strike. In answer to the strike, a company spokesperson, Jim Small, said, "Indonesia could be reaching a point where it is pricing itself out of the market" (Global Exchange, 1998).

Yet the existence of the semi-periphery doesn't simply serve as a conversion point; it has a structural role in the world-system. Because the core, periphery, and semi-periphery share similar economic, political, and ideological interests, the semi-periphery acts as a buffer that lessens tension and conflict between the core and periphery nations. "The existence of the third category means precisely that the upper stratum is not faced with the *unified* opposition of all the others because the middle stratum is both exploited and exploiter" (Wallerstein, 2000, p. 91, emphasis original).

Kondratieff Waves

Since 1450, world-economies have moved through four distinct phases. These phases occur in what are called *Kondratieff waves* (K-waves), named after Nikolai Kondratieff, a Russian economist writing during the early twentieth century. Kondratieff noticed patterns of regular, structural change in the world-economy. These waves last 50 to 60 years and consist of two phases, a growth phase (the A-cycle) and a stagnation phase (the B-cycle).

Much of what drives these phases in modern economic world-systems comes from the cycles of exploitation and accumulation that we've already talked about. During the A-cycle, new products are created, markets expanded, labor employed, and the political and economic influence of core states moves into previously external areas—new geographic areas are brought into the periphery for labor and materials (imperialism). At 25 to 30 years into the A-cycle, profits begin to fall due to overproduction, decreasing commodity prices, and increasing labor costs. In this B-cycle, the economy enters a deep recession. Eventually, the recession bottoms out and small businesses collapse, which leaves fewer firms and greater centralization of capital accumulation (quasi-monopolistic conditions), which, in turn, sets the stage for the next upswing in the cycle (A2-cycle) and the next recession (B2-cycle). Historically, these waves reach a crisis point approximately every 150 years. Each wave has its own configuration of core and periphery states, with generally one dominant state, at least initially.

Wallerstein sees these waves as phases in the development of the world-system. Within each phase, three things occur: The dominant form of capitalism changes (agricultural → mercantilism → industrial → consolidation); there is a geographic expansion as the division of labor expands into external areas; and a particular configuration of core and periphery states emerges. There have been four such phases thus far in the world-system. In Figure 9.1, I've outlined the different phases and their movement through time. I've also noted some of the major issues and the

Figure 9.1   World-Systems Phases

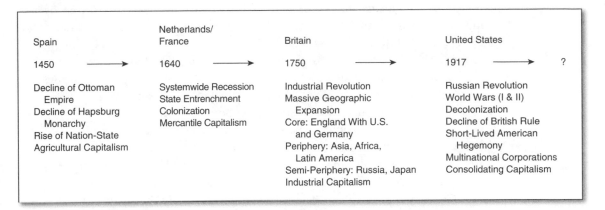

hegemonic core nations for easy comparison. Wallerstein (2004) uses the term *hegemonic* to denote nations that for a certain period of time,

> were able to establish the rules of the game in the interstate system, to domi-nate the world-economy (in production, commerce, and finance), to get their way politically with a minimal use of military force (which however they had in goodly strength), and to formulate the cultural language with which one discussed the world. (p. 58)

I'm not going to go into much historic detail here. You can read Wallerstein's (1974, 1980, 1989) three-volume work for the specifics. But briefly, phase one occurred roughly between 1450 and 1640, which marks the transition from feudalism and world-empires to the nation-state. Both the Ottoman Empire and the Hapsburg dynasty began their decline in the sixteenth century. As the world-empires weak-ened, Western Europe and the nation-state emerged as the core, Spain and the Mediterranean declined into the semi-periphery, and northeastern Europe and the Americas became the periphery. During this time, the major form of capitalism was agricultural, which came about as an effect of technological development and eco-logical conditions in Europe.

The second phase lasted from 1640 to 1750 and was precipitated by a system-wide recession that lasted approximately 80 years. During this time, nations drew in, centralized, and attempted to control all facets of the market through mercantilism, the dominant form of capitalism in this phase. Mercantilism was designed to increase the power and wealth of the emerging nations through the accumulation of gold, favorable trade balances, and through foreign trading monopolies. These goals were achieved primarily through colonization (geographic expansion). As with the previous period, there was a great deal of struggle among the core nations, with a three-way conflict among the Netherlands, France, and England.

The third phase began with the Industrial Revolution. England quickly took the lead in this area. The last attempt by France to stop the spread of English power was Napoleon's continental blockade, which failed. Here capitalism was driven by industry, and it expanded geographically to cover the entire globe. Wallerstein places the end of the third phase at the beginning of World War I and the beginning of the fourth phase at 1917 with the Russian Revolution. The Russian Revolution was driven by the lack of indigenous capital, continued resistance to industrializing from the agricultural sector, and the decay of military power and national status. Together these meant that "the Russian Revolution was essentially that of a semi-peripheral country whose internal balance of forces had been such that as of the late nineteenth century it began on a decline towards a peripheral status" (Wallerstein, 2000, p. 97). During this time, the British Empire receded, due to a number of factors including decolonization, and two states in particular vied for the core position: Germany and the United States. After World War II, the United States became the leading core nation, a position it enjoyed for two decades.

Hegemonic or leading states always have a limited life span. Becoming a core nation requires a state to focus on improving the conditions of production for capitalists; but staying hegemonic requires a state to invest in political and military might. Over time, other states become economically competitive and the leading state's economic power diminishes. In attempts to maintain its powerful position in the world-system, the hegemonic state will resort first to military threats and then to exercising its military power (note the increasing U.S. military intervention over the past 25 years). The "use of military power is not only the first sign of weakness but the source of further decline," as the capricious use of force creates resentment first in the world community and then in the state's home population as the cost of war increases taxation (Wallerstein, 2004, pp. 58–59).

Thus, the cost of hegemony is always high, and it inevitably leads to the end of a state's position of power within the world-system. For the United States, the costs came from the Cold War with the USSR; competition with rising core nations, such as Japan, China, and an economically united and resurgent Western Europe; and such displays of military might as the Korean, Vietnam, Gulf, and Iraq wars. The decline of U.S. hegemony since the late 1960s has meant that capitalist freedom has actually increased, due to the relative size and power of global corporations. There are many multinational corporations now that are larger and more powerful than many nations. These new types of corporation "are able to maneuver against state bureaucracies whenever the national politicians become too responsive to internal worker pressures" (Wallerstein, 2000, p. 99). The overall health of world capitalism has also meant that the semi-periphery has increased in strength, facilitating growth into the core.

The Modern Crisis

There are several key points in time for the world-system, such as the Ottoman defeat in 1571, the Industrial Revolution around 1750, and the Russian Revolution in 1917. Each of these events signaled a transition from one capitalist regime to another.

Wallerstein argues that one such event occurred in 1968, when revolutionary movements raced across the globe, involving China, West Germany, Poland, Italy, Japan,
Vietnam, Czechoslovakia, Mexico, and the United States. So many nations were
caught up in the mostly student-driven social movements that, collectively, they have
been called the first world revolution. They were certainly powerful and extensive.

Wallerstein (1995) argues that these worldwide movements came out of the
tension that has long existed between "two modernities—the modernity of technology and the modernity of liberation" (p. 472). Modernity grew out of the
Enlightenment and positivistic philosophy. The Enlightenment refers to a period of
European history from the late 1600s to the late 1700s that was characterized by the
assumption that the knowledge of most worth is based on reason and observation
(science) rather than faith (religion). Thinkers in the Enlightenment believed that,
through reason, humans could control not only the physical universe but society as
well. This was a positivist view of life as compared to fatalistic perspectives of religion. Humans could make a difference; humans could change their life course and
not be subject to an impenetrable god. Part of this hope lay in technology: tools
through which humanity could control the material universe and improve the
physical standard of living. This hope was, of course, embodied in science and its
offshoots, such as medicine.

The other pronounced hope of modernity concerned equality and was embodied in the nation-state; this is the second modernity. Many social scientists saw their
place in this grand scheme of equality. For example, Harriett Martineau (1838/
2003), one of the very first sociologists, argued that "every element of social life
derives its importance from this great consideration . . . the relative amount of
human happiness" (p. 25). For Martineau, the ultimate test of any society and its
state is how well it measures up to this one great consideration. Nevertheless, modern society, especially in the United States, was founded on a contradiction: inalien-
able rights but only for a select group.

Wallerstein tells us that the upheavals of 1968 were directed at this contradiction
and the failure of society to fulfill the hope of modernity: liberation for all. Students
by and large rejected much of the benefits of technological development and proclaimed society had failed at the one thing that truly mattered: human freedom.
The material benefits of technology and capitalism were seen as traps, things that
had blinded people to the oppression of blacks, women, and all minorities. And this
critique wasn't limited to technologically advanced societies:

> In country after country of the so-called Third World, the populaces turned
> against the movements of the Old Left and charged fraud. . . . [The people of
> the world] had lost faith in their states as the agents of a modernity of liber-
> ation. (Wallerstein, 1995, p. 484)

The 1968 movements in particular rejected American hegemony because of its
emphasis on material wealth and hypocrisy in liberation.

In Wallerstein's scheme, the collapse of Communism was simply an extension of
this revolt, one that most clearly pointed out the failure of state government to

produce equality for all: "Even the most radical rhetoric was no guarantor of the modernity of liberation, and probably a poor guarantor of the modernity of technology" (p. 484). Interestingly, Wallerstein sees the collapse of Leninism as a disaster for world capitalism. Leninism had constrained the "dangerous classes," those groups oppressed through capitalist ideology and practice. Communism represented an alternative hope to the contradictions found in capitalist states. With the alternative hope gone, "The dangerous classes may now become truly dangerous once again. Politically, the world-system has become unstable" (p. 484).

Structurally, the upheavals of 1968 occurred at the beginning of a K-wave B-cycle. In other words, the world was standing at the brink of an economic downturn or stagnation, which lasted through the 1970s and 1980s. As we've seen, such B-cycles occur throughout the Kondratieff wave, but this one was particularly deep. The 20-year economic stagnation became an important political issue because of the prosperity of the preceding A-cycle. From 1945 to 1970, the world experienced more economic growth and prosperity than ever. Thus the economic downturn gave continued credence and extra political clout to worldwide social movements. Economically, the world-system responded to the downturn by attempting to roll back production costs by reducing pay scales, lowering taxes associated with the welfare state (education, medical benefits, retirement payments), and re-externalizing input costs (infrastructure, toxicity, raw materials). There was also a shift from the idea of developmentalism to globalization, which calls for the free flow of goods and capital through all nations.

However, while the world-system is putting effort into regaining the A-cycle, there are at least three structural problems hindering economic rebound. First, as we've noted, there are limits to exporting exploitation. Four hundred years of capitalism have depleted the world's supply of cheap labor. Every K-wave has brought continued geographic expansion, and it appears that we have reached the limit of that expansion. More and more of the world's workforce is using their political power to increase the share of surplus labor they receive. Inevitably, this will lead to a sharp increase in the costs of labor and production and a corresponding decrease in profit margins. Remember, capitalism is defined by continual accumulation. This worldwide shift, then, represents a critical point in the continuation of the current capitalist system.

Second, there is a squeeze on the middle classes. Typically, the middle classes are seen as the market base of a capitalist economy. And, as we've seen, a standard method of pulling out of a downturn is to increase the available spending money for the middle classes, either through tax breaks or through salary increases. This additional money spurs an increase in commodity purchases and subsequently in production and capital accumulation. However, this continual expanding of middle-class wages is becoming too much for firms and states to bear. One of two things must happen: Either these costs will be rolled back or they will not. If they are not reduced, "both states and enterprises will be in grave trouble and frequent bankruptcy" (Wallerstein, 1995, p. 485). If they are rolled back, "there will be significant political disaffection among precisely the strata that have provided the strongest support for the present world-system" (p. 485).

Third, as we've noted, accumulation is based on externalizing costs. Two of those costs, raw material depletion and toxicity, have natural limits and it appears that we might be reaching them. Global warming, ozone rupture, destruction of the rain forests, and land degradation from waste are themes with which we are all familiar. Nowhere does the idea of natural limits come out more clearly than in the work of Peter Vitousek, professor of biosciences at Stanford University.

Vitousek, Ehrlich, Ehrlich, and Matson (1986) argue that directly (through consumption) and indirectly (through toxic waste), human beings presently use up about 40% of the world's net primary production (NPP), which represents the rate of production of biomass that is available for consumption by all plants and animals. In other words, of the total amount of energy available for life on this planet, human beings use 40% of it. Predicting the earth's long-term ability to support human life is difficult to calculate, because it depends on the wealth of the population and the kinds of technologies supporting it, but we can see that humans use up a hugely disproportionate amount of the earth's resources (we are but one of some 5–30 million animal species on the planet) and we can see that the resources of the earth are finite.

But limits aren't the only concern; toxic waste has been accumulating for years. Typically, firms take the cheapest way of handling waste—dump it on someone else's property—until public outcry motivates governments to pass laws restricting dumping. But the laws are not retroactive, and it appears difficult to assign responsibility. The result is that government, not industry, tends to pay for the bulk of cleanup. According to an article in the *Washington Post*, "The number of toxic or hazardous sites requiring federal attention continues to grow, and Congress will have to spend at least $14 billion to $16.4 billion over the coming decade just to keep pace with the problem" (Pianin, 2001, p. A19).

Structural and Cultural Signs of the End

Wallerstein argues that world-systems enter a time of chaos during transition periods. How things change or into what form is not predictable. A world-system runs its cyclical courses through the Kondratieff wave, with periods of growth and stagnation, finally ending in collapse. A new configuration emerges out of this rubble, but, unlike Marx, Wallerstein offers no clear predictions. However, Wallerstein does argue that the uprising of 1968 marked the beginning of the end of the current world-system. We can see not only the clear marks of the dialectical cycles near the end of a 150-year Kondratieff wave, we can also see that the structural supports upon which capitalism has been built are limited and nearing exhaustion.

There are also cultural and structural signs that indicate that the system is in the uncertainty of transition. Wallerstein points to two cultural signs: the introduction of complexity theory in science and postmodern theory in the social sciences. In the past 15 years or so, a significant number of physical scientists and mathematicians have turned against the causal predictability of Newtonian physics. Newtonian physics postulated a universe run according to universal laws—laws that in all time and in every place could explain, predict, and control the physical features of the cosmos. Currently, many scientists are saying that Newtonian physics is a special case of reality; it fits only in circumstances that are clearly circumscribed or limited. The tools of science must therefore incorporate more flexible schemes with wider scopes of application. And so today we hear of complexity theory, chaos theory, strange attractors, fuzzy logic, and so on. Wallerstein's (1995) point is this: "The natural world and all its phenomena have become historicized" (p. 486). That is, the scientific view of the universe has historically changed: The old science was built on a mechanistic, linear view of the universe; the new science is not linear nor is it mechanistic.

The idea of a historicized science is an oxymoron, at least from the initial perspective of science. Science assumed that the universe is empirical and operates according to law-like principles. These principles could be discovered and used by humans to understand, predict, and control their world. Science was in the business of producing abstract and universal truths, not truths that only hold under certain conditions. The historicity of society has always been an argument against the possibility of social science, precisely because the factors that influence human behavior and society change according to the context. The hard, laboratory sciences have now become susceptible to the same critique: According to complexity theory, all knowledge is contextual and contingent; nothing is universal and certain. "Hence the new science raises the most fundamental questions about the modernity of technology" (Wallerstein, 1995, p. 486).

The scene in the social sciences has followed suit and become even less certain than it was before. In the past 25 years, the most vocal and influential voice in the social sciences has been postmodernism (see Chapter 14). Postmodernism in its most radical form, as it was brought into the social sciences, argues that the social world in technologically advanced societies is a virtual or hyper-real world. The cultural signs, symbols, and images that we use aren't connected to any social reality. Most of them come not from real social groups in face-to-face interaction, but are, in fact, produced by media and advertising concerns.

As a result of this cultural fragmentation and the new doubts in science, all grand narratives are held in distrust. Grand or meta-narratives are stories that attempt to embrace large populations of people. Typically, grand narratives are generated by political groups (as in nationalism and national identities). In their place, postmodernism advocates polyvocality, or many voices. Postmodernism argues that all voices are equal and should be given equal weight. These voices are of course linked to specific groups, such as men, women, blacks, Chicanos, and all the subdivisions within the groups, such as bisexual-Chicano-Catholic males. There is thus an ethical dimension to postmodernism—"It is a mode of rejecting the modernity of technology on behalf of the modernity of liberation" (Wallerstein, 1995, p. 487).

The two structural signs that indicate we are in a time of chaotic transition are financial speculation and worldwide organization of social movements. There has been limited success in rolling back costs and reducing the press on profits, but not nearly what was needed or hoped for. As a result, capitalists have sought profit in the area of financial speculation rather than production. Many have taken great profits from this kind of speculation, but it also "renders the world-economy very volatile and subject to swings of currencies and of employment. It is in fact one of the signs of increasing chaos" (Wallerstein, 2004, p. 86).

On the political scene, since 1968 there has been a shift from movements for electoral changes to the "organization of a movement of movements" (Wallerstein, 2004, p. 86). Rather than national movements seeking change through voting within the system, radical groups are binding together internationally to seek change within the world-system. Wallerstein offers the World Social Forum (WSF) as an example. It is not itself an organization, but a virtual space for meetings among various militant groups seeking social change.

Another indicator of this political decentralization is the increase in terrorist attacks worldwide, such as the strike on the World Trade Center, September 11, 2001, and the bomb attacks on London, July 7, 2005. The terrorist groups themselves are decentralized, nonstate entities, which makes conflict between a state like the United States and these entities difficult. Nation-states are particular kinds of entities defined by a number of factors, most importantly by territory, rational law, and a standing military. These factors and the political orientation they bring mean that nation-states are most efficient at confronting other nation-states, ones that have specified territories, that legitimate rational law, and that have modern militaries. Almost everything about the terrorist groups that the United States is facing is antithetical to these qualities of the nation-state. The United States is a centralized state and the terrorists are decentralized groups. These differences in social structure and relation to physical place make it extremely difficult for the United States to engage the terrorists—there is no interface between the two—let alone defeat or make peace with them.

But more than that, the attacks of September 11 have energized politically right-wing groups in the United States. It has allowed them to cut ties with the political center and "to pursue a program centered around unilateral assertions by the United States of military strength combined with an attempt to undo the cultural evolution of the world-system that occurred after the world revolution of 1968 (particularly in the fields of race and sexuality)" (Wallerstein, 2004, p. 87). This, along with attempts to do away with many of the geopolitical structures set in place after 1945 (like the United Nations), has "threatened to worsen the already-increasing instability of the world-system" (p. 87).

These issues are the reason that Wallerstein (1999) talks about the demise of **world-systems theory.** Remember, world-systems theory is a critical perspective of global capitalism. As global capitalism fails, the insights that world-systems thinking can give us will become less significant. Yet in the remaining years of global capitalism, world-systems theory gives us a critical perspective for social involvement.

What will follow the 400-year reign of capitalism is uncertain. World-systems theory, as Wallerstein sees it, is meant to call our attention to thinking in structural time and cyclical processes; it is meant to lift our eyes from the mundane problems of our lives so that we can perceive the world-system in all its historical power to set the stage of our lives; it is intended to give us the critical perspective to have eyes to see and ears to hear the Marxian dynamics still at work within the capitalist system; and, finally, it is intended to spur us to action. Unlike C. Wright Mills (1956), Wallerstein is not saying that "great changes are beyond [our] control"; rather, he means that "fundamental change is possible . . . and this fact makes claims on our moral responsibility to act rationally, in good faith, and with strength to seek a better historical system" (Wallerstein, 1999, p. 3). Because the system is in a period of transition where "small inputs have large outputs" (p. 1) and "every small action during this period is likely to have significant consequences" (Wallerstein, 2004, p. 77), we must make diligent efforts to understand what is going on; we must make choices about the direction in which we want the world to move; and we must bring our convictions into action, because it is our behaviors that will affect the system. In Wallerstein's (2004) words,

> We can think of these three tasks as the intellectual, the moral, and the political tasks. They are different, but they are closely interlinked. None of us can opt out of any of these tasks. If we claim we do, we are merely making a hidden choice. (p. 90)

Summary

- Wallerstein sees his work more in terms of a type of analysis than a specific theory. His point is that it is the principles of analysis that drive the theorizing rather than the other way around. There are two main features of Wallerstein's perspective: globality and historicity. Globality conceptualizes the world in system terms, which cut across cultural and political boundaries. Historicity sees history in terms of structural time and cyclical time within the structures, rather than focusing on events, people, and linearity.

- In terms of theory, Wallerstein takes a Marxian approach. He focuses on the division of labor, exploitation, and the processes of accumulation and overproduction. In Marxian theory, exploitation is the chief source of profit. Thus, capitalists are intrinsically motivated to increase the level of exploitation. And since wages tend to go up as capitalist economies mature, reducing the level of exploitation and profit, there is therefore a constant tendency to export exploitation to nations that have a less developed capitalist economy, thus increasing the worldwide division of labor.

- Capitalist accumulation implies that capital is invested for the purpose of creating more capital, which in turn is invested in order to create more capital. In modern capitalism, this process of accumulation is augmented by the state. The state specifically bears the costs associated with transportation, toxicity, and the exhaustion of materials. More powerful states additionally provide conditions that facilitate quasi-monopolies, thus increasing capitalists' profits and the rate of accumulation.

- Overproduction is endemic to capitalism as well. Because they are driven by the capitalist need for accumulation, commodification (the process through which material and nonmaterial goods are turned into products for sale) and production are intrinsically expansive. Capitalists will continue to create new and produce existing commodities until the market will no longer bear it, thus creating more supply than demand.

- Taken together, the processes of exploitation and the division of labor and the dynamics of accumulation and overproduction create a scenario in which there is a continual movement of products and labor from more powerful to less powerful nations.

- In the world-economy, there are four types of nations: the core, semi-periphery, the periphery, and external areas. In general, exploitation and mass production of least-profitable goods move from the core to the external areas. However, because this is a system, there is also a move of nations as they transition from external to peripheral to core. Eventually, there will be no more areas to exploit with low-profit mass production, which will lead to system breakdown.

- The world-economy thus tends to go through cycles of expansion, depression, and breakdown. These cycles reach a crisis about every 150 years. According to Wallerstein, the world is now in its fourth phase of world economics. The last phase began in 1917, with the United States as the world-economy's core nation. Wallerstein marks the beginning of the end of this phase with the social upheavals of 1968. In addition to the social movements, the world-economy entered a cycle of depression that was particularly deep and lasted for about 20 years. While the world-economy is actively trying to come back from this economic depression, there are three factors that are inhibiting this attempt: the system limits to exploitation; the middle-class squeeze; and the limited ability of states to pick up externalized costs. Thus, Wallerstein argues that the world-system is on the brink of collapse and is currently experiencing the chaotic period that always precedes such an end.

TAKING THE PERSPECTIVE

I said something in the beginning of this chapter that I now need to put in context. Wallerstein prefers the word *globality* to *globalization.* The reason for this is that the term is generally thought of in ahistorical, market economy terms. For example, the 2001 Nobel Prize winner in Economic Sciences, Joseph E. Stiglitz (2003), defines *globalization* as

> the closer integration of the countries and peoples of the world which has been brought about by the enormous reduction of costs of transportation and communication, and the breaking down of artificial barriers to the flows of goods, services, capital, knowledge, and (to a lesser extent) people across borders. (Stiglitz, 2003, p. 9)

Notice that in this definition the focus is on the market flow of goods, services, capital, and so forth; that there is no mention of system (other than "closer integration") nor is there any sense of history. The latter two are of specific concern to Wallerstein and world-systems theorists because without the ideas of history and system, the descriptions of globalization are atheoretical (without theory). World-systems analysis, on the other hand, can be theoretical precisely because it understands the phenomena using the general dynamics of systems theory that are able to account for historical changes and predict future outcomes.

(Continued)

(Continued)

Wallerstein intentionally uses the hyphen in *world-systems theory* to emphasize that he is talking about systems that constitute a world or a distinct way of existing. This approach looks at society as an interrelated whole, with every internal part systemically influencing the others. A systems approach additionally places emphasis on the relationship between the system and its environment. Thus, world-systems analysis argues that nations or collectives change in response to systemic factors that press upon it from the outside. For example, according to world- systems analysis, Peru isn't "modernizing" because it is something every nation will do; Peru is modernizing because it is caught in a global capitalist system that is pressuring it to change. Thus, world-systems analysis focuses on factors that cut across cultural and political boundaries and create an "integrated zone of activity and institutions which obey certain systemic rules" (Wallerstein, 2004, p. 17).

If social actors such as nations, institutions, and groups are related to each other through a specific system, then the history of that system is extremely important for understanding how the system is working presently. Wallerstein picked up the notions of structural time and cyclical process from French historian and educator Fernand Braudel (1981–1984). Braudel criticized event-dominated history as being too idiographic and political; this is the kind of history with which we are most familiar. The prefix "idio" specifically refers to the individual or one's own. Idiographic knowledge, then, is focused on unique individuals and their events. An example of this event history approach is to understand U.S. history in terms of things like Abraham Lincoln and the Civil War and Martin Luther King Jr. and the civil rights movement. Such an understanding doesn't see changes through history as the result of systematic social facts, but, rather, it perceives historical change as occurring through unique events and political figures—in other words, idiographic history is atheoretical.

Braudel felt that this kind of history is dust and tells us nothing about the true historical processes. Yet Braudel also criticized the opposite approach, nomothetic knowledge. The word *nomothetic* is related to the Greek word *nomos,* which means law. The goal in seeking nomothetic knowledge, like that of science, is to discover the abstract and universal laws that underpin the physical universe. According to Braudel, when nomothetic knowledge is sought in the social sciences, it more often than not creates mythical, grand stories that legitimate the search for universal laws instead of explaining historical social history.

Wallerstein's idea of *historicity* lies between the ideographic focus on events and the law-like knowledge of science. Rather than focusing on events, Wallerstein's approach concentrates on the history of structures within a world-system. For example, capitalism is a world-system that has its own particular history. There have always been people who have produced products to make a profit, but the capitalism of modernity, the kind that Weber (1904–1905/2002) termed "rational capitalism," is unique to a particular time period. An account of rational capitalism from its beginnings, from around the sixteenth century, that would include all the principal players (such as nations, firms, households, and so forth) and their systemic relations is what Wallerstein has in mind.

Historicity thus includes the unique variable of time. In taking account of world-systems rather than event history, historicity is centered upon structural time and the cyclical time within the structures. Wallerstein is telling us that structures have histories, and it is the history of structures with which we should be concerned, rather than events, because structures set the frames within which human behavior and meaning take place. Structures have life spans, they are born and they die, and within that span there are cyclical processes.

BUILDING YOUR THEORY TOOLBOX

Learning More—Primary Sources

- Wallerstein built his theory through three volumes of historical data (*The Modern World-System,* I, II, III). The historical breadth is impressive and convincing, but I would suggest you begin your reading of Wallerstein with his later works:

  o *The End of the World as We Know It: Social Science for the Twenty-First Century,*University of Minnesota Press, 1999.

  o *World-Systems Analysis: An Introduction,* Duke University Press, 2004.

  o A good chapter-length introduction to this perspective is provided by Christopher Chase-Dunn, "World-Systems Theorizing," in *Handbook of Sociological Theory,* edited by Jonathan H. Turner, Kluwer, 2002.

Check It Out

- *Globalization:* For an overview of globalization studies in sociology, read Saskia Sassen's *A Sociology of Globalization,* W. W. Norton, 2007. For a simple yet satisfying introduction to a more general approach, see Manfred B. Steger's *Globalization: A Very Short Introduction,* Oxford, 2009. And from an economist's perspective, Joseph E. Stiglitz's *Globalization and Its Discontents,* W. W. Norton, 2003.

Seeing the World

- Write a 250-word synopsis of the theoretical perspective of world-systems theory.

- After reading and understanding this chapter, you should be able to define the following terms theoretically and explain their theoretical importance to world-systems analysis: *modern capitalism, globalization, systems, exploitation, dialectical materialism, division of labor, externalized costs, quasi-monopolies, overproduction, world-empires, world-economies, core states, periphery states, semi-periphery states, Kondratieff waves, world-systems theory*

- After reading and understanding this chapter, you should be able to answer the following questions (remember to answer them *theoretically*):

  o What are the central features that link national economies into a global system?

  o In what ways do states externalize costs and help create quasi-monopolies?

  o What are the Marxian economic dynamics in back of the relationships among the core, semi-periphery, periphery, and external areas? Explain how these dynamics work and how they are related to the demise of capitalism.

  o What are Kondratieff waves and how do they factor into global changes?

(Continued)

(Continued)

- Beginning with the events in 1968, explain Wallerstein's crisis of modernity. What are the structural and cultural signs that the system is failing?

- In the face of this crisis, what recommendations does Wallerstein have for political involvement? Be certain to explain his rationale for saying these recommendations will influence the system.

Engaging the World

- In reference to his work, Wallerstein (2000) has said, "My intellectual biography is one long question for an adequate explanation of contemporary reality that I and others might act upon" (p. xv). In keeping with Wallerstein, I have only one question to put to you: After reading Wallerstein, how will you engage your world?

Weaving the Threads

- Consider the approaches to inequality given us by Chafetz, Bourdieu, and now Wallerstein, and then answer the following questions: What kinds of inequalities or scarce resources are the most important in each theory? What kinds of structures perpetuate these inequalities? How is social change possible for each of these theorists? Can these three theories complement one another?

CHAPTER 10

The Network Society:

Manuel Castells

(1942–)

A s we saw in Chapter 9, our social situation has dramatically changed since the beginning of modernity and the time of "classical" theory—it appears as if our lives are impacted by systems that are global in size. Wallerstein's theory, however, fits rather well in the modern mold. He continues to talk about capitalism in terms of commodification, exploitation, and the relations of production—it's the global division of labor that connects us, according to Wallerstein. And nation-states continue to play a significant role especially in facilitating capitalist growth; and capitalism is still centered on production. All of these issues can be found in Marx's theory; in fact, the basic theoretical move that Wallerstein makes is to move Marxian dynamics from the national to international level. But what if society is no longer based on our usual ideas of social structure, capitalist production, and political states? What if there's another system, one that was utterly outside the comprehension of classical theorists such as Marx, Weber, and Durkheim? What if rather than empirical, concrete reality being supremely important, it is something less tangible and more virtual in terms of time and space? What if the ideas of American, German, or Mexican society are less viable than ever before? What if civil society and democratic nations are no longer feasible? These are the possibilities that Manuel Castells asks us to consider.

THEORIST'S DIGEST

Brief Biography

Manuel Castells (1942–) was born in La Mancha, Spain, and grew up in Valencia and Barcelona. In college, he studied law and economics and received his PhD in sociology and another in human sciences from the University of Paris–Sorbonne in 1967. While in Paris, he was a political activist, fighting against Franco's dictatorship. He taught sociology at the University of Paris from 1967 to 1979. In 1979, he took a professorship at the University of California, Berkeley; then, in 2003, he moved to the University of Southern California Annenberg School for Communication. Castells has written 22 books, coauthored 21, and has over 100 articles published in academic journals. His most influential works are his trilogy, *The Information Age: Economy, Society, and Culture*, which has been translated into over 23 languages. Among his many awards and distinctions is the C. Wright Mills Award from the American Society for the Study of Social Problems, the Robert and Helen Lynd Award from the American Sociological Association, the National Medal of Science from Catalonia, and the Lifelong Research Award from the Committee on Computers and Information Technology of the American Sociological Association.

Central Sociological Questions

Castells' early work focuses on the issue of urban space. He uses a Marxian approach to understand how social conflicts transform the urban landscape. This initial concern with space and politics led him to consider how both are affected by information technologies. In the work we focus on here, Castells asks, How does the intrusion of computer networks impact the space in which people connect and express issues of power and identity?

Simply Stated

Castells argues that computer and information technologies have dramatically impacted human existence. These technologies have lifted out social relationships, the work of capitalism, and political activism from the boundaries of the nation-state. What we mean by society, then, is more in keeping with the dictates of computer networks than the modern ideas of national society and democracy. Importance and power in a network are determined by how much information, symbols, and imagery a position can hold and process. The basis of class has changed as well, from production to managing work and flows of capital. Political activities have also shifted from the content of a political platform to control of image and negative information.

Key Ideas

Keynesian economics, information technology, the logic of networks, annihilation of time and place, power, class, politics, identities, legitimizing identity, resistance identity, project identity, civil society, symbol mobilizers, new democracy

Concepts and Theory: Information Technology

Castells' idea is that the information revolution that began in the 1980s has restructured capitalism and created a global society that is connected via networks. Prior to World War II, the capitalist system had played out its Marxist dynamics and was in a worldwide, inexorable depression—there was no way out. Socialist movements were gaining power globally, and there was a good chance that capitalism would have collapsed had it not been for the war. During the Great Depression of the 1930s, John Maynard Keynes (1936) published a new theory of economics. The basic tenet of *Keynesian economics* is that the state can moderate the effects of free-market capitalism through controlling interest rates and by investing in the economic infrastructure, thus becoming a major consumer. But, Castells argues, Keynesian economics, just like laissez-faire capitalism before it, had built-in contradictions and limitations, which came to a head by the 1970s and resulted in rampant inflation.

From the 1970s into the 1990s, massive efforts at restructuring capitalism were under way. There were four goals: (1) Deepen the logic of profitability; (2) improve the profitability of both capital and labor; (3) globalize commodity and labor markets; and (4) use the state to maximize the profitability of the national economy, even at the cost of social programs and education. Essential to this project was flexibility, such as "just-in-time" (JIT) inventory strategies, and adaptability. Castells (2000b) argues that this attempt at restructuring would have been extremely limited without the new information technology.

By *new information technology*, Castells has in mind computer technologies, both hardware and software, which, when coupled with the Internet, have connected humanity in a way that was up to this point unthinkable. As a result of information technology, space and time have become more abstract and infinitely less meaningful in terms of patterning and organizing social connections. We can, for example, have virtual face-to-face meetings with people in China, England, the United States, and Argentina at the same "time." Further, and perhaps more importantly, information has become the focal point of economic practices and growth. As the name indicates, information technologies act on information. In industrial societies, technologies act on the production process. For example, Ford's assembly-line technology, along with mass-produced, interchangeable parts, broke down the process of making a car into a series of simple tasks that unskilled workers could perform. So profound was the effect of this technology on economic production that it became known as "Fordism."

Information technologies, however, act upon information. As an example, let's consider something that falls a bit outside of Castells' concerns, but that most of us can relate to: music recording and playback. Before the digital age, music was recorded using analog technologies. Analog recording stores music as a continuous wave in or on the media (phonograph record or magnetic tape). It's called analog because the waves imprinted on the media are *analogous* to the sound waves of the music (the same basic idea applies to video recordings). In digital recording, the music is translated into discrete numbers or data. The first step in this information technology was developed in 1937 by British scientist Alec Reeves—he invented Pulse Code Modulation, one of the platforms upon which today's digital technology is based; and every step since then has involved innovations in how technology can store, transmit, and play back information. The production of these technologies for consumption is a secondary move: In a network society, technical innovation is focused primarily on producing and reproducing information—commodification comes later.

The most important informational technologies have focused on computers and communication. Ever since the first digital computer was invented in the early 1940s, each new technology has been directed at storing and using information. Castells (2000b) argues that this move to information technologies is having and will continue to have pervasive effects because human activity is based on information. There have been three major technological advances that have fundamentally influenced knowledge and information: the alphabet (written language), the printing press, and the computer. We know that the effects of the first two advances were tremendous. Civilization itself is indebted to written language, and the advent of the printing press led to the rise and spread of the Protestant Reformation, the Renaissance, and the Scientific Revolution. In addition, because the first commercially viable printed book was the Bible, and there was no comparable text in Asian countries, mechanized printing did not take hold as rapidly there, which in turn facilitated the European advantage over the East in the Industrial Revolution and technological domination. The printing press also influenced the way in which people think. The transmission of information changed from artistic expression (with hand printing) to chiefly textual. This shift facilitated the conversion from metaphorical to linear thinking. Castells is concerned with the third technological advancement in communication and information—the computer—and its influence in structuring society.

Power, Politics, and Class in the Network Society

The most significant effect of computer technology Castells sees is that *the logic of networks* will be the basis of the new social system. The idea of a network is rather straightforward. It is a set of interconnected points or "nodes," and nodes are simply places where the threads or paths of the network cross. Networks can be made up of any number of things, like networks of exchange. Castells is concerned with information networks, the nodes of which are points where information is held or processed. This kind of network is possible because of computer and communication technologies, and it is defined by those technologies.

Let's think for a moment about a computer network. Because the basic properties of networks are the same, you can choose any network, such as AIM (America Online Instant Messenger), the network at your place of work, the Internet as a whole, and so on. Networks are open and extremely flexible structures. They can be of almost any size and can change without threatening the balance of the whole. Networks have no center, and they work on the binary inclusion/exclusion model: That is, a node is either in the network or not; if a node ceases to function, it's eliminated and the network is rearranged—for example, your computer can move into or out of a network without affecting the network as such. There is no distance between nodes and no time element; rather than distance, such as between my computer and yours, what matters in networks are restrictions on the flow of information, and time, if used at all, is simply a marker of flow (e.g., when you sent your email). A node becomes important in a network either because it can hold and process information more efficiently, or because it functions as a switch that connects different networks. Once programmed, networks function automatically and impose their logic on all the social actors using it.

Such computerized informational networks have redefined the material basis of life in our society. All animals, including humans, are fundamentally related to time and space, but computing and network technologies have changed that relationship. Rather than the biological clock of human existence, or the mechanical clock of the industrial age, new communication technologies *annihilate time and place*. Rather than the essentialness of place, new information technologies have reoriented us to a space of flows, where exists the "organizational possibility of organizing the simultaneity of social practices without geographic contiguity" (Castells, 2000a, p. 14). Thus, social organization is set free from the confines of time and space. This freedom is so profound in its implications that Castells (2000b) marks the information age as the beginning of human history, "if by history we understand the moment when . . . our species has reached the level of knowledge and social organization that will allow us to live in a predominantly social world" (pp. 508–509).

Power in any such network is dramatically reorganized from the hierarchical model of bureaucracies and social inequalities. Power in networks is a function of a node's ability to find, hold, and process information. Nodes that can act as switches between informational networks are power-holders: "Since networks are multiple, the inter-operating codes and switches between networks become the fundamental sources in shaping, guiding, and misguiding societies" (Castells, 2000b, p. 502). More importantly, the informational network has provided the structure for the core activities of a global economy. Currently, the bulk of capital accumulation results from financial flows rather than production. Profit from production and consumption, from organizations and institutions, is extracted and reverted to the financial flows. Capital is then invested globally, following interests of greatest return, which are increasingly based on speculation and money markets rather than real goods and services. Financial flows are thus based on theoretical knowledge and timeliness of information. This "electronically operated global casino" decides the "fate of corporations, household savings, national currencies, and regional economies" (Castells, 2000b, p. 503).

The network society has dramatically affected *class* as well. It results first in capitalism without capitalists. The legal owners of any large business—Marx's definition of capitalists—are found in investment funds and individual portfolios, both of which are subject to networks of speculative management. The corporate managers don't make up a capitalist class either, because they do not control, nor do they know about, the movements of capital in networks of financial flows. Rather than a class that holds and uses capital, the global capital network is a network of networks that "are ultimately dependent upon the nonhuman capitalist logic of an electronically operated, random processing of information" (Castells, 2000b, p. 505).

The working class has likewise been redefined by the logics of networks. Labor has become exceedingly general. Rather than the specified labor of production, it's labor as a generic part of speculative capitalism—labor becomes a piece on the global chessboard of capital flows. Capital and labor increasingly exist in different spaces and times: capital in the space of flows and the instant/constant time of computerized communication, and labor in the space of places and the time of clocks and daily life. "At its core, capital is global. As a rule, labor is local" (Castells, 2000b, p. 506). What becomes organized through networks is work, rather than labor. The work of organizations is carried on in network fashion. Each contributing member is a node, and the network as a whole can be made up of individuals; segments of businesses; or entire companies, large or small. They can be dispersed over thousands of miles and exist in different clock-time zones. All this and more can be coordinated for a single project, thus forming an informational network. As soon as the project is finished, the nodes are disconnected and reorganized for other work. The work process is thus globally integrated but fragmented locally, resulting in the individuation of labor, increased flexibility, and instability of work.

The organizational logic of communication and informational technologies has reformed *politics* as well. In most places around the world, people now get their information about political candidates through the media, which has become the platform for politics. In a media-saturated environment, capturing attention becomes the single most important scarce resource. Politics thus becomes personalized in the cult of personality, "and image-making is power-making" (Castells, 2000b, p. 507). In the spectacle of image, with a public (an audience) dulled by a constant barrage of images and information, the most effective messages are negative: "assassination of opponents' personalities, and/or of their supporting organizations" (2000a, p. 13). Thus, the information of value in politics is anything that will spark a scandal. An entire network revolves around finding, protecting, and leaking this valued information. "Politics becomes a horse race, and a tragicomedy motivated by greed, backstage manoeuvres [sic], betrayals, and, often, sex and violence— a genre increasingly indistinguishable from TV scripts" (p. 13).

Politics cannot but influence the *state,* and the politics of spectacle and reliance on the media undermine its legitimacy and power. In response, personalities begin to build informational networks and systems of deference around themselves, further challenging the legitimacy of the state. State power is also challenged by the global flows of money and information. Part of this has to do with the pure size of capital flows and the volatility of money markets, but more basically, since the nation-state has always been defined in terms of "subordinating to orderly domination . . . a 'territory'" (Weber, 1922/1968, p. 901), the breakdown of time and space (territory) by the network society deeply undermines the power of the state. In response, states partner with other nations and build multinational and international organizational, informational networks, such as the World Trade Organization, NATO, the International Monetary Fund, and so on. The result is that "the new state is no longer a nation-state" (Castells, 2000a, p. 14); rather, it is a network state created out of negotiated decision making and power sharing.

Concepts and Theory:
Networks, Identities, and Democracy

For Castells, *identities* are clusters of cultural traits that function to provide meaning for people. In order to see the implications of this, think back to the fundamental attributes of meaning from Chapter 3. Meaning isn't any *thing*—it isn't in an action or a word, it isn't inherent within an experience, nor is it located in any object. Rather, meaning is that which actions, words, and so on express or sign, and signs always point away from themselves—therefore, *meaning is never the thing-in-itself*. And meaning constitutes our reality: "No longer can man confront reality immediately. . . . [It] seems to recede in proportion as man's symbolic activity advances. Instead of dealing with the things themselves, man is in a sense constantly conversing with himself" (Cassirer, 1944, p. 42).

If meaning isn't the actual thing or event, then meaning is achieved or created, and one of the functions of identity is to provide a basis for the construction of biographical narratives of meaning. Castells (2004) defines three different types of identities: The first type, the *legitimizing identity*, is the kind found in the dominant institutions of society. Legitimations are stories or narratives that provide a moral or ethical basis for social power. Legitimizing identities, then, are those around which individuals construct meaning and a sense of self that are related to and legitimate civil society. Obvious examples include the president of the United States, corporate CEOs, male and female genders, heterosexuality, professor, and so on.

The second type in Castells' scheme is *resistance identity*. This type of identity normally comes out of a sense of exclusion from the institutions of civil society and is bound up with the formation of communities of resistance that give members a sense of solidarity and the ability to form countercultures and ideology. These communities and identities can center around such issues as religious views and other status inequities. Because they are resistance identities, they create strong boundaries of inclusion and exclusion and thus work to "exclude the excluders." It's important to note that resistance identities aren't necessarily concerned with social change; they are reactionary and seek to establish an identity where identity has been denied.

This is where the issue of meaning that we talked about above becomes important. Identities provide a meaningful ordering and framework for life. When identities are denied, or controlled to the point of redefining the person, the existential questions of life and purpose come to the forefront—conversely, when identities are unproblematic, the questions of existence are effectively silenced; legitimating identities don't tend to provoke existential questions in those claiming them. Under conditions of exclusion, resistance identities function as cultural, emotional, and psychological strongholds. Their purpose isn't to change, but to proclaim. Often these identities are born out of "the pride of self-denigration" (Castells, 2004, p. 9) and shout back at institutions with proclamations such as "black is beautiful" or "I am woman, hear me roar."

The third type of identity that concerns Castells is the *project identity*. This is an identity associated with social projects of change: "In this case, the building of identity is a project of a different life" (Castells, 2004, p. 10). Project identities produce subjects, but subjects, Castells is very clear about, are not individuals. *Webster's* (2002) defines *subject* variously as "the material from which a thing is formed," "the theme of a discourse or predication," "something that sustains or is embodied in thought or consciousness," or "something that forms a basis (as for action, study, discussion, or use)." Castells' use of the term *subject* captures all of the above. Subjects are collective actors that form the material of our sense of self and our involvement with the world. These subjects are the themes of the discourse of social change; they are the mental and emotional focus through which identity and meaning are sustained in consciousness; and, especially in the case of project identities, the subject forms the basis for action, study, and discussion.

The Network Society and the Crisis in Democracy

Castells (2004) defines *civil society* as "a set of organizations and institutions, as well as a series of structured and organized social actors, which reproduce . . . the identity that rationalizes the sources of structural domination" (p. 8). While civil society isn't identical with the state, it exists in relation to the state; and the state is the "object of citizenship" (p. 402). However, the state is suffering a crisis of legitimation in the network society. Its sovereignty has been undermined by "global flows and trans-organizational networks of wealth, information, and power" (p. 402); by the spectacle of politics; and by the state's increasing inability to fulfill its commitments to the safety net of minimal benefits, including unemployment, retirement income, health care coverage, insuring bank deposits, and so forth. These effects of the network society have created a crisis of legitimation for the nation-state and, by extension, legitimizing identities and democracy.

There are two important effects growing out of this legitimation crisis. First, "a growing majority of citizens do not feel that democracy will help them very much in addressing the issues that confront them in their daily lives" (Castells, 2004, p. 413). One measure of this is what is commonly called voter apathy. In 1960, about 61% of the television sets in the United States were tuned to the October presidential debates, and voter turnout for the presidential election was almost 65% of the adult population. By the year 2000, fewer than 30% of the televisions tuned to the presidential debates, and voter turnout had dropped to 51% (Patterson, 2002).

The second outcome of the legitimation crisis is the ascent of resistance identities. Remember how Castells conceptualizes identities: They function to create meaning. In this case, resistance identities are created to counter the loss of meaning and direction that accompanies the legitimation crisis. To help us get a clear sense of resistance identities in the network society, let's think through the example of gender in Western nations. Prior to the women's suffrage movement of the 1800s and early 1900s, being a "woman" was by and large a legitimizing identity. The identity bound all women together and situated them in the discourse of patriarchy. The identity thus legitimated the family structure as well as the unequal power relations between men and women. The suffrage movements worked to create a project identity committed to gaining equal rights for women, in particular, the right to vote and the right to higher education. In the 1960s, a second wave of feminism emerged to address the unofficial discrimination and inequalities that still existed for women. Equal opportunities for work and political power, equal pay, cultural representations, and control over their bodies were some of the issues. Both the first and second waves of feminism had project identities.

Beginning in the early 1990s, another wave of feminism arose, mostly among young women who had grown up with benefits achieved by the first two waves of feminism. These women also were most affected by the new information and communication technologies. Feminism for these women is different. Rather than having specific political, economic, or social goals, third-wave feminism challenges the definitions of woman, femininity, and feminism, which are seen as creating a sense that all women are essentially the same. All essentializing theories are rejected, including feminist theory, gender theory, conflict theory, and so on. The focus is on deconstructing such totalizing identities and discourses and insisting on diversity. Rather than either a legitimizing or project identity, third-wave feminism denies the possibility of a woman's identity: "Since no monolithic version of 'woman' exists, we can no longer speak with confidence of 'women's issues'; instead, we need to consider that such issues are as diverse as the many women who inhabit our planet" (Dicker & Piepmeier, 2006, p. 107).

While being able to trace the history of feminist identity is enlightening, most resistance identities don't have this evolving background. Today, most resistance identities are formed around such things as religious fundamentalism, geographic region, music styles, and so on. An example that has both region and music is found in Jeff Foxworthy's comments at the 2007 Country Music Television awards ceremony, held in Nashville, Tennessee. Here are a few lines from his speech:

> I like country music because it's about the things in life that really matter. . . . It's about love, family, friends, with a few beers. . . . It doesn't take political sides even on things as ugly as war. Instead, it celebrates the men and women who go to fight 'em. . . . It's about kids and how there ain't nothing like 'em. . . . Country folks love their kids and they will jack you up if you try to

mess with 'em. . . . Country music doesn't have to be politically correct. We sing about God because we believe in Him. . . . It's real music, sung by real people for real people. The people that make up the backbone of this country. . . . You can call us rednecks if you want, we're not offended, 'cause we know what we are all about. We get up and go to work, we get up and go to church, and we get up and go to war when necessary. (Foxworthy, quoted in Martin, 2007)

Foxworthy defined the country music identity by "building trenches of resistance and survival on the basis of principles different from, or opposed to, those permeating the institutions of society" (Castells, 2004, p. 8). Without specifically saying so, the statement builds strong boundaries of exclusion for anyone outside country music or the values proclaimed, and it simultaneously builds a sense of community and solidarity for country music fans. Within that solidarity, it allows little if any diversity: "In contrast to pluralistic, differentiated civil societies, cultural communes display little internal differentiation" (p. 70). That is one of the qualities of resistance identities: They provide a strong cultural center, a clear sense of right and wrong, a solid ground for meaning.

Resistance identities in the network society are acts of cultural resistance, with no real political or economic goals. Much like a third-wave feminist concerned with expressing gender, Foxworthy's country music fan is concerned with the meanings surrounding identity. They both draw a line in the sand and proclaim, this is who I am. Moreover, as you can see with both examples, resistance identities are individualized. There's a sense of cultural community that accompanies these identities, and there are clear meanings associated with them, but neither of them requires or implies that members actually group together. You can be a country music fan and believe in the boundaries that Foxworthy proclaims, and never once get together with other fans. Further, if and when you do get together, the focus will probably be on music and beer, "With a cheap woman and two-timin' man thrown in for spice" (Foxworthy, quoted in Martin, 2007). The center of discussion would probably not be political activism. If you do talk about ideas or values with which you disagree, it likely won't be with any intent of creating a project to bring about change. It will simply be a ritual that generates high levels of emotional energy that will make your identity and beliefs feel more sacred. Resistance identities thus create a strong sense of meaning in a world where meanings are becoming delegitimized and fragmented.

With the sources of legitimizing identities weakened or gone, the shared identities necessary for democracy are no longer present. Further, and this is extremely important to note, project identities in and of themselves are suffering the same fate as legitimizing identities, because both share the same social basis: the civil sphere and democratic government defined by the nation-state. What Castells' theory implies is that that form of society is gone or receding; social connections now being made through the network society that is not bounded or limited by the state. The structural, systemic bases of participatory democracy as understood from the eighteenth century through the ending decades of the twentieth are gone. And resistance identities by themselves are nothing more than emotional constructs that give individuals and small groups a sense of meaning and purpose.

However, resistance identities can form the basis of new project identities. In fact, Castells (2004) argues that resistance identities could "be *the main potential source* of social change in the network society" (p. 70, emphasis added). These new project identities do not come out of the industrial era's "identities of civil society" (p. 422) but may emerge from the intense interactions around cultural resistance. For example, while there's an emphasis on choice in what passes as gender (expressions of femininity) in third-wave feminism, there are also a good number of third wavers who are deeply involved in political activism, not always for women's rights. So, for instance, a third-wave feminist may have a project identity built around environmental issues—specifically feminist-as-environmentalist—yet at the same time she expresses her gender identity as resistance. However, there is nothing about resistance identities that necessarily implies project identities. Resistance identities thus represent a further danger to the idea of participatory democracy. Rather than creating new project identities, these resistance communes could simply maintain their inward gaze, occupied only with keeping the meaningfulness of their own identities. Castells (2004) ironically characterizes such narcissism as "inducing a process that might transform communal heavens into heavenly hells" (p. 70).

Among the resistance identities Castells (2004) lists as possibilities for project identities are religious communes, ethnicity, gender, territorial identities, environmentalism, and so on. Again, please notice that the content—what the identity is about—is virtually unimportant, in terms of it being the basis of a project identity. The deciding factor between resistance and project identities is the intent to bring change. In other words, project identities have projects. Project identities in the network society, however, don't generally work the same as in industrial society. As we've seen, the network society implies a new form of power. Rather than the political power of civil society, network power resides in codes of information and images of representation. Conflict over power in the network society is a battle for people's minds: "Whoever, or whatever, wins the battle of people's minds will rule, because mighty, rigid apparatuses will not be a match, in any reasonable timespan, for the minds mobilized around the power of flexible, alternative networks" (Castells, 2004, p. 425).

According to Castells, there are two types of *symbol mobilizers,* those social actors able to influence information and imagery. First, there are the Prophets, symbolic personalities that can create information and imagery and mobilize the network. Recent examples include Bono of U2 (and his work on AIDS and developing nation debt forgiveness), Angelina Jolie (protesting use of landmines, helping refugees), and Sting (and his work with Amazonia, helping to save the Amazon rain forests). The second and more important avenue for mobilizing symbols and information around project identities is the decentralized activity of the network itself. The Internet can of course be used to gather people together for rallies, demonstrations, and so on. But its greatest impact is on people's awareness, thinking, and feelings about the project issue. In contrast to the Prophet motif, this "impact on society rarely stems from a concerted strategy, masterminded by a center" (Castells, 2004, p. 427). Decentralized, flexible networks of information and communication around issues of environmentalism, women's lives, sweatshop working conditions, refugees, human rights violations, and so on produce and distribute news, ideas, insights, explanations, strategies, and images around the world, thus impacting the way people see and interface with the world.

This network of social change is the breeding ground for a *new democracy*. Its form is different, without the "orderly battalions, colorful banners, and scripted proclamations" (Castells, 2004, p. 428) of civil society; and it's thus difficult to recognize. But for the same reason, there is a continuing

> subtle pervasiveness of incremental changes of symbols processed through multiform networks, away from the halls of power. It is in those back alleys of society, whether in alternative electronic networks or in grassrooted networks of communal resistance, that I have sensed the embryos of a new society, labored in the fields of history by the power of identity. (Castells, 2004, p. 428)

Summary

- Castells argues that society and capitalism went through significant restructuring between the 1970s and 1990s. Essential to this restructuring were new information technologies. This new technology lifted capital and social relations from the embeddness of time and space—they redefined the material basis of human life—and allowed for an almost infinite number of reconstructions. The accumulation of capital shifted then from production to financial flows. Capital is then invested globally, following interests of greatest return, which are increasingly based on speculation and money markets rather than real goods and services.

- The basis of social connections changed and is now subject to the logic of networks. Within this logic, connections are created by nodes rather than people situated in time and place. A node is important because of the amount of information it holds and processes or the way it connects to other elements within the network. Actual people as traditionally understood in terms of a situated lifeworld become of secondary importance: A person becomes important in the network as he or she functions as a network node.

- Thus power in a network is determined by a node's ability to find, hold, and process information; and, more importantly, the node's ability to act as a switch between informational networks. Class is established more by a node's capability to organize work or direct flows of speculative capital than by production. Politics in the network society are a function of image-making and negative information, which is able to capture attention in the network. The politics of the state, then, are dependent upon network-based media personalities. The sovereignty of the state is also deconstructed by the importance of global flows of money and information, both of which fall outside the ability of the state to regulate efficiently.

- As a result of these changes in power and politics, the legitimacy of the state is questioned. And as a result of this crisis in legitimation, the majority of citizens no longer believe that traditional democracy addresses the problems faced in daily life. Additionally, resistance identities become increasingly important. In the network society there are three forms of identity: legitimating, resistance, and project. Legitimating and project identities are based on the modern ideal of state-based emancipatory politics; the former established and the latter seek to reform the distribution of civil rights. As the centrality of the state and emancipatory politics decline, so do the importance and power of legitimating and project identities. Resistance identities—which are formed around existential questions and meaning—ascend in practice and significance. However, in and of themselves, resistance identities are not political and are individualized, which in turn threatens the possibility of participatory democracy. However, in the network society resistance identities represent the best possibility for the reforming of project identities. Resistance identities can be used to mobilize information and imagery, which can bring incremental changes and shifts in network power.

TAKING THE PERSPECTIVE

Castells is one of those unique theorists for whom there is little antecedent and little if any extended work. The focus of this theory is simply too new. However, generally speaking, his concerns are well founded in the history of social theory. From the outset, sociological theorists have been concerned with defining and then analyzing society. As noted in Chapter 1, the idea of society as a macro-level entity existing above and influencing face-to-face social situations is distinctly modern. And early sociologists spent a good deal of theoretical energy defining and explicating the dynamics of such an entity; it is most explicitly present in Durkheim's work. That approach is where we get our notions of social structure and institutions. However, all that work had as its background assumption the defining feature of the nation-state—society in modern terms is intrinsically linked to the democratic state defined by territory and the exclusive use of legitimated coercive power. Castells' work, even more than Wallerstein's, proposes a new base for and understanding of society.

Castells is also concerned with identity, which, again, is a central issue of modern theorists. Stuart Hall (1996) notes that identity in the Enlightenment "was based on a conception of the human person as a fully centered, unified individual, endowed with the capacities of reason, consciousness, and action" (p. 597). This sense of identity, then, became the basis of the citizen and national identity; an American, for example, capable of participatory democracy. This notion of identity as well was based upon the sovereignty of the state, an institution where the politics of democracy could be played out and legitimated power of the state could be directed toward equality and social justice.

As we've seen, Castells argues for a new and different basis of society and thus identity. Society—social connections—is no longer based on identities that are situated and lived in real time and place. Rather, he argues that the majority of our sociability is created through information technology networks, which transcend national borders and thus redefine power, class, and politics. So, while his concerns are clearly modern and well established, he takes us in new directions and asks that we rethink the ideas that have dominated and led the social sciences for almost 200 years.

(Continued)

(Continued)

In terms of his theoretical approach, Castells means his theory to be used as an analytic heuristic, somewhat like Bourdieu in intent. This approach implies two things. First, unlike Wallerstein, Castells' theory isn't meant to be predictive; rather, it's a way of seeing and analyzing the social world. Second, the theory is a "work in progress open to rectification by empirical research" (Castells, 2000a, p. 6). His work, then, is quite literally intended to provide ideas and concepts "to be used in the building of a sociological theory able to grasp emerging forms of social organization and conflict" (p. 6).

BUILDING YOUR THEORY TOOLBOX

Learning More—Primary Sources

- The foundation of Castells' work is found in his three-volume work concerning the network society: *The Rise of the Network Society, The Power of Identity,* and *The End of Millennium.*

Learning More—Secondary Sources

- Though portions of Castells' work appear in many texts, there are very few secondary sources focused exclusively on him. I can suggest

    o *Manuel Castells (Key Contemporary Thinkers),* by Felix Stalder, Polity Press, 2006.
    o *Conversations with Manuel Castells,* by Castells and Martin Ince, Polity Press 2003.

Check It Out

- Castells' Web page at USC Annenberg:
    o http://annenberg.usc.edu/Faculty/Communication/CastellsM.aspx
- There are two wonderful videos featuring Manual Castells on YouTube:
    o http://www.youtube.com/watch?v=0GBB7U5mvOw
    o http://www.youtube.com/watch?v=qrOABiFUdOg

Seeing the World

- After reading and understanding this chapter, you should be able to define the following terms theoretically and explain their theoretical importance to Castells' theory of the network society: Keynesian economics, information technology, the logic of networks, annihilation of time and place, power, class, politics, identities, legitimizing identity, resistance identity, project identity, civil society, symbol mobilizers, new democracy

- After reading and understanding this chapter, you should be able to answer the following questions (remember to answer them *theoretically*):

  o Explain how three major technological advances have fundamentally influenced knowledge and information. Pay special attention to how the logic of networks have altered the way in which people are socially organized.

  o Explain how computer/information technologies have fundamentally altered power, politics, and class.

  o Explain how the sovereignty of the state is challenged through computer/information technologies.

  o Clarify the differences among legitimizing, resistance, and project identities.

  o Explain how civil society has changed as a result of computer and information technologies. In your explanation be sure to explicate the new democracy.

Engaging the World

- Use Castells' notions about legitimizing, resistance, and project identities to analyze at least three identities you claim.

- Using your explanation of how civil society has changed, draw out at least three implications for democracy. In other words, how has the possibility of democracy changed as a result of the process involved in the network society?

- Propose a project that would fit into Castells' notion of the new democracy. The project topic can be anything, so pick something you really care about. Using Castells' theory, explain how your project could potentially influence society.

- Speculate about possible effects of Castells' idea of the network society on sociology and other social disciplines

Weaving the Threads

- Using Wallerstein and Castells, explain how democracy and politics have changed as a result of globalization. How has the state been decentered from the social project of modernity? How have political identities and personal practices been redefined?

- How is the modern idea of society challenged by Castells and Wallerstein? How would you now define society?

- How has capitalism changed as a result of the network society? Focus your discussion on capital and class.

- Compare and contrast Wallerstein's and Castells' theories in terms of political involvement. Which do you think is more viable and why?

- Compare and contrast Castells' theory of politics and identities with that of Wilson and Chafetz. What does the network society imply about the identities and politics of race and gender?

Part IV

Modernity and Postmodernity

Modernity and Reason:

Jürgen Habermas

(1929–)

S ocieties change—there's no doubt about that. But there is a great deal of debate about how societies change. In this book, for example, we've considered theories that say that society changes incrementally through each interaction and we've looked at theories that argue that society changes as the result of massive systemic pressures. Jürgen Habermas argues that society can change because people choose to change it. This vision of social change seems simple enough. In fact, it is the idea in back of democracy and a major reason why people vote. But we've already begun to see that this idea isn't as straightforward as it might seem. Within the boundaries of a national economic system, race, gender, and class all resist change.

In Chapter 7, Wilson showed us that the lives of blacks in the United States will change only if systemwide changes are made in the mode of economic production; and Chafetz demonstrated that voluntaristic change will have little effect on gender inequality without structural changes that lay outside the ability of individuals to influence. In Chapter 8, Pierre Bourdieu revealed how the hidden structure of habitus works below the level of awareness to replicate our class position.

On a global level, Immanuel Wallerstein (Chapter 9) alerts us to the possibility that the social system may be too complex for us to actually guide. And Manuel Castells in Chapter 10 is hopeful only in the tenuous possibility that resistance identities may form project identities through symbol mobilizers. Looking ahead to our next chapter, Anthony Giddens (1990) argues that modernity is like a runaway train, with no one at the helm; he asks, "Why has the generalising of 'sweet reason' not produced a world subject to our prediction and control?" (p. 151). In fact, from this point on in our book, reason and the audacious attempt of humans to control their world will be called into question again and again. The modern world is perhaps "not one in which the sureties of tradition and habit have been replaced by the certitude of rational knowledge" (Giddens, 1991, p. 3).

In response to such critiques, Erich Fromm (1955)—an associate with the Frankfurt School—points the way to a hope through critical theory:

> But all these facts are not strong enough to destroy faith in man's reason, good will and sanity. As long as we can think of other alternatives, we are not lost; as long as we can consult together and plan together, we can hope. (p. 363)

In many ways, Habermas is one of the last, great modernists. Can we take control of society and move it to become better, more humane, and truly free? Can reason prevail in the face of the alienating forces of modernity? Habermas thinks so, and gives us theoretical reasons for our doing the same.

THEORIST'S DIGEST

Brief Biography

Jürgen Habermas was born on June 18, 1929, in Düsseldorf, Germany. His teen years were spent under Nazi control, which undoubtedly gave Habermas his drive for freedom and democracy. His educational background is primarily in philosophy, but also includes German literature, history, and psychology. In 1956, Habermas took a position as Theodor Adorno's assistant at the Institute of Social Research in Frankfurt, which began his formal association with the Frankfurt School of critical thought. In 1961, Habermas took a professorship at the University of Heidelberg, but returned to Frankfurt in 1964 as a professor of philosophy and sociology. From 1971 to 1981, he worked as the director of the Max Planck Institute, where he began to formalize his theory of communicative action. In 1982, Habermas returned to the institute in Frankfurt, where he remained until his retirement in 1994.

Central Sociological Questions

Born out of the political oppression of Nazi Germany, Habermas is driven to produce a social theory of ethics that would not be based on political or economic power and would be universally inclusive. He is a critical theorist who sees humankind's hope of rational existence within the inherent processes of communication. Specifically he asks, how can the civil sphere of democracy be revitalized so that participatory democracy can move forward?

Simply Stated

As a result of organized capitalism, the commodification of mass media, and the scientific study of society and human relations, democracy has been disabled through the colonization of the lifeworld and public sphere. However, the qualities inherent in critical theory and communication could form the base for the revitalization of civil society and participatory democracy as they are enacted in speech communities.

Key Ideas

Legitimacy, authority, lifeworld, liberal capitalism, depoliticized class, public sphere, pragmatic consensus, organized capitalism, legitimation crisis, colonization of the lifeworld, steering, generalized media of exchange, colonization of the public sphere, public opinion, analytic knowledge, interpretive knowledge, critical theory, speech communities, communicative action, civil society

Concepts and Theory: Capitalism and Legitimation

Drawing on Karl Marx's theory of capitalism, Max Weber's ideas of the state and legitimation, Edmund Husserl's notion of the lifeworld, and Talcott Parsons' view of social systems, Habermas gives us a model of social change and modernity. You are by now generally familiar with Marx's theory of capitalism and Parsons' argument concerning the ways in which system components are integrated. But let me take a moment to talk about Weber's and Husserl's contributions to Habermas' theory.

Legitimations are stories, narratives and myths, that a society tells that justify some portion of socially created reality. A Weberian concern with **legitimation** is specifically, though not exclusively, focused on power, authority, and the state. In order for a system of domination like the state to work, people must believe in it. Part of the reason behind this need is the cost involved in the use of power. If people don't believe in authority to some degree, they will have to be forced to comply through coercive power. The use of coercive power requires high levels of external social control mechanisms, such as monitoring (you have to be able to watch and see if people are conforming) and force (because they won't do it willingly). To maintain a system of domination not based on legitimacy costs a great deal in terms of technology and manpower. In addition, people generally respond in the long run to the use of coercion by either rebelling or giving up—the end result is thus contrary to the desired goal.

In contrast to coercive power, *authority* implies the ability to require performance that is based upon the performer's belief in the rightness of the system, which is where legitimacy comes in. Legitimacy provides people with the moral basis for believing in the system. So, for example, your professor tells you that you will be taking a test in 2 weeks. And in 2 weeks you show up to take the test. No one has to force you; you simply do it because you believe in the right of the professor to give tests. And that's Weber's point: Social structures can function because of belief in a cultural system. The state, because it is almost exclusively defined in terms of power, is especially dependent upon legitimacy.

The concept of **lifeworld** originally came from Edmund Husserl. Habermas uses it to refer to the individual's everyday life—the world as it is experienced immediately by the person, a world built upon culture and social relations, and thus filled with historically and socially specific meanings. The purpose of the lifeworld is to facilitate communication: to provide a common set of goals, practices, values, languages, and so on that allow people to interact, to continually weave their meanings, practices, and goals into a shared fabric of life.

Liberal Capitalism and the Hope of Modernity

Drawing from Marx and Weber, Habermas argues that there have been two phases of capitalism, liberal capitalism and organized capitalism. Each phase is defined by the changing relationship between capitalism and the state. In *liberal capitalism,* the state has little involvement with the economy. Capitalism is thus able to function without constraint. Liberal capitalism occurred during the beginning phases of capitalism and the nation-state.

Capitalism and the nation-state came into existence as part of sweeping changes that redefined Western Europe and eventually the world. Though they began much earlier, these changes coalesced in the seventeenth and eighteenth centuries. Prior to this time, the primary form of government in Europe was feudalism, brought to Europe by the Normans in 1066. Feudalism is based on land tenure and personal relationships. These relationships, and thus the land, were organized around the monarchy with a clear social division between royalty and peasants. Thus, in the lifeworld of the everyday person in feudal Europe one's personal obligations and relationship to the land were paramount. The everyday person was keenly aware of his or her obligations to the lord of the land (the origin of the word landlord). This was seen as a kind of familial relationship and fidelity was its chief goal. Notice something important here: People under feudalism were subjects of the monarchy, not citizens.

Capitalism came about out of an institutional field that included the state, Protestantism, and the Industrial Revolution. The nation-state was needed to provide the necessary uniform money system and strong legal codes concerning private property; the Protestant Reformation created a culture with strong values centered on individualism and the work ethic; and the Industrial Revolution gave to capitalism the level of exploitation it needed.

Habermas argues that together the nation-state and capitalism *depoliticized class* relations, proposed equality based on market competition, and contributed strongly to the emergence of the public sphere. The term *class* first came into the English language in the seventeenth century (see Williams, 1983, pp. 60–69). At that time, it had reference mainly to education; our use of *classic* and *classical* to refer to authoritative works of study came from this application. The true modern use of the term *class* came into existence between 1770 and 1840, a time period that corresponds to the Industrial Revolution as well as the French and American political revolutions.

Almost everything about society changed during this time, in particular the ideas of individual rights and accountability and the primacy of the economic system. The modern word *class*, then, carries with it the ideas that the individual's position is a product of the social system and that social position is made rather than inherited. "What was changing consciousness was not only increased individual mobility, which could be largely contained within the older terms, but the new sense of a society or a particular social system which actually created social division, including new kinds of divisions" (Williams, 1983, p. 62).

Thus, class is no longer a political issue, it is an economic one—class relations are no longer seen in terms of personal relations and family connections, but rather as the result of free market competition. Under capitalism and the civil liberties brought by the nation-state, all members of society are seen equally as citizens and economic competitors. Any differences among members in society are thus believed to come from economic competition and market forces, rather than birthright and personal relationships. Clearly, liberal capitalism brought momentous changes to the lifeworld: It became a world defined by democratic freedoms and responsibilities. Social relationships were no longer familial but, rather, legal and rational. The chief goal for the person in this lifeworld was full democratic participation. According to Habermas, the mechanism for this full participation is the public sphere.

The combination of the ideals of the Enlightenment, the transformation of government from feudalism to nation-state democracy, and the rise of capitalism created something that had never before existed: the public sphere. The **public sphere** is a space for democratic, public debate. Under feudalism, subjects could obviously complain about the monarchy and their way of life, and no doubt they did. But grumbling about a situation over which one has no control is vastly different than debating political points over which one is expected to exercise control. Remember, this was the first time Europe or the Americas had citizens, with rights and civic responsibilities; there was robust belief and hope in this new person, the citizen. The ideals of the Enlightenment indicated that this citizenry would be informed and completely engaged in the democratic process, and the public sphere is the place where this strong democracy could take place.

Habermas sees the public sphere as existing between a set of cultural institutions and practices on the one hand and state power on the other. The function of the public sphere is to mediate the concerns of private citizens and state interests. There are two principles of this public sphere: access to unlimited information and equal participation. The public sphere thus consists of cultural organizations such as journals and newspapers that distribute information to the people; it contains both political and commercial organizations where public discussion can take place, such as public assemblies, coffee shops, pubs, political clubs, and so forth. The goal of this public sphere is *pragmatic consensus.*

Thus, during liberal capitalism, the relationship between the state and capitalism can best be characterized as laissez-faire, which is French for "allow to do." The assumption undergirding this policy was that the individual will contribute most successfully to the good of the whole if left to his or her own aspirations. The place of government, then, should be as far away from capitalism as possible. In this way of thinking, capitalism represents the mechanism of equality, the place where the best are defined through successful competition rather than by family ties. During liberal capitalism, then, it was felt that the marketplace of capitalism had to be completely free from any interference so that the most successful could rise to the top. In this sense, faith in the "invisible hand" of market dynamics corresponded to the evolutionist belief in survival of the fittest and natural selection.

Organized Capitalism and the Legitimation Crisis

Such was the ideal world of capitalism and democracy coming out of the Enlightenment. The central orienting belief was progress; humankind was set free from the feudalistic bonds of monarchical government, and each individual would stand or fall based on his or her own efforts. In addition to economic pursuit, these efforts were to be focused on full democratic participation. Each citizen was to be fully and constantly immersed in education—education that came not only from schools but also through the public sphere. The hope of modernity was thus invested in each citizen and that person's full participation—people believed that rational discourse would lead to decisions made by reason and guided by egalitarianism.

Two economic issues changed the relationship between the economy and the state, which, in turn, had dramatic impacts on the lifeworld and public sphere. First, rather than producing equal competitors on an even playing field, free markets tend to create monopolies. Thus, by the end of the nineteenth and beginning of the twentieth centuries, the United States' economy was essentially run by an elite group of businessmen who came to be called "robber barons." Perhaps the attitude of these capitalists is best captured by the phrase attributed to William H. Vanderbilt, a railroad tycoon: "The public be damned." These men emphasized efficiency through Taylorism (named after Frederick Taylor, the creator of scientific management) and economies of scale. The result was large-scale domination of markets. These monopolies weren't restricted to the market; they extended to vertical integration as well. With vertical integration, a company controls before-and-after manufacture supply lines. One example is Standard Oil, who at this time dominated the market, owned wells and refineries, and controlled the railroad system that moved its product to market.

The response of the U.S. government to widespread monopolization was to enact antitrust laws. The first legislation of this type in the United States was the Sherman Antitrust Act of 1890. In part the act reads,

Every contract, combination in the form of trust or otherwise, or conspiracy, in restraint of trade or commerce among the several States, or with foreign nations, is declared to be illegal. . . . Every person who shall monopolize, or attempt to monopolize, or combine or conspire with any other person or persons, to monopolize any part of the trade or commerce among the several States, or with foreign nations, shall be deemed guilty of a felony.

However, capitalists fought the act on constitutional grounds and the Supreme Court prevented the government from applying the law for a number of years. Eventually the Court decided for the government in 1904, and the Antitrust Act was used powerfully by both presidents Theodore Roosevelt and William Taft. This regulatory power of the U.S. government was further extended under Woodrow Wilson's administration and the passing of the Clayton Antitrust Act in 1914.

The second economic issue that modified the economy's relationship with the state was economic fluctuations. As Karl Marx had indicated, capitalist economies are subject to periodic oscillations, with downturns becoming harsher as they cycle through time. By the late 1920s, the capitalist economic system went into severe decline, creating worldwide depression in the decade of the thirties. What came to be called "classic economics" fell out of favor and a myriad of competitors clamored to take its place. Eventually, the ideas of John Maynard Keynes took hold and were explicated in his 1936 book, *The General Theory of Employment, Interest and Money.* His idea was simple, and reminiscent of Marx: Capitalism tends toward overproduction— the capacity of the system to produce and transport products is greater than the demand. Keynes' theory countered the then popular belief in the invisible hand of the market and argued that active government spending and management of the economy would reduce the power and magnitude of the business cycle.

Keynes' ideas initially influenced Franklin D. Roosevelt's belief that insufficient demand produced the Depression, and after World War II Keynes' ideas were generally accepted. Governments began to keep statistics about the economy, expanded their control of capitalism, and increased spending in order to keep demand up. This new approach continued through the 1950s and 1960s. While the economic problems of the 1970s cast doubt upon Keynesian economics, new economic policies have continued to include some level of government spending and economic manipulation.

Thus, due to the tendency of completely free markets to produce monopolies and periodic fluctuations, the state became much more involved in the control of the economy. *Organized capitalism,* then, is a kind of capitalism where economic practices are controlled, governed, or organized by the state. According to Habermas, the change from liberal to organized capitalism, along with the general dynamics of capitalism (such as commodification, market expansion, advertising, and so on), have had three major effects.

First, there has been a shift in the kind and arena of crises. As we've seen, liberal capitalism suffered from economic crises. Under organized capitalism, however, the economy is managed by the state to one degree or another. This shift means that the crisis, when it hits, is a crisis for the state rather than the economy. It is specifically a *legitimation crisis* for the state and for people's belief in rationality.

There are two things going on here in the relationship between the state and the economy: The state is attempting to organize capitalism, and the state is employing scientific knowledge to do so. Together, these issues create crises of legitimation and rationality rather than simply economic disasters. Nevertheless, Habermas argues that the economy is the core problem: Capitalism has an intrinsic set of issues that continually create economic crises. However, due to the state's attempts to govern the economy, what the population experiences are ineffectual and disjointed responses from the state rather than economic crises. More significantly, in attempting to solve economic and social problems, the state increasingly depends upon scientific knowledge and technical control. This reliance on technical control changes the character of the problems from social or economic issues to technical ones.

Concepts and Theory: The Colonization of Democracy

The other two important effects concern the lifeworld and the public sphere. In our discussion of legitimation and rationality crises, we can begin to see the changes in the lifeworld. The lifeworld of liberal capitalism was constructed out of a culture that believed in progress through science and reason. In this lifeworld, the person was expected to be actively involved in the democratic process. However, the general malaise that grows out of the crisis of legitimation reduces people's motivation and the meaning they attach to social life.

Colonization of the Lifeworld

In addition, according to Habermas, a **colonization of the lifeworld** is taking place due to the political and economic systems. To understand what Habermas means, we have to step back a little. As I've already noted, Habermas gives us a theory that involves social evolution. In general, social evolutionists argue that society progresses by becoming more complex: Structures and systems differentiate and become more specialized. The evolutionary argument is that this specialization and complexity produce a system that is more adaptable and better able to survive in a changing environment.

One of the problems that comes up in differentiated systems concerns coordination and control, or what Habermas refers to as *steering*. In complex social systems, the institutions and structures have different values, roles, status positions, languages, and so forth (this is precisely what it meant by structural differentiation). Differentiated social structures tend to go off in their own direction. We have seen that Talcott Parsons (Chapter 2) felt this problem was solved through *generalized media of exchange*. The idea of media is important, so let's consider it again for a minute. *Merriam-Webster's* (2002) defines medium (media is plural) as "something through or by which something is accomplished, conveyed, or carried on." For example, language is a form of media: It's the principal medium through which communication is organized and carried out. Different social institutions or structures use different media. In education, for instance, it's knowledge and in government it's power. These are the instruments or media through which education and government are able to perform their functions.

For Parsons, the solution to the problem of social integration and steering is for the different social subsystems to create media that are general or abstract enough that all other institutions could use them as means of exchange. We can think about this like boundary crossings. Visualize a boundary between different social structures or subsystems, such as the economy and education. How can the boundary between economy and education be crossed? Or, using a different analogy, how can the economy and education talk to each other when they have different languages and values?

Habermas is specifically concerned with the boundaries between the lifeworld and the state and economy. In Habermas' terms, Parsons basically argues that the state and economy use power and money, respectively, as media of exchange with the lifeworld. If you think about this for a moment, it seems to make sense. You exist in your lifeworld, so what does the economy have that you want? You might start a list of all the cars, houses, and other commodities that you want, but what do they all boil down to? Money. And how does the economy entice you to leave your lifeworld and go to work? Money. So, money is the medium of exchange between the lifeworld and the economy. The same logic holds for the boundary between the lifeworld and the state: Power is what the state has and what induces us to interact with the state. However, Habermas (1981/1987) sees a problem:

> I want to argue against this—that in the areas of life that primarily fulfill functions of cultural reproduction, social integration, and socialization, mutual understanding cannot be replaced by media as the mechanism for coordinating action—that is, it cannot be technicized—though it can be expanded by technologies of communication and organizationally mediated— that is, it can be rationalized. (p. 267, emphasis original)

Habermas is arguing that there is something intrinsic about the lifeworld that cannot be reduced to media, such as money and power, "without sociopathological consequences" (p. 267). Let me give you an easy example from a different issue: having sex. Most people would agree that you cannot "technicize" this behavior using the medium of money without fundamentally changing the nature of it; there is a clear distinction between making love with your significant partner and having sex with a prostitute. Habermas is making the same kind of argument about humanity and communication in general. For him, the sphere of mutual understanding, the life-world, cannot be reduced to power and money without essentially changing it.

Yet Habermas isn't arguing that Parsons made a theoretical mistake. Parsons saw himself as an empiricist and merely sought to describe the social world. So in this sense, Parsons was right: There is something going on in modernity that tries to mediate the lifeworld. Habermas takes this idea from Parsons and argues that in imposing their media on the lifeworld, the state and economy are fundamentally changing it. The lifeworld, by definition, cannot be mediated through money or power without deeply altering it.

According to Habermas, the lifeworld is naturally achieved through consensus. This is basically the same thing that symbolic interactionists argue. Remember, interactions emerge and are achieved by individuals consciously and unconsciously negotiating meaning and action in face-to-face encounters. This negotiation, or consensus building, occurs chiefly through speech. Thus, using money or power fundamentally changes the lifeworld. In Habermas' (1981/1987) words, it is colonized: "The mediatization of the lifeworld assumes the form of a colonization" (p. 196).

This idea of the colonization of the lifeworld is perhaps one of Habermas' best-known and most provocative concepts. Using *Merriam-Webster's* (2002) again, a *colony* is "a body of people settled in a new territory, foreign and often distant, retaining ties with their motherland or parent state . . . as a means of facilitating established occupation and [governance] by the parent state." Habermas is arguing that the modern state and economic system (capitalism) have imposed their media upon the lifeworld. In this sense, money and power act just like a colony—they are means through which these distant social structures seek to occupy and dominate the local lifeworld of people.

Habermas (1981/1987, p. 356) argues that four factors in organized capitalism set the stage for the colonization of the lifeworld. First, the lifeworld is differentiated from the social systems. Historically, there was a closer association between the lifeworld and society; in fact, in the earliest societies they were coextensive; in other words, they overlapped to the degree that they were synonymous. As society increases in differentiation and complexity, the lifeworld becomes decoupled from institutional spheres. Second, the boundaries between the lifeworld and the different social subsystems become regulated through differentiated roles. Keep in mind that social roles are scripts for behavior. In traditional societies, most social roles were related to the family. So, for example, the eldest male would be the high priest—the family and religious positions would be filled and scripted by the same role. This kind of role homogeneity made the relationship between the lifeworld and society relatively nonproblematic, and, more importantly, it served to connect the two spheres.

Third, the rewards for workers in organized capitalism in terms of leisure time and expendable cash offset the demands of bureaucratic domination. "Wherever bourgeois law visibly underwrites the demands of the lifeworld against bureaucratic domination, it loses the ambivalence of realizing freedom at the cost of destructive side effects" (Habermas, 1981/1987, p. 361). And fourth, the state provides comprehensive welfare. Worker protection laws, social security, and so forth reduce the impact of exploitation and create a culture of entitlement where legal subjects pursue their individual interests and the "privatized hopes for self-actualization and self-determination are primarily located . . . in the roles of consumer and client" (p. 350).

For simplicity's sake, we can group the first two and last two items together. The first two factors are generally concerned with the effects of complex social environments. The more complex the social environment, due to structural differentiation, the greater will be the number and diversity of cultures and roles with which any individual will have to contend. This in turn dismantles the connections among the elements that comprise the lifeworld: culture, society, and personality.

The second two factors concern the effects of the state's position under organized capitalism. Under organized capitalism, the state protects the capitalist system, the capitalists, and the workers. In doing so, the state mitigates some of the issues that would otherwise produce social conflict and change. But perhaps more importantly, the state further individualizes the person. The roles of consumer and client, both associated with a climate of entitlement, overshadow the role of democratic citizen.

As a result of these factors, everything in organized capitalism that informs the lifeworld, such as culture and social positions, comes to be defined or at least influenced by money and power. Money and power have a certain logic or rationality to them. Weber talked about four distinct forms of rationality, two of which are pertinent here: instrumental and value rationality. Instrumental-rational action is behavior that is determined by pure means and ends calculation. For example, your action in coming to the university might be considered instrumentally rational if being here is a means to the goal of obtaining a good job or career. Value-rational behavior is action that is based upon one's values or morals. If there is no way you could get caught paying someone to write your term paper for you, then it would be instrumentally rational for you to do so. It would be the easiest way to achieve a desired end. However, if you don't do that because you believe it is dishonest, then your behavior is being guided by values or morals.

Value rationality is specifically tied to the lifeworld and instrumental rationality to the state and economy. Thus, a good deal of what happens when the lifeworld is colonized is the ever-increasing intrusion of instrumental rationality and the emptying of value rationality from the social system. The result is that "systemic mechanisms—for example, money—steer a social intercourse that has been largely disconnected from norms and values. . . . [And] norm-conformative attitudes and identity-forming social memberships are neither necessary nor possible" (Habermas, 1981/1987, p. 154). In turn, people in this kind of modern social system come to value money and power; money and power are seen as the principal means of success and happiness. Money is used to purchase commodities that are in turn used to construct identities and impress other people. Rather than being a humanistic value, respect becomes something demanded rather than given, a ploy of power rather than a place of honor.

To see the significance of this, let's recall the ideal of the lifeworld of modernity. When the lifeworld changed in the move from traditional to modern society, it took on new priorities and importance. The lifeworld was ideally to be dominated by democratic freedoms and responsibilities and occupied by citizens fully engaged in reasoning out the ways to fulfill the goals of the Enlightenment—progress and equality—through communication and consensus building. As Habermas (1981/1987) says, "The burden of social integration [shifts] more and more from religiously anchored consensus to processes of consensus formation in language" (p. 180).

As you can see, using money or power as steering media in the lifeworld is the antithesis of open communication and consensus building. One of the results of this situation is that the lifeworld decouples from or becomes incidental to the social system, in terms of its integrative capacities. A lifeworld colonized by money and power cannot build consensus through reasoning and communication;

people in this kind of lifeworld lose their sense of responsibility to the democratic ideals of the Enlightenment.

Colonization of the Public Sphere

This process is further aggravated by developments in the public sphere. As we've seen, the public sphere and its citizens came into existence with the advent of modernity. Citizens "are endowed by their Creator with certain unalienable Rights." This phrasing in the U.S. Declaration of Independence is interesting because it implies that these rights are moral rather than simply legal. There is a moral obligation to these rights that expresses itself in certain responsibilities:

> Whenever any Form of Government becomes destructive of these ends, it is the Right of the People to alter or to abolish it, and to institute new Government, laying its foundation on such principles and organizing its powers in such form, as to them shall seem most likely to affect their Safety and Happiness.

Thus the most immediate place for involvement for citizens is the public sphere. In that space between power on the one hand and free information on the other, citizens are meant to engage in communication and consensus formation. It is in that space that discussion and decisions about any form of government are to be made. However, a *colonization of the public sphere* has taken place in much the same way as the lifeworld. Specifically, the public sphere, which began in the eighteenth century with the growth of independent news sources and active places of public debate, transformed into something quite different in the twentieth century. It became the place of public opinion—something that is measured through polls, used by politicians, and influenced by a mass media of entertainment.

There are two keys here. First, *public opinion* is something that is manufactured through social science. It's a statistic, not a public forum or debate that results in consensus. Recall what we saw earlier about how Habermas views the knowledge of science, even social science—its specific purpose is to control. Transforming consensus in the public sphere into a statistic makes controlling public sentiment much easier for politicians, both subjectively and objectively.

The second key issue I want us to see is the shift in news sources. Most of the venues through which we obtain our news and information today are motivated by profit. In other words, public news sources aren't primarily concerned with creating a democratic citizenry or with making available information that is socially significant. As such, information that is given out is packaged as entertainment most of the time. In a society like the United States, the consumers of mass media are more infatuated with "wicked weather" than the state of the homeless.

Concepts and Theory: A Democratic Hope

When we began our discussion, I mentioned that Habermas still holds out the promise of modernity. This hope is anchored in three areas: critical theory, speech communities, and civil society. The ideas and proposals in back of these are rather straightforward. Achieving them, however, is difficult under the conditions created by organized capitalism, where the possibility and horizon of moral discourse are stunted.

The Hope of Critical Theory

Habermas argues that there are three kinds of knowledge and interests: empirical, *analytic knowledge* that is interested in the technical control of the environment (science); hermeneutic or *interpretive knowledge* that is interested in human understanding and cooperation; and critical knowledge that is interested in emancipation. Because scientific knowledge seeks to explain the dynamic processes found within a given phenomenon, social science is historically bound. That is, it sees things only as they currently exist. That being the case, scientific knowledge of human institutions and behaviors can only describe and thus reinforce existing political arrangements (since society is taken "as is").

Further, positivistic social science is blind to its own conditions of knowledge: It uncritically places itself fully within the political and economic framework of modernity and then proclaims to express objective truth or knowledge. Remember the first assumption of science: The universe is empirical and objective. It's out there and we can observe it objectively and discover how it works. By definition, human beings aren't objective; they are subjectively oriented toward meaning. Nor is society "out there" in the same way the moon is. We can study the moon objectively because it truly exists apart from us; if human beings had never existed, the moon would be exactly the same. But this can't be said about society. Human beings make up society; it exists only because of us. Therefore we can't stand outside of it to create objective knowledge—attempts to study society objectively end in denying the only questions that really matter about society: What values should guide society? What are the possibilities?

Critical theory, on the other hand, purposefully stands within the social world where the dramas of oppression and social justice are played out. Rather than aligning itself with the assumption of objectivity, as social science has done, critical knowledge embraces the democratic project as its foundation. Its values, then, are known, questioned, and at the center of the production of critical knowledge, rather than hidden and denied as in social science. The intent of critical knowledge is to further the democratic project and social justice by exposing the distortions, misrepresentations, and political values found in our knowledge and speech.

The Hope of Speech Communities

Speech communities or situations are the basis for ethical reasoning and occur under certain guidelines of communication. Before we get to those guidelines, we need to consider what Habermas calls *communicative action:* action with the intent to communicate. Habermas makes the point that all social action is based on communication. However, to understand Habermas' intent, it might be beneficial to consider something that looks like social communication but isn't. We can call this strategic speech. Strategic speech is associated with instrumental rationality, and it is thus endemic within the lifeworld of organized capitalism as well as the social system.

In this kind of talk, the goal is not to reach consensus or understanding, but rather for the speaker to achieve his or her own personal ends. For example, the stereotypical salesperson or "closer" isn't trying to reach consensus; he or she is trying to sell something (a more immediate example is the student explaining why he or she missed the test). In strategic talk, speech isn't being practiced simply as communication; communication is being used to achieve egocentric ends, which is contrary to the function of communication: "Reaching understanding is the inherent telos [ultimate end] of human speech. Naturally, speech and understanding are not related to one another as means to end" (Habermas, 1981/1984, p. 287).

Communicative action within an ideal speech situation is based upon some important assumptions. As we are reviewing these assumptions, keep in mind that Habermas is making the argument that communication itself holds the key and power to reasoned existence and emancipatory politics. Communication has intrinsic properties that form the basis of human connection and understanding. Habermas points out that every time we simply talk with someone, in every natural speech act, we assume that communication is possible. We also assume that it is possible to share intersubjective states. These two assumptions sound similar but are a bit different. Communication simply involves your assuming that your friend can understand the words you are saying. Sharing intersubjective states is deeper than this. With intersubjectivity, we assume that others can share a significant part of our inner world—our feelings, thoughts, convictions, and experiences.

A third assumption we make in speech acts is that there is a truth that exists apart from the individual speaker. In this part of speech, we are making validity claims. We claim that what we are saying has the strength of truth or rightness. This is an extremely important point for Habermas and forms the basis of discourse ethics and universal norms. All true communication is built upon and contains claims to validity, which inherently call for reason and reflection. Further, these claims assume validity is possible; that truth or rightness can exist independent of the individual, which implies the possibility of universal norms or morals; and that validity claims can be criticized, which implies that they are in some sense active and accountable to reason. Validity claims also facilitate intersubjectivity in that they create expectations in both parties. The speaker is expected to be responsible for the reasonableness of his or her statement, and the hearer is expected to accept or reject the validity of the statement and provide a reasonable basis for either.

These assumptions are basic to speech: We assume that we can communicate; we assume we can share intersubjective worlds; and we assume that valid statements are possible. What Habermas draws out from these basic assumptions of speech is that it is feasible to reasonably decide on collective action. This is a simple but profound point: Intrinsic to the way humans communicate is the hope of decisive collective action. It is possible for humanity to use talk in order to build consensus and make reasoned decisions about social action. This is both the promise and hope of modernity and the Enlightenment.

Ethical reason and substantive rationality are thus intrinsic to speech, but it isn't enough in terms of making a difference in organized capitalism. As with all critical theorists, Habermas has a praxis component. Praxis for Habermas is centered in communication and the creation of ideal speech situations. Here communication is a skill, one that as democratic citizens we need to cultivate in order to participate in the civil society. As we consider these points of the ideal speech community, notice how many of them have to do more with listening than with speaking. In an ideal speech situation,

- Every person who is competent to speak and act is allowed to partake in the conversation—full equality is granted and each person is seen as an equal source of legitimate or valid statements
- There is no sense of coercion; consensus is not forced; and there is no recourse to objective standings such as status, money, or power
- Anyone can introduce any topic; anyone can disagree with or question any topic; everyone is allowed to express opinions and feelings about all topics
- Each person strives to keep his or her speech free from ideology

Let me point out that this is an ideal against which actual speech acts can be compared and toward which all democratic communication must strive. The closer a community's speech comes to this ideal, the greater is the possibility of consensus and reasonable action.

> If we assume that the human species maintains itself through the socially coordinated activities of its members and that this coordination has to be established through communication . . . then the reproduction of the species also requires satisfying the conditions of a rationality that is inherent in communicative action. (Habermas, 1981/1984, p. 397)

The Hope of Civil Society

Ideal speech communities are based upon and give rise to civil society. **Civil society** for Habermas is made up of voluntary associations, organizations, and social movements that are in touch with issues that evolve out of communicative action in the public sphere. In principle, civil society is independent of any social system, such as the state, the market, capitalism in general, family, or religion. Civil society, then, functions as a midpoint between the public sphere and social interactions. The elements of civil society provide a way through which the concerns developed in a robust speech community get expressed to society at large. One of the more important things civil society does is to continually challenge political and cultural organizations in order to keep intact the freedoms of speech, assembly, and press that are constitutionally guaranteed. Examples of elements of civil society include professional organizations, unions, charities, women's organizations, advocacy groups, and so on.

Habermas gives us several conditions that must be met for a robust civil society to evolve and exist.

- It must develop within the context of liberal political culture, one that emphasizes equality for all, and an active and integrated lifeworld.
- Within the boundaries of the public sphere, men and women may obtain influence based on persuasion but cannot obtain political power.
- A civil society can exist only within a social system where the state's power is limited. The state in no way occupies the position of the social actor designed to bring all society under control. The state's power must be limited and political steering must be indirect and leave intact the internal operations of the institution or subsystem.

Overall, Habermas rekindles the social vision that was at the heart of modernity's birth. Modernity began in the fervor of the Enlightenment and held the hope that humanity could be the master of its own fate. There were two primary branches of this movement, one contained in science and the other in democratic society. In many ways, science has proven its worth through the massive technological developments that have occurred over the past 200 years or so. However, Habermas argues that the hope of democracy has run aground on the rocks of organized capitalism. Further, the use of positivistic science to understand society and human relations rationalizes us away from seeing society as we ought and from true social discourse concerning issues of ethical and moral concern. In communicative action and civil society, he points the way to a fully involved citizenry reasoning out and charting their own course. But what Habermas gives us is an ideal—not in the sense of fantasy, but in the sense of an exemplar vision. In his theory, it is the goal toward which societies and citizens must strive if they are to fulfill the promise of modernity. Habermas, then, lays before us a challenge, "the big question of whether we could have had, or can now have, modernity without the less attractive features of capitalism and the bureaucratic nation-state" (Outhwaite, 2003, p. 231).

Summary

- Habermas' theory of modernity is in the tradition of the Frankfurt School of critical theory. His intent is to critique the current arrangements of capitalism and the state, while at the same time reestablishing the hope of the Enlightenment, that it is possible for human beings to guide their collective life through reason.

- Habermas argues that modernity has thus far been characterized by two forms of capitalism: liberal and organized. The principal difference between these two forms is the degree of state involvement. Under liberal capitalism, the relationship between the state and capitalism was one of laissez-faire. The state practiced a hands-off policy in the belief that the invisible hand of market competition would draw out the best in people and would result in true equality based on individual effort. However, laissez-faire capitalism produced two counter-results: the tendency toward monopolization and significant economic fluctuations due to overproduction. Both unanticipated results prompted greater state involvement and oversight of the capitalist system.

• Organized capitalism is characterized by active government spending and management of the economy. This involvement of the state in capitalism facilitates three distinct results, all of which weaken the possibility of achieving the social promise of modernity:

1. A crisis of legitimation and rationality. Because the state is now involved in managing the economy, fluctuations, downturns, and other economic ills are perceived as problems with the state rather than the economy. When they occur, these problems threaten the legitimacy of the state in general. In addition, because the state uses social scientific methods to forecast and control economies, belief in rationality is put in jeopardy. These crises in turn reduce the levels of meaning and motivation felt by the citizenry.

2. The colonization of the lifeworld. The lifeworld is colonized by the state and economy, as the media of power and money replace communication and consensus as the chief values of the lifeworld.

3. The reduction of the public sphere to one of public opinion. This occurs principally as the media have shifted from information to entertainment value and as the state makes use of social scientific methods to measure and then control public opinion.

• However, Habermas argues that the hope of social progress and equality can be embraced once again through communicative action and a robust civil society. Communication is based upon several assumptions, the most important of which concern validity claims—these inherently call for reason and reflection. Together, such assumptions lead Habermas to conclude that the process of communication itself gives us warrant to believe it is possible to reach consensus and rationally guide our collective lives.

• Communicative action is also a practice. True communicative action occurs when full equality is granted and each person is seen as an equal source of legitimate or valid statements; objective standings such as status, money, or power are not used in any way to persuade members; all topics may be introduced; and each person strives to keep his or her speech free from ideology.

• Communicative action results in and is based upon a robust civil society. Civil society is made up of mid-level voluntary associations, organizations, and social movements. Such organizations grow out of educated, rational, and critical communicative actions and become the medium through which the public sphere is revitalized. A civil society is most likely to develop under the following conditions: A liberal political culture is present that emphasizes education, communication, and equality; men and women are prevented from obtaining or using power in the public sphere; the state's power is limited.

TAKING THE PERSPECTIVE

As we saw in Chapter 2, critical theory took its cue and impetus from the inhumanity of Nazism and the Holocaust. And these forces of destruction only became more widespread through World War II and its aftermath: the American destruction of Hiroshima and the continued threat of nuclear annihilation, and the atrocities of Stalinism and the subsequent Cold War. These were forces of destruction not just of human life but of human spirit as well. The hope with which the twentieth century began lay in ashes by the end. Even the student "revolutions" of 1968 were smothered under the weight of state-sponsored capitalism, incessant commodification and advertising, and the spread of lifeless, homogeneous popular culture through the mass media. To continue to hope in participatory democracy and social justice seemed naive at best; and more generally the hope was swept under the rug of political apathy and the unceasing hunger for cultural stimulation with which the twenty-first century began. The face of humanity revealed during the twentieth century was as different as the one hoped for in the eighteenth century as the darkness of Hades is from the splendor of paradise.

That was critical theory's defining moment. The skepticism and critique born out of those historical moments are the weight that it bears, not as a burden (though burdensome it is) but as that which gives it presence and propels it forward. Having said that, there are questions about "whether it has any coherence as a 'school' of thought at all" (Ray, 1990, p. x). There have been at least three and maybe four phases that the Frankfurt School has gone through. And there are many works that have a sense of critical theory about them but owe little to the actual School itself. However, I think there are four issues around which most critical theory gathers.

First, there is an emphasis on the relationship between history and society on the one hand and social position and knowledge on the other. To understand any society, you must first understand its historical path and the structural arrangements within it. The knowledge and political interests that people hold within any society are based upon a person's social position within a historically specific social and cultural context.

Second, critical theory specifically critiques positivism and the idea that knowledge can be value-free. With humans, all knowledge is based on and reflects values. Positivistic knowledge through social science is simply blinded to its own biases and is but a reification of method. The supreme use of reason is emancipation, bringing equality and freedom to all humankind. The purpose, then, of theory and sociology is not understanding, not control, but emancipation. Critical theory, then, is always applied to the human condition.

Third, the work of critical theory is open-ended and is simply and only dependent upon and guiding by critical thinking. Overall the work of the Frankfurt School and those who have followed indicate that it isn't possible to clearly, truthfully, and accurately plan out the right path for humanity; there is no right society, no goal toward which we strive. The idea that there is lies at the base of why "social science" is an oxymoron—control in order to bring freedom, objectification to understand the subject. But not only is the idea wrongheaded, humans living in rationalized, commodified, mediated culture are too entwined with the spirit of the age to see clearly. We can but see dimly at best. Critical theory and critical thinking are meant to help us examine and deconstruct our thoughts and thinking. The goal of critical theory is subversion:

"The project of Critical Theory has been to develop ways of thinking so subversive of dominant legitimations, that to understand them was to resist them" (Ray, 1990, p. xviii).

This leads to the fourth quality, which is found particularly in Habermas: The vehicle for social change is participatory democracy guided by critical theory and thought. Most of what passes as "democracy" is nothing but oligarchy by the powerful elite. This rule by few produces a false totality, which, in truth, is antagonistic and held together by oppressive power. In contrast, the intent of social democracy is the intellectual and practical involvement of all its citizens.

BUILDING YOUR THEORY TOOLBOX

Learning More—Primary Sources

- See the following works by Jürgen Habermas:

  - *The Theory of Communicative Action, Vol. 1: Reason and the Rationalization of Society,* Beacon Press, 1984; *Vol. 2: Lifeworld and System: A Critique of Functionalist Reason,* Beacon Press, 1987.

  - *The Philosophical Discourse of Modernity: Twelve Lectures,* MIT Press, 1990.

  - *The Structural Transformation of the Public Sphere: An Inquiry Into a Category of Bourgeois Society,* MIT Press, 1991.

Learning More—Secondary Sources

- For secondary resources see:

  - *Habermas's Critical Theory of Society,* by Jane Braaten, SUNY Press, 1991.

  - *Habermas and the Public Sphere,* edited by Craig Calhoun, MIT Press, 1993.

  - *Habermas: A Critical Introduction,* by William Outhwaite, Stanford University Press, 1995.

Check It Out:

- Strong coverage of critical theory in the social disciplines and philosophy:

  - http://plato.stanford.edu/entries/critical-theory/
- Online resource for readings from various critical theorists:

  - http://www.uiowa.edu/~commstud/resources/critical_authors.html
- Habermas on YouTube:

  - http://www.youtube.com/watch?v=jB16ALNh18Q

  - http://www.youtube.com/watch?v=oTCuRlz22g4

(Continued)

(Continued)

Seeing the World

- Write a 250-word synopsis of the theoretical perspective critical theory.

- After reading and understanding this chapter, you should be able to define the following terms theoretically and explain their theoretical importance to Habermas' theory: *legitimacy, authority, lifeworld, liberal capitalism, depoliticized class, public sphere, pragmatic consensus, organized capitalism, legitimation crisis, colonization of the lifeworld, steering, generalized media of exchange, colonization of the public sphere, public opinion, analytic knowledge, interpretive knowledge, critical theory, speech communities, communicative action, civil society*

- After reading and understanding this chapter, you should be able to answer the following questions (remember to answer them *theoretically*):

  o Explain the differences between liberal and organized capitalism. Pay particular attention to the changing relations between the state and economy.

  o Define the lifeworld and its purpose, and explain how it became colonized.

  o Define the public sphere and explain how it came about, its purpose, and its colonization.

  o What is communicative action and how does it form the basis of value-rational action?

  o Define ideal speech situations (or communities) and explain how they give rise to civil society.

  o What is civil society? What are the conditions under which it can survive? How is it important to a democratic society?

Engaging the World

- Using your favorite Internet search engine, look up "participatory democracy." How would Habermas' ideal speech community fit this model? Does the Internet provide greater possibilities for ideal speech situations to develop? How could Internet communities be linked to civil society?

- Racial, ethnic, gender, sexual identity, and religious groups have all been and are being disenfranchised in modern society. How does the ideal speech situation "enfranchise" these groups? In other words, how does the ideal speech situation do away with the possibility of disenfranchised groups?

- What social group do you belong to that most nearly approximates the ideal speech community?

- How can you begin your own praxis?

Weaving the Threads

- You have now had several theoretically informed assessments of and guidelines for participatory democracy. Write a one-page synopsis of the assessments and principles for reinvigorating democracy for each of the following: Wallerstein, Castells, and Habermas.

CHAPTER 12

Runaway Modernity:

Anthony Giddens

(1938–)

As we've seen, modernity began as a time when human beings believed they could control the physical and social worlds in order to life human existence. We've also seen, and are aware from simply living in this age, that there are problems. Yet Anthony Giddens takes us on another path, not pointing to the issues that have come up along the way, but, rather, the idea of modernity contains intrinsic contradictions that make it impossible to fulfill its own reason for existence. According to Giddens (1990), modernity is a juggernaut, "a runaway engine of enormous power which, collectively as human beings, we can drive to some extent but which also threatens to rush out of our control and which could rend itself asunder" (p. 139). The word *juggernaut* comes from the Hindi word *Jagannātha*, which refers to a representation of the god Vishnu or Krishna—the lord of the universe. Every year the god's image would be paraded down the streets amid crowds of the faithful, dancing and playing drums and cymbals. It's thought that at times believers would throw themselves under the wheels of the massive cart, to be crushed to death in a bid for early salvation. A juggernaut, then, is an irresistible force that demands blind devotion and sacrifice.

This image of an irresistible force conjures up the thrilling ride of the roller coaster, with its twin sensations of trust and danger, but the juggernaut of modernity isn't as controllable or predictable as a roller coaster. Here we can see a chief difference between Giddens and Habermas: For Habermas, rational control is central to modernity and imminently possible, inherent in the very act of communication; but for Giddens, modernity is almost by definition out of control. The intent of modernity is progress—but the effect of modernity is the creation of mechanisms and processes that become a runaway engine of change. And we, like the devotees of Jagannātha, are drawn to modernity's power and promise.

> The ride is by no means wholly unpleasant or unrewarding; it can often be exhilarating and charged with hopeful anticipation. But, so long as the institutions of modernity endure, we shall never be able to control completely either the path or the pace of the journey. In turn, we shall never be able to feel entirely secure, because the terrain across which it runs is fraught with risks of high consequence. (Giddens, 1990, p. 139)

THEORIST'S DIGEST

Brief Biography

Anthony Giddens was born January 18, 1938, in Edmonton, England. He received his undergraduate degree with honors from Hull University in 1959, studying sociology and psychology. Giddens did his master's work at the London School of Economics, finishing his thesis on the sociology of sport in 1961. From then until the early 1970s, Giddens lectured at various universities including the University of Leicester, Simon Fraser University, the University of California at Los Angeles, and Cambridge. Giddens finished his doctoral work at Cambridge in 1976. He remained at Cambridge through 1996, during which time he served as dean of Social and Political Sciences. In 1997, Giddens was appointed director of the London School of Economics and Political Science. Giddens is the author of some 34 books that have been translated into well over 20 languages. Giddens is also a member of the Advisory Council of the Institute for Public Policy Research (London, England) and has served as advisor to British prime minister Tony Blair.

Central Sociological Questions

Giddens is a political sociologist, driven by both political questions and political involvement. While his early work certainly contained a typical Marxian interest in class, his later work is much more concerned with the political ramifications of globalization and what he characterizes as the juggernaut of modernity or the runaway world. Given the juggernaut of modernity, he asks, how are interactions and behaviors patterned over time? How can people become politically involved? In order to answer those questions, Giddens must first understand the essence of society. In this, Giddens seeks an ontology of the social world: What kinds of things go into the making of society? Precisely how does it exist?

Simply Stated

Society is not made up of objective structures that determine and pattern action across time and space. Rather, because the human world is a constructed world, people are psychologically motivated to routinize their behaviors and to see them as belonging in specific social places. In traditional society, these were assured through kinship, community, and religion. But modern society has rendered those ineffectual through radical reflexivity, the emptying of time and space, disembedding of social relationships, and globalization. The result is that the certitude of traditional society has been replaced with tenuous social relations, individualized and uncertain projects of self-actualization, and lifestyle politics rather than the politics of emancipation.

Key Ideas

Structuration theory, duality of structure, social structures, normative rules, signification codes, authoritative resources, allocative resources, time–space distanciation, modalities of structuration, domination, institutional orders, reflexive monitoring, rationalization of action, discursive consciousness, practical consciousness, routinization, regionalization, ontological security, radical reflexivity, separation of time and space, disembedding mechanisms, symbolic tokens, expert systems, reflexive project of the self, bodily regimes, organization of sensuality, pure relationships, emancipatory politics, life politics, mediated experiences.

Concepts and Theory:
The Reality of Society and Its People

I usually address the perspective of the theorist later in the chapter. But with Giddens, I need to put it first. In order to understand the power of what Giddens says about modernity, we have to understand his perspective first. We've seen that the social project of modernity is based on the existence of two factors: society and free agents. In order to use science to understand and guide society, society must exist as an object capable of being studied and discovered. And in order to guide society through democracy, citizens had to have the power of reason and the ability to make free choices. We have come across critiques of this already. But Giddens proceeds in a different direction. His understanding of modernity is based on a distinct understanding of what society is and how people can affect it. He also reformulates the problem of social order. And we have to grasp these issues before we can appreciate his theory of modernity. His understanding of society and social actors is called **structuration theory**.

The Way Society Exists

Here's the simple version: Society doesn't exist as objective structures; rather, it is continually built or structured by reflexive social actors (people). That might sound familiar, and it should. Giddens uses insights from the material we covered in Chapters 3 to 5: symbolic interaction, ethnomethodology, and dramaturgy. It might also sound simple, but be careful. In using and explaining these insights he explains their ontology. The word *ontology* means the study of existence. So Giddens explains the fundamental reality in back of symbolic interaction, ethnomethodology, and dramaturgy. He does so because it's important for us to understand the way society exists to truly grasp what is going on in modernity. Giddens introduces a number of new terms in this section; and it's always difficult reading through such material. But there are two things I want you to keep in mind. First, if you understood Chapters 3–5, you already have a basic understanding of what Giddens is talking about; he is just taking you one more step. The second thing to keep in mind is the simple version I started this paragraph with. Giddens just builds on that, so if you feel lost, come back to the simple model and see where it fits in. And, take it one step at a time.

Step 1: Understanding Two Things at Once

Giddens draws on ethnomethodology for this idea; and it simply says that social things exist together, not apart. Like Bourdieu, Giddens argues that the subject–object divide (or agent–structure) is a false dichotomy, created to explain away the complexity of human practice. Giddens (1986) says, "Human social activities, like some self-reproducing items in nature, are recursive" (p. 2). It's like the chicken and egg question, which in some ways is a silly one. When you have the egg, you have the chicken. They are one and the same, just in different phases. So, to follow the analogy, it's like this: Social actors produce social reality, but the mere fact that you have "social actors" presumes an already existing social world.

The primary insight of Giddens' structuration theory is that social structures and agency are recursively and reflexively produced: They are continuously brought into existence at the same moment through the same behaviors. Rather than seeing structure and agency as a dualism, as two mutually exclusive elements, Giddens proposes a duality—two analytically distinguishable parts of the same thing. The *duality of structure* indicates that structure is both the medium and the outcome of the social activity or conduct that it reflexively organizes.

"This is a difficult concept to understand, so let me give you an example." And I just did. I put the first sentence of this paragraph in quotation marks because it is our example. Any time we write or speak a sentence, we do a couple of things. First, and most obviously, we create the sentence. The second and less obvious thing we do is re-create the rules through which the sentence was made in the first place. This is a little tricky, so pay close attention. In order to put together a sentence, we have to follow the rules. If we don't, the sentence won't make any sense and it won't really be a sentence. Thus, in order to exist as a sentence, the line of words must be formed according to the rules. Yet, at the same moment we create the sentence, we also re-create the rules through which the sentence was made in the first place.

You might say, "Wait a minute, the rules existed before the sentence." Did they? You learned the rules in school and those rules are found in English grammar texts, right? In fact, we often refer to the grades between the primary levels and high school as "grammar school" because that's where you learn the rules of grammar. But is that really where you learned the rules? If it was, it would imply that you couldn't form a sentence before reaching that point in school. But the fact is you could form sentences well before you "learned the rules"; further, studies have shown that 5- and 6-year-olds make use of very complex grammars. In truth, the rules you learned in school are the rules you already knew. The difference is that the rules found in grammar texts are formalized interpretations of the rules that already exist in the language itself; grammars and dictionaries are produced by academics based on the study of language. Note that grammarians study the language to discover the rules—the rules are already there in the language. The rules for making the sentence are in the sentence itself—the expression and the structure are created in the same moment. According to Giddens, the same is true about social agents and structures.

Step 2: The Stuff of Social Structures

Here Giddens simply says that social structures aren't things that exist apart from people; *social structures* exist in the ways that people use rules and resources. There are two kinds of rules: normative rules and codes of signification. Keep in mind that in both cases these "rules" are fluidly embedded in social practices. They don't exist abstractly or independently. Giddens also notes that rules may be consistently or rarely invoked, tacit or discursive, informal or formal, and weakly or strongly sanctioned. You should be familiar with *normative rules*—they are rules that govern behavior, such as the norm against littering. But signification codes require a bit of explanation.

Signification codes are rules through which meaning is produced. In our sentence illustration above, the signification code is lodged in the practices of speaking and writing. One example of the consequence of these codes or rules is the rhetoric of political spin-doctors. Spin-doctors want to guide us so that we interpret events in a specific manner; but in doing so they must abide by generally accepted rules of interpretation. If they don't, then chances are good that we won't buy their "spin." It's important to mention that these rules are historically and culturally specific. That's why interpretations can change over time. There are also two kinds of resources: authoritative and allocative. *Authoritative resources* are made up of such things as techniques or technologies of management, organizational position, and expert knowledge. Allocative resources come from the control of material goods or the material world. Resources, then, involve the control of people and supplies.

I've pictured the duality of structure in Figure 12.1. A we've seen, Giddens argues that structure and agency are mutually formed in the same act. Just as in our sentence example, the rules and resources that are used in social encounters both create and are found in the interaction and structure. The act of social co-presence is possible only through the use of social rules and resources—and the rules and resources exist only in the act of social co-presence. Thus, structure and agency are mutually constructed through the use of the exact same rules and resources, as noted by all the two-headed arrows in the figure.

Figure 12.1   Duality of Structure

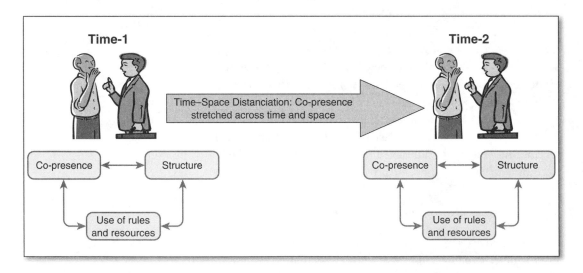

Step 3: Expressing Structure and Creating Social Order

We want to see two things in this step. First, Giddens talks about the problem of social order that Parsons and Garfinkel were concerned about as really just a problem of time and space. If we're all together at once in one place, it's easy to see how we make sure everybody acts together. The problem of order comes about when different interactions are separate either through geographic space or time. Notice the large arrow linking the two sets of interactions in Figure 12.1. The arrow indicates how behaviors and encounters are patterned over time. Giddens (1986) rephrases the problem of patterning action in terms of **time–space distanciation**: "*The fundamental question of social theory . . . is to explicate how the limitations of individual 'presence' are transcended by the 'stretching' of social relations across time and space*" (p. 35, emphasis added). The idea of time–space distanciation refers to the ways in which physical co-presence is stretched through time and space. This is a fairly unique and graphic way of thinking about patterning behaviors. We can think of Giddens' idea as an analogy: If you've ever played with Silly Putty or bubble gum by stretching it out, then you can see what he is talking about. What this analogy implies is that the interactions at Time-1 and Time-2 appear patterned because they are made out of the same materials that are stretched out over time and space.

The second thing Giddens wants us to see here is his answer to the question in the quote above: How does it happen? His answer is found in his idea of **modalities of structuration**. The word *modality* is related to the word *mode,* which refers to a form or pattern of expression, as in someone's mode of dress or behavior. For example, in writing this book, I'm currently in my academic mode. Modalities of structuration, then, are simply ways in which rules and resources are knowingly used by people in interactions.

I've pictured a bit of what Giddens is getting at in Figure 12.2. Notice that there are three elements in the circle: social practices, modalities, and structures.

Figure 12.2   Modalities of Structuration

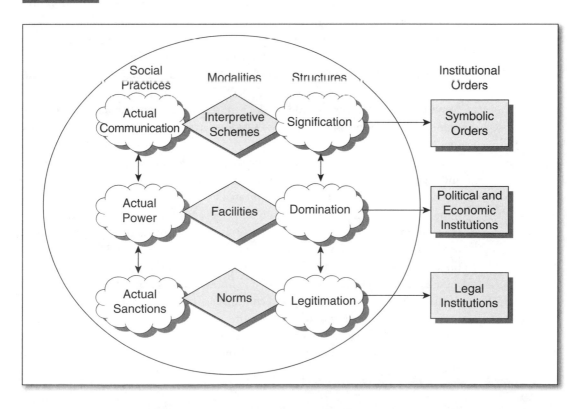

Modalities of structuration are ways in which structure and practice (or agency) are expressed. I've indicated that relationship by the use of overlapping diamonds. In a loose way, we can think of structures as the music itself; the modalities as the mode of reproduction, as in analog or digital; and the social practices as the musician. As you can see, Giddens gives us three modalities or modes of expression (interpretive schemes, facilities, and norms), corresponding on the one hand to three social practices (communication, power, and sanctions), and on the other to structures (signification, domination, and legitimation).

This isn't as complicated as it might seem. Let's use the example of you talking to your professor in class. Let's say that in this conversation you refuse to take the test that he or she has scheduled. The professor reacts by telling you that you will fail the course if you don't take the test. What just happened? You can break it down using Giddens' modalities of structuration, following the model in Figure 12.2. First, there were actual social practices that involved communication and sanctions. Your communication was interpreted using a scheme that both you and your professor know. For convenience sake, let's call this scheme "meanings in educational settings." You know this interpretive scheme because it is part of the general signification structure of this society at the beginning of the twenty-first century. Second, the professor invoked sanctions based on norms of classroom behavior. Again, you both know these norms because they are part of the legitimation structure of this society.

I'm sure you were able to follow this discussion through the model without any difficulty. And I'm also sure that you didn't have any trouble with any of the phrases I used in the above explanation. Things like "society at the beginning of the twenty-first century" sound reasonable and familiar. But remember, the first principle of structuration theory is duality, not dualism. So when we use the term *society* or *structure*, we are not talking about something separate from social practices. Like our sentence illustration, the actual conversation between you and the professor, and the interpretive schemes and the structure of signification, all come into existence at the same moment. Apart from signification and interpretation, communication can't exist; and likewise, without actual communication, interpretation and communication can't exist. Obviously, the same is true for the sanctions that the professor invoked.

In terms of Giddens' definition of structure as rules and resources, signification and legitimation are more closely tied to rules and domination is more linked to resources (facilities). *Domination* is expressed as actual power through the facilities of authoritative and allocative resources. For example, part of the way the actual power of the university over me as a professor is expressed is through the facilities of classroom space, computer and Internet access, and so forth. By encircling all these elements together and by using two-headed arrows, I'm indicating that all these processes—the social practices, modalities, and structures—are reflexive and recursive. That is, they mutually and continuously influence one another.

Part of what I want you to see in Figure 12.2 is the connectedness of all social practices, modalities, and structures. They are all tied up together and expressed and produced in the same moment. Further, the recursive and interpenetrated nature of these facets of social life is what Giddens means by institutionalization, or the stretching out of co-presence across time and space. Remember, human life is ongoing. The process that I've placed a circle around in Figure 12.2 works like a ball that just keeps rolling downhill. It is this continuity of recursive practices and structures that stretches interactions across time and space. Comparing Figure 12.1 and Figure 12.2, we can think of the two men talking as moments in which we stopped the ball and looked inside. The arrow between the two sets of interactions depicts the movement of the ball between those two moments.

There's one other thing that we need to notice from Figure 12.2. All of this action of institutionalization results in different *institutional orders*. While there are some terms in there that look familiar, like "economic institutions," they aren't the same as we usually think of them. Many sociologists think of institutions as substantive and distinct (or "differentiated," in functionalist terms). In other words, most sociologists treat institutions as if they are real, separate objects with independent effects. However, Giddens is saying that institutions don't exist as substantive things or objects and they aren't truly separate and distinct. Notice that the different institutional orders are all made from the same fabric; it's just cut or put together differently in each case. They all draw from the same structures (rules and resources) of signification (S), domination (D), and legitimation (L), but emphasizing one of the elements over the others produces different kinds of institutional orders.

Making Society and Hiding It—How Much Do We Really Know?

Blumer, Garfinkel, and Goffman all agree that we actually create society in face-to-face interactions. So, that's not news for us. What Giddens is going to do is go deeper, behind the scenes to see what's going on inside us as we achieve social order and reality. Some of it we're aware of, but probably not in the way you think. And some of it works below the level of our awareness. Giddens argues that there are three important things going on in interactions: reflexive monitoring of action, rationalization of action, and motivation for action. Giddens thinks of these tasks as being "stratified," or as having different levels of awareness. The behavior that we're most aware of is *reflexive monitoring*. In order to interact with one another, people must watch the behaviors of other people, monitor the flow of the conversation, and keep track of their own actions. As part of this routine accomplishment, we can also provide reasons for what we do; that is, we can provide a rationalization of our own actions.

In talking about *rationalization of action*, Giddens makes a distinction between discursive and practical consciousness. The word *discursive* is related to discourse or conversation. But it has a deeper meaning as well: It's a discourse marked by analytical reasoning. So *discursive consciousness* refers to the ability to give a reasoned verbal account of our actions. It's what we know and can express about social practices and situations. This consciousness is clearly linked to reflexive monitoring of the encounter and the rationalization of action—discursive consciousness is our awareness of these two.

Practical consciousness refers to the knowledge that we have about how to exist and behave socially. However, people can't verbally express this knowledge. Social situations and practices are extremely complex, according to Giddens, and they thus require a vast and nuanced base of knowledge, and we have to act more by intuition than by rational thought. This idea isn't as difficult as it might seem. We can think of the ability to perform an opening ritual ("Hey, how's it going?") as part of this practical consciousness. People know *how* to perform an opening ritual, but most people can't rationally explain *why* they do it.

There's an important point to note about discursive and practical consciousnesses: They aren't necessarily linked. At first glance, it might appear that discursive consciousness is our ability to explain what practical consciousness tells us to do. But notice what I said above about practical consciousness: "People can't verbally express this knowledge." So discursive consciousness (the explanation) isn't necessarily associated in any real way with practical consciousness (the actions). We know how to act and we know how to explain our action, but both of these issues are part of the social interaction, not part of the unconscious motivations of the actor.

The All-Important Unconscious Motivation

Practical consciousness is bound up with the production of routine. It's like driving a car or riding a bicycle; most of what is involved is done out of habit or practical consciousness. In the same way, most of what we do socially on a daily basis is routine. Routinization "is a fundamental concept in structuration theory" (Giddens 1986, p. xxii) and refers to the process through which the activities of day-to-day life become habitual and taken for granted. *Routinization,* then, is a primary way in which face-to-face interactions are stretched across time and space (Figure 12.1). Or put another way, routinization is one of the main ways through which the modalities of structuration are institutionalized (Figure 12.2). Part of the way we routinize activities is through *regionalization,* which is the zoning of time and space in relation to routinized social practices. In other words, because we divide physical space up, we can more easily routinize our behaviors. Thus, certain kinds of social practices occur in specific places and times. Regionalization varies by form, character, duration, and span.

The form of the region is given in terms of the kinds of barriers or boundaries that are used to section it off from other regions. The form allows greater or lesser possible levels of co-presence. When you stop and talk with someone in the hallway, there is a symbolic boundary around the two of you that is fairly permeable; it is very possible that others could join in. However, when you go into the men's or women's restroom, there is a physical and symbolic barrier that explicitly limits the possibility of co-presence.

The character of the region references the kind of social practices that can typically take place within a region. For example, people have lived in houses for centuries, but the character of the house has changed over time. In agrarian societies, the home was the center of the economy, government, and family; but in modern capitalist societies, the home is the exclusive domain of family and is thus private rather than public.

The duration and span of the region refer to the amount of geographic space and to the length or kind of time. Certain regions are usually available for social practices only during certain parts of the day or for specific lengths of time; the bedroom is an example in the sense that it is usually associated with "sleep time." Regions also span across space in varying degrees. So, a coliseum gives unique opportunities for co-presence and social activities when compared to an airplane.

We come now to what actually patterns structuration and time–space distanciation—Giddens calls it **ontological security**. As we've seen, the word *ontology* refers to existence, so ontological security is simply being secure in the reality we've created. But even though that sounds simple, it's pretty amazing. We create reality, then we make ourselves feel secure that the created reality is actually real. The truth of the matter is that the reality of the human world is existentially moored in meaning, which is fallible, mutable, and uncertain. As the philosopher Ernst Cassirer (1944) puts it,

> No longer can man confront reality immediately; he cannot see it, as it were, face to face. Physical reality seems to recede in proportion as man's symbolic activity advances. Instead of dealing with the things themselves man is in a sense constantly conversing with himself. (p. 42)

According to Giddens, if people ever notice this about their reality, they will suffer deep psychological angst. We are motivated, then, as a result of this unconscious psychological insecurity about the socially created world, *to make the world routine and thus taken for granted*. Note that this anxiety is unconscious—it isn't usually experienced; but when it is, it is felt as a diffuse, general sense of unease.

According to Giddens (1990), ontological security refers to the feelings of "confidence that most humans [sic] beings have in the continuity of their self identity and in the constancy of the surrounding social and material environments of action" (p. 92). Giddens argues that the fundamental trust of ontological security is generally produced in early childhood and maintained through adult routines. Because most of the social practices in our lives are carried out by routine, we experience trust in the world, due to its routine character, and we can take for granted the ontological status of the world. In premodern societies, trust and routine in traditional institutions covered up the contingency of the world. Kinship and community created bonds that reliably structured actions through time and space. Religion provided a cosmology that reliably ordered experience. And tradition itself structured social and natural events, because tradition by definition is routine.

Now we're about to take our final step in our journey to understand society and its people. Remember the fundamental problem of social order? It's time–space distanciation. And remember why it's a problem? Because according to Giddens there are no such things as objective social structures that coerce us to act in certain ways. So, how and why do we do it? The how is structuration but the why is extremely important. The ultimate force behind us solving the problem of time–space distanciation is our deep-seated need for ontological security. That need drives us to routinize and regionalize behaviors.

Traditional societies provided routinization and regionalization without fail through kinship, community, and religion. However, in modern societies *none of these institutional settings produces a strong sense of trust and ontological security.* According to Giddens, those needs are met differently: Routine is integrated into abstract systems, pure relationships substitute for the connectedness of community and kin, and reflexively constructed knowledge systems replace religious cosmologies— but not with the certainty or the psychological rewards of premodern institutions. The result is that ontological insecurity—anxiety regarding the "existential anchoring of reality" (Giddens, 1991, p. 38)—is a greater possibility in modern rather than traditional societies.

Concepts and Theory: The Contours of Modernity

We have now laid the groundwork for Giddens' understanding of how society works in general: Actors are motivated to routinize social actions and interactions by the psychological need for ontological security. These routines serve to stretch out face-to-face encounters through time and space as actors use different modalities to express the social structures of signification, domination, and legitimation through their social practices. This constant structuration produces different institutional orders that, along with regionalization, work to stabilize routine. Routinization and the institutional orders that it generates stabilize time–space distanciation and thus give the individual a continual basis of trust in her or his social environment, which, in turn, provides the individual with ontological security.

Thus, in Giddens' scheme, society isn't structured; that is, it doesn't exist as an obdurate object with an independent existence. The important point here is that society by its nature is continually susceptible to disruption or change. This constant possibility is, of course, what creates the diffuse and unconscious sense of insecurity that people have about the reality of society. However, this possibility is also what makes modernity an important issue, for both the process of structuration and for the person. In the next section, we will think about how living in modernity influences our experience of our self and others. But for now simply think about how the dynamic quality of modernity radically changes structuration and time–space distanciation. There are four analytically distinct factors that produce the dynamism of modernity: radical reflexivity, the separation of time and space, disembedding mechanisms, and globalization. As we'll see, though we can separate these areas analytically, they empirically reinforce one another.

Radical Reflexivity

Giddens sees reflexivity as a variable, rather than a static condition. He argues that modernity creates a level of *radical reflexivity.* Previous to this time, people didn't think much about society. In fact, the entire idea of society as an entity unto itself wasn't really conceived of until the work of people like Montesquieu and Durkheim. Today, we are quite aware of society and we think deliberatively about our nation and the organizations and institutions in which we participate.

Progress and reflexivity are intrinsically related. It only takes a moment's reflection to see that progress demands reflexivity. It is endemic in modernity because every social unit must constantly evaluate itself in terms of its mission, goals, and practices. However, the hope of progress never materializes—the ideal of progress means that we never truly arrive. Every step in our progressive march forward is examined in the hopes of improving what we have achieved. Progress becomes a motivating value and a discursive feature of modernity, rather than a goal that is ever reached.

Here's a real-life example. Chances are good that you are attending an accredited college or university. Schools of higher education are certified by regional accrediting organizations. Being accredited allows you as a student to qualify for federal financial aid and to transfer credits from one college to another, and it allows professors to apply for federal grants for research. At my university, we just finished with our reaccreditation self-study. This self-study took 2 years to complete. Even though 2 years seems like a long time, we actually began preparing for the self-study the 2 years previous by evaluating our mission statement in light of what we knew to be the new criteria of accreditation.

Out of the first study came a new mission statement that was then used during the following study to reevaluate every aspect of the university (notice the reflexive element). The self-study produced recommendations for the next 10 years, and the study and its recommendations were scrutinized by a committee of academics and administrators sent by our regional affiliation. Changes were and will be implemented as a result of the study. The interesting thing to me is that 80% to 90% of the study deals with things that are only tangentially related to actual learning, which is what we think the university is about. Most of the study addresses symbolic or political issues that have little to do with what happens in the classroom or in your learning experience. The greater proportion of the changes, then, would not have come about except for their symbolic or political values and reflexive organization.

Modern organizations are bureaucratic in nature and are thus bound up with rational goal setting, recursive practices, and continual reflexivity. For example, the reaccreditation study I just mentioned will be repeated in 10 years and every 10 years thereafter. This year my department is doing its self-study, and it gets repeated every 5 years. When I worked for Denny's restaurants as a manager, we had corporate plans that helped form the regional plans that helped create the unit plans, which strongly influenced my personal plans as a manager. Depending on the level, those plans were systematically evaluated every 1 to 5 years. Modern organizations, institutions, and society at large are thus defined through the continued use of reflexive evaluation.

One further point about radical reflexivity: It forms part of our basic understanding of knowledge and rational life. Modern knowledge is equivalent to scientific knowledge, and part of what makes knowledge scientific is continual scrutiny and systematic doubt. This understanding of knowledge is woven into the fabric of our culture. Every child in the United States receives training in what is called scientific literacy. According to the National Academy of Sciences (1995),

> This nation has established as a goal that all students should achieve scientific literacy. The *National Science Education Standards* are designed to enable the nation to achieve that goal. They spell out a vision of science education that will make scientific literacy for all a reality in the 21st century.

Thus, children in the United States are systematically trained to be reflexive about knowledge in general.

Emptying Time and Space

In this section, it is very important for you to keep in mind what Giddens means by *time–space distanciation*—it's his way of talking about how our behaviors and actions are patterned and are thus somewhat predictable. Therefore, whatever happens to time and space in modernity influences the patterns of interaction that make up society. With that in mind, Giddens argues that the *separation of time and space* is crucial to the dynamic quality of modernity.

In order to understand how time and space can be emptied, we have to begin by thinking about how humans have related to time and space for most of our existence. Up until the beginnings of modernity, time and space were closely linked to natural settings and cycles. People have always marked time, but it was originally associated with natural places and cycles. The cycle of the sun set the boundaries of the day, the cycle of the moon marked the month, and the year was noted by the cycles of the seasons. But the week, which is the primary tool we use to organize ourselves today, exists nowhere in nature. It's utterly abstract in terms of nature. Something similar may be said about the mechanical clock. Previous to the invention and widespread use of the mechanical clock, people regulated their behaviors around the moving of the sun. (See Roy, 2001, pp. 40–45; McCready, 2001.)

Thus, in modern societies, time and space have become abstract entities that have been emptied of any natural connections. Further, the concept of space itself has become stretched out and more symbolic than physical. As I mentioned, modernity is distinguished by the belief in progress. Progress implies change, and the emptying of time and space "serves to open up manifold possibilities of change by breaking free from the restraints of local habits and practices" (Giddens, 1990, p. 20). Making time and space abstract has also aided in another distinctive feature of modernity, the bureaucratic organization. Our lives are subject to rational organization precisely because time and space are emptied of natural and social relations. My students and I can all meet at 9:45 a.m. in the Graham building, Room 308, for class because time and space have been emptied. And Boeing manufacturing in California can order parts from a steel plant in China to be ready for assembly beginning in January because time and space are abstract.

The emptying of time and space means that time–space distanciation can be increased almost without limit, which is one of the defining characteristics of modernity. Traditional societies are defined by close-knit social networks that create high levels of morality and an emphasis on long-established social practices and relationships. Any social form that could break with the importance of tradition would have to be built upon something other than close-knit social groups. Modernity, then, is defined as the time during which greater and greater distances are placed between people and their social relations. As we'll see, increasing time–space distanciation and escalating reflexivity mutually reinforce one another, and together they create the dynamism of modernity—the tendency for continual change.

Institutions and Disembedding Mechanisms

In discussing the transition from traditional to modern society, many sociologists talk about structural differentiation, especially functionalists. The problem that Giddens sees in institutional differentiation is that it can't give a reasoned account of a central feature of modernity: radical time–space distanciation. However, thinking about institutions in terms of disembedding mechanisms does. Thus, Giddens claims that the distinction between traditional and modern institutions isn't differentiation so much as it is embedding versus disembedding. *Disembedding mechanisms* are those practices that lift out social relations and interactions from local contexts. Again, let's picture a kind of ideal type of traditional society where most social relationships and interactions take place in encounters that are firmly entrenched in local situations. People would live in places where they knew everybody and would depend upon people they knew for help. Distant situations, along with distant others, were kept truly distant. There are two principal mechanisms that lifted life out of its local context: symbolic tokens and expert systems.

Symbolic tokens are understood in terms of media of exchange that can be passed around without any regard for a specific person or group. There are a few of these kinds of tokens around, but the example par excellence is money. Money creates a universal value system wherein every commodity can be understood according to the same value system. Of necessity, this value system is abstract; that is, it has no intrinsic worth. In order for it to stand for everything, it must have no value in itself. The universal and abstract nature of money frees it from constraint and facilitates exchanges over long distances and time periods. Thus, by its very nature, money increases time–space distanciation. And, the greater the level of abstraction of money, such as through credit and soft currencies, the greater will be this effect.

The other disembedding mechanism that Giddens talks about is *expert systems*. Let's again think about a traditional community. If you lived in a traditional community and were going to have a baby, to whom would you go? If in the same group you experienced marital problems, where would you go for advice? If you wanted to know how to grow better crops or appease the gods or construct a building or do anything that required some form of social cooperation, where would you go? The answer to all these questions, and all the rest of the details of living life, would be your social network. If you wanted to grow better crops, you might go to your friend Paul whose fields always seem full and alive. For marital advice, you would probably go to your grandparents; for childbirth help, you'd go to the neighbor's wife who had been practicing midwifery for as long as you can remember.

Where do we go for these things today? We go to experts—people that we don't personally know who have been trained academically in abstract knowledge. But we don't really have to "go to" an expert to be dependent upon expert systems of knowledge. For instance, I have no idea how to construct a building that has many levels and can house a myriad of classrooms and offices, yet I'm dependent upon that expert knowledge every time I go to my office or teach in a classroom. Every time we turn on a computer or flick a light switch or start our car or go to buy food at the grocery store—in short, every time we do anything that is associated with living in modernity—we are dependent upon abstract, expert systems of knowledge. Systems of expert knowledge are disembedding because they shift the center of our life away from local contexts to dependence on abstract knowledge and distant others, who sometimes never appear.

Globalization

Giddens argues that four institutions in particular form the dynamic and time period of modernity: capitalism, industrialism, monopoly of violence, and surveillance. In terms of the dynamic of modernity, capitalism stands out. Capitalism is intrinsically expansive. It is driven by the perceived need for profit, which in turn drives the expansion of markets, technologies, and commodification.

Industrialization is of course linked to capitalism, but it has its own dynamics and relationships with the other institutional spheres. Industrialism, the monopoly of coercive power, and surveillance feed one another and create what is generally referred to as the industrial-military complex. A military complex is formed by a standing army and the parts of the economy that are oriented toward military production. Once a coercive force begins to use technology, it becomes not only dependent upon industrialism but also provides a constant impetus for more and better technologies of force and surveillance. A military complex by its very existence is not only available for protection, it is also in its best interests to instigate aggression whenever possible in order to expand its own base and the interests of its institutional partners.

From Chapter 9, you already know that capitalism naturally implies relationships among various nations, and if you take a moment, you'll see that the military complex also implies international relations. Thus, the institutional dimensions of modernity are explicitly tied up with globalization. Giddens (1990) defines globalization as "the intensification of worldwide social relations which link distant localities in such a way that local happenings are shaped by events occurring many miles away and vice versa" (p. 64). Globalization is thus defined in terms of a dialectic relation between the local and the distant that further stretch out co-presence through time and space. The four dimensions of globalization, according to Giddens, are the world capitalist economy, the world military order, the international division of labor, and the nation-state system.

In order to help us get a handle on what Giddens is arguing, I've drawn out the chief processes that we've been talking about in Figure 12.3. Most all of the factors on the far left of the model are interrelated in some way. For example, the use of bureaucratic, rational management increases in the presence of world capitalism and expert systems. But to draw out all the relationships at that level would defeat the purpose of the model as a heuristic device. I have indicated the mutual effects at the next level. All of these dynamics—radical reflexivity, separation of time and space, disembedding, globalization—mutually imply and affect one another. For example, as time and space are separated from the actual, institutions can further remove the social from the local, which in turn allows more abstract connections at the global level. These all mutually reinforce one another and build the dynamism of modernity. Collectively, this figure and all that it implies answers the question, "Why are change and discontinuity endemic in modernity?" Use Figure 12.3 to think through that question and Giddens' theory of modernity.

Figure 12.3 Dynamism of Modernity

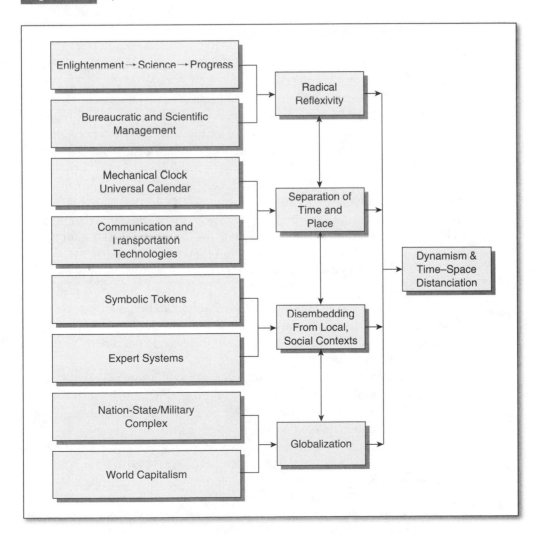

Concepts and Theory: The Experience of Modernity

It is extremely difficult to see the effects of modernity in our own lives. We live our lives as if they are essential, as if there were nothing more to us than our inner personality and experiences. Yet sociology teaches us that we are social beings created for and out of social relations. And the sociological imagination encourages us to see the intersections of biography, history, and society. Giddens paints a portrait of the modern individual and asks us to look behind (or in front of) our own subjective experiences and understand them as finding their roots in a particular social organization called modernity. Modernity is characterized by endemic reflexivity and time–space distanciation. What this implies for the person is that the individual and her or his subjective experiences have been lifted out of densely packed social networks and required to do increasing amounts of personal work. This personal work centers on the reflexive project of the self, life politics, and intimate relations.

The Reflexive Project of the Self

In times previous to modernity, the self was deeply embedded in the social. People were caught up in and saw themselves only in terms of the group. The self was an extension of the group just as certainly as your arm is an extension of your body. The individual life was not only seen as part of the group, but its trajectory was also plotted and marked socially. So, for example, a boy knew for certain when he had changed from a boy to a man—he went through a rite of passage. Such is not the case today.

In modernity, the individual stands alone. The individual is "free." You, for example, are free to express yourself in any number of ways. You have a plethora of potential identities and experiences open to you. But at the same time, you no longer have any institutional markers to guide you or to define your "progress," and there are no institutions that are directly responsible for you. In the *reflexive project of the self,* you have to reflexively define your own options and opportunities with regard to social and personal change. The self is no longer an entity embedded in known and firm social and institutional relationships and expectations. This shift from the traditional, social self with clear institutional guidelines to the individual reflexive project was brought about because of the dynamics of modernity that we reviewed in the previous section.

The body is drawn into this reflexive project as well. Before radical modernity, the body was, for the most part, seen as either the medium through which work was performed or a vehicle for the soul. In either case, it was of little consequence and received little attention unless it became an obstacle to work or salvation. In radical modernity, on the other hand, the body becomes part of self-expression and helps to sustain "a coherent sense of self-identity" (Giddens, 1991, p. 99). The body becomes wrapped up with the reflexive project of the self in four possible ways: appearance, demeanor, sensuality, and through bodily regimes. We covered the first two ways in our chapter on Goffman, so we will just take time to review the last two.

The body is involved in the self-project through *bodily regimes.* In radical modernity, "we become responsible for the design of our own bodies" (Giddens, 1991, p. 102). The body is no longer a simple reflection of one's work but can become a canvas for a self-portrait. Capitalism, mass media, advertising, fashion, and medical expert knowledge have produced an overabundance of information about how the body works and what kinds of behaviors result in what kinds of body images. We are called upon to constantly review the look and condition of our body and to make adjustments as necessary. The adjustments are carried out through various body regimes of diet, exercise, stress-reducing activities (yoga, meditation), vitamin therapies, skin cleansing and repair, hair treatments, and so forth.

With the *organization of sensuality,* Giddens has in mind the entire spectrum of sensual feeling of the body, but the idea is particularly salient for sexuality. Together, mass education, contraceptive technologies, decreasing family size, and women's political and workforce participation created the situation where "today, for the first time in human history, women claim equality with men" (Giddens, 1992, p. 1). Giddens links women's freedom with the creation of an "emotional order" that contains "an exploration of the potentialities of the 'pure relationship'" and "plastic sexuality" (pp. 1–2). The idea of plastic sexuality captures a kind of sexuality that came into existence as sex was separated from the demands of reproduction. Plastic sexuality is an explicit characteristic of modernity. For the first time in history, sexuality could become part of self-identity. We should also note that since sexuality is part of the reflexive project of the self, it is subject to reflexive scrutiny and intentional exploration.

Pure Relationships

To begin our discussion of pure relationships, let's think about friendship. Giddens points out that early Greeks didn't even have a word for friend in the way we use it today. The Greeks used the word *philos* to talk about those who were the most near and dear, but this term was used for people who were in or near to family. And the Greek *philos* network was pretty well set by the person's status position; there was little in the way of friends as we think of them, as personal choices.

In languages that did have a word for friend, these friends were seen within the context of group survival. Friends were the in-group and others were the out-group. The distinction was between friend and enemy, or, at best, stranger. Keep in mind that groups were far more important then than they are now because individual survival was closely tied to group affiliations and resources. A friend was someone you turned to in time of need; thus the values associated with friendship were honor and sincerity. Today, however, because of disembedding mechanisms and increased time–space distanciation, not all friends are understood in terms of in-group membership and actual assistance. The individual can have distant friends and is enabled and expected to take care of himself or herself (the reflexive project).

A fundamental change has thus occurred in friendships: from friendship with honor based on group identity and survival to friendship with authenticity based on a mutual process of self-disclosure. Rather than trust being embedded in social networks and rituals, trust in modernity has to be won, and the means through which this is done is self-evident warmth and openness. By implication, this authenticity and self-regulation provide the personal, emotional component missing in trust in the abstract systems of modernity.

Intimate relations in modernity are thus characterized by *pure relationships*—friendships and intimate ties that are entered into simply for what the relationship can bring to each person. Remember that traditional relationships were first set by existing networks and institutions and the motivation behind them was usually social, not personal. For example, most marriages were motivated by politics or economics (not by love) and were arranged for the couple by those most responsible for the social issues in question (not by the couple themselves). This is the way in which modern relationships are pure: They occur purely for the sake of the relationship. Most of our relationships are not anchored in external conditions, like the politically or economically motivated marriage. Rather, they are "free-floating." The only structural condition for a friendship or marriage is proximity: We have to be near enough to make contact. But with modern transportation and communication technologies, our physical space is almost constantly in motion and can be quite far-ranging, and we have "virtual" space at our fingertips.

In addition to the free-floating and pure nature of these relations, they are also reflexively organized, based on commitment and mutual trust, and focus on intimacy and "self" growth. Like the reflexive project of the self, relationships are reflexively organized; that is, they are continually worked at by the individuals, who tend to consult an array of sources of information. The number of possible sources for telling us how to act and be in our friendships and sexual relations is almost endless. Daytime television is filled with programming that explores every facet of relationships; the magazine rack at the local supermarket is a cornucopia of surveys and advice on how to have the best (fill in the blank with any aspect of an intimate relationship); it's estimated that over 2,000 new self-help book titles are published every year in the United States; and the Internet resources available for improving relationships are innumerable. Most of us have taken a relationship quiz with our partner at some point (if you haven't, just wait, it's coming), and all of us have asked of someone the essential question for relationships that are reflexively organized: "Is everything all right?" This kind of communication is a moral obligation in pure relationships; the gamut of communication covers everything from the mundane ("How was your day at work?") to the serious ("Do you want to break up with me?").

Choice and Life Politics

Along with the accelerating changes in modernity, there has been a shift from emancipatory politics to life politics. *Emancipatory politics* is concerned with liberating individuals and groups from the constraints that adversely affect their lives. In some ways, this type of political activity has been the theme of modernity—it was the hope that democratic nation-states could bring equality and justice for all. And, in some respects, this theme of modernity has failed. We are more than ever painfully aware of how many groups are disenfranchised.

Life politics, by way of contrast, is the politics of choice and lifestyle. It is not based on group membership and characteristics, as is emancipatory politics; rather, it is based on personal lifestyle choices. We have come to think of choice as a freedom we have in the United States. But it is more than that—it has become an obligation. Choice is a fundamental element in contemporary living. This principality of choice is based on disembedding mechanisms and time–space distanciation, and results in, as we've seen, the reflexive project of the self. Part of that project comes to be centered on the politics of choice.

Mass media also plays a role in creating choice by facilitating mediated experiences. *Mediated experiences* are in contrast to social experiences that take place in face-to-face encounters and are created as people are exposed to multiple accounts of situations and others with whom they have no direct association through time and space. Every time you watch television or read a newspaper, you are exposed to lives to which you have absolutely no real connection. Like so many other features of modernity, this stretches out co-presence but it also creates a collage effect. The pictures and stories that we receive via the media do not reflect any essential or social elements. Instead, stories and images are juxtaposed that have nothing to do with one another. The picture we get of the world, then, is a collage of diverse lifestyles and cultures, not a direct representation.

As a result of being faced with this collage, what happens to us as individuals? One implication is that the plurality of lifestyles presented to us not only allows for choice—it necessitates choice. In other words, what becomes important is not the issue of group equality, but, rather, the insistence on personal choice. What is at issue in this milieu is not so much political equality (as with emancipatory politics) as inner authenticity. In a world that is perceived as constantly changing and uprooted, it becomes important to be grounded in one's self. Life politics creates such grounding. It creates "a framework of basic trust by means of which the life-span can be understood as a unity against the backdrop of shifting social events" (Giddens, 1991, p. 215). Life politics, then, helps to diminish the possibility and effects of ontological insecurity.

A good example of life politics is veganism—the practice of not eating any meat or meat by-products. Not only is eating flesh avoided, but also any products with dairy, eggs, fur, leather, feathers, or any goods involving animal testing. One vegan I know summed it up nicely when she said, veganism "is an integral component of a cruelty-free lifestyle." It is a political statement against the exploitation of animals, and for some it is clearly a condemnation of capitalism—capitalism is particularly responsible for the unnatural mass production of animal flesh as well as commercial animal testing. Yet, for most vegans, it is a lifestyle, one that brings harmony between the outside world and inner beliefs, and not necessarily part of a collective movement.

However, it would be wrong to conclude that life politics is powerless because it does not result in a social movement. Quite the opposite is true. Life politics springs from and focuses attention on some of the very issues that modernity represses.

What life politics does is to "place a question mark against the internally referential systems of modernity" (Giddens, 1991, p. 223). Life politics asks,

> Seeing that these things are so, what manner of men and women ought we to be? In traditional society, morality was provided by the institutions, especially religion. Modernity has wiped away the social base upon which this kind of morality was based. Life politics "remoralizes" social life and demands "renewed sensitivity to questions that the institutions of modernity systematically dissolve." (p. 224)

Rather than asking for group participation, as does emancipatory politics, life politics asks for self-realization, a moral commitment to a specific way of living. Rather than being impotent in comparison to emancipatory politics, life politics "presage[s] future changes of a far-reaching sort: essentially, the development of forms of social order 'on the other side' of modernity itself" (p. 214).

Summary

- According to Giddens, the central issue for social theory is to explain how actions and interactions are patterned over time and space; or, to use Giddens' terms, social theory needs to explain how the limitations inherent within physical presence are transcended through time–space distanciation. There are two primary ways through which this occurs: the dynamics of structuration and routinization.

- Structuration occurs when people use specific modalities to produce both structure (rules and resources of signification, domination, and legitimation) and practice (physical co-presence). Thus, the very method of structuration reflexively and repeatedly links structure and person and facilitates time–space distanciation.

- Routinization is psychologically motivated by a diffuse need for ontological security. The reality of society is precarious because it depends on structuration, which is reflexive and recursive. In other words, the process of structuration doesn't reference anything other than itself and it depends on ceaseless interactional work. This precariousness is unconsciously sensed by people, which, in turn, motivates them to routinize their actions and interactions and to link their routines to physical regions and institutional orders, which further add stability.

- Routinization was unproblematically achieved in traditional societies. People rarely left their regions and the institutional orders were slow to change. Modernity, however, is characterized by dynamism and increasing time–space distanciation. Dynamism and time–space distanciation are both directly related to radical reflexivity, extreme separation of time and place, the disembedding work of modern institutions, and globalization. These factors are related to the proliferation of science and progress, bureaucratic management, the mechanical clock and universal calendar, communication and transportation technologies, symbolic tokens and expert systems of knowledge, the military complex, and world capitalism.

- As a result of radical modernity, the individual is lifted out of the social networks and institutions that socially situated the self by acquiring certain identities, knowledge, and life course markers. The modern individual is given the reflexive project of the self that is only internally referential. As part of the reflexive project of the self, the individual involves himself or herself in strategic life planning using expert systems of knowledge and mediated experiences, all of which are permeated with pervasive doubt. The reflexive project of the self involves constant evaluation and reevaluation based on possible new information (ever revised by experts and available through mass media) and self-reflection (How am I doing? Should I be feeling this way?). The reflexive project includes lifestyle politics in which the individual must reflexively work her or his way through continuously presented and expanding arenas of social existence. Individuals, then, become hubs for social change as they reflexively order their life in response to a constantly changing political landscape.

BUILDING YOUR THEORY TOOLBOX

Learning More—Primary Sources

- To learn more about Giddens' theory of structuration, you should read *The Constitution of Society,* University of California Press, 1986.
- For Giddens' theory of modernity, I recommend *Modernity and Self-Identity: Self and Society in the Late Modern Age,* Stanford University Press, 1991.

Learning More—Secondary Sources

- An excellent encounter with Giddens' theory (not just a review) is Stjepan Gabriel Mestrovic's *Anthony Giddens: The Last Modernist,* Routledge, 1998.

Check It Out

- *Fluid modernity:* For an approach that is neither modern nor postmodern, I recommend you read Zygmunt Bauman, especially *Liquid Modernity,* Polity Press, 2000; and *Postmodernity and Its Discontents,* New York University Press, 1997.
- Check out Giddens on YouTube:
  - http://www.youtube.com/watch?v=n-9rDFN2zPU
  - http://www.youtube.com/watch?v=c61pmOxRlTs

(Continued)

(Continued)

Seeing the World

- Write a 250-word synopsis of the theoretical perspective of structuration theory.

- After reading and understanding this chapter, you should be able to define the following terms theoretically and explain their theoretical importance to Giddens' ontology of society and theory of modernity: *structuration theory, duality of structure, social structures, normative rules, signification codes, authoritative resources, allocative resources, time–space distanciation, modalities of structuration, domination, institutional orders, reflexive monitoring, rationalization of action, discursive consciousness, practical consciousness, routinization, regionalization, ontological security, radical reflexivity, separation of time and space, disembedding mechanisms, symbolic tokens, expert systems, reflexive project of the self, bodily regimes, organization of sensuality, pure relationships, emancipatory politics, life politics, mediated experiences*

- After reading and understanding this chapter, you should be able to answer the following questions (remember to answer them *theoretically*):

  o What is time–space distanciation and why is it the central question for Giddens? How does modernity affect time–space distanciation?

  o What are social structures, in Giddens' scheme? How do they exist and what do they do?

  o What are modalities of structuration? What are the three modalities? What is the function of modalities of structuration?

  o What are the three institutional orders and how are they created?

  o What are practical and discursive consciousnesses and how do they fit in with reflexive monitoring?

  o What is the unconscious motivation in human interaction? What specific processes come about due to this motivation? How does each process vary? What are their effects?

  o What are the main processes that produce the dynamic of modernity? There are at least four. Define each process and explain how it contributes to the dynamic character of modernity.

  o What is the reflexive project of the self? How did it become individualized? How is the body involved and why do you think the body is important in this project?

  o Explain the differences between emancipatory and lifestyle politics. Why is lifestyle politics more prevalent today than emancipatory?

Engaging the World

- Giddens is one of the architects and proponents of what is known as the "third way" in politics. Using your favorite Internet search engine, look up "third way." What is the third way and how is Giddens involved? How can you see it related to his theory?

Weaving the Threads

- Compare and contrast Giddens' theory of structuration with Bourdieu's constructivist-structuralism approach. Specifically, how are patterns of behavior replicated in the long run? How does each one overcome the object–subject dichotomy? Do you find one approach to be more persuasive? Why or why not?

- Compare and contrast Habermas' and Giddens' views of modernity. I recommend you start with their defining characteristics of modernity and review the issues that are implied in the definitions. After you've worked your way through these comparisons, define modernity and its chief problems.

- In Chapter 11 I asked you to write a one-page synopsis of the assessments and principles for reinvigorating democracy for Wallerstein, Castells, and Habermas. Do the same now for Giddens (remember that modernity and democracy are tied up together). Now compare, contrast, and evaluate these explanations. Based on your evaluation, synthesize these theories and create a single assessment of the democratic project of modernity. Evaluate the potential for reinvigorating democracy.

- Check the index in this book and look up the different definitions and explanations of "social structures." Evaluate each of these approaches and create what you feel to be a clear, robust, and correct definition-explanation of social structures. Justify your theory.

CHAPTER 13

Defining the Possible and Impossible:

Michel Foucault
(1926–1984)

P ower. It's an uneasy word, especially in a democracy. Power in a democracy is supposed to flow from the citizenry up to government. Yet when it appears in social theory, it's usually an explanation about why power works in ways perhaps not in keeping with a democracy. Some theorists see power as an element of social structure—something attached to a position within the structure, like the power that comes with being the president of the United States. In this scheme, power is something that a person can possess and use. Other theorists have defined power as an element of exchange. Others have seen power more in terms of influence. This is a more general way in which to think of power, because many types of social relationships and people can exercise influence.

Michel Foucault defines power differently from most that have come before him. Foucault asks us to see power in knowledge. That in itself isn't unusual. Marx saw a connection between power and knowledge; he called it ideology and false consciousness. Weber also recognized that knowledge and power are connected. He specifically saw that knowledge could be used as power the more society became bureaucratized. Foucault takes this idea of power and knowledge much further than either Marx or Weber. For Foucault, power is hidden and treacherous. It is found in truth and discourse, and carried out in bodies, minds, and subjectivities.

THEORIST'S DIGEST

Brief Biography

We should begin this brief biography by noting that Foucault would balk at the idea that we need to know anything about the author in order to understand his work. Further, Foucault would say that any history of the author is something that we use in order to validate a particular reading or interpretation. Having said that, Foucault was born on October 15, 1926, in Poitiers, France. Foucault studied at the École Normale Supérieure and the Institut de Psychologie in Paris. In 1960, returning to France from teaching posts in Sweden, Warsaw, and Hamburg, Foucault published *Madness and Civilization,* for which he received France's highest academic degree, doctorat d'État. In 1966, Foucault published *The Order of Things,* which became a best-selling book in France. In 1970, Foucault received a permanent appointment at the Collège de France (France's most prestigious school) as chair of History of Systems of Thought. In 1975, Foucault published *Discipline and Punishment* and took his first trip to California, which came to hold an important place in Foucault's life, especially San Francisco. In 1976, Foucault published the first volume of his last major work, *The History of Sexuality.* The two other volumes of this history, *The Use of Pleasure* and *The Care of the Self,* were published shortly before Foucault's death in 1984.

Central Sociological Questions

In Foucault's (1984/1990b) own words, "As for what motivated me.... It was curiosity—the only kind of curiosity, in any case, that is worth acting upon with a degree of obstinacy: not the curiosity that seeks to assimilate what it is proper for one to know, but that which enables one to get free of oneself. After all, what would be the value of the passion for knowledge if it resulted only in a certain amount of knowledgeableness and not, in one way or another and to the extent possible, in the knower's straying afield of himself?" (p. 8). In brief, Foucault was interested in how ideas and subjectivities come into existence and how they limit what is possible. But Foucault's search was not simply academic, though it was that. As the above quote tells us, Foucault sought to understand his own practices "in relationship of self with self and the forming of oneself as a subject" (p. 6).

Simply Stated

Foucault's basic premise is that human reality is language. There's an old adage that says, "There are three sides to every story: yours, mine, and the truth." Because language is human reality, Foucault would say that there are only two sides; the truth of any event or thing isn't available to humans because of our deep dependence and use of language. This implies that any claim to represent the truth (such as my trying to convince you that my story is the right one) is an expression of power. Social power is expressed and imposed through what passes as legitimated knowledge, which orders the world around us, and through discourse, which orders our subjective positions. Modernity brought with it a specific kind of power in that the individual disciplines himself or herself—modern power is practiced from within. Modern power is also distinct in that the person is objectified by these internal practices.

Key Ideas

Truth games, counter-histories, archaeology, genealogy, episteme, discourse, governmentality, objectification, panopticon, microphysics of power, medical gaze

Concepts and Theory: The Truth About Truth

The truth about truth is that it is used to exercise **power**. Thus Foucault's interest in truth isn't abstract or philosophical. Rather, Foucault is interested in analyzing what he calls *truth games*. His use of "games" isn't meant to imply that what passes as truth in any historical time is somehow false or simply a construction of language. Foucault feels that these kinds of questions can only be answered, let alone asked, after historically specific assumptions are made. In other words, something can only be "false" once a specific truth is assumed; Foucault is involved in uncovering how truth is assumed. Specifically, Foucault's interest in truth concerns the game of truth: the rules, resources, and practices that go into making something true for humans.

The idea of practice is fairly broad and includes such things as institutional and organizational practices as well as those of academic disciplines—in these practices, truth is formed. The idea also refers to specific practices of the body and self—these are where power is exercised. Most of us use the word *practice* to talk about the behaviors we engage in to prepare for an event, like band practice for a show. But practice has another meaning as well. This meaning is clear when we talk about a medical practice. When you go to your physician, you see someone who is "practicing" medicine. In this sense, practice refers to choreographed acts that interact with bodies—sets of behaviors that together define a way of doing something. This is the kind of practice in which Foucault is interested.

Uncovering Truth

Foucault uncovered truth games by constructing what he called *counter-histories*. When most of us think of history, we think of a factual telling of events from the past. We are aware, of course, that sometimes that telling can be politicized, which is one reason we have "Black History Month" here in the United States—we are trying to make up for having left people of color out of our telling of history. But most of us also think that the memory model is still intact; it's just getting a few tweaks. Foucault wants us to free history from the model of memory. He really doesn't say anything directly about whether any particular history is more or less true; that's not an issue for him. History in all its forms is part of and generated by discourse. Thus, Foucault's concern is how the idea of true history is used. What Foucault wants to produce for us is a counter-history—a history told from a different point of view from the progressive, linear, memory model.

The important questions then become, why is one path taken rather than another? Why is the present filled with one kind of discourse rather than others? And what has been the cost of taking this path rather than all the other potentialities? Thus, a counter-history identifies:

> the accidents, the minute deviations—or conversely, the complete reversals—the errors, the false appraisals, and the faulty calculations that gave birth to those things that continue to exist and have value for us; it is to discover that truth or being does not lie at the root of what we know and what we are, but the exteriority of accidents. (Foucault, 1984, p. 81)

Foucault uses two terms to talk about his counter-history, archaeology and genealogy. Though the distinctions are sometimes unclear, *archaeology* seems to be oriented toward uncovering the relationships among social institutions, practices, and knowledge that come to produce a particular kind of discourse or structure of thought. *Genealogy* may be better suited to describe Foucault's (1984) work that is concerned with the actual inscription of discourse and power on the mind and body: "Genealogy, as an analysis of descent, is thus situated within the articulation of the body and history. Its task is to expose a body totally imprinted by history and the process of history's destruction of the body" (p. 83). We could say that archaeology is to text what genealogy is to the body. In both cases, there is an analogy to digging, searching, and uncovering the hidden history of order, thought, madness, sexuality, and so on. The hidden history isn't necessarily more accurate—it's simply a counter-story that is constructed more in an archaeological mode than a historical one.

Why So Critical?

What is Foucault's point in constructing counter-histories? Part of what he wants to do is expose the contingencies of what we consider reality, but to what end? Many critical perspectives are based on assumptions of what would make a better society. In other words, there must be something to which the current situation is compared to demonstrate what it is lacking. But Foucault sees it otherwise. For him, *the critical perspective in itself is sufficient because it opens up possibilities.* In fact, Foucault would argue that a utopian scheme only attempts to replace one system of impoverishment with another. The point is to keep possibilities always open, to keep people critically examining their life and knowledge system so that they can perpetually be open to the possibility of something else.

According to Foucault's scheme, an important part of what creates knowledge, order, and discourse is the presence of "blank spaces." Foucault (1966/1994b) pictures knowledge as a kind of grid. The boxes in the grid are the actual linguistic categories, like mammal, flora, mineral, human, black, white, male, and female. We are familiar with those parts of the grid; they form part of our everyday language. However, there is actually a more important part of the grid: the part of the grid that creates the order—the blank spaces between the categories. "It is only in the blank spaces of this grid that order manifests itself in depth as though already there, waiting in silence for the moment of its expression" (p. xx). The true power of a discourse or knowledge system is in the spaces between the categories. As Eviatar Zerubavel (1993) notes,

> Separating one island of meaning from another entails the introduction of some mental void between them. . . . It is our perception of the void among these islands of meaning that makes them separate in our mind, and its magnitude reflects the degree of separateness we perceive among them. (pp. 21–22)

These spaces are revealed most clearly in transgression. As an illustration, let's think about a little boy of about 3 or 4 years of age. He is playful, playing with the toys he's been given and emulating the role models he sees on TV and among the neighborhood children. But one day his father comes home and finds him playing with dolls. His father grabs the doll away and tells his son firmly that boys do not play with dolls. In this instance, the category of gender was almost invisible until the young boy unwittingly attempted to cross over the boundary or space between the categories. The meaning and power of gender waited "in silence for the moment of its expression."

This idea of space is provocative. A more Durkheimian way of thinking about categories would conceptualize the space between them as a boundary or wall. Using the idea of boundary to think about the division between categories is fruitful: Walls separate and prevent passing. The young boy in our example certainly came up against a wall, and many of us have felt the walls of gender, race, or sexism. But the idea of walls makes the use of categories and knowledge seem objective, as if they somehow exist apart from us, and this is not what Foucault has in mind.

Notice that the boy in our example was unaware of the "wall" until his father showed it to him. From Foucault's position, the wall of gender was erected in the father's gendered practices. Foucault's idea of space helps us think about the practices of power. Space, in this sense, is empty until it is filled—seeing space between categories rather than a wall makes us wait to see what will go there and how it goes there. Space is undetermined. Something can be built in space but the space itself calls our attention to potential. Foucault's research, his critical archaeology, fills in that potential—he tells us how that space became historically constructed in one way rather than any of the other potential ways.

Foucault's counter-history actually creates a space of its own. On one side, Foucault's archaeology of modernity uncovers the fundamental codes of thought that establish for all of us the order that we will use in our world. On the other side, Foucault sets the sciences and philosophical interpretations that explain why such an order exists. Between these two domains is a space of possibilities, a space wherein a critical culture can develop that sufficiently frees itself "to discover that these orders are perhaps not the only possible ones or the best ones" (Foucault, 1966/1994b, p. xx).

In other words, through the archaeology of knowledge, Foucault wants to not only expose the codes of knowledge that undergird everything we do, feel, and think; he also wants to set loose the idea that things might not be as they are. He wants to free the possibility of thinking something different. That possibility of thought exists in the critical space between—but in this case the space isn't specified, as it is in already existing orders. Foucault doesn't necessarily have a place he is taking us; he doesn't really have a utopian vision of what knowledge and practice ought to be. His critique is aimed at freeing knowledge and creating possibility; it's aimed at creating an empty space that is undetermined.

Concepts and Theory: The Practices of Power

According to Foucault, power isn't something that a person possesses, but it is something that is part of every relationship. Foucault tells us that there are three types of domains or practices within relationships: communicative, objective, and power. Communication is directed toward producing meaning; objective practices are directed toward controlling and transforming things—science and economy are two good examples; and practices of power, which Foucault (1982) defines as "a set of actions upon other actions" (p. 220), are directed toward controlling the actions and subjectivities of people. Notice where Foucault locates power—*it's within the actions themselves,* not within the powerful person or the social structure. Foucault uses the double meaning of "conduct" to get at this insight: Conduct is a way of leading others (to conduct an orchestra, for example) and also a way of behaving (as in "Tommy conducted himself in a manner worthy of his position."). Thus, we conduct others through our conduct.

However, Foucault's intent is not to reduce power to the mundane, the simple organization of human behavior across time and place. Rather, Foucault's point is that power is exercised in a variety of ways, many of which we are unaware. Power, then, becomes insidious. Power acts in the normalcy of everyday life. It acts by imperceptible degrees, exerting gradual and hidden effects. In this way, the exercise of power entices us into a snare that feels of our own doing. But how is power exercised? Where does it exist and how are we enticed? Foucault argues that power is exercised through the epistemes (underlying order) and discourses found in what passes as knowledge. The potential and practice of power exists in these epistemes and discourses that set the limits of what is possible and impossible, which in turn are felt and expressed through a person's relationship with himself or herself, in subjectivities—the way we feel about and relate to our inner self—and the disposition of the body.

The Power of Order

Order is an interesting idea. We order our days and lives; we order our homes and offices; we order our files and our bank accounts; we order our yards and shopping centers; we order land and sea—in short, humans order everything. How do we order things? One of the ways is linguistically: "Indeed, things become meaningful only when placed in some category" (Zerubavel, 1993, p. 5). But a deeper and more fundamental question can be asked: How do we order the order of things? In other words, what scheme or system underlies and creates our categorical schemes? We may use categories to order the world around us, but where do the categories get their order?

To introduce us to this question, Foucault (1966/1994b) tells a delightful story of reading a book that contains a Chinese categorical system that divides animals into those "(a) belonging to the Emperor, (b) embalmed, (c) tame, (d) sucking pigs, (e) sirens, (f) fabulous, (g) stray dogs, (h) included in the present classification, (i) frenzied, (j) innumerable, (k) drawn with a very fine camelhair brush, (l) et cetera, (m) having just broken the water pitcher, (n) that from a long way off look like flies" (p. xv). The thing that struck Foucault about this system of categories was the limitation of his own thinking—"the stark impossibility of thinking that" (p. xv, emphasis original). In response, Foucault asks an important set of questions: What sets the boundaries of what is possible and impossible to think? Where do these boundaries originate? What is the price of these impossibilities what is gained and what is lost?

Foucault argues that there is a fundamental code to culture, a code that orders language, perception, values, practices, and all that gives order to the world around us. He calls these fundamental codes epistemological fields or the episteme of knowledge in any age. **Episteme** refers to the mode of thought's existence, or the way in which thought organizes itself in any historical moment. An episteme is the necessary precondition of thought. It is what exists before thought and that which makes thought possible. This foundation of thought is not held consciously. It is undoubtedly this preconscious character of the episteme that makes thought believable and ideas seem true.

Further, rather than seeing thought and knowledge as results of historical, linear processes, Foucault argues that discontinuity marks changes in knowledge. Most of us think that the knowledge we hold accumulated over time, that we have thrown out the false knowledge and replaced it with true knowledge as we progressively learned how things work. This evolutionary view of knowledge actually comes from the culture of science. It is the way we want to see our knowledge, not necessarily the way it is. Foucault argues that knowledge doesn't progress linearly. Rather, what we know and how we know it is linked to historically specific patterns of behavior, institutional arrangements, and economic and social practices that set the rules and conditions of discourse and the limits of our possibilities. And that historical path is marked by rupture: discontinuities and sudden, radical changes.

The importance of what Foucault is saying is that this idea of rupture implies that knowledge and truth are purely functions of institutional arrangements and practices and not the result of any real quest for truth. Thus, what counts as truth in any age—our own included—comes about through historically unique practices and institutional configurations. This implies not only that knowledge is socially constructed, but also, and more importantly, that *knowledge is nothing more and nothing less than the exercise of power*. This pure power is put into effect through discourse and the taken-for-granted ordering of human life.

The Power of Discourse

Discourse refers to languages and behaviors that are specific to a social issue, like the discourse of race. In simple terms, a discourse is a way of talking about things. If you want to discuss music with a group of musicians, for instance, there is an acceptable discourse or language that you would use. It would include such words as *key, modes, transposing,* and so on. This discourse would be different from the one you would use to talk about baseball. You wouldn't normally tell your baseball team to hit the field and "tune up," nor would you tell a violinist to "bunt."

Foucault's interest in the idea of discourse is a bit more significant. First, he wants us to see beneath the surface of the word choice between "bunt" and "tune up." Foucault is interested in the rules and practices that underlie the words and ideas that we use. Discourse sets the possibilities of thought and existence. There is an obvious link between language and thought: We think in language. So, a discourse, with its underlying rules and practices, gives us a language with which to think and talk. That's a commonsensical statement, and we might be tempted just to accept it at face value. But using discourse as the basis of thought sets the boundaries of what is possible and impossible for us to think, so it is more profound than it might first appear.

The second thing that discourse does is to determine the position a person or object must occupy in order to become the subject of a statement. "I'm a man" is such a statement. For me to be a man, I must meet the conditions of existence that are set down in the discourse of gender. I not only have to meet those conditions for you; I must meet them for me as well, because the discourse sets out the conditions of subjectivity, how we think and feel about our self. Subjects, and the accompanying inner thoughts and feelings, are specific conditions within the discourse. As we locate ourselves within a discourse, we become subject to the discourse and thus subjectively answer ourselves through the discourse.

This work of positioning that discourse accomplishes is one of its most powerful acts. Think about it this way: It is extremely difficult to talk to someone about anything without positioning yourself within a discourse. There are discourses surrounding sports, family, gender, race, class, self-improvement, medicine, mass media, cars, trucks, and on and on. Once you begin to converse using a discourse, you automatically occupy a position within it that tells you how to think, feel, and act.

The third thing that Foucault wants us to see about discourse is that it is used instead of coercive force to impose order on a social group. Critically speaking, social order is always a problem for the elite in any society. One way to subjugate a population is through physical coercion. However, as we saw in Chapter 11, the use of force is costly and produces contrary effects. Discourse is used instead of force and is thus characterized by a will to truth and a will to power. In other words, there is political intention behind truth and power. What passes as truth and how truth is validated are dependent upon the discourse. And discourse intrinsically contains a will to power.

Let me give you a dramatic example. The attacks of September 11, 2001, were perpetrated by men who are either "terrorists" or "freedom fighters," depending on the discourse that is used. Within these discourses are legitimations and methods of reasoning that create these two different social meanings. Further, the discourses create the subjective experience of all the different peoples involved. The substance of one discourse is captured by the title of the report generated by the U.S. government: *The National Commission on Terrorist Attacks Upon the United States.* Clearly, the discourse in the United States defines the perpetrators as terrorists and the subjective experience of those in the United States as being innocently attacked. The substance of the other discourse is revealed in the title and opening lines of a document confiscated by the police in Manchester, England, during a search of an Al Qaeda member's home. The title of the document is *Declaration of Jihad,* and the opening lines are addressed to "those champions who avowed the truth day and night" (*Al Qaeda Training Manual,* n.d.). One discourse creates the meaning of attack and terrorist; the other creates the meaning of holy war and champion.

The Power of Objectification

For Foucault, then, power is not so much a quality of social structures as it is the practices or techniques that become power as individuals are turned into subjects through discourse. Foucault intends us to see both meanings of the noun "subject": as someone to control, and as one's self-knowledge. Here Foucault's unique interest is quite clear—perhaps the most insidious form of power is that which is exercised by our self over how we think and feel; it is the power we exercise in the name of others over our self.

In an interesting analysis, Foucault uses the state to illustrate both meanings of subject. State rule is usually understood in terms of power over the masses. While this is a true characteristic of the state, Foucault argues that the modern state also exercises individualization techniques that exercise power over the subjectivity of the person. Foucault talks about this form of ruling as **governmentality:** "The government of the self by the self in its articulation with relations to others" (Foucault, 1989, as quoted in Davidson, 1994, p. 119). Governmentality was needed because of the shift from the power of the monarch to the power of the state.

Under a monarchy, the power of the queen or king was absolute and he or she required absolute obedience, but the scope of that control was fairly narrow. The nation-state "freed" people from the coercive control of the monarchy but at the same time broadened its scope of control. The nation-state is far more interested in controlling our behaviors today than monarchies were 300 years ago. In governmentality, the individual is enlisted by the state to exercise control over himself or herself. This is partly achieved through expert, professional knowledge that comes from medicine and the social and behavior sciences. The state supports such scientific research, and the findings are employed to extend control, particularly as the individual uses and consults medicine, psychology, and other sciences.

A fundamental part of Foucault's argument about the practices of power is the historical shift to *objectification*. Obviously, if power is intrinsic to human affairs of all kinds, then people have always exercised power. However, the practice of power became something different and more insidious due to historical changes that objectified the subject of power. We are all probably familiar with the transitive verb "to objectify." It means to make something an object that isn't an object, and it also means to exist apart from any internal relationship. Interestingly, most of us are probably not familiar with the transitive verb "to subjectify." As a case in point, my word processor just highlighted "subjectify" as a misspelled word, yet it is a real word that appears in exhaustive dictionaries. We just rarely use the word, nor do we think about things becoming subjectified—we assume that we subjectively relate to everything about ourselves. But, according to Foucault, that is not the case in modernity. Today, we relate to our self, our body, and our sexuality as objects.

Foucault's work is found in a series of books that provide a counter-history to some of the objectifying power practices found in Western societies. These books detail madness and rationality, abnormality and normality, medicine and the clinic, penal discipline and punishment, psychiatry and criminal justice, and the history of sexuality. In general, these works document how you and I exercise power over our bodies and subjectivities. While I don't have the luxury of introducing you to all of Foucault's archaeology and genealogy, it is important for us to talk about a few of his concepts so that you can get a sense of how Foucault's theoretical ideas get played out. We'll first be looking at how power is exercised over our body and then over our inner, subjective life.

Concepts and Theory: Disciplining the Body

Foucault's intent in his book *Discipline and Punish* is to map a major shift in the way in which Western society handles crime and criminals. The shift is from punishment and torture to discipline. Foucault paints a graphic comparative picture in the first seven pages of this book. The first part of the picture is an account of the public torture and killing of a man named Damiens on March 2, 1757. Damiens had been convicted of murder and sentenced to having his flesh torn from his body with red-hot pincers, followed by various molten elements (such as lead, wax, and oil) poured into the open wounds. The hand that held the knife with which he had committed the murder was burnt with sulfur. Finally, he was drawn and quartered by four horses and his body burnt to ashes and the ashes scattered to the winds.

The second image in Foucault's picture is a set of 12 rules for the daily activities of prisoners in Paris. The rules covered the prisoners' entire day and included such things as prayer, Bible reading, education, bathing, recreation, and work. These rules were in use a mere 80 years after the public torture of Damiens. The shortness of the time period indicates that the change isn't due to gradual adjustment and progress, but rather to abrupt shifts in knowledge, perception, and power.

Foucault uses this graphic comparison to point out a fundamental change that occurred in Europe and the United States. Most of us would look at these differences and attribute the change to a dawning of compassion and a desire to treat people more humanely. Foucault, on the other hand, looks deeper and more holistically at the shift. This change not only affected the penal system; it was a fundamental social change as well. During this period of time, from the eighateenth to nineteenth centuries (also known as the Enlightenment), science gained its foothold in society. Society as a whole began to embrace what we call scientism—the adaptation of the methods, mental attitudes, and modes of expression typical of scientists. Scientism values control, and control is achieved by objectifying the world and reducing it to its constituent parts. The gaze of the scientist is thus penetrating, particularizing, and objectifying. This kind of gaze results in universal technologies that allow humans to regularize and routinize their control of the world.

The shift, then, was not due to society becoming more compassionate and humane; the shift from punishment to discipline was a function of scientism and the desire to more uniformly control the social environment. As Foucault (1975/1995) says, the primary objective of this shift was

> to make of the punishment and repression of illegalities a regular function, coextensive with society; not to punish less, but to punish better; to punish with an attenuated severity perhaps, but in order to punish with more universality and necessity; to insert the *power to punish more deeply into the social body*. (p. 82, emphasis added)

This new way of discipline and control is best characterized by Jeremy Bentham's panopticon. The word **panopticon** is a combination of two Greek words. The first part, "pan," comes from the word *pantos,* meaning "all." The second part comes from the word *optikos,* meaning "to see." Together, panopticon literally means "all-seeing." There is actually an optical instrument called the panopticon that combines features of both the microscope and telescope, allowing the viewer to see things both up close and far away, thus seeing all.

Jeremy Bentham developed a different kind of panopticon—a building for prisons. Bentham's panopticon was a round building with an observation tower or core that optimized surveillance. The building was divided into individual prison cells that extended from the inner core to the outer wall. Thus, each cell had inner and outer windows; each prisoner was thus backlit by the outer window, allowing for easy viewing. "They are like so many cages, so many small theatres, in which each actor is alone, perfectly individualized and constantly visible" (Foucault, 1975/1995, p. 200). The tower itself was fitted with venetian blinds, zigzag hallways, and partitioned intersections among the observation rooms in the tower. These made the tower guards invisible to the prisoners who were being observed. The purpose of the panopticon was to allow seeing without being seen. Here "inspection functions ceaselessly. The gaze is alert everywhere" (p. 195).

Foucault isn't really interested in the panopticon as such. He sees the idea of the panopticon as illustrative of a shift in the fundamental way people thought and the way in which power is practiced. In terms of crime and punishment, it involved a shift from the spectacle of torture (which fit well with monarchical power) to regulation in prison (which fits well with the nation-state); from seeing crime as an act against authority to an act against society; from being focused on guilt (did he or she do it?) to looking at cause (what social or psychological factors influenced the person?); and, most importantly, from punishment to discipline—more specifically, to the self-discipline imposed by the ever-present but unseen surveillance of the panopticon.

Foucault (1975/1995) refers to this kind of control as the *microphysics of power* and sees this as the explicit link between knowledge and power: "There is no power relation without the correlative constitution of a field of knowledge, nor any knowledge that does not presuppose and constitute at the same time power relations" (p. 27). The microphysics of power is exercised or practiced as knowledge is produced, appropriated by groups for use, distributed to the population through education and mass media (such as books, magazines, and the Internet), and then retained internally by those that others want to control.

The Disciplines of the Human Sciences

Obviously, all of society was not put into a physical panopticon, but society was placed within a symbolic or institutional system of surveillance. In another word play, Foucault argues that the discipline associated with panopticon surveillance of the entire population comes from the disciplines, in particular the human sciences. The modern episteme created the possibility of the human sciences, such as psychiatry, psychology, and sociology. The human has been the subject of thought and modes of control for quite some time, but in every case the human was seen holistically or as part of the universal scheme of things. In the modern episteme, however, mankind becomes the object of study, not as part of an aesthetic whole, but as a thing in its own right.

This discourse of science serves to objectify and control the individual. Psychiatry and psychology used the mechanical model of the universe to gaze inside the psyche of the person; sociology and political science looked at the external circumstances of humanity. Thus, both the internal motivations and reasons behind action as well as the external factors became the objects of science in order to fulfill its chief goal, which is control. Statistics are used to quantify and categorize;

psychotherapy and psychological testing are used to probe and catalog; all of the disciplines and their methodologies are brought into "discipline" in order to fulfill this primary goal of control.

Foucault (1982) finds the human sciences particularly interesting because they are "modes of inquiry which try to give themselves the status of sciences" (p. 208). The human sciences are thus not true science; they only take on the guise of science. The human sciences did not grow out of scientific questions; they grew out of the modern episteme. Simply put, during the time that people began to talk about society and psychology, the kind of knowledge that was seen as real and valuable was science. So, in order to be accepted, the social and behavioral disciplines had to take on the guise of science.

More specifically, Foucault argues that there are three areas of knowledge in the modern episteme: mathematical and physical sciences, life and economic sciences, and philosophy. The human sciences grew out of the space created by these three knowledge systems. Asking scientific questions about things like biology and physics, which have some basis in the objective world, set the stage for those same questions to be asked about the questioner. Further, each of these sciences pursues knowledge in a distinctive manner, each with its own logic. The human sciences, on the other hand, must borrow from each of these because they have no unique domain or methodology. The human sciences stand in

> relation to all the other forms of knowledge . . . at one level or another, [they use] mathematical formalization; they proceed in accordance with models or concepts borrowed from biology, economics, and the sciences of language; and they address themselves to that mode of being of man which philosophy is attempting to conceive. (Foucault, 1966/1994b, p. 347)

Therefore, the precariousness or uncertainty of the human sciences isn't due to, "as is often stated, the extreme density of their object" (Foucault, 1966/1994b, p. 348), rather, their uncertainty of knowledge is due to the fact that they have no true method of their own—everything is borrowed. The validity of knowledge is in some way always related to methodology. What we know is an effect of how we know. Because the human sciences don't have their own methodology, the knowledge generated is without any basis—in the end, it is purely an expression of power that can be explicitly used by the state to control populations, but is more generally part of the control people exercise over themselves in modernity.

As such, we generally see and understand ourselves in Western cultures from the human science model. We listen endlessly to public opinion polls and voting predictions, and they become constant topics of conversation for us. Our bookstores, magazine racks, and Internet chat rooms are filled with ever-increasing numbers of self-help books, advice, and groups. We understand the family in terms of such psychosocial models as the "functional family," and we raise our children according to the latest findings. Almost everything that we think, feel, and do is scrutinized by a human science, and we are provided with that knowledge so that we too can understand our own life and its circumstances.

The Discipline of Medicine

But the human sciences are not alone in their objectification of humanity; they are aided by a culture produced by the *medical gaze*. The modern medical gaze is different from that of the eighteenth century. At that time, disease was organized into hierarchical categories such as families, genera, and species. In some ways the patient was superfluous to the disease. The doctor's gaze, then, was directed not so much at the patient as at the disease. Diseases transferred to the body when their makeup combined with certain qualities of the patient, like their temperament. Symptoms existed within the disease itself, not the patient. This way of seeing where symptoms live implies that the patient's body could actually get in the way of the doctor seeing the symptoms. For example, if the patient was old, then the symptoms associated with being elderly could obscure the doctor's view of the symptoms associated with the disease. The medical gaze, then, was directed at the disease, not the body.

However, by the nineteenth century, the modern medical gaze had come to locate disease within the patient. Disease was no longer seen to exist within its own world apart from the body; from this new clinical point of view, disease is located within the body and is constituted by its symptoms. The patient can't get in the way of the symptoms; the symptoms and disease are the same and exist within the body. This shift in discourse created the clinical gaze, an objectifying way of seeing that looks within and dissects the patient. With the clinical gaze, "Western man could constitute himself in his own eyes as an object of science" (Foucault, 1963/1994a, p. 197).

Modern medicine is thus created through a gaze that makes the body an object, a thing to be dissected, either symbolically or actually, in order to find the disease within it. The culture of the clinical gaze helped to create a general disposition in Western society to see the person as an object. This disposition, along with the human sciences, made the practices of power much more effective and treacherous—objects that can be thrown away are much easier to control than subjects who demand continuing emotional and psychic connections.

Disciplining Sex

Thus, bodily regimens of exercise and diet, self-understanding and regulation of feelings and behaviors, all stem from medicine and the human sciences, which Foucault tells us make up the panopticon of modernity. But Foucault is interested in something deeper than the control of the body—he wants to document how we as individuals exercise social power over the way we relate to our own selves. Nowhere is this more clearly seen than in Foucault's counter-history of sexuality. In order to understand Foucault's intent, we will now briefly review Greek and modern ideas of sexuality.

Greek Sexuality

Ancient Greece was the birthplace of democracy and Western philosophy. There was, in fact, a connection between democracy and philosophy. In Athens, in response to an upheaval by the masses against their tyrannical leader, a politician named Cleisthenes introduced a completely new organization of political institutions called democracy (the rule of common people). Through democratic elections, the elite incrementally lost their advantage in the assemblies and the common people ruled. Unfortunately, the masses were susceptible to impassioned speech and ended up making several decisions that conflicted with one another or entailed high costs. This series of crises created a desire in the elite for absolutes: What are the truths upon which all decisions and governance should be based? Truth obviously couldn't be found simply through rhetoric; they believed that there had to be some absolutes upon which decisions could be based.

Along with other factors, this impetus helped produce the Greek notion of the soul. For the Greek, the idea of the soul captured all that is meant by the inner person: his or her mind, emotions, ethics, beliefs, and so on. But in reading Plato, it's also clear that the soul was seen to be hierarchically constructed. Within the soul, the mind is preeminent and alone is immortal. The emotions and appetites, though part of the soul, are lesser and mortal. Thus, reason is godlike and education, especially philosophy, is important for proper discipline.

It is important that we see the emphasis here. The mind, emotions, and bodily appetites are viewed hierarchically, but they are all seen as part of the soul. In order to get a sense of the relationships within the soul, let's take a look at a conversation that Plato (1993) sets up between Socrates and a group of students. Socrates speaks first:

> "Do you think that it's a philosopher's business to concern himself with what people call pleasures—food and drink, for instance?"
>
> "Certainly not, Socrates," said Simmias.
>
> "What about those of sex?"
>
> "Not in the least." . . .
>
> "Then it is your opinion in general that a man of this kind is not preoccupied with the body, but keeps his attention directed as much as he can away from it and towards the soul?"
>
> "Yes, it is." . . .
>
> "Then when is it that the soul attains to truth? When it tries to investigate anything with the help of the body, it is obviously liable to be led astray."
>
> "Quite so."
>
> "Is it not in the course of reasoning, if at all, that the soul gets a clear view of reality?"
>
> "Yes." (pp. 117–118)

Notice how Socrates views sex: He puts it on the same level as eating and drinking. Sex isn't something set aside and special. It is simply seen as a bodily appetite, on a par with eating and drinking. And these aren't a direct concern for the philosopher—they are only of indirect concern. If the bodily appetites get in the way of the search for reality or truth, then they are of concern, but only then. The point is to keep the mind free. A person shouldn't be preoccupied with the body, because too much attention on the body and its appetites will take his or her attention away from the quest for truth. This bit of dialogue sets us up well for the way Foucault talks about sex in Greek society.

In Greek society, sexuality existed as *aphrodisia*. This Greek word is obviously where we get our term *aphrodisiac,* but it had a much broader meaning for the Greeks. Foucault notes that neither the Greeks nor the Romans had an idea of "sexuality" or "the flesh" as distinct objects. When we think of sex, sexuality, or the flesh, we usually have in mind a single set of behaviors or desires. The Greeks, while they had words for different kinds of sexual acts and relations, didn't have a single word or concept under which they could all fit. The closest to that kind of umbrella term is *aphrodisia,* which might be translated as "sensual pleasures" or "pleasures of love," and more accurately the works and acts of Aphrodite, the goddess of love.

These works of Aphrodite, perhaps like the works of any god or goddess, cannot be fully categorized. To do so would limit the god. This lack of a catalog or objective specification of sexuality is exactly Foucault's point. In modern, Western society, particularly as expressed through Christianity, there is a definite way to index those things that are sexual, or the "works of the flesh." This identifiability is extremely important for the Western mind because sex is a moral issue; it, above all other things, defines immoral practices. So, what counts and doesn't count as sexual is imperative for us, but wasn't for the Greeks.

The Greeks also employed the idea of *chresis aphrodision* to sexuality: The phrase means "the use of pleasures." The Greeks' use of pleasure was guided by three strategies: need, timeliness, and status. The strategy of need once again highlights Socrates' approach to sexual practices. As we've seen, in ancient Greece, the relationship to one's body was to be characterized by moderation; but every person's appetites and abilities to cope are different. Thus, the Greek strategy was for the individual to first know his need—to understand what the body wants, what its limits are, and how strong the mind is.

The second strategy is timeliness and simply refers to the idea that there are better and worse times to have sexual pleasures. There was a particularly good time in one's life, neither too young nor too old; a good time of the year; and good times during the day, usually connected with dietary habits. The issue of time "was one of the most important objectives, and one of the most delicate, in the art of making use of the pleasures" (Foucault, 1984/1990b, p. 57). The last strategy in the use of pleasures was status. The art of pleasure was adapted to the status of the person. The general rule was that the more an individual was in the public eye, the more he should "freely and deliberately" adapt rigorous standards regarding his use of pleasures.

Rather than seeing sexuality as moral, the Greeks saw it in terms of ascetics. Ascetics refer to one's attitude or relationship toward one's self, and for the Greek this was to be characterized through strength. The word *ascetics* comes from the Greek *asketikos,* which literally translated means "exercise." The idea here is not simply something we do, as in exercising control; it also carries with it a picture of active training. Here we see the Greek link between masculinity and virility. The virile man in Greek society was someone who moderated his own appetites. He was the man who voluntarily wrestled with his body in order to discipline his mind. The picture we see is that of an athlete in training. For example, the athlete knows that eating chocolate or ice cream can be very pleasurable. But while in training, the athlete willingly forgoes those pleasures for what he or she sees as a higher good. The result of this training is *enkrateia,* the mastery of one's self. It's a position of internal strength rather than weakness.

Training is always associated with a goal; there is an end to be achieved or a contest to be won. In this case, the aim of the Greek attitude toward sexuality is a state of being, something that becomes true of the individual in his daily life. This is the teleology, or ultimate goal, of sexuality, the fourth structuring factor that defines a person's relationship to sex. The goal for the Greek was freedom. We can again see this idea in the conversation with Socrates. Truth and reality were things to be sought after. Too much emphasis on sex, just like eating and drinking, can get in the way of this search. As Socrates (Plato, 1993) said, "surely the soul can reason best when it is free of all distractions such as hearing or sight or pain or pleasure of any kind" (p. 118).

Western Modern Sexuality

The Western, modern view of sex is quite different from the Greek. It is, in fact, quite different from that which developed in the East. Where Eastern philosophy and religion developed a set of practices intended to guide sexual behavior to its highest and most spiritual expression and enjoyment (for instance, Kama sutra), the West developed systems of external control and prohibitions. Of course, a great deal of the impetus toward this view of sex was provided by the Christian church.

Part of this movement came from Protestantism with its emphasis on individual righteousness and redemption. Rather than being worthy of God because of Church membership and sacraments, Protestantism singled the individual out and made his or her moral conduct an expression of salvation and faith. But an important part was also played by the Counter-Reformation, a reform movement in the Catholic Church.

Confession and penance are sacraments in the Catholic Church. They are one of the ways through which salvation is imparted to Christians. The Counter-Reformation increased the frequency of confession and guided it to specific kinds of self-examination, designed to root out the sins of the flesh down to the minutest detail:

> sex . . . [in all] its aspects, its correlations, and its effects must be pursued down to their slenderest ramification: a shadow in a daydream, an image too slowly dispelled, a badly exorcised complicity between the body's mechanics and the mind's complacency: everything had to be told. (Foucault, 1976/1990a, p. 19)

This was the beginning of the Western idea that sex is a deeply embedded power, one that is intrinsic to the "flesh" (*the* vehicle of sin par excellence, as compared to the Greek idea of bodily appetites), and one that must be eradicated through inward searching using an external moral code and through outward confession.

While these Christian doctrines would have influenced the general culture, they would have remained connected to the fate of Christianity alone had it not been for other secular changes and institutions beginning in the eighteenth century, most particularly in politics, economics, and medicine. With the rise of the nation-state and science, population became an economic and political issue. Previous societies had always been aware of the people gathered together in society's name, but conceiving of the people as the population is a significant change. *The idea of population transforms the people into an object that can be analyzed and controlled.*

In this transformation, science provided the tools and the nation-state the motivation and control mechanisms (ability to tax, standing armies, and so on). The population could be numbered and analyzed statistically, and those statistics became important for governance and economic pursuit. The population represented the labor force, one that needed to be trained and, more fundamentally, born. At the center of these economic and political issues was sexuality:

> It was necessary to analyze the birthrate, the age of marriage, the legitimate and illegitimate births, the precocity and frequency of sexual relations, the ways of making them fertile or sterile, the effects of unmarried life or of the prohibitions, the impact of contraceptive practices [and so on]. (Foucault, 1976/1990a, pp. 25–26)

In the latter half of the nineteenth century, medicine and psychiatry took up the sex banner as well. Psychiatry, especially through the work of Freud, set out to discover the makeup of the human mind and emotion, and it began to catalog mental illnesses, especially those connected with sex. It conceptualized masturbation as a perversion at the core of many psychological and physical problems, homosexuality as a mental illness, and the maturation of a child in terms of successive sexual issues that the child must resolve on the way to healthy adulthood. In short, psychiatry "annexed the whole of the sexual perversions as its own province" (Foucault, 1976/1990a, p. 30). Law and criminal justice also bolstered the cause, as society sought to regulate individual and bedroom behaviors. Social controls popped up everywhere that "screened the sexuality of couples, parents and children, dangerous and endangered adolescents—undertaking to protect, separate, and forewarn, signaling perils everywhere, awakening people's attention, calling for diagnoses, piling up reports, organizing therapies. These sites radiated discourses aimed at sex" (pp. 30–31).

All of these factors worked to change the discourse of Western sexuality in the twentieth century. Sex went from the Greek model of a natural bodily appetite that could be satisfied in any number of ways, to the modern model of sex as the insidious power within. At the heart of this change is the confession, propagated by Catholicism and Protestantism and picked up by psychiatry, medicine, educators, and other experts. Confessional rhetoric is found everywhere in a society that uses Victorian prudishness as its backdrop for incessant talk about sex in magazines, journals, books, movies, and reality television shows. Repression is used as a source of discourse, and sex has become the topic of conversation—a central feature in Western discourse, and the defining feature of the human animal. Sex is suspected of "harboring a fundamental secret" concerning the truth of mankind (p. 69).

In the modern discourse of sex, sexuality has become above all an object, a truth to discover and a thing to control. In this, sex has followed the use and development of science in general and the human sciences in particular: "The project of a science of the subject has gravitated, in ever narrowing circles, around the question of sex" (Foucault, 1976/1990a, p. 70). This form of objective control ("bio-control") over the intimacy of humanity came through science and is linked with the development of the nation-state and capitalism. While capitalism and the nation-state seem to be firmly established and the need for such control not as great, what we are left with is a way of constructing our self as the moral subject of our sexual behavior. We have inherited a certain kind of subjectivity from this discourse, a particular way of relating to our self and sexuality. This legacy of the modern discourse of sexuality sees sex as a central truth of the self, as an object that must be studied and understood. Further, the modern discourse of sexuality tells us that this part of us is intrinsically dangerous. It is at best an amoral creature and at worst a defiled beast that treads upon sacred and moral ground.

Summary

- Foucault takes the position that knowledge and power are wrapped up with one another; each produces and reinforces the other. Power as exercised and expressed through discourse creates the way in which we feel, act, think, and relate to our self. Likewise, the knowledge of any epoch defines what is mentally, emotionally, and physically possible. Foucault sees the practices involved in power and knowledge as games of truth—the use of specific rules and resources through which something is seen as truth in any given age. The games of truth that Foucault is particularly interested in are the ones that involve the practices through which we participate in the domination of our subjectivity.

- Much of Foucault's work is in the form of counter-history. The generally accepted model of history is that of history as memory: History is our collective memory of events. We also usually think of history as slowly progressing in a linear fashion. Foucault argues that history is far from a memory of linear events—history is power in use. It's a myth that is constructed according to specific values. Foucault proposes a counter-history, one that focuses on abrupt episodes of change and the way in which knowledge changes in response to various power regimes. Foucault uses an archaeological approach to uncover the practices that are associated with discourse and ways of thinking, and he uses a genealogical approach to uncover how discourse and power are inscribed on the body and mind.

- Foucault argues that the knowledge people hold is based upon historical epistemes. Episteme means the underlying order; Foucault uses it to refer to the way thought organizes itself in any historical period of time. Discourses are produced within historical epistemes. A discourse is a way of talking about something that is guided by specific rules and practices, that sets the conditions for our subjective awareness, and that subjugates through a will to truth and power.

- While power is found in all human practice, Foucault is particularly interested in the unique power of modernity. This expression of power is associated with changes in government, medicine, the institution of the human sciences, changes in the Western discourse of sexuality, and changes in the penal system. The change from rule by monarchy to rule by the nation-state demanded a new form of governmentality, one in which the individual watches over his or her own behaviors, one that increases control while preserving the illusion of freedom. This governmentality was aided by the human sciences through the ideas of population, an essentializing and mechanistic model of the person, and the value of expert knowledge. Governmentality was also produced through a new medical "gaze," which located symptoms and disease within the body, panoptical practices in controlling criminality, and changes in sexuality promoted by the Catholic confessional and Protestant individualism. Together, these created a discourse of governmentality that objectifies and controls through her own practices.

TAKING THE PERSPECTIVE

Obviously most of the theories we've looked at beginning in Chapter 7 have been critical of society in one way or another. This is especially true of Jürgen Habermas, whose base is critical theory. Yet there is a fundamental difference between those critiques and the one offered by Foucault. With the others there is a sense of some substance or presence, but with Foucault one gets a sense of absence. For example, with Foucault there isn't truth, only truth games; and there isn't history, just counter-histories. One way to understand this absence is to simply say that Foucault has other concerns, and that undoubtedly is part of it. But there's something deeper, more basic in back of Foucault's approach: Foucault approaches the social world as a poststructuralist.

In order to understand **poststructuralism**, we must first look to structuralism (since the "post" denotes that it comes after structuralism. Structuralism argues that there are deep structures that underlie and generate observable phenomena or events. This is a more radical statement than is usually made when we talk about structure in sociology (such as Parsons' structural-functionalism). For many sociologists, social structures are seen as influencing our lives; they help account for the patterned nature of human action and interaction. But social structures are usually seen as one of several influences. While we can talk about the poles of the debate in terms of structure versus agency, most sociologists acknowledge that interactions, culture, and structure all influence our behavior.

On the other hand, structuralism sees the power of structure as absolute. These structures work below the level of consciousness, and they don't simply influence or even determine our behaviors; they generate, create, and produce them. Everything that we see, think, feel, and do are in reality events or manifestations of the structure. While this may sound depressing to some of us, for structuralists this idea represented a ray of hope. As the linguistic structuralist Claude Lévi-Strauss (1963) put it, "Structural linguistics will certainly play the same renovating role with respect to the social sciences that nuclear physics, for example, has played for the physical sciences" (p. 33). It is the criticism of this belief and hope that forms the core of poststructuralism.

The basic premise of poststructuralism is that language signifies rather than represents. In other words, language doesn't refer to or represent any actual reality—all we have is language. Yet people have always sought a center for language—we have wanted language to be a response to the real world, to be tied down, moored, centered in reality. This center is what brings presence to language. The use of "presence" here functions as a technical term; it implies being or existence. In other words, humans have always sought a center to their linguistic schemes that would make language authentic, true, or real. Ideas such as essence, existence, substance, subject, transcendence, consciousness, God, man, and so forth have given language a reason for its existence, a firm foundation upon which to stand, and an "invariable presence" (Derrida, 1967/1978, pp. 279–280).

But there are two problems with this idea or desire. First, a center that moors language to some reality is by definition outside of the totality of language. The idea of a monotheistic God is a good example. God is seen to exist outside of time, space, and language, and because of that external existence, believers think that He gives reason for the universe in its totality (including time, space, and language). The clearest expression of this sort of centering is the doctrine of plenary inspiration, the belief that every single word written in the Bible was directly inspired or dictated by God.

However, the external nature of the center reveals a contradiction. A center that is located outside the whole is by definition not inside and thus cannot be at the center of the totality. In other words, language is the totality of human existence—we think, feel, and see linguistically. But humans have always looked outside of language for the center or reason of language. There's part of us that knows this, but we usually ascribe it to being "wrong." We say things like "people used to talk about the earth being flat, but they were wrong." Poststructuralism wants us to see that there's never a chance of being "right" because those "truths" or "centers" are always and ever, by definition, outside language. What we see in the idea of a center is a desire to master anxiety—anxiety about the human mode of existence. Since this is so, "the entire history of the concept of structure . . . must be thought of as a series of substitutions of center for center" (Derrida, 1967/1978, p. 279). Thus, logically, there is no center to language, no firm foundation upon which to stand.

The second issue that poststructuralists want to bring to our attention is that a rupture has occurred in the history of language. Amongst all the other critiques of capitalism, race, gender, and so on, there came a time when language itself was critiqued. Writing is a profound process. Through writing, we inscribe or write the world around us. That's what happens when we use language to understand and make meaning out of the physical world and our experiences—we put the meaning on it; the meaning isn't "there" for language to represent. Writing/language is so profound that it writes its own critique. Think of it this way: If you were a linguist and

(Continued)

(Continued)

wanted to critique language, what's the only thing you use? You would have to use language; you would write the critique of writing *by writing it*—here language inscribes upon itself. The rupture is that moment in time when language itself was critiqued, and it without question reveals the absolute reflexive nature of language.

Thus, rather than language being centered in an independent reality, language is inherently self-referential, creating a world of oppressive power relations (Foucault's point). The implications of this are as follows:

- Poststructuralism rejects the belief in essentializing ideas that conceptualize the social world or a portion of it as a universal totality—rather, the social world is fragmented and historically specific (general social theories are thus impossible and oppressive).

- Poststructuralism denies the possibility of knowing an independent or objective reality—rather, the human world and knowledge are utterly textual or discursive

- Poststructuralism discards the idea that texts or language have any true meaning—rather, texts are built around difference and carry a surplus of meaning (humanity is thus left with nothing but interpretation and interpretations of interpretation—this book is an interpretation of others' interpretations of a social world; and as you read, you produce yet another interpretation).

- Poststructuralism rejects the idea of universal human nature developed out of the Enlightenment—rather, the meaning of the human subject is historically specific and is an effect of discourse, with the discourses of an age producing the possible bodies and subjectivities of the person.

Beyond that, Lemert (1990) points us to four uses of poststructuralism in sociology. He says that in the social sciences, we typically solve the problems or questions we pose with "reference to ideas like 'empirical reality'" (p. 244). Poststructuralism shatters the idea of a center; our texts therefore can't legitimately make reference to an empirical reality because every reality for humans is a written (inscribed) one. Thus, what we have isn't an empirical reality; it is a textual reality. What, then, can we conclude? Lemert gives us four propositions for poststructuralist sociology:

1. That theory is an inherently discursive activity

2. That the empirical reality in relation to which theoretical texts are discursive is without exception textual

3. That empirical texts depend on this relationship to theoretical texts for their intellectual or scientific value

4. That in certain, if not all, cases a discursive interpretation yields more, not less, adequate understanding (p. 244)

BUILDING YOUR THEORY TOOLBOX

Learning More—Primary Sources

- Among Foucault's "must reads" are
  - o *The History of Sexuality, Vol. I: An Introduction,* Vintage, 1990.
  - o *The Order of Things: An Archaeology of the Human Sciences,* Vintage, 1994.
  - o *Discipline and Punish: The Birth of the Prison,* Vintage, 1995.
  - o *The Birth of the Clinic: An Archaeology of Medical Perception,* Vintage Books, 1994.
  - o *The Essential Foucault,* edited by Paul Rabinow and Nikolas S. Rose, New Press, 2003.

Learning More—Secondary Sources

- I recommend the following, in order of accessibility:
  - o *Michel Foucault,* by Sara Mills, Routledge, 2003.
  - o *The Cambridge Companion to Foucault,* edited by Gary Gutting, Cambridge, 1994.
  - o *Foucault,* by Gilles Deleuze, University of Minnesota Press, 1988.

Check It Out

- *Power and knowledge: On Civilization, Power, and Knowledge: Selected Writings,* by Norbert Elias, edited by Stephen Mennell and Johan Goudsblom, University of Chicago Press, 1998.
- Foucault on the Web: http://www.theory.org.uk/ctr-fouc.htm

Seeing the World

- After reading and understanding this chapter, you should be able to define the following terms theoretically and explain their theoretical importance to Foucault's theory of power: *truth games, counter-histories, archaeology, genealogy, episteme, discourse, governmentality, objectification, panopticon, microphysics of power, medical gaze*
- After reading and understanding this chapter, you should be able to answer the following questions (remember to answer them *theoretically*):
  - o Explain Foucault's connection between power and knowledge. How does he conceptualize power? How does knowledge function as power? What are the unique characteristics of modern power?
  - o What does Foucault mean by "the order of things"? Explain how his "counter-histories" are used to expose this order.

(Continued)

(Continued)

   o Define discourse and explain how it provides a subjective position for the speaker.

   o Explain the place of the social sciences (human disciplines) in creating govern-
      mentality and the microphysics of power.

   o Describe how sex and sexuality changed between ancient Greek society and modern
      Western society.

   o Write a 250-word synopsis of the theoretical perspective poststructuralism.

Weaving the Threads

- Using the index of this book, find the different ways power is defined and used theoretically. Evaluate each of these ways and create a theory of power that you think best
  explains it. Justify your answer.

- Compare and contrast Foucault's idea of governmentality and Anthony Giddens' notion
  of the reflexive project of the self. Explain why you think these two ideas are distinct.
  Together, what do they imply about how we relate to the "self" in modernity?

- Power is a taken-for-granted part of what you learned about race, gender, and class in
  Chapters 7 and 8. What ways do you see Foucault's theory of power elaborating what
  you know about social inequality?

CHAPTER 14

The End of Everything:

Jean Baudrillard

(1929–2007)

I n August 1990, the United States along with 33 other nations declared war on Iraq. The cost of the Gulf War was more than $60 billion and involved over 1 million troops. Though the numbers are still uncertain, it's estimated that well over 100,000 people died as a result of the campaign. Before the invasion, Jean Baudrillard published an article titled "The Gulf War Will Not Take Place." During the campaign Baudrillard published another article, "The Gulf War Is Not Taking Place." After the war, the new piece by Baudrillard was called "The Gulf War Did Not Take Place." He later published a book by the same title: *The Gulf War Did Not Take Place.*

Baudrillard isn't saying that guns weren't fired and people didn't die. Baudrillard's point in this provocative book is that for the world this was a mediated war. The mass media provided continuous television coverage, but that coverage was packaged and presented in such a way as to lure audiences to watch (the medium is the message). The "news," then, was a commodification of what happened on the ground. What the world saw wasn't the reality of the war but a hyperreality designed to stimulate rather than inform: "It is a masquerade of information: branded faces delivered over to the prostitution of the image, the image of an unintelligible distress. . . . It is not war taking place over there but the disfiguration of the world" (Baudrillard, 1995, p. 40)

Baudrillard's striking analysis of the Gulf War is based a postmodern perspective. Often, postmodernism is often confused with poststructuralism, which we considered in Chapter 13. And there are some similarities. Both are concerned with culture generally and language particularly, and both argue that culture and language function without any physical or objective reality in back of them. There are, I think, two main differences between them. First, they each locate the reasons for the lack of reality in different places. Poststructuralism generally considers the intrinsic characteristics of language itself, while social postmodernism usually looks to such factors as capitalism and mass media as the culprits.

Second, they each focus on different effects of the state of culture. For instance, Foucault argues that rather than referring to any physical reality, language contains political discourses that function to exercise power over the person. Baudrillard, on the other hand, sees culture as absolutely void of any significance at all, political or otherwise. Any meaning or power in culture has been stripped away by incessant commodification, advertising, and the trivializing effects of mass media.

> The systems of reference for production, signification, the affect, substance and history, all this equivalence to a "real" content, loading the sign with the burden of "utility," with gravity—its form of representative equivalence—all this is over with. (Baudrillard, 1976/1993b, p. 6)

THEORIST'S DIGEST

Brief Biography

Jean Baudrillard was born in Reims, France, on July 29, 1929. Baudrillard studied German at the Sorbonne University, Paris, and was professor of German for 8 years. During that time, he also worked as a translator and began his studies in sociology and philosophy. He completed his dissertation in sociology under Henri Lefebvre, a noted Marxist-humanist. Baudrillard began teaching sociology in 1966, eventually moving to the Université de Paris-X Nanterre as professor of sociology. From 1986 to 1990, Baudrillard served as the director of science for the Institut de Recherche et d'Information Socio-Économique at the Université de Paris-IX Dauphine. Beginning in 2001, Baudrillard was professor of the philosophy of culture and media criticism at the European Graduate School in Saas-Fee, Switzerland. Baudrillard is the author of several international best sellers, among them are *Symbolic Exchange and Death*, *Simulacra and Simulation*, *Seduction*, *America*, and *The Gulf War Did Not Take Place*. Baudrillard died March 6, 2007.

Central Sociological Questions

Baudrillard is essentially concerned with the relationship between reality and appearance; this is an issue that has plagued philosophers and theorists for eons. Baudrillard's unique contributions to this problem concern the effects of mass media and advertising. Baudrillard, then, is deeply curious about the effects of mass media on culture and the problem of representation: Has capitalist-driven mass media pushed appearance to the front stage in such a way as to destroy reality? Is there a difference between image and reality in postmodernity?

Simply Stated

Culture is meant to express social meanings and create social relationships, both of which happen through the use of symbols. And symbols work as they are intended when connected to real people in real situations. However, as a result of commodification, advertising, and mass media, cultural symbols have been cut off from their social embeddness and have become free-floating, without any specific social reference. Because human nature is principally oriented toward symbolic meaning, people have been left without any real meaning. This void is filled with mass media and electronic stimulations, which need to be produced in ever more spectacular and plasticine fashion. The person himself or herself is left without any solid, social identities and must cobble together an image-based self.

Key Ideas

Postmodern, human nature, symbolic exchange, use-value, exchange-value, sign-value, commodity fetish, sign fetish, consumer society, labor of consumption, simulacrum, free-floating signifiers, hyperreality, death of the subject, fragmenting identities

Concepts and Theory:
Human Nature, Symbols, and Production

Baudrillard is both fun and frustrating, and usually at the same time. He, more than any other postmodern writer I know, exemplifies what he is writing about. "Baudrillard's writings are a kind of intellectual Disneyland, neither true nor false" (Danto, 1990, p. 48). Baudrillard is part of the postmodern landscape. Reading his many books and articles is an experience in cultural implosion. Yet at the same time, he tells us something about the society and people living in postmodernity, something very few say with as much insight or art. Baudrillard's writings are part play and part purpose. Yet we're going to say something definite and hopefully meaning-ful about Baudrillard in this chapter. We're going to focus on the purposeful part of his writings—but keep in mind the playful part too (think about it: I'm proposing to say something meaningful about meaninglessness). To understand Baudrillard, we must begin with his view of human nature; and he began with Marx.

Though Baudrillard began as a Marxist, the disappointing results of the 1968 student uprisings made him question economic Marxism. Baudrillard ends up viewing Marxism as actually substantiating certain aspects of the capitalist mental-ity. There are a few ways that Baudrillard sees Marx as doing this. First, his theory of species being argues that human beings are by nature economic producers, and that true consciousness comes through being intimately involved in the production process. The product of this kind of species production acts like a mirror that reflects human nature back to people. In making this kind of argument, Marx is giving ultimate legitimation to the entire capitalist scheme of production. Marx reduced humankind to economic producers, just the way capitalism does. Baudrillard (1973/1975) argues that "in order to find a realm beyond economic value (which is in fact the only revolutionary perspective), then *the mirror of pro-duction* in which all Western metaphysics is reflected, must be broken" (p. 47, emphasis original).

The way Baudrillard breaks this mirror is by focusing on humankind's symbolic nature. Baudrillard argues that humans are basically oriented toward **symbolic exchange**: the exchange of gifts, actions, signs, and so on for their symbolic rather than material value. Here, Baudrillard is making the same kind of argument about human nature that Durkheim (1912/1995) did: Humans are symbolic creatures oriented toward meaning rather than production.

A good example of the value of symbolism in traditional societies is the preva-lence of transition rituals, as in the conversion from boy to manhood. In the ritual of attaining manhood, the actual behaviors themselves are immaterial, whether it is wrapping a sack of fire ants around the hands or mutilating the penis. Any object or set of behaviors can have symbolic value. What matters is what the ritualized actions symbolize for the group. Symbolic exchange formed part of daily life in pre-capitalist societies: the exchange of food, jewelry, titles, clothing, and so on were all involved in a symbolic "cycle of gifts and countergifts" (Baudrillard, 1973/1975, p. 83). Symbolic exchange thus established a community of symbolic meanings and recip-rocal relations among a group of people.

Baudrillard also claims that human nature is wrapped up in excess. Like Marx, Baudrillard sees humanity as capable of creating their own needs. That is, the needs of other animals are set; but the potential needs of humans are without limit. For example, today I "need" an iPod and an HDTV plasma screen; a few years ago I didn't. And I can't even begin to imagine what I will need in 5 years. However, unlike Marx, Baudrillard sees excess as an indicator of human boundlessness. Wrapped up in this sense of excess, I think, is transcendence: the ability to reach above the mundane, which is in itself a symbolic move.

In place of species being, Baudrillard proposes excess: Rather than being bound up with survival, production, and materialism, human nature is found in excess and exuberance. Douglas Kellner (2003) summarizes Baudrillard's point of view nicely: "humans 'by nature' gain pleasure from such things as expenditure, waste, festivities, sacrifices and so on, in which they are sovereign and free to expend the excesses of their energy (and thus follow their 'real nature')" (p. 317). Baudrillard argues that these human characteristics were given license and support in precapitalist societies. However, the modernist demands of rationality and restraint in the beginning years of capitalism are the antithesis of symbolic exchange and excess.

Commodities as Signs

Another set of Marxian ideas that Baudrillard specifically inverts is the labor theory of value. A theory of economic value explains from where the value of goods comes. In order to talk about this issue, Marx used two terms: use-value and exchange-value. *Use-value* refers to the actual function that a product contains, or its material makeup, while *exchange-value* refers to the rate of exchange one commodity bears when compared to other commodities. The interesting thing for Marx is that when reduced to monetary value, exchange-value is much higher than use-value. In other words, you get paid less to produce a product than it sells for. Yet Marx argued that exchange-value wasn't simply decided by market fluctuations. Something more stable is involved—something common to all commodities. Marx's argument is that human labor creates exchange-value and is the source of capitalist profit.

Baudrillard counters by arguing that Marx is continuing to focus on materialist, and thus capitalist, ideas. Like species being, use-value is completely bound up with the idea of products. Use-value is oriented to a materialist world alone. It is filled with practical use that is used up in consumption. It has no value or meaning other than material. And, like species being, the idea of use-value validates the basic tenets of capitalism—the truth of human life is rooted in economic production and consumption. Exchange-value is materialist as well, because exchange-value is based on human, economic production. The idea of exchange-value also legitimates and substantiates instrumental rationality, the utilitarian calculations of costs and benefits. Again, rather than critiquing capitalism, Baudrillard sees Marx as legitimating it.

> The Marxist seeks a *good use* of economy. Marxism is therefore only a limited petit bourgeois critique, one more step in the banalization of life toward the "good use" of the social! . . . Marxism is only the disenchanted horizon of capital—all that precedes or follows it is more radical than it is. (Baudrillard, 1987, p. 60, emphasis original)

In place of use- and exchange-values, Baudrillard proposes the idea of *sign-value*. Commodities are no longer purchased for their use-value, and exchange-value is no longer simply a reflection of human labor. Each of these capitalist Marxian values has been trumped by signification. In postmodern societies, commodities are now purchased and used more for their sign-value than for anything else. As you can see, postmodernity is part of the linguistic turn in sociology.

In order to be able to compare these differences, I've laid them out in Table 14.1. I'll explain the historical transitions in a moment, but symbolic exchange was pre-eminent in traditional, noncapitalistic societies. Baudrillard will refer to this time period as the first and second phases of the sign. Use-value and exchange-value were dominant during the early stages of capitalism and began what Baudrillard calls the consumer society (the third stage of the sign). Sign-value corresponds to postmodernity, the fourth stage of the sign. I'd like you to notice the shifts in "meanings." Symbolic exchange has personal meaning: Its meaning is strong and clear for those participating. Under capitalism, meaning shifts to instrumental and market concerns—what will this object do for me, and what can I gain from it? In postmodernity, "meaning" shifts to signs in relation to other signs. This latter idea is Derrida's point exactly; Baudrillard is simply seeing it as part of a historical progression. But Baudrillard also takes Derrida's notion a step further.

Table 14.1   Value Chart

	Symbolic Exchange	Use-Value	Exchange-Value	Sign-Value
Essence	Gift	Function	Economy	Consumption
Value	Symbol	Instrument	Commodity	Sign
Meaning	Relation to subject	What object does	Market worth	Relation to other signs
Examples	Wedding ring	Automobile as transportation	The book costs $19.95	Clothing as fashion

Sign Fetish

Let's look at one more idea from Marx before moving to Baudrillard's theory. Marx was very critical of the process of commodification. A commodity is simply something that is sold in order to make a profit. *Commodification as a process* refers to the way more and more objects and experiences in the human world are turned into products for profit. To see what Marx means, simply compare your life with that of your great-grandparents. Chances are that many more of the objects and experiences in your life are purchased rather than made; they exist as commodities in your world. Commodification is intrinsic to capitalism.

Increasing commodification leads to *commodity fetish*. Marx used the term *fetish* in its pre-Freudian sense of idol worship. The idea here is that the worshipper's eyes are blinded to the falsity of the idol. Marx's provocative term has two implications that are related to one another. First, in commodity fetish, people misrecognize what is truly present within a commodity. By this Marx meant that commodities and commodification are based on the exploitation of human labor, but most of us fail to see it. Second, in commodity fetish there is a substitution. For Marx, the basic relationship between humans is that of production. But in commodity fetish, the market relations of commodity exchange are substituted for the productive or material relations of persons. The result is that rather than being linked in a community of producers, human relationships are seen through commodities, either as buyers and sellers or as a group of like consumers. Commodification and its fetish are among the primary bases of alienation, which, according to Marx, separate people from their own human nature as creative producers and from one another as social beings.

Again, Baudrillard argues that Marx's concern was misplaced and actually motivated by the capitalist economy. Marx's entire notion of the fetish is locked up with species being and material production. With commodity fetish, we don't recognize the suppressive labor relations that underlie the product and its value, and we substitute an alienated commodity for what should be a product based in our own species being. In focusing exclusively on materialism, "Marxism eliminates any real chance it has of analyzing the *actual process of ideological labor*" (Baudrillard, 1972/1981, p. 89, emphasis original). According to Baudrillard, ideology isn't based in or related to material relations of production, as Marx argued. Rather, ideology and fetishism are both based in a "*passion for the code*" (p. 92, emphasis original).

One way to understand what Baudrillard is talking about is to go back to Table 14.1. Human nature is symbolic and oriented toward meaning. In symbolic exchange, real meaning and social relationships are present. However, capitalism and changes in media have pushed aside symbolic exchange and in postmodernity have substituted sign-value. And, as we've seen with Derrida, sign-value is based on textual references to other signs, nothing else. The fetish, then, is the human infatuation with consuming sign-vehicles that are devoid of all meaning and reality. Thus, ideology "appears as a sort of cultural surf frothing on the beachhead of the economy" (Baudrillard, 1972/1981, p. 144). Signs keep proliferating without producing substance. This simulation of meaning is what constitutes ideology and fetish for Baudrillard. This implies that continuing to use the materialist Marxian ideas of fetish and ideology actually contributes to capitalist ideology, because it displaces analysis from the issues of signification.

Concepts and Theory: The Death of Meaning

Baudrillard's (1981/1994) theory is based on a fundamental assumption: "Representation stems from the principle of the equivalence of the sign and of the real" (p. 6). What Baudrillard means is that it is possible for signs to represent reality, especially social reality. Think about it this way: What is the purpose of culture? In traditional social groups, culture was created and used in the same social context. For the sake of conversation, let's call this "grounded culture," the kind of culture that symbolic exchanged is based on. In a society such as the United States, however, much of our culture is created or modified by capitalists, advertising agencies, and mass media. We'll call this "commodified culture."

Members in traditional social groups were surrounded by grounded culture; members in postmodern social groups are surrounded by commodified culture. There are vast differences in the reasons why grounded versus commodified culture is created. Grounded culture emerges out of face-to-face interaction and is intended to create meaning, moral boundaries, norms, values, beliefs, and so forth. Commodified culture is produced according to capitalist and mass media considerations and is intended to seduce the viewer to buy products. With grounded culture, people are moral actors; with commodified culture, people are consumers. Postmodernists argue that there are some pretty dramatic consequences, such as cultural fragmentation and unstable identities (for a concise statement, see Allan & Turner, 2000).

Four Phases of the Sign

Beginning with this idea of grounded or representational culture, Baudrillard posits four phases of the sign. The first stage occurred in premodern societies. The important factor here is that language in premodern societies was not mediated. There were little or no written texts and all communication took place in real social situations in face-to-face encounters. In this first phase, the sign represented reality in a profound way. There was a strong correlation or relationship between the sign and the reality it signified, and the contexts wherein specific signs could be used were clear. In this stage, all communicative acts—including speech, gift giving, rituals, exchanges, and so on—were directly related to and expressive of social reality. Here is the birthplace of symbolic exchange.

The second phase of the sign marked a movement away from these direct kinds of symbolic relationships. It gained dominance, roughly speaking, during the time between the European Renaissance and the Industrial Revolution. While media such as written language began previous to the Renaissance, it was during this period that a specific way of understanding, relating to, and representing the world became organized. Direct representation was still present, but certain human ideals became to make inroads. Art, for example, was based on observation of the visible world and yet contained the values of mathematical balance and perspective. Nowhere is this desire for mathematical balance seen more clearly than in Leonardo da Vinci's work *Proportions of the Human Figure*. Thinking of some of da Vinci's other paintings, such as the *Mona Lisa* and *The Last Supper*, we can also see that symbols were used to convey mystery and intrigue.

The Killing Fields of Capitalism

The third phase of the sign began with the Industrial Revolution. This is the period of time generally thought of as modernity. The Industrial Age brought with it a proliferation of consumer goods never before seen in the history of humanity. It also increased leisure time and produced significant amounts of discretionary funds for more people than ever before. These kinds of changes dramatically altered the way produced goods were seen. Here is where we begin to see the widespread use of goods as symbols of status and power. Thorstein Veblen (1899) termed this phenomenon *conspicuous consumption.*

Baudrillard (1970/1998) characterizes this era as the beginning of the **consumer society.** Here is where commodities begin their trek toward sign-value, and symbolic exchange becomes buried under an avalanche of commodified signs. In the consumer society, social relations are read through a system of commodified signs rather than symbolic exchange. Commodities become the sign-vehicles in modernity that carry identity and meaning (or its lack). For example, in modern society the automobile is a portable, personal status symbol. Driving an SUV means something different from driving a Volkswagen Beetle, which conveys something different from driving a hybrid. As this system becomes more important and elaborated, a new kind of labor eventually supplants physical labor, the *labor of consumption.* This doesn't mean the work involved in finding the best deal. The labor of consumption is the work a person does to place himself or herself within an identity that is established and understood in a matrix of commodified signs.

Baudrillard's point is that most if not all of shopping done in the consumer society is driven by sign-value. Every commodity sits in a signed relationship with other commodities—from garden rocks for sale with the word "imagine" etched into them, to tractors, to clothing, to cheese, to the way you listen to music (on records, CDs, MP3 players), to where you shop, and even to what you carry your purchases home in (plastic, paper, or canvas reusable bags). The principal form of labor, then, in the consumer society is the work expended in being able to recognize the "correct" sign-values in the ever-changing schemes of commodified signs.

The fourth stage of the sign began shortly after World War II and continues through today. This fourth stage occurs in postindustrial societies. As such, there has been a shift away from manufacturing and toward information-based technologies. In addition, and perhaps more importantly for Baudrillard, these societies are marked by continual advances and an increasing presence of communication technologies and mass media. Mediated images and information, coupled with unbridled commodification and advertising, are the key influences in this postmodernity. The cultural logic has shifted from the logic of symbolic exchange in precapitalist societies, to the logic of production and consumption in capitalist societies, and finally now to the logic of simulation. For Baudrillard (1976/1993b), postmodernity marks the end of everything:

> The end of labor. The end of production. . . . The end of the signifier/ signified dialectic which facilitates the accumulation of knowledge and of meaning. . . . And at the same time, the end simultaneously of the exchange value/use value dialectic which is the only thing that makes accumulation and social production possible. . . . The end of the classical era of the sign. (p. 8)

Baudrillard (1981/1994) posits that the postmodern sign has "no relation to any reality whatsoever: it is its own pure simulacrum" (p. 6). These kinds of signs are set free from any constraint of representation and become a "play of signifiers . . . in which the code no longer refers back to any subjective or objective 'reality,' but to its own logic" (Baudrillard, 1973/1975, p. 127). Thus, in postmodernity, a fundamental break has occurred between signs and reality. Signs reference nothing other than themselves; they are their own reality and the only reality to which humans refer. These seem like brash and bold claims, but let's look at Baudrillard's argument behind them.

Concepts and Theory: Simulating Reality

Baudrillard argues that there is something intrinsic in transferring information that breaks it down. This is an important point: Anytime we relate or convey information to another, there is a breakdown. So fundamental is this fact that Baudrillard makes it an equation: information = entropy. Baudrillard argues that information destroys its base. The reason for this is twofold. First, information is always about something; it isn't that thing or experience itself. Information by definition, then, is always something other than the thing itself. Second, anytime we convey information, we must use a medium, and it is impossible to put something through a medium without changing it in some way. Even talking to your friend about an event you experienced changes it. Some of the meaning will be lost because language can't convey your actual emotions, and some meaning will be added because of the way your friend individually understands the words you are using.

Mass Media and Advertising

Mass media is the extreme case of both these processes: Social information is removed innumerable times from the actual events, and capitalist mass media colors things more than any other form. One of the reasons behind this coloration is that mass media expends itself on the staging of information. Every medium has its own form of expression—for newspapers it's print and for television it's images. Every piece of information that is gleaned by the public from any media source has thus been selected and formed by the demands of the media. This is part of what is meant by the phrase "the medium is the message."

Further, mass communication comes prepackaged in a meaning form. What I mean by that is that information is staged and the subject is told what constitutes his or her particular relationship to the information. The reason for this is that media in postmodernity exist to make a profit, not to convey information. "Information" is presented more for entertainment purposes than for any intellectual ones. The concern in media is to appeal to and capture a specific market segment. That's why Fox News, CNN, and National Public Radio are so drastically different from one another—the information is secondary; its purpose is to draw an audience that will respond to appeals by capitalists to buy their goods. The presentation of information through the media is a system of self-referencing simulation or fantasy. Thus, "information devours its own content. It devours communication and the social" (Baudrillard, 1981/1994, p. 80).

There is yet another important factor in this decisive break—advertising: "Today what we are experiencing is the absorption of all virtual modes of expression into that of advertising" (Baudrillard, 1981/1994, p. 87). The act of advertising alone reduces objects from their use-value to their sign-value. For Marx, the movement from use-value to exchange-value entails an abstraction of the former; in other words, the exchange-value of a commodity is based on a representation of its possible uses. Baudrillard argues that advertising and mass media push this abstraction further. In advertising, the use-value of a commodity is overshadowed by a sign-value. Advertising does not seek to convey information about a product's use-value; rather, advertising places a product in a field of unrelated signs in order to enhance its cultural appearance. As a result of advertising, we tend to relate to the fragmented sign context rather than the use-value. Thus, in postmodern society, people purchase commodities more for the image than for the function they perform.

Let's think about the example of clothing. The actual use-value of clothing is to cover and keep warm. Yet right now I'm looking at an ad for clothing in *Rolling Stone*, and it doesn't mention anything about protection from the elements or avoiding public nudity. The ad is rather interesting in that it doesn't even present itself as an advertisement at all. It looks more like a picture of a rock band on tour. We could say, then, that even advertising is advertising itself as something. On the sidebar of the "band" picture, it doesn't talk about the band. It says things like "jacket, $599, by Avirex; T-shirt, $69, by Energie," and so on. Most of us won't pay $599 for a jacket to keep us warm; but we might pay that for the status image that we think the jacket projects. Baudrillard's point is that we aren't connected to the basic human reality of keeping warm and covered; we aren't even connected to the social reality of being in a rock band (which itself is a projected image of an idealized life). We are simply attracted to the images.

Seduction and Stimulation

Baudrillard further argues that many of the things we do today in advanced capitalist societies are based largely on images from past lives. For example, most people in traditional and early industrial societies worked with their bodies. Today, increasing numbers of people in postindustrial societies don't work with their bodies, they work out their bodies. The body has thus become a cultural object rather than a means to an end. In postindustrial society, the body no longer serves the purpose of production; rather, it has become the subject of image creation: We work out in order to alter our bodies to meet some cultural representation.

Clothing too has changed from function to image. In previous eras, there was an explicit link between the real function of the body and the clothing worn—the clothing was serviceable with reference to the work performed or it was indicative of social status. For example, a farmer would wear sturdy clothing because of the labor performed, and his clothing indicated his work (if you saw him away from the field, you would still know what he did by his clothing). However, in the postmodern society, clothing itself has become the creator of image rather than something merely serviceable or directly linked to social status and function.

Let's review what we know so far: In times past, the body was used to produce and reproduce; clothing was serviceable and was a direct sign of work and social function. In postmodern society, however, bodies have been freed from the primary burden of labor and have instead become a conveyance of cultural image. The body's "condition" is itself an important symbol, and so is the decorative clothing placed upon the body. Now here is where it gets interesting: In the past, a fit body represented hard work and clothing signed the body's work, but what do our bodies and clothing symbolize today? Today, we take the body through a workout rather than actually working with the body. We work out so we can meet a cultural image—but what does this cultural image represent?

In times past, if you saw someone with a lean, hard body, it meant the person lived a mean, hard life. There was a real connection between the sign and what it referenced. But what do our spa-conditioned bodies reference? Baudrillard's point is that there is no real objective or social reference for what we are doing with our bodies today. The only reference to a real life is to that of the past—we used to have fit bodies because we worked. Thus, in terms of real social life, today's gym-produced bodies represent the past image of working bodies. Further, what does this imply about the clothes we wear? The clothes themselves are an image of an image that doesn't exist in any kind of reality. Baudrillard calls this **simulacrum**, an image of an image of a "reality" that never existed and never appears.

Thus, what we buy today aren't even commodities in the strictest sense. They are what Fredric Jameson calls **free-floating signifiers**. Free-floating signifiers are signs and symbols that have been cut loose from their social and linguistic contexts, and thus their meaning is at best problematic and generally nonexistent. In such a culture, tradition and family can be equated with paper plates (as in a recent television commercial) and infinite justice with military retribution (as in the U.S. president's initial characterization of the Iraq conflict).

Rather than representing, as signs did in the first phase, and rather than creating meaningful and social relations, as symbolic exchange did, commodified signs do nothing and mean nothing. They have no referent, and their sign-context, the only thing that could possibly impart meaning, is constantly shifting because of mass media and advertising. As they are, these signs cannot provoke an emotional response from us. Emotions, then, develop "a new kind of flatness or depthlessness, a new kind of superficiality in the most literal sense . . . [which is] perhaps the supreme formal feature of all the postmodernisms" (Jameson, 1984, p. 60).

These free-floating signs and images don't represent reality; they create hyperreality. Part of the hyperreality is composed of the commodities that we've been talking about. But a more significant part is provided by the extravagance of media entertainment, like Las Vegas and Disneyland. **Hyperreality** is a way of understanding and talking about the mass of disconnected culture. It comes to substitute for reality. In hyperreality, people are drawn to cultural images and signs for artificial stimulation. In other words, rather than being involved in social reality, people involve themselves with fake stimulations. Examples of such simulacra include artificial Christmas trees, breast implants, airbrushed Playboy Bunnies, food and drink flavors that don't exist naturally, and so on.

A clear example of this kind of hyperreality is reality television. Though predated by *Candid Camera*, the first reality show in the contemporary sense was

An American Family, shown on Public Broadcasting Service stations in the United States. It was a 12-installment show that documented an American family going through the turmoil of divorce. The show was heavily criticized in the press. Today, reality shows are prevalent. Though the numbers are difficult to document, between the year 2000 and 2005 there were some 170 new reality shows presented to the public in the United States and Great Britain, with the vast majority being shown in the United States. The year 2004 saw reality programming come of age, as there were nine reality shows nominated for 23 Emmy awards.

The interesting thing about reality programming is that there is no reality. However, it presents itself as a representation of reality. For example, the show *Survivor* placed 16 "castaways" on a tropical island for 39 days and asked, "Deprived of basic comforts, exposed to the harsh natural elements, your fate at the mercy of strangers . . . who would you become?" (*Survivor* Show Concept, n.d.). But the "castaways" were never marooned nor were they in any danger (as real castaways would be). And the game rules and challenges read more like *Dungeons and Dragons* than a real survivor manual, with game "challenges" and changes in character attributes for winning (like being granted "Immunity"). So, what do the images of reality programming represent? Perhaps they are representations of what a fantasy game would look like if human beings could really get in one. The interesting thing about reality programming, and fantasy games for that matter, is the level of involvement people generate around them. This kind of involvement in simulated images of nonreality is hyperreality.

The significance of the idea of hyperreality is that it lets us see that people in postmodernity seek stimulation and nothing more. Hyperreality itself is void of any significance, meaning, or emotion. But, within that hyperreality, people create unreal worlds of spectacle and seduction. Hyperreality is a postmodern condition, a virtual world that provides experiences more involving and spectacular than everyday life and reality.

Sign Implosion

Baudrillard characterizes the simulacrum and hyperreality of postmodernity as an implosion. Where in modernity there was an explosion of signs, commodities, and distinctions, postmodernity is an implosion of all that. In modernity, there were new sciences like sociology and psychology; in postmodernity, the divisions between disciplines have collapsed along with an increasing preference for and growth of multidisciplinary studies. In modernity, there were new distinctions of nationality, identity, race, and gender; in postmodernity, these distinctions have imploded and collapsed upon themselves. Postmodernity is fractal and fragmented, with everything seeming political, sexual, or valuable—and if everything is, then nothing is. Baudrillard claims that this implosion of signs, identities, institutions, and all firm boundaries of meaning have led to the end of the social.

What Baudrillard is saying is that the proliferation, appropriation, and circulation of signs by the media and advertising influence the condition of signs, signification, and meaning in general. In the first stage of the sign, signs had very clear and specific meanings. But as societies and economic systems changed, different kinds of media and ideas were added. In the postmodern age, the media used to communicate information become utterly disassociated from any kind of idea of representation. Everywhere a person turns today in a postmodern society there are media. Cell phones, computers, the Internet, television, billboards, "billboard clothing" (clothing hocking brand names), and the like surround us. And every medium is commodified and inundated with advertising. In postmodernity, we are hard-pressed to find any space or any object that isn't communicating or advertising something beyond itself.

All of this has a general, overall effect. Signs are no longer moored to any social or physical reality; all of them are fair game for the media's manipulation of desire. Any cultural idea, image, sign, or symbol is apt to be pulled out of its social context and used to advertise and to place the individual in the position of consumer. As these signs are lifted out of the social, they lose all possibility of stable reference. They may be used for anything, for any purpose. And the more media that are present, and the faster information is made available (like DSL versus dialup computer connections), the faster signs will circulate and the greater will be the appropriation of indigenous signs for capitalist gain, until there remains no sign that has not been set loose and colonized by capitalism run amok. All that remains is a yawning abyss of meaninglessness—a placeless surface that is incapable of holding personal identity, self, or society.

Let's take a single example—gender. Gender has been a category of distinction for a good part of modernity. Harriet Martineau, the first person to ever use the word "sociology" in print, saw some 80 years before women won the right to vote that the project of modernity necessarily entailed women's rights. So close is the relationship between the treatment of women and the project of modernity for Martineau (1838/2003), that to her it becomes one of the earmarks of civilization: "Each civilized society claims for itself the superiority in its treatment of women" (p. 183). When gender first came up as an issue of equality, specifically in terms of a woman's right to vote, there was little confusion about what gender and gender equality meant. It was common knowledge who women were and what that very distinct group wanted.

But as modernity went on, things changed. In the United States after the 1960s, the single category of gender broke down. Various claims to distinction began to emerge around gender: The experience of gender is different by race, by class, by sexuality, and so on. The category imploded, with all the implicit understandings that went along with it. Today, when confronted by a person who appears to be a woman, the observing individual may be unsure. Is the "woman" really a woman or a man trapped in a woman's body? Or, is the "woman" a transsexual, who has physically been altered or symbolically changed (as with someone like RuPaul)? In postmodernity, the given cues of any category or object or experience cannot be taken at face value as indicative of a firm reality. All of the signs are caught up in a whirlwind of hyperreality.

In postmodernity, very few if any things can be accepted at face value. Meaning and reality aren't necessarily what they appear, because signs have been tossed about by a media without constraint, driven by the need to squeeze every drop of profit out of a populace through the proliferation of new markets with ever-shifting directions, cues, signs, and meanings in order to present something "new."

I've pictured my take of Baudrillard's argument in Figure 14.1. Let me emphasize that my intention with this diagram is simply to give you a heuristic device; it's a way to order your thinking about Baudrillard's theory. One of the best things about postmodern theory is that it is provocative, and part of the reason that it's provocative is that it isn't highly specified. There's a way, then, that this kind of picture stifles the postmodern; there's also a way in which something like this is quite modernist: It seeks to reduce complexity by making generalizations. So, I present this figure with some trepidation, but with the intent of giving you a place to "hang your hat." (In other words, if you're feeling at all lost and uncomfortable, then you need a modernist moment.)

As you can see, I've divided Baudrillard's thought into three main groups: signification, social factors, and social practices. I see Baudrillard as weaving these themes throughout his opus. And I've organized these ideas around the notion of sign phases. Generally speaking, the first two phases of the sign were fairly well grounded in the social. People were clearly involved in face-to-face social networks, the principal form of labor was material, commodities basically contained use- and exchange-values, and humanity was deeply entrenched in symbolic exchange.

Figure 14.1   Baudrillard's Sign Stages

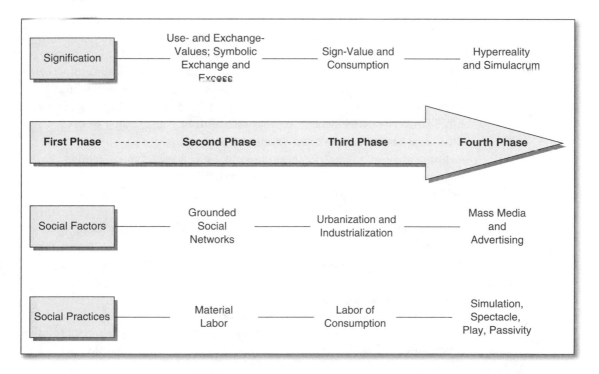

The third phase of the sign comes about as the result of capitalism and the nation-state. The strong social factors in this era were urbanization and industrialization; people began to spend increasing amounts of time doing consumption labor; and the value of commodities shifted from use- to sign-value. As communication and transportation technologies increased, mass media and advertising became the important factors in social change. In a world of pure sign, signs no longer signify; it's all hyperreality and simulacrum, the fourth stage of the sign.

Concepts and Theory: The Postmodern Person

Baudrillard argues that these postmodern processes produced the *death of the subject*. The subject he has in mind is that of modernity—the individual with strong and clear identities, able to carry on the work of democracy and capitalism. That subject, that person, is dead in postmodern culture. With the increase in mass media and advertising, there has been a corresponding decrease in the strength of all categories and meanings, including identities. What is left is a mediated person, rather than the subject of modernity. As Kenneth Gergen (1991) puts it, "one detects amid the hurly-burly of contemporary life a new constellation of feelings or sensibilities, a new pattern of self-consciousness. This syndrome may be termed multiphrenia, generally referring to the splitting of the individual into a multiplicity of self-investments" (pp. 73–74). This is an important idea, and one that appears in the work of a number of postmodernists. So let's take a moment to consider it fully.

One of the fundamental ways in which identity and difference are constructed is through exclusion. In psychology, this can by and large be taken for granted: I am by definition excluded from you because I am in my own body. For sociologists, exclusion is a cultural and social practice; it's something we do, not something we are. This fundamental point may sound elementary to the extreme, but it's important for us to understand it. In order for me to be me, I can't be you; in order for me to be male, I can't be female; in order for me to be white, I can't be black; in order to be a Christian, I can't be a Satanist; ad infinitum.

Cultural identity is defined in opposition to, or as it relates to, something else. Identity and self are based on exclusionary practices. The stronger the practices of exclusion, the stronger will be the identity; and the stronger my identities, the stronger will be my sense of self. Further, the greater the exclusionary practices, the more real will be my experience of identities and self. Hence, the early social movements for equality and democracy had clear practices of exclusion. It gave the people the strength of identity to make the sacrifices necessary to fight.

Fragmenting Identities

The twist that postmodernism gives to all this is found in the ideas of cultural fragmentation and de-centered selves and identities. In many ways, the ideas of gender and race are modernist: They collapse individualities into an all-encompassing identity. However, a person isn't simply female, for example—she also has many identities that crosscut that particular cultural interest and may shift her perceptions of self and other in one direction or another. For us to claim any of these identities—to claim to be female, black, male, or white—is really for us to put ourselves under the umbrella of a grand narrative, stories that deny individualities in favor of some broader social category. Grand narratives by their nature include very strong exclusionary tactics.

More to the point, the construction of centered identities is becoming increasingly difficult in postmodernity. Postmodernists argue that culture in postindustrial societies is fragmented. Since culture and identity are closely related, if the culture is fragmented, then so are identities. The idea of postmodernism, then, makes the issues of gender and race very complex. Clear racial and gender identities may thus be increasingly difficult to maintain. The culture has become more multifaceted, and so have identities. This means that we have greater freedom of choice, which we think we enjoy, but freedom of choice also implies that the distinctions between gender and racial identities aren't as clear or as real as they once were. Thus, social movements around race and gender become increasingly difficult to produce in postmodernity.

How, then, are postmodern identities constructed? Zygmunt Bauman (1992) argues that as a result of de-institutionalization, people live in complex, chaotic systems. Complex systems differ from the mechanistic systems in that they are unpredictable and not controlled by statistically significant factors. In other words, the relationships among the parts are not predictable. For example, race, class, and gender in a complex system no longer produce strong or constant effects in the individual's life or self-concept.

Thus being a woman, for instance, might be a disability in one social setting and not have any meaning at all in another, and race, class, and gender might come together in a specific setting in unique and random ways. Within these complex systems, groups are formed through unguided self-formation. In other words, we join or leave groups simply because we want to. And the groups exist not because they reflect a central value system, as a modernist would argue; rather, they exist due to the whim and fancy of their members and the tide of market-driven public sentiment.

The absence of any central value system and firm, objective evaluative guides tends to create a demand for substitutes. These substitutes are symbolically, rather than actually or socially, created. The need for these symbolic group tokens results in what Bauman (1992, pp. 198–199) calls "tribal politics" and defines as self-constructing practices that are collectivized but not socially produced. These neo-tribes function solely as imagined communities and, unlike their premodern namesake, exist only in symbolic form through the commitment of individual "members" to the idea of an identity.

But this neo-tribal world functions without an actual group's powers of inclusion and exclusion. It is created through the repetitive and generally individual or imaginative performance of symbolic rituals and exists only so long as the rituals are performed. Neo-tribes are thus formed through concepts rather than actual social groups. They exist as imagined communities through a multitude of agent acts of self-identification and exist solely because people use them as vehicles of self-definition: "Neo-tribes are, in other words, the vehicles (and imaginary sediments) of individual self-definition" (Bauman, 1992, p. 137).

Play, Spectacle, and Passivity

All that we just covered is caught up in the social practices of postmodernity. Opposition is impossible because postmodern culture has no boundaries to push against; it is tantamount to pushing against smoke. Further, the acting subject is equally as amorphous. Thus, according to Baudrillard, there's little place in postmodernity to grab ahold of and make a difference. Most things turn out to be innuendo, smoke, spam, mistakes . . . a smooth surface of meaninglessness and seduction. Baudrillard (1993a) leaves us with a few responses: play, spectacle, and passivity.

What can you do with objects that have no meaning? Well, you can play with them and not take them seriously. "So, all that are left are pieces. All that remains to be done is to play with the pieces. Playing with the pieces—that is postmodern" (Baudrillard 1993a, p. 95). How do we play in postmodernity? What would postmodern play look like? Here's an example: People in postmodern societies intentionally engage in fleeting contacts. Consider the case of "flash mobs." According to Wikipedia.com, "A flash mob is a group of people who assemble suddenly in a public place, do something unusual or notable, and then disperse. They are usually organized with the help of the Internet or other digital communications networks" (Flash Mob, n.d.). Sydmob (n.d.), an Internet group facilitating flash mobs in Sydney, Australia, asks, "Have you ever been walking down a busy city street and noticed the blank look on people's faces? How about on public transport? That look of total indifference is unmistakable; it's the face of [a] person feeling more like a worker bee than a human being. Have you ever felt like doing something out of the ordinary to see their reaction?"

In this play, spectacle becomes important. Georg Simmel, a classic theorist ahead of his time, gives us the same insight. Simmel (1950) argues that "life is composed more and more of these impersonal contents and offerings that tend to displace the genuine personal colorations and incomparabilities. This results in the individual's summoning the utmost in uniqueness and particularization, in order to preserve his most personal cores. He has to exaggerate this personal element in order to remain audible even to himself" (p. 422). Echoing Simmel, Zygmunt Bauman (1992) notes that "to catch the attention, displays must be ever more bizarre, condensed and (yes!) disturbing; perhaps ever more brutal, gory and threatening" (p. xx).

The remaining postmodern practice is a kind of resistance through passivity—refusing to play. There's an old American slogan from the Vietnam era that says, "Suppose they gave a war and nobody came?" This is similar to what Baudrillard has in mind with resistance through passivity. Rather than attempting to engage postmodern culture, or responding in frustration, or trying to change things, Baudrillard advocates refusal or passive resistance. And perhaps like the war that no one shows up for, postmodernity will simply cease.

Summary

- Baudrillard uses Marx's notion of use- and exchange-value to argue that commodities are principally understood in postmodernity in terms of their sign-value.

- Baudrillard proposes four stages of the sign. In the first two stages, the sign adequately represented reality, and social communities were held together through the reciprocity of symbolic exchanges. People were also able to practice "excess"—the boundless potential of humanity—through festivals, rituals, sacrifices, and so on.

- Modernity began in the third phase of the sign with the advent of capitalism and industrialization. Baudrillard characterizes modernity as the consumer society. Within such a society, labor shifts to techniques of consumption with an eye toward sign identification. Modernity also brought rationalization and constraint, the antithesis of symbolic exchange and excess.

- In postmodernity, the increasing presence and speed of mass media, along with ever-increasing levels of commodification and advertising, push all vestiges of meaning out of signs. Mass media tends to empty cultural signs because the natural entropy of information is multiplied and because signification is suppressed in favor of media concerns of production. Advertising pushes this process of emptying further: Advertising sells by image rather than use, which implies that commodities are placed in unrelated sign contexts in order to fit a media-produced image. These detached and redefined images are pure simulacra. Postmodern society is inundated by media technology and thus an immense amount of this kind of signification and culture, most of which references and produces a hyperreality.

- Baudrillard's postmodern condition is found in simulation, spectacle, play, and passivity. Baudrillard claims that the central subject of modernity—the person as the nexus of national and economic rights and responsibilities—is dead. In the place of the subject stands a media terminal of fragmented images. What remains is play and spectacle. As signs move ever faster through the postmodern media, their ability to hold meaning continues to disintegrate. Thus, in order to make an impression, cultural displays must be more and more spectacular. In such a climate, the hyperreality of media becomes more enticing, with greater emotional satisfaction than real life—but these media images must continue to spin out to ever more radical displays. Playing with empty signs or intentionally disengaging are the only possible responses.

TAKING THE PERSPECTIVE

In these sections I try to give you a sense of the theoretical perspective as a whole that an individual theorist is using. However, there's a problem with trying to do this with postmodernism. Recall what Baudrillard said? Systems of reference are gone. So, because culture is fragmented and free-floating for postmodernists, "postmodernism" can't reference any single, cohesive idea. We're not left being silenced, however. Just keep in mind that in this small section I will of necessity (and by definition!) be leaving a good deal out.

The word *postmodernism* was first used in Hispanic literary criticism in the 1930s, it gained currency in the visual arts and architecture by the 1960s and early 1970s, and it made its way into social theory with the French publication of Jean-François Lyotard's *The Postmodern Condition* in 1979 (see Anderson, 1998). As I said, postmodernism is a word that denies its ability to function as a word. There does, however, seem to be one organizing feature: No matter what field we're talking about, postmodernism is always understood in contrast to modernism.

Modernity and *postmodernity* are terms that are used in a number of disciplines. In each the meaning is somewhat different, but it is also generally the same: Modernity is characterized by unity, and postmodernity is distinguished by disunity. In modern literature, for example, the unity of narrative is important. Novels move along according to their plot, and while there might be twists and turns, most readers are fairly confident in how time is moving and where the story is going. Postmodern literature, on the other hand, doesn't move in predictable patterns of plot and character. Stories will typically jump around and are filled with indirect and reflexive references to past styles or stories. The purpose of a modern novel is to convey a sense of continuity in story; the purpose of a postmodern work is to create a feeling of disorientation and ironic humor.

In the social world, modernity is associated with the Enlightenment and defined by progress; by grand narratives and beliefs; and through the structures of capitalism, science, technology, and the nation-state. To state the obvious, postmodernism is the opposite or critique of all that. According to most postmodern thought, things have changed. Society is no longer marked by a sense of hope in progress. People seem more discouraged than encouraged—more filled with a blasé attitude than optimism.

In a late capitalist society, rather than providing a basis of meaning, "Culture has necessarily expanded to the point where it has become virtually coextensive with the economy itself . . . as every material object and immaterial service becomes [an] inseparably tractable sign and vendible commodity" (Anderson, 1998, p. 55). Thus, capitalism has colonized culture and turned meaning into goods that are bought and sold. At the same time, these processes make culture less real. As we saw in the quote from Baudrillard at the beginning of this chapter, signs in advanced capitalism don't represent anything; they have no utility or reality. They are commodified images that serve little more function than to seduce us into consumerism.

The same is true for self and identity: "As an older industrial order is churned up, traditional class formations have weakened, while segmented identities and localized groups, typically based on ethnic or sexual differences, multiply" (Anderson, 1998, p. 62). However, these segmented relationships "pull us in a myriad directions, inviting us to play such a variety of roles that the very concept of an 'authentic self' with knowable characteristics recedes from view. The fully saturated self becomes no self at all" (Gergen, 1991, p. 7).

Taken together, then, we can define social postmodernism as a critical form of theorizing that is concerned with the unique problems associated with culture and the subject in advanced capitalistic societies.

BUILDING YOUR THEORY TOOLBOX

Learning More—Primary Sources

- I suggest that you start off with some of Baudrillard's more theoretical works:
  - *For a Critique of the Political Economy of the Sign,* Telos Press, 1981.
  - *The Mirror of Production,* Telos Press, 1975.
  - *Simulacra and Simulation,* University of Michigan Press, 1994.
- There is also a good reader out:
  - *Baudrillard: A Critical Reader,* edited by Douglas Kellner, Blackwell, 1994.

Learning More—Secondary Sources

- Baudrillard secondary sources include:
  - *Jean Baudrillard: From Marxism to Postmodernism and Beyond,* by Douglas Kellner, Stanford University Press, 1990.
  - *Jean Baudrillard (Routledge Critical Thinkers),* by Richard Lane, Routledge, 2009.

Check It Out

- *What about Disneyland?* To find out about Baudrillard's take on Disneyland, either read *America,* by Baudrillard, Verso, 1989, or type "Disneyland and Baudrillard" into your Internet search engine.
- An in-depth look at Baudrillard's philosophy: http://plato.stanford.edu/entries/baudrillard/

(Continued)

(Continued)

Seeing the World

- Write a 250-word synopsis of the theoretical perspective of postmodernism.

- After reading and understanding this chapter, you should be able to define the following terms theoretically and explain their theoretical importance to Baudrillard's theory of postmodernity: *human nature, symbolic exchange, use-value, exchange-value, sign-value, commodity fetish, sign fetish, consumer society, labor of consumption, simulacrum, free-floating signifiers, hyperreality, death of the subject, fragmenting identities*

- After reading and understanding this chapter, you should be able to answer the following questions (remember to answer them *theoretically*):

    o How does Baudrillard argue that Marx actually affirms and legitimates capitalism? How does Baudrillard invert Marx's argument?

    o Explain how ideology and fetishism are based on a passion for the code.

    o What are the four stages of the sign? Be certain to explain their characteristics and the social factors that helped bring them about.

    o What is the consumer society? What labor is specific to the consumer society?

    o How do mass media and advertising empty the sign of all meaning and reference?

    o How have social identities imploded in postmodernity? What are the ramifications for political change?

    o Explain why play, spectacle, and passivity make sense in Baudrillard's postmodernity.

Engaging the World

- Using your favorite search engine, type in "nostalgia and postmodern." What place does nostalgia have in postmodernity? How does Baudrillard talk about it? Give at least three examples of how this part of postmodernity is affecting your life.

- Analyze your lifeworld using Baudrillard's theory. What elements of simulacrum and hyperreality are present? What implications do you think these have for the way you understand the world and yourself?

Weaving the Threads

- Compare and contrast the idea of the death of the subject and postmodern identities (neo-tribes) with Giddens' theory of the reflexive project of the self. Which do you think more accurately describes the issues surrounding identities and selves in late and post-modernity? Why? (Remember to justify your answer *theoretically*.)

- Compare and contrast the political implications of Giddens' late modernity and Baudrillard's postmodernity. Which do you think more accurately reflects the current conditions? Why?

- What implications do Blumer's and Baudrillard's theories have for one another? In other words, what implications do commodified, free-floating signifiers have for face-to-face symbolic interaction?

- What implications does Baudrillard's theory have for impression management (Chapter 5)?

Part V

Identity Politics

Racial Wounds and the Niggerization of America:

Cornel West

(1953–)

I want to start this chapter by telling you why Cornel West is included in this book. The first and most obvious reason is that West is speaking to a black America that is in the political, economic position that Wilson describes in Chapter 7. West delineates the cultural and psychological effects of the black upward mobility that Wilson tells us about. The second reason flows from the first:

Together, Wilson and West show us how structure and culture come together, which has been a continuing thorny issue for theorists of society. The third reason is that West gives us a model of Christianity in modernity. Modern democracy began with the separation of church and government, especially in the United States. One reason for this separation is that typically religion is a top-down approach; that is, God and religious texts tell us what to believe and how to act. And democracy is a bottom-up approach: Power to rule flows up from the people. West gives us a model of how Christianity can work hand in hand with a democracy founded on equal participation and rights (and this is important because democracy was never meant to function without religion). Finally, West is included because his concern is deeper and broader than just race. Race is important not only for racial equality, but also because race is at the heart of American democracy. As West (1999) says, "To be American is to raise perennially the frightening democratic question: What does the public interest have to do with the most vulnerable and disadvantaged in our society?" (p. xix).

THEORIST'S DIGEST

Brief Biography

Cornel West was born in Tulsa, Oklahoma, in 1953. He began attending Harvard University at 17 and graduated 3 years later, magna cum laude. His degree was in Near Eastern languages and literature. West obtained his PhD at Princeton, where he studied with Richard Rorty, a well-known pragmatist. West has taught at Union Theological Seminary, Yale Divinity School, the University of Paris, Harvard, and is currently at Princeton. Among his most significant works are *Race Matters* and *Democracy Matters: Winning the Fight Against Imperialism*. His recent works include *Keeping Faith: Philosophy and Race in America* and a rap CD, *Never Forget: A Journey of Revelations*.

Central Sociological Questions

Cornel West's life is committed to not only the race question in America, but to the democratic ideals of open and critical dialogue, the freedom of ideas and information, and compassion for and acceptance of diverse others. His passion, then, is to expose antidemocratic energies wherever they made be found. In this chapter he specifically asks two questions: How has capitalist marketing affected black Americans? and How has 9/11 affected democracy in America?

Simply Stated

West is concerned about race and democracy in the United States. Since the civil rights era of the 1960s, blacks have experienced greater political participation and economic upward mobility than ever before. While these changes have had obvious positive effects, they have also worked to weaken the traditional black community and create a crisis in black leadership.

Since the 1960s, African Americans have been subjected to intense marketing with an ever-expanding number of commodities. As a result, market moralities have replaced traditional black cultural armor and have created a sense of black nihilism. In response to these threats, West calls for a reenergizing of moral reasoning, coalition strategy, and mature black identity. West is also focused on greater democratic good in the United States. He argues that this has been threatened as a result of 9/11. The threat isn't terrorism, but, rather, the American response to terrorism, which has produced antidemocratic dogmas that threaten the very core of democracy. Here West calls for resurrecting Socratic questioning, commitment to prophetic justice, and a tragicomic commitment to hope.

Key Ideas

False consciousness, pragmatism, existentialism, democratic faith, modern capitalist markets, market saturation, black cultural armor, market moralities, ontological wounds, existential angst, black nihilism, politics of conversion, crisis in black leadership, three kinds of leadership styles, racial reasoning, moral reasoning, mature black identity, coalition strategy, postdemocratic age, Constantinian Christianity, prophetic Christianity, democracy, free-market fundamentalism, aggressive militarism, escalating authoritarianism, Socratic questioning, democratic armor, commitment to prophetic justice, tragicomic commitment to hope

Concepts and Theory: Prophetic Democracy

For most of the people in this book it is important to know where they're coming from: Understanding their theoretical perspective helps us understand the actual theory. One particular example is Anthony Giddens (Chapter 12). There we saw that we couldn't truly understand the forces of modernity until we had a good grasp of how society is made, through structuration rather than structure. With Cornel West it may even be more important. West's perspective—the way he looks at and interfaces with the social world—is unique. By blending elements from Karl Marx, pragmatism, existentialism, and Christianity, West sees things that few people ever do. So, as with Giddens, West's perspective comes here rather than at the end.

Marx and the Commodification of Consciousness

For West (1999), Marxian thought is an "indispensable tradition for freedom fighters" (p. 212). West is particularly interested in Georg Lukács' expansion of the Marxian relationship between commodities and **false consciousness**. Lukács (1923/1971) developed Marx's ideas and argued that the process of commodification affects every sphere of human existence and is the "central, structural problem of capitalist society in all its aspects" (p. 83). Under these circumstances, value is determined not by any intrinsic feature of human activity or relationships, but rather by the impersonal forces of markets, over which individuals have no control. The objects and relations that will truly gratify human needs are hidden, and the commodified object is internalized and accepted as reality. Thus, commodification results in a consciousness based on reified, false objects. This Lukácsian "reified mind" does not attempt to transcend its false foundation, but through rationalization and calculation "progressively sinks more deeply, more fatefully and more definitively into the consciousness of man" (p. 93)—in other words, people caught in consumerism tend to justify unending buying by any means possible.

One of the classic Marxian problems has to do with overcoming false consciousness with class consciousness. For both Marx and Lukács, the only group of people who can overcome false consciousness is the working class. The only way to truly see the whole is by standing outside of it—thus, only the proletariat can conceive of the social system in its entirety: "The proletariat represents the true reality, namely the tendencies of history awakening into consciousness" (Lukács, 1923/1971, p. 199). The working class by its very position of alienation is capable of seeing the true whole, the knowledge of class relations from the standpoint of the entire society and its system of production and social relations. Bourgeois thought is simply an ahistorical acceptance of its own ideology and status quo.

Obviously, there is a tension here. On the one hand, commodification results in false consciousness, and on the other hand, the workers—those who suffer the effects of commodification the most—are the only ones who can see the problem for what it is. There is also another problem: the "overwhelming resources of knowledge, culture and routine which the bourgeoisie undoubtedly possesses" (Lukács, 1923/1971, p. 197). Thus, though the working and middle classes are capable of grasping the whole, they are susceptible both to psychological false consciousness and the cultural resources of the elite. However, these cultural resources are not controlled by the elite exclusively. West draws from another mid-twentieth-century Marxist, Antonio Gramsci (1928/1971), to argue that the ability to rule does not depend on material relations alone, as in classic Marxian thought. Social change will involve a war of cultural positions—a battle for people's minds, not overt conflict.

Culture, then, takes on a critical value for West. Generally, this cultural position is important in race theory in two ways. First, it is the place of revolutionary work. As we've seen, according to this tradition of Marxian thinking, there is first a battle for the mind in any social change. There must be a critical intelligence. West sees this type of consciousness as part of the project of modernity itself, specifically the American democratic experiment. "My conception of what it means to be modern is shot through with a sense of the dialogical—the free encounter of mind, soul and body that relates to others in order to be unsettled, unnerved and unhoused" (West, 1999, pp. xvii–xviii). As we will see, this kind of culture doesn't just create itself, especially in capitalist countries. Critical awareness comes out of specific kinds of culture-producing practices, most notably community, religion, and public discourse.

The second way culture is important for race theory is its long heritage. Many of the early publications by people of color and women were in the form of literature. Harriet Beecher Stowe's *Uncle Tom's Cabin* and Charlotte Perkins Gilman's *The Yellow Wallpaper* are good examples. While the work of W. E. B. Du Bois is obviously scholastic, it is permeated with poems, songs, and literary references. For example, Du Bois' powerful *The Souls of Black Folk* begins with the lyrics and music notes of a song. Du Bois' other major work, *Darkwater,* begins with a credo, a confession of faith.

The choice on the part of these authors to produce literary work may have been due to the structural constraints placed upon political minorities, but it is also true that the plight of the disenfranchised often may be best communicated through means that can impact emotion and not simply cognition. Oppression isn't simply a fact; it is a profound experience. West (1999) points this out when he says that "our great truth tellers [are] mainly artists" (p. xix).

Further, the troubles themselves cry out for creative release. Note the way West (1999) describes music, the "highest expression" of human history:

> Music at its best achieves this summit because it is the grand archaeology into and transfiguration of our guttural cry, the great human effort to grasp in time . . . our deepest passions and yearnings as prisoners of time. Profound music leads us—beyond language—to the dark roots of our scream and the celestial heights of our silence. (p. xvii)

Now notice how Marx (1844/1978a) describes religion: "*Religious* suffering is at the same time an *expression* of real suffering and a *protest* against real suffering. Religion is the sigh of the oppressed creature, the sentiment of a heartless world, and the soul of soulless conditions. It is the *opium* of the people" (p. 54, emphasis original). The last part of that quote is what most people are familiar with, but taken in context it achieves a much fuller meaning. These intense forms of culture—music and religion—both articulate something about the human condition that is difficult to express elsewhere. This link between profound experience and deep cultural expression may be one reason why music and religion have occupied such prominent places in African American culture.

Pragmatic Democracy

We discussed pragmatism in Chapter 3, but let's review it here. Briefly, *pragmatism* is the American philosophy that developed out of the cultural devastation of the Civil War as a way of understanding truth. Truth in pragmatism is specific to a community. It arises out of the collective's physical work and communication. Thus, pragmatism is based on common sense and the belief that "truth and knowledge shifts to the social and communal circumstances under which persons can communicate and cooperate in the process of acquiring knowledge" (West, 1999, p. 151).

Thus, in pragmatism, human action and decisions aren't determined or forced by society, ideology, or preexisting truths. Rather, decisions and ethics emerge out of a consensus that develops through interaction. This is the pragmatism that West (1999) latches onto. It is a

> culture of creative democracy . . . where politically adjudicated forms of knowledge are produced in which human participation is encouraged and for which human personalities are enhanced. Social experimentation is the basic form, yet it is operative only when those who must suffer the consequences have effective control over the institutions that yield the consequences. (p. 151)

Questioning Existence

I want to start our consideration of *existentialism* by asking you a question: Have you ever wondered why you exist, or what the meaning of life is? If so (and most of us have), you've experienced the essence of existentialism. Existentialism starts with the problem of being or existence and argues that the very question or problem creates existence. As far as we know, human beings are the only animal that questions its existence; all other animals simply exist. But human beings ask, and in asking we create human existence as a unique experience. Thus, the answer to the question can only be found in the being asking it.

Here's a simple analogy. Let's say I come to you with a cup of coffee and declare that it tastes like mud. And I then ask, "Why does this coffee taste like mud?" You taste the coffee and tell me that it tastes fine. "Okay," I say, "but why does it taste like mud?" Startled, you respond by telling me once again that the coffee doesn't taste like mud. And I insist, "Why does the coffee taste like mud?" Eventually, you would probably get frustrated and tell me that the muddy coffee is my problem, not yours. Why is it my problem? Because I'm the only one that thinks the coffee tastes like mud. Both the problem and its solution can only exist inside of me. The same is true for the question of existence.

Two ideas are prominent in existentialism: struggles or suffering, and authenticity or being (existence). These ideas find space between such tensions as the individual versus the social, subjective versus objective, liminal experiences (such as death) and nihilism, and situated thought versus reason. Whatever the tensions may be, the resolution is found within the person himself or herself. As we've seen, pragmatism argues that there is no absolute truth, only truths that are arrived at socially, truths that provide practical answers to real problems. Truth for pragmatists, then, is socially practical. In contrast to pragmatism, existentialism argues that there are no social truths and truth exists emotionally, not objectively. Truths such as history and science—social, practical truths—belong to society or to the crowd. As such, they are objective and indifferent. Truth in existentialism is determined by individual authenticity—by a passionate, and generally absurd, leap of faith.

This issue of subjective authenticity is exemplified by the biblical story of Abraham (see Søren Kierkegaard's *Fear and Trembling*). The story goes that one day God came to Abraham and commanded him to kill his son. For Abraham, there appeared to be little to justify such a command. In fact, Abraham had every reason to doubt that the command even came from God, since even Satan himself can appear as an angel of light. Even so, Abraham prepared to kill his son and offer his life on an altar of burning wood. With little or no objective evidence, what drove Abraham to make the sacrifice? Biblical believers would say faith, and existentialism agrees. Truth isn't something that exists objectively; truth is that which is embraced passionately in its uncertainty, in all its absurdity.

To be human—*to exist as a human*—then, is to embrace existence passionately in spite of the affront brought by irresolvable struggles. To be human is to hold tight to faith when there is no reason. Truth is discovered and exists only in the passionate embrace of authenticity, existing in the truth of one's own self. This existential faith is not found in anything outside the individual; it is found within the limits of the human soul. West (1999) puts it this way: "To be human is to suffer, shudder and struggle courageously in the face of inevitable death" (p. xvi).

West combines both pragmatism and existentialism in a call to *democratic faith.* According to West, the issues we struggle with are social issues—the oppression of humanity by humanity, found in such inequalities as racism and sexism. And these problems must be struggled with and resisted collectively, through community and religion and dialogue. But the faith that West (1999) is interested in comes from the individual soul, because the struggle will always be there. It's part of being human and modern: "The very meaning of being modern may be the lack of any meaning, that our quest for such meaning may be the very meaning itself—without ever arriving at any fixed meaning" (p. xviii). West isn't necessarily discounting the possibility of solving the problem of racism. But he recognizes these struggles as an essential part of being human. Thus, we cannot pin our hopes and actions on the solution, on the democratic victory over racism. Rather, hope comes from within, as a result of maintaining faith when there is no objective reason for faith.

Democratic Christianity

Cornel West is a Christian whose faith informs everything he is, thinks, and does—but he is a particular kind of Christian. Because Christianity is a broad, multifaceted religion, there are any number of ways that we can understand the faith. One way is to see where it focuses its energies. If we look at Christianity in this way, we can create a continuum. On one end of this continuum of focus is the kind of Christianity that is centered on the afterlife. This kind of Christianity takes its lead from Paul's injunction to the Colossians: "Since, then, you have been raised with Christ, set your hearts on things above, where Christ is seated at the right hand of God." Here the issues of this life are of little concern, except to keep one's self unto God. At the other end of this continuum is the Christianity that focuses on this present life. This opposite pole takes as its model the Christ in the temple who in rage overturned the tables of the moneychangers and drove them out with a whip. Here Christianity is deeply involved in issues of social justice and reform (one example of this is Liberation Theology, http://liberationtheology.org/).

The first perspective is an example of the kind of religion that Marx criticized. Its model is the "meek and mild Jesus" who taught that the proper response to oppression is to turn the other cheek. Marx argued that this form of religion serves to maintain the status quo. With this perspective, suffering in this life is not to be avoided or changed—it is a gift from God to purge the believer, to test and temper the believer's faith. Marx didn't see the possibility of the second perspective. On this end of the continuum, religion is an agent of social change, and righteousness is a social quality, not simply an individual one. Here God's righteous indignation is expressed through His Children in order to create the Kingdom of God on earth. Of course these two poles of my continuum and the examples of Christ can overlap in any individual, as they do in Cornel West. West is clearly oriented toward the social change pole, yet he finds inspiration in both models of Jesus.

West finds deep insight in the example of Christ as the long-suffering Son of God on earth. Remember that West's perspective is informed by existential authenticity: passionate faith in the presence of continuous struggle. For West (1999), the life of Jesus is the ideal model for such a faith: "The concrete example of the love and compassion of Jesus rendered in the biblical Gospel narratives constitutes the most absurd and alluring mode of being in the tragicomic world" (p. xvi). One of the principal forms of expression for this absurd existence is love. West's (1993/2001) dedication of his book *Race Matters* to his son is a moving example of this tenet of his faith: "To my wonderful son Clifton Louis West who combats daily the hidden injuries of race with the most potent of weapons—love of self and others" (p. vii).

The second way West's Christianity is expressed is through prophetic thought. This is where we find the Christ in the temple. We would be wrong to see the love, compassion, and patience that West espouses as what we usually think of as meek and mild. In West's Christianity, love and anger coexist in equal amounts. The most potent weapon may be love, but West (1993/2001) also chastens the black leaders of today for their "relative lack of authentic anger" (p. 58). And he doesn't pull punches with the state of religion: West (1999) tells us that he wrote his second book, *Prophetic Fragments,* in order to "convey my moral outrage at the relative indifference of American religion to the challenging of social justice beyond charity" (p. 357). West is angry, but it is a slow anger, a settled rage based on a sense of social righteousness.

This orientation toward this present life gives West's Christianity one further characteristic: skepticism. His prophetic utterances are not born out of any sense of absolute truth; rather, their genesis is found in the pragmatic truth and suffering of this life. "For me," he says, "there is always a dialectic of doubt and faith, of skepticism and leap of faith" (West, 1999, p. 215). In the end, this "inescapable demon of doubt" enables West to love his way "through the absurdity of life and the darkness of history" (p. xvi) and to see the American experiment as "fueled with a religion of vast possibility," (p. xviii) rather than a closed dogmatism. West thus sees faith and his prophetic anger as intertwined with skepticism, resulting from human interaction within communities and religions, founded on uncertainty and struggle, rather than based on unshakable truth. Here we clearly see West's philosophy and Christianity come together.

Concepts and Theory: Black Existence in America

West gives us two basic structural influences on blacks in the United States: the economic boom and expansion of civil rights for blacks in the 1960s, and the saturation of market forces. In terms of the economic and political well-being of blacks in the United States, West is simply saying that they both increased, particularly during the boom of the 1970s. For example, the U.S. Census Bureau (n.d.) reports that black, male, median income increased from $9,519 in 1950 to $17,055 in 1970, as measured in 2003 dollars. These changes helped define blacks as a viable market group, one with disposable income and market-specific products. In some obvious ways, these changes have benefited the black experience in America. However, the development of black economic markets has also had significant negative effects.

As a way of distributing goods and services, markets have been a part of human history for millennia. *Modern, capitalist markets,* however, have a couple of unique characteristics. Modern capitalism, you'll remember, is defined by the endless accumulation of capital to create more capital. Because capital is its own goal, it's never achieved (capital to generate capital to generate capital and so on endlessly). This drive implies that the need for profit is insatiable and thus continues to increase. Because markets are the mechanism through which profit and capital are gained, modern capitalist markets are intrinsically expansive: They expand vertically (through accessories for an existing product), horizontally (producing new products within a market), and geographically (extending existing markets to new social groups). A second unique characteristic of modern capitalism is related to the factor of expanding markets: Capitalists are driven to create a never-ending stream of new or different commodities. Keep in mind that commodification is a process that converts more and more of the human lifeworld into something that can be bought and sold, and it creates new "needs" within the consumer. Human beings are not just the only animal capable of economic production; we are also the only species able to create new psychological drives and needs for the new products. There's a sense in which markets are without any morals whatsoever: They aren't restricted by any kind of ethic—they can be used to sell Bibles or guns to terrorists. This quality makes them applicable to any situation or product. However, as we will see, the absence of any ethical restrictions implies and creates a morality of its own. And these market moralities are particularly destructive for black Americans.

Black Nihilism

West characterizes this market expansion into the black community as a kind of *market saturation.* He first argues that the market saturation of the black population has stripped away community-based values and substituted market moralities. Earlier I mentioned that markets are amoral. But this is in a restricted sense only—markets can be used for anything. Markets do, however, convey some specific cultural ideas and sensibilities. In classical theory, for example, Max Weber was extremely interested in how markets and bureaucracies create rational rather than affective culture, and Georg Simmel saw markets as contributing to cultural signs becoming frivolous.

West argues that being a focus for market activity, commodification, and advertising has changed black culture in America. Prior to market saturation, blacks had a long history of community and tradition. They were equipped with a kind of *black cultural armor* that came via black civic and religious institutions. This armor consisted of clear and strong structures of meaning and feeling that "embodied values of service and sacrifice, love and care, discipline and excellence" (West, 1993/2001, p. 24). While this is specific to black Americans, it's important to note that this general shift from community-based traditional culture to less meaningful and more pliable culture was a concern of many social theorists of modernity. We find this idea of cultural shift repeatedly in classical theory. The basic idea is that culture has dramatically changed through processes accompanying urbanization and commodification. Rather than being meaningful, normative, and cohesive, culture is trivialized, anomic, and segmented.

West is making this same kind of argument, so he follows a strong theoretical tradition. West, however, is pointing out that while the dispersion of community and the emptying of culture may have affected much of modern society during the beginning and middle stages of modernity and capitalism, the black community in America wasn't strongly influenced by these changes until after the 1960s. Until then, blacks continued to rely on community-based relations and religiously influenced culture. As a result of the twin structural influences of civil rights and upward mobility, blacks moved out of black communities and churches. The structural bases for cultural armor were weakened as a result.

In place of cultural armor, blacks have since been inundated with the *market moralities* of conspicuous consumption and material calculus. The culture of consumption orients people to the present moment and to the intensification of pleasure. This culture of pleasure uses seduction to capitalize "on every opportunity to make money" (West, 1993/2001, p. 26). It overwhelms people in a moment where the past and future are swallowed up in a never-ending "repetition of hedonistically driven pleasure" (p. 26). Further, the material calculus argues that the greatest value comes from profit-driven calculations. Every other consideration, such as love and service to others, is hidden under the bushel of profit.

As I've mentioned, most of these cultural ramifications of markets and commodification have also been present in other groups. But in West's (1993/2001) opinion, two issues make these effects particularly destructive for blacks. First, black upward mobility and the presence of the black middle class concern only a small sliver of the pie. Most of the black citizens of the United States still suffer under white oppression. The other issue that makes the black experience of market saturation distinct is the "accumulated effect of the black wounds and scars suffered in a white-dominated society" (p. 28). In other words, there is a historical and cultural heritage, no matter how much the immediacy of market saturation and pleasure tries to deny it—much of the history of the United States was built on the oppression of blacks, over the 188 years from 1776 to 1964.

Obviously, these two factors influence one another. Healing from past wounds can only take place in a present that is both nurturing and repentant, a place that does not replicate hurts from the past. According to West (1993/2001), this isn't happening for blacks in America: Cultural beliefs and media images continue to attack "black intelligence, black ability, black beauty, and black character in subtle and not-so-subtle ways" (p. 27). And, as noted earlier, black upward mobility is still limited. For example, in 2002 over 30% of black children lived under the poverty line, compared to 12.3% of white children (Statistical Abstract of the United States, 2002).

In the abstract, West's argument so far looks like this: black upward mobility + increased civil rights → weakening of civic and religious community base → substitution of market moralities for cultural armor—all of which takes place within the framework of the black legacy in the United States and continued oppression. "Under these circumstances black existential *angst* derives from the lived experience of ontological wounds and emotional scars" (West, 1993/2001, p. 27, emphasis original). The *ontological wounds* that West is speaking of come from the ways in which black reality and existence have been denied throughout the history of the United States.

In general, *existential angst* refers to the deep and profound insecurity and dread that comes from living as a human being. Recall our discussion about existentialism: To be human is to suffer, to know we suffer, and to question the reason for suffering. West employs the idea of angst to describe the uniquely black experience of living under American capitalism and democracy. Black experience is deeply historical, yet the past and the future are buried under the market-driven pleasures of the moment; black experience is fundamentally com-munitarian, yet that civic and religious base is overwhelmed by market individ-ualisms; black experience is painfully oppressive, yet it is countered only by increasing target marketing and consumerism. Thus, West argues that the result of market saturation and morality for blacks is a deeply spiritual condition of despair and insecurity.

Because blacks no longer have the necessary culture, community, or leadership, this angst cannot be used productively. It is instead turned inward as anger. And this anger is played out in violence against the weak. Righteous anger, turned against the oppressor in hopes of liberation, becomes increasingly difficult to express. **Black nihilism** denies the hope in which this anger is founded. With no viable path, this anger is turned inward and found in black-against-black violence, especially against black women and children.

Crisis in Black Leadership

However, nihilism can be treated. West argues that it is a disease of the soul, one that cannot be cured, as there is always the threat of relapse. This disease must be met with love and care, not arguments and analysis. What is required is a new kind of politics, a *politics of conversion*, which reaches into the subversive memory of black people to find modes of valuation and resistance. Politics of conversion is centered on a love ethic that is energized by concern for others and the recognition of one's own worth. This kind of politics requires prophetic black leaders who will bring "hope for the future and a meaning to struggle" (West, 1993/2001, p. 28). There is, however, a *crisis in black leadership.*

For West, there is a relationship between community and leadership. Strong leaders come out of vibrant communities. With the breakdown of the black com-munity, black leaders don't have a social base that is in touch with the real issues. There is thus no nurturing of critical consciousness in the heart of black America. Rather, much of the new black leadership in America comes out of the middle class. And black middle-class life is "principally a matter of professional consci-entiousness, personal accomplishment, and cautious adjustment" (West, 1993/2001, p. 57). West maintains that what is lacking in contemporary black leadership is anger and humility; what is present in overabundance is status anxiety and concerns for personal careers.

West divides contemporary black leaders into two general types—politicians and academics—with *three kinds of leadership styles:* race-effacing managerial leaders, race-identifying protest leaders, and race-transcending prophetic leaders. There are some differences between politicians and academics, but by and large they express the same leadership styles.

The managerial/elitist model is growing rapidly in the United States. This style of leadership is one that has been co-opted by bureaucratic norms. He or she navigates the political scene through political savvy and personal diplomacy. Race is downplayed in the hopes of gaining a white constituency. In academia, the elitist sees himself or herself as having a kind of monopoly over the sophisticated analysis of black America. But the analysis is flat and mediocre because of the intellectual's desire to fit into the university system. In both cases, whether under political savvy or academic abstraction, race is effaced.

The second type of leader, the protest leader, capitalizes on the race issue but in a very limited way, in a kind of "one-note racial analyses" (West, 1993/2001, p. 68). Here "Black" becomes all-powerful. West characterizes these leaders as "confining themselves to the black turf, vowing to protect their leadership status over it, and serving as power brokers with powerful nonblack elites" (p. 60). In this context, racial reasoning reigns supreme.

Racial reasoning is a way of thinking that is concerned with equality more as a group right rather than a general social issue. For West, racial reasoning begins with an assumption of the black experience. The discourse of race, then, centers on black authenticity: the notion that some black experiences and people are really black while others aren't. Racial reasoning results in blacks closing ranks, but again it is around a one-note song rather than a symphony of color. Racial reasoning results in black nationalist sentiments that "promote and encourage black cultural conservatism, especially black patriarchal (and homophobic) power" (1993/2001, p. 37). Closing the ranks thus creates a hierarchy of acceptability within a black context: the black subordination of women, class divisions, and sexual orientation within black America.

Leadership for Equality

These two kinds of black leaders have promoted political cynicism among black people, and have dampened "the fire of enraged local activists who have made a difference" (West, 1993/2001, p. 68). Part of black nihilism, or nothingness, is this sense of ineffectuality, of being lost in a storm too big to change. What is needed, according to West, are black leaders founded on moral reasoning rather than racial reasoning.

Moral reasoning is the stock and trade of race-transcending prophetic leaders. Prophetic leadership does not rest on any kind of racial supremacy, black or white. It uses a *coalition strategy,* which seeks out the antiracist traditions found in all peoples. It refuses to divide black people over other categories of distinction and rejects patriarchy and homophobia. Such an approach promotes moral rather than racial reasoning.

This prophetic framework of moral reasoning is also based on a *mature black identity* of self-love and self-respect that refuses to put "any group of people on the pedestal or in the gutter" (West, 1993/2001, p. 43). Moral reasoning also uses subversive memory, "one of the most precious heritages [black people] have" (West, 1999, p. 221). It recalls the modes of struggling and resisting that affirmed community, faith, hope, and love, rather than the contemporary market morality of individualism, conspicuous consumption, and hedonistic indulgence.

Both the coalition strategy and mature black identity are built at the local level. West (1999) sees local communities as working "from below and sometimes beneath modernity" (p. 221), as if local communities can function below the radar of markets and commodification. It is within vibrant communities and through public discourse that local leaders are accountable and earn respect and love. Such leaders merit national attention from the black community and the general public, according to West.

In this framework, the liberal focus on economic issues is rejected as simplistic. Likewise, the conservative critique of black immorality is dismissed as ignoring public responsibility for the ethical state of the union. In their places, West proposes a democratic, pragmatically driven dialogue. As I mentioned earlier, West doesn't propose absolutes. His is a prophetic call to radical democracy and faith, to finally take seriously the declaration that all people are created equal.

Together, moral reasoning, coalition strategy, and mature black identity create the black cultural armor. West's use of "armor" is a biblical reference. Christians are told in Ephesians 6:13 (New International Version) to "put on the full armor of God, so that when the day of evil comes, you may be able to stand your ground, and after you have done everything, to stand." There the threat was the powers of darkness in heavenly places; here the threat is black nihilism in the heart of democracy. These two battles are at least parallel if not identical for West. The fight for true democracy is a spiritual battle for the souls of humankind that have been dulled by market saturation, especially the souls of black America. West (1993/2001) exhorts black America to put on its cultural armor—a return to community life and moral reasoning along with coalition strategy and mature black identity—so as to "beat back the demons of hopelessness, meaninglessness, and lovelessness" and create anew "cultural structures of meaning and feeling" (p. 23).

Concepts and Theory: The Postdemocratic Age

West's (2004) newest work is an indictment of American democracy in the wake of 9/11. He argues that the terrorist attack on September 11, 2001, provided the spark to an already existing fire bed of antidemocratic dogmas and an emasculated political process. West notes that the political scene in the United States has recently been dominated by an illicit marriage of corporate and political elites (a plutocracy) and the Christian Right. Among the plutocratic elite, "salesmanship to the demos has taken the place of genuine democratic leadership" (p. 3). Given the choice between two political alternatives that are both dependent upon corporate favor, people are increasingly choosing to opt out of the democratic process, both in terms of voting and critical dialogue. West characterizes this as a **postdemocratic age**—"the waning of democratic energies and practices in our present age of the American empire" (p. 2).

West (2004) sees the emptiness of the American political culture, created by market saturation and a dearth of leadership, as giving place to the Christian Right. People are reaching out for a sense of meaning and purpose. The Christian Right provides that, but its righteousness is misguided and its perspective "narrow, exclusionary, and punitive" (p. 66). Specifically, the rhetoric of Christian fundamentalism is used to legitimate three antidemocratic dogmas: free-market fundamentalism, aggressive militarism, and authoritarianism. As Berger and Luckmann (Chapter 8) argue, religion provides the strongest legitimation of any belief or idea—any fundamentalism is the most powerful force behind any religious legitimation. In addition, West (2004) argues that the Christian Right is perverting the soul of American democracy, "because the dominant forms of Christian fundamentalism are a threat to the tolerance and openness necessary for sustaining any democracy" (p. 146).

Yet, as we noted in the discussion about West's perspective, West is a Christian. But he sees vast differences between what he calls Constantinian Christianity and prophetic Christianity. *Constantinian Christianity* is named after the Roman emperor Constantine, who converted to Christianity in 312 CE. The various accounts differ on some of the specifics, but all agree that Constantine received a vision of Christ just before the Battle of the Milvian Bridge. As a result, Constantine commanded that a purple silk banner hanging from a crosspiece on a pike (representing Christ) be placed as his new battle standard. Eventually, because of Constantine, Christianity became the official religion of the Roman Empire. The state then used the church as an instrument of imperial policy, and the church used the state as a means of imposing its religious rule. Constantinian Christianity, then, is a "terrible co-joining of church and state" (West, 2004, p. 148) that robs the church "of the prophetic fervor of Jesus and the apocalyptic fire of that other Jew-turned-Christian named Paul" (p. 147).

West (2004) argues that as a result of the marriage between church and state, Christianity has been invested with an "insidious schizophrenia." On the one hand, there are the Constantinian elements occupied with power, privilege, and possession, a Christianity that has "been on the wrong side of so many of our social troubles, such as the dogmatic justification of slavery and the parochial defense of women's inequality" (p. 149). West argues that the Christian Right, including the Christian Coalition and the Moral Majority, is the shining example of Constantinian Christianity in America.

On the other hand are the elements of prophetic Christianity, most clearly seen in Social Gospel churches. *Prophetic Christianity* holds up wisdom, justice, and freedom for all humanity as its virtues. It isn't concerned with power; it is concerned with promoting equality and respecting and supporting every cultural group's unique heritage and way of life. In making his case for the differences between Constantinian and prophetic Christianity, West (2004) argues that the strongest movements for equality have been led by prophetic Christians, including "the abolitionist, women's suffrage, and trade-union movements in the nineteenth century and the civil rights movement in the twentieth century" (p. 152).

> I do not want to be numbered among those who sold their souls for a mess of pottage—who surrendered their democratic Christian identity for a comfortable place at the table of the American empire while, like Lazarus, the least of these cried out and I was too intoxicated with worldly power and might to hear, beckon, and heed their cries. To be a Christian is to live dangerously, honestly, freely. . . . This is the kind of vision and courage required to enable the renewal of prophetic, democratic Christian identity in the age of the American empire. (West, 2004, p. 172)

Three Antidemocratic Dogmas

Before we begin this section, we should take a moment to define what West means by democracy. *Democracy* is not simply the freedom to vote—the freedom to vote democratically is based on the presence of at least three elements. Together, these elements give democracy a forward vision—the hope of future progress gained through rejecting the shackles of the past and the continual process of enlightenment. The first element of democracy is open and critical dialogue. The democracy of the United States is built upon such dialogue, as is evident in the Declaration of Independence and the First Amendment to the Constitution. The second element is necessitated by the first: the freedom of ideas and information necessary for democratic dialogue and questioning. Democracy cannot exist in an environment where knowledge and thought are hidden in darkness.

Third, the necessity of dialogue and the freedom of ideas imply compassion for and acceptance of diverse others. A democratic government exists in order to preserve the freedoms and rights of diverse others. Any kind of government can protect its borders and provide infrastructure, but West argues that a democratic government is especially well-suited to guard the freedoms of its citizens in the face of oppression. This protection is the defining feature of a democratic government and its sole reason for existence. Note that acceptance is not the same as tolerance. Tolerated voices aren't allowed an equal footing in dialogue. But American democracy goes further than acceptance. In the roots of American democracy there is desire for alternative voices. Consider these words from "The New Colossus," by Emma Lazarus:

> Not like the brazen giant of Greek fame
>
> With conquering limbs astride from land to land;
>
> Here at our sea-washed, sunset gates shall stand
>
> A mighty woman with a torch, whose flame
>
> Is the imprisoned lightning, and her name
>
> Mother of Exiles. From her beacon-hand

Glows world-wide welcome; her mild eyes command

The air-bridged harbor that twin cities frame,

"Keep, ancient lands, your storied pomp!" cries she

With silent lips. "Give me your tired, your poor,

Your huddled masses yearning to breathe free,

The wretched refuse of your teeming shore,

Send these, the homeless, tempest-tossed to me,

I lift my lamp beside the golden door!"

As we've seen, West takes seriously the idea that culture can exist and act like a structure. This position implies first that culture can develop autonomously and second that culture can have its own set of effects in concert with or independent of other social structures. In this case, the social structural issues that concern West are the rising plutocracy and the Christian Right. West is also still concerned with the saturation of market forces. In addition, West sees the terrorist attacks of 9/11 as a key event in pushing the United States toward a postdemocratic society.

There are three cultural dogmas with which West is concerned: free-market fundamentalism, aggressive militarism, and escalating authoritarianism. We'll talk about each of these in a moment, but first notice West's use of religious terms. First, these cultural issues are dogmas. While *dogma* can have a more general meaning, in religious circles it is a technical term with a very specific meaning. Dogmas are officially established religious doctrines. They serve not only to distinguish one belief system from another, but they are also the guiding lights for religious practice. West is telling us that these cultural elements function like religious dogma: They dictate and legitimate certain beliefs and practices. And these beliefs, practices, and legitimations are held to be fundamental to a certain way of life—in this case, the American way of life.

The second religious term that West uses is *fundamentalism*, and it is used in reference to the first cultural belief: free markets. Interestingly enough, though we may now talk about Islamic fundamentalists, the term was first used in reference to Protestant Christianity. Christian fundamentalism began in the United States during the nineteenth century in response to several millennialist movements (belief in the second coming and 1,000-year reign of Christ). It spread during the latter part of the nineteenth century because of Protestant concerns over Catholic immigration, labor unrest, and biblical criticism. There are several beliefs that are common to fundamentalism, including the literal interpretation of the Bible, the physical second coming of Christ, physical resurrection, and so on. But *what people believe is not as important as how people believe*—fundamentalism is characterized by absolute certainty and militant conservatism.

In terms of free markets, West (2004) is arguing that American culture has developed a militant belief in them—a *free-market fundamentalism*. Free markets are perceived to be the mechanism for bringing about international cooperation, modernization, happiness, true competition, the good life, and so forth. This glorification

of the market leads to a corporate-dominated society where the interests of capitalism are equated with democracy and corporate leaders are seen as the highest expression of democratic good. The current idea of free markets seems to be shielded by a
faith that borders on worship; little is done in the face of the estimated $300 billion
cost of white-collar crime (Legal Information Institute, n.d.). Market fundamentalism also "redefines the terms of what we should be striving for in life, glamorizing
materialistic gain, narcissistic pleasure, and the pursuit of narrow individualistic pre-
occupations"; in the end, it "trivializes the concern for public interest" (p. 4).

West's (2004) point is that this dogmatic belief in free-market fundamentalism
blinds people to any other concern except market moralities. Because of this single-
sightedness, individuals caught up in this belief are willing to make any sacrifice
necessary to "succeed at any cost" (p. 27). The irony of this blind chase for profit is
that it is based on faith in free markets, which implies that even "corporate elites are
not fully in control of market forces" (p. 27) and market forces are a power unto
themselves. The effects of unfettered market forces are beginning to show in terms
of environmental pollution and the emptying out of democratic energies.

Part of the drain on democratic energies comes from nihilism. Just as West
(2004) saw black nihilism as a result of the saturation of market forces and market
moralities, he also argues that Americans as a whole are suffering from "psychic
depression, personal worthlessness, and social despair" (p. 26). Nihilism comes
about because (1) people are caught in the ambivalence of believing in free markets
while recognizing their inevitable costs (such as white-collar crime); (2) unceasing
market expansion and market moralities create a situation where meaning and
knowledge are continually overturning and are stripped of any continuity or stability; (3) market moralities are void of any sense of right or wrong (which is the
definition of moral); and (4) market moralities have corrupted the principles of
representative democracy all the way to the top:

> Our politicians have sacrificed their principles on the altar of special interests;
> our corporate leaders have sacrificed their integrity on the altar of profits;
> and our media watchdogs have sacrificed the voice of dissent on the altar of
> audience competition. (West, 2004, p. 28)

The next antidemocratic dogma that West explains is *aggressive militarism*.
Although the roots of both this and the next dogma (authoritarianism) go deeper,
the immediate stimulus is the terrorist attacks of 9/11. West (2004) sees 9/11 as a
watershed moment for American democracy: "The ugly events of 9/11 should have
been an opportunity for national self-scrutiny" (p. 12). Why did the terrorists
attack the United States? What ideas are so meaningful that men would not only
kill but lay down their own lives to communicate? What are the social, political,
and historical backgrounds? Did U.S. imperialist behavior play a role? But rather
than becoming positively responsive, West points out, the citizens of this nation
either killed any hope of communication in a "simplistic and aggressive 'with us or
against us' stance" (p. 12) or were silenced by the single-note dogmatism of
American fundamentalism.

Thus, rather than democratic questioning, the United States turned to the dogma of aggressive militarism. The new national policy of war became defined in terms of the "preemptive strike," where in the presence of even faulty intelligence it is in the nation's best interest to attack first. In practice, this policy is evidenced by unilateral intervention, colonial invasion, and armed occupation of foreign soil and people. West clarifies the costs of such actions: At the international level, the use of unmasked violence tends to create further instability; at the national level, the dogma of militarism results in expanded police power, further development of the prison-industrial complex, and increased legitimation of male power and violence; at the ethical level, such elite-driven war actions are always paid for most dearly in the disproportional deaths of youth coming from lower classes and populations of color.

The third member of this trinity of antidemocratic dogma is *escalating authoritarianism.* West argues that the American belief in authoritarianism is rooted in the understandable paranoia about terrorism, the long-standing fear of individuals having too many liberties, and the deep-seated distrust of any social or cultural differences. The events of 9/11 rekindled and deepened these fears. The results have gone in the exact opposite direction from democracy: Dramatic increases in governmental surveillance, especially within schools and universities, and decreases in legal protections of individual citizens—these two are coupled with and amplified by decreases in the oversight of government activities.

West sees an analogy here. In America, he sees black people as having been "niggerized." To be niggerized is to be dehumanized, and blacks in this country have been designated and treated as "nigger" for over 350 years. They have been made "to feel unsafe, unprotected, subject to random violence, and hated" (West, 2001, p. 20). In short, blacks have been terrorized by white America. Now, the entire United States has been niggerized. As a result of the terrorism of 9/11, Americans in general feel unsafe, unprotected, subject to random violence, and hated. The comparison West wants to make is between the black response to terrorism and the current American response to terrorism.

West (1999) characterizes the current response to 9/11 as the gangsterization of America. A gangster mentality is one that makes things a "question of getting over . . . instead of getting better, and that gangster mentality promotes a war against all" (p. 218). This gangsterization of America not only concerns aggressive militarism and escalating authoritarianism, it also involves market moralities and fetishes that come out of free-market fundamentalism. These dogmas have produced "an unbridled grasp at power, wealth, and status" that have snuffed the democratic light from the very nation that is its chief advocate—"we are experiencing the sad American imperial devouring of American democracy" (West, 2004, p. 8).

Putting On the Democratic Armor

To combat the nihilist threat, to overcome the niggerization and gangsterization of America, West exhorts us to put on the democratic armor. There are three elements to this defensive covering: Socratic questioning, prophetic justice, and tragicomic commitment to hope. Socrates never wrote a word. What we know of the *Socratic questioning* came to us through Plato, his student. Plato presents the Socratic method as a way of discovering ethical truths. It is a method of inquiry that uses critical questions as its tool—imagine a class where the professor didn't lecture but only asked questions. The purpose of the method is to question every idea until its underlying assumptions are exposed. The assumptions are then questioned in terms of their logical relationship to other assumptions. In this process, those involved agree to accept any answer that is logically reasoned. In other words, what matters most is the process, not the product. There aren't predetermined truths that the "teacher" is attempting to impose. Questioning and logic, then, are both method and goal.

I'm sure you can see why West advocates Socratic questioning as a primary piece in the democratic citizen's armor. Democracy for West is based upon and can only prosper when critical questioning is its driving force. As West points out, critical questioning was the wellspring of America's first document, the Declaration of Independence: Without it, not only would the United States not have been born; the United States as a truly democratic nation could not continue to exist.

West gives us at least two guidelines for this quest. First, we must engage in a critical and open-minded assessment of the history of every dogma (see Foucault, Chapter 13, for this kind of archaeology of ideas). Remember that West takes seriously the structural weight of culture. One of the things that means is that ideas and dogmas do not exist as some kind of soliloquy or solo performance. They have a history. Uncovering that history exposes ideology's contingent and political base.

The second guideline that West gives us is the race lens. The history of ideas and the race lens go hand in hand. There are a number of frames through which we could uncover the heritage of democratic ideas in America. But the race lens is perhaps the most powerful, because whether we look at the oppression of gays, women, workers, or the near genocide of Native Americans, what we find at the core is "the deeply antidemocratic and dehumanizing hypocrisies of white supremacy" (West, 2004, p. 14).

However, remember West's (2004) purpose in advocating the race lens: to incite critical inquiry. The purpose, then, is not to create "sentimental stories of pure heroes of color and impure white villains"; this would "simply flip the script and tell new lies about ourselves" (p. 15). Rather, using the race lens should unsettle Americans. It should bring into sharp relief the distinctions between Constantinian America and democratic America. It should humble America in the realization that today's dogmas are just as destructive to the democratic spirit as racism. It should make Americans reject dogmas of any kind. According to West, democracy never gets it right; what is right about democracy is its process: "All democracies are incomplete and unfinished" (p. 204). In short, the race lens should prompt neverending Socratic, pragmatic questioning and parrhesia—freedom of speech.

West points out something extremely important about democracy and freedom of speech. The men who founded America feared the masses or demos. Plato feared the demos as well and advocated the rule of philosopher-kings. These elite feared chaos and anarchy. The masses were seen as uneducated and capable of being easily persuaded. West (2004) tells us that the "genius of the Founding Fathers" of the United States was to still grant and protect Socratic questioning and freedom of speech (p. 211). What this means is that democracy is founded on a tension between elites and the demos, and this tension is always and necessarily there. If either side becomes too dominant (as with the current American plutocracy), the dialogue that democracy is founded on comes to a halt.

Socratic questioning and *commitment to prophetic justice* are intertwined. Many people, when they think of a prophet, conceive of a person telling and foretelling absolute truth. This is not what West has in mind. West's idea of prophetic vision can't be related to truth because of his notion of Socratic questioning and because of the prominence he gives pragmatism. A commitment to prophetic justice is first a call away from indifference. Prophetic justice is a commitment—it is in its essence engagement. Every example we have of prophets indicates that they are people who are utterly involved—think of John the Baptist or Siddhartha Gautama, the Buddha.

For West (2004), this prophetic commitment is to "justice of an oppressed people" (p. 17). To talk about this justice, West invokes the model of jazz. In jazz, every player has a distinct voice. It isn't like a symphony where individual voices are swallowed up in sections and the presence of the whole. Jazz is based on virtuosity and improvisation within a single melodic structure. All members are playing the same song, but each gives his or her own take. Commitment to justice, then, is first a commitment to polyvocality, the presence and honoring of many voices. True democracy can never oppress or disenfranchise; to the degree that a nation does, it is no longer democratic. The test of democracy is in how many voices are being silenced.

A commitment to justice also implies a commitment to one's own self. This commitment is a

> matter of finding one's own distinctive voice, one's own precious individuality that is not reduced to rugged, rapacious, ragged individualism. But rather is constituted by bouncing up against other voices within a community just like a jazz quartet, where if you haven't found your distinctive voice, it's time for you to practice more. (West, 2000)

Practicing for jazz entails an understanding of music theory so deep that it frees the player to intuitive improvisation. Thus, a democratic commitment to prophetic justice entails a commitment to true and continuous education.

Together, polyvocality and self-education create fire—they both produce and validate prophetic speech. Only when a person is committed to diversity in community and to the edification of education can he or she speak. When one is dedicated to this fire, he or she must speak, and in the fire of polyvocality and self-education others will listen.

The third portion of the democratic cultural armor is a *tragicomic commitment to hope*. To explain this armor, West draws on the musical genre of the blues. Most of us know that both blues and jazz came out of black culture, but many of us don't recognize or like to think about the fact that they came out of the black experience of white oppression. Yet this is West's point exactly: Jazz and blues are the freest music forms in America, yet they were created by an enslaved people. Blues specifically gives expression to tragicomic hope.

The blues originated in the back-and-forth call of slaves working the fields. The call at once gave voice to pain and hope to the soul. Grief was expressed in the call, yet the cadence gave rhythm and thus lightness to the work. Individual suffering was expressed, affirmed, and given meaning in a community of sufferers. "The root of blues is the human experience and psyche itself" (Erlewine, 1999, p. v), and its essence is "to stare painful truths in the face and persevere without cynicism or pessimism" (West, 2004, p. 21).

Tellingly, the blues was born out of terrorism: the terrorist suppression of blacks by white supremacist slave owners. West tells us that we are at a crossroads brought about by yet another kind of terrorism: the attacks of 9/11. According to West (2004), we have begun down the wrong road, toward a postdemocratic society. Even so, "Our fundamental test may lie in our continuing response to 9/11" (p. 8). America's move toward the road of democracy begins with the blues:

> The blues forges a mature hope that fortifies us on the slippery tightrope of Socratic questioning and prophetic witness in imperial America. . . . This kind of tragicomic hope is dangerous—and potentially subversive—because it can never be extinguished. . . . It is a form of elemental freedom that cannot be eliminated or snuffed out by any elite power. (pp. 216, 217)

Summary

- West draws on four traditions in organizing his thought: cultural Marxism, pragmatism, existentialism, and Christianity. Marx's theory of commodification and market expansion are key elements in West's theory as well. But West also draws upon the critical Marxian view of culture—culture is used to oppress in often hidden ways, but it can also be used to bring change. From pragmatism, West takes the idea of practical values emerging from collective dialogue. He sees pragmatism as a key philosophy in the American democratic experiment. From existentialism, West draws the ideas of subjective authenticity and passionate absurdity. And from Christianity, he takes love for self and others and the prophetic outcry for mercy and justice.

- Since the 1960s, blacks in the United States have on the one hand enjoyed increased economic and political freedoms, but on the other have become the victims of market saturation. Market saturation has changed the primary orientations of blacks. Previously, blacks were strongly oriented to civic and religious institutions and the traditional ties of family and home. Market saturation has infested the black community with market moralities: fleeting hedonistic pleasure and monetary gain. The effects of markets are exaggerated for blacks because of the black heritage in America. The mix of past wounds, the continuing racial prejudice, and market moralities creates black nihilism (a sense of hopelessness and meaninglessness associated with living as a black person in the United States).

- West exposes a crisis in black leadership, arguing that most black leaders fall under either the managerial/elitist model or that of protest leaders. With protest leaders, racial reasoning is paramount, which promotes ethics based on skin color alone, rather than on moral or justice issues. West calls on prophetic leaders who will transcend race and return to moral reasoning. These leaders must begin in the community, at the grassroots level, where they can participate in pragmatic community dialogue, build up trust, and maintain accountability.

- West argues that since 9/11, America has entered a postdemocratic age. There are three dogmas that have worked to bring this about: free-market fundamentalism, aggressive militarism, and escalating authoritarianism. To return to democracy, West argues that we must put on the democratic armor: Socratic questioning, prophetic justice, and tragicomic commitment to hope.

BUILDING YOUR THEORY TOOLBOX

Learning More—Primary Sources

- See the following works by Cornel West:
  - *Race Matters,* Vintage Books, 1993.
  - *Democracy Matters: Winning the Fight Against Imperialism,* Penguin Books, 2004.
  - *The Cornel West Reader,* Basic Civitas Books, 1999.

Learning More—Secondary Sources

- Cornel West: *The Politics of Redemption (Key Contemporary Thinkers),* by Rosemary Cowan, Polity Press, 2003.

Check It Out

- There are a good number of clips of Cornel West on YouTube. Search the site and check out a few of them.
- Cornel West has put out a hip-hop CD. Find information at http://www.cornelwest.com/.

Seeing the World

- Write a 250-word synopsis of the theoretical perspective West synthesizes from Marx, pragmatism, existentialism, and Christianity. Hint: Don't keep these four issues separate. Bring them together and state them as a single perspective.
- After reading and understanding this chapter, you should be able to define the following terms theoretically and explain their theoretical importance to West's theories:

false consciousness, pragmatism, existentialism, democratic faith, modern capitalist markets, market saturation, black cultural armor, market moralities, ontological wounds, existential angst, black nihilism, politics of conversion, crisis in black leadership, three kinds of leadership styles, racial reasoning, moral reasoning, mature black identity, coalition strategy, postdemocratic age, Constantinian Christianity, prophetic Christianity, democracy, free-market fundamentalism, aggressive militarism, escalating authoritarianism, Socratic questioning, democratic armor, commitment to prophetic justice, tragicomic commitment to hope

- After reading and understanding this chapter, you should be able to answer the following questions (remember to answer them *theoretically*):

  o West takes very specific things from Marxian theory, pragmatism, existentialism, and Christianity. Explain what those are and how they influence his work.

  o How can culture act as a structure?

  o What are the three structural forces influencing blacks in America today?

  o Why did market saturation affect the black community in unique ways?

  o What is black nihilism, where does it come from, and how is it affecting blacks in the United States today?

  o Why is there a black leadership crisis? What are politics of conversion?

  o What is racial reasoning? How does moral reasoning counter racial reasoning?

  o What is West's critique of the Christian Right? How is the Christian Right an example of Constantinian Christianity?

  o What are the three elements of democracy?

  o How are free-market fundamentalism, aggressive militarism, and escalating militarism creating a postdemocratic age?

  o How has the United States as a whole been niggerized and gangsterized?

  o What is the democratic armor? How will each piece help overcome the postdemocratic age?

  o How does West use the concepts of jazz and blues?

Engaging the World

- Become involved in campus efforts to end discrimination. Check and see if you have an office of multicultural affairs. Find out what other campus organizations are involved in ending discrimination.

- If you're African American, explore how your values and sense of self are impacted by market moralities. If you're not African American, how have market moralities affected you?

(Continued)

(Continued)

- What does West's critique of political leadership imply generally about what we should expect from leaders in a democratic society? Analyze the current national leadership using West's criteria. Think especially about Barack Obama. Where would you place him in West's scheme? Search the Internet to discover West's opinion of Obama.

Weaving the Threads

- Evaluate Wilson's class-based proposals using West's theory of black nihilism.
- Synthesize Wilson and West into a general theory of racial inequality.
- Compare and contrast Foucault's and West's theories of subjective experience. How can these theories be brought together to give us greater insight into how individual, subjective experiences are formed in this period of modernity?

Text, Power, and Women:

Dorothy E. Smith

(1926–)

Gender inequality has been studied by sociologists ever since the time of Harriet Martineau. In 1837, she published her study of America. For Martineau (1837/2005), one of the key tests of civilization and democracy in a society is the condition of women: "If the test of civilization be sought, none can be so sure as the condition of that half of society over which the other half has power" (p. 291). Granted, since that time the topic of gender has come in and out of favor with the discipline as a whole. Nevertheless, it's safe to say that gender inequality as a topic of study has been a central concern since the 1970s; and, sociologists have done countless studies and published innumerable articles, books, and essays on the subject since then.

But, what if a good many of them actually worked to suppress women rather than liberate them? Dorothy E. Smith asks us to consider this possibility. She argues that the way in which women are dominated isn't solely through the social structures with which Janet Saltzman Chafetz told us about in Chapter 7. No, gender inequality also works through the social and behavioral sciences as they create *knowledge about women* in opposition to *women's knowledge*. This body of knowledge claims objectivity and thus authority "not on the basis of its capacity to speak truthfully, but in terms of its specific capacity to exclude the presence and experience of particular subjectivities" (Smith, 1987, p. 2). Smith wants to begin with and center social and behavioral research on the actual lived experiences of people and their encounter with texts, rather than on the texts that deny the very voices they claim to express.

THEORIST'S DIGEST

Brief Biography

Dorothy E. Smith was born in Northallerton, Yorkshire, Great Britain, in 1926. She earned her undergraduate degree in 1955 from the London School of Economics. In 1963, Smith received her PhD from the University of California at Berkeley. She has taught at Berkeley, the University of Essex, and the University of British Columbia. She is currently Adjunct Professor at the University of Victoria. In recognition of her contributions to sociology, the American Sociology Association (ASA) honored Smith with the Jessie Bernard Award in 1993 and the Career of Distinguished Scholarship Award in 1999. Her book *The Everyday World as Problematic* has received two awards from the Canadian Sociology and Anthropology Association: the Outstanding Contribution Award and the John Porter Award, both given in 1990.

Central Sociological Questions

Smith is centrally concerned with how the daily lives of men and women are quite often different. Yet, when gender is studied from a social scientific perspective, the distinct experiences and knowledge of women are written out. The relations of ruling, then, continue to be exerted even under the guise of gender inequality. "My research concern is to build an ordinary good knowledge of the text-mediated organization of power from the standpoint of women in contemporary capitalism" (Smith, 1992, p. 97).

Simply Stated

Smith argues that the social and behavioral sciences have systematically developed an objective body of knowledge about the individual, social relations, and society in general. This body of knowledge claims objectivity and thus authority "not on the basis of its capacity to speak truthfully, but in terms of its specific capacity to exclude the presence and experience of particular subjectivities" (Smith, 1987, p. 2). Because of this exclusion, social scientific texts are nothing more than an expression of the relations of ruling that continue to oppress women. Smith wants to center research on the actual lived experiences of women, and their encounters with these texts.

Key Ideas

Practices of power, new materialism, texts, facticity, standpoint, constitutive work, relations of ruling, fault line, relations of ruling, institutional ethnography

Concepts and Theory: The Problem With Facts

As with Giddens and West, I'm putting Smith's perspective up front rather than at the end of the chapter. The main reason I'm doing this with Smith is because in many ways her theory and perspective are the same; as you'll see, it's hard to talk of one apart from the other. Plus, she gives us a different account of how gender inequality is achieved than did Chafetz (Chapter 7); again, because she sees the world a bit differently.

Method, Not Theory

In 1992, *Sociological Theory*, the premier theoretical journal of the American Sociological Association, presented a symposium on the work of Smith. Though Smith had been publishing for quite some time, her dramatic impact on sociology came with the publications in 1987 of *The Everyday World as Problematic: A Feminist Sociology* and in 1990 *The Conceptual Practices of Power: A Feminist Sociology of Knowledge*. Being the subject of a special issue in *Sociological Theory* so soon after the publication of two major works attests to the impact that Smith's perspective was having on sociology. Among the commentators in that special issue were Patricia Hill Collins, Robert Connell, and Charles Lemert, each a significant theorist in her or his own right. However, Smith (1992) critiqued each of these theorists as having misinterpreted her work: "Each constructs her or his own straw Smith" (p. 88).

Of course, Collins, Connell, and Lemert had their own individual issues, but Smith (1992) argues that they universally misconstrued her work as theory rather than method. "It is not . . . a totalizing theory. Rather it is a *method of inquiry*, always ongoing, opening things up, discovering" (p. 88, emphasis original). This is obviously an important point for us to note at the beginning of our discussion of Smith's work. She doesn't give us a general theory, not even a general theory of gender oppression. Smith gives us a method, but it isn't a method in the same sense as data analysis—Smith's is a theoretical method. It's a method grounded in a theoretical understanding of the world that results in theoretical insights. Further, for Smith these theoretical insights are themselves continually held up to evaluation and revision.

In general, Smith's work is considered "standpoint theory." As we'll see below, that's a fairly accurate description of what she does. But Smith argues that thinking about standpoint theory theoretically makes the idea too abstract and it defeats the original intent. Like Pierre Bourdieu, Smith is very interested in the *practices of power*. She is interested in what happens on the ground in the lived experiences of women, more so than the abstract words of sociological theory.

Let me give you an example that might help us see the distinction that Smith is making. Not so long ago I was talking to a friend of mine who plays and builds drums. We were talking about the special feeling that comes from building the instrument you play. There's a kind of connection that develops between the builder and the wood, a connection that is grounded in the physical experience of the wood. I agreed with what he said and told him that kind of knowledge is called kinesthetic. But I was painfully aware that there was a real difference between what we were each talking about. He has actually worked with the wood out of which he builds his drum kits; though I play guitar, I have never experienced that kind of connection with my instrument. I had the word for what he was talking about, but he had the actual experience.

Smith is arguing that something happens when we formalize and generalize our concepts. We can quickly move out of the realm of real experience. As such, it is possible for concepts to play a purely discursive role. Just like in my example of kinesthetic knowledge, we can talk about things of which we only have discursive or linguistic knowledge. Thus, I can talk about the intuitive connection that exists between a musician and an instrument that he or she has built, but I have no actual knowledge of it. It's purely theoretical for me.

Obviously, there are no significant consequences of my woodworking example. But in the social world, there can be important ramifications, and that's the point that Smith wants us to see. **Standpoint** theory isn't a theory per se; it's a method of observation that privileges the point of view of actual people over theoretical, abstract knowledge. That may sound commonsensical and you may agree with it, but Smith would contend that most of what you and I know about the social world is like my knowledge of building a musical instrument.

In thinking about Smith's approach, it is important to note that she doesn't see herself as arguing against abstractions. To one degree or another, theory is usually abstracted. When we talk about theory being abstract, we mean that it is not simply a statement or restatement of the particulars. In a fundamental way, then, most theories and theoretical terms exist outside of the actual situation as generalizations. For example, there is a significant difference between saying "LaToya went to Food Lion to do the food shopping" and "women generally do the grocery shopping." The first statement is particular; it refers to the behaviors of a specific person at a definite location and time. In that sense, the statement is limited and not theoretically powerful. The second statement, because it is abstract, is more theoretically powerful. Most theory is at least somewhat abstract; it's the best way for us to say something significant about what is going on. Because she focuses on the actualities of lived experience, Smith's standpoint theory can be read to mean that abstractions are themselves bad. But that isn't her intent.

Nor is she interested in simply discrediting or deconstructing the knowledge or relations of ruling. Quite a bit of critical theory is aimed at these issues. For example, chances are good that much of what you've learned in other classes about gender or race is a historical account of how patriarchy or racism came about and how it functions to oppress people. The intent in these courses is to discredit sexism or racism by deconstructing their ideological and historical bases. But discrediting isn't Smith's specific intent either.

Smith argues that in both these cases, abstractions and ideological deconstruction, the critique by itself isn't enough; it doesn't tell the actual story. Theory in both forms plays itself out in the everyday, actual world of people, and that is Smith's concern. Insofar as theory and ideology mean anything, they mean something in everyday life, whether that life is the researcher's or that of ordinary women. Like I said, Smith is interested in where the rubber meets the road. In this case, the "rubber" is made up of theoretical abstractions and ideological knowledge that governs, and the "road" is the actual experiences of women. Thus, Smith isn't interested in doing away with abstractions per se, nor is she simply interested in exposing the relations of ruling; doing so is not enough, and it runs the risk of replicating the problem, as we will soon see.

The New Materialism

As we've seen in other chapters, Marx's materialism argues that there is a relationship between one's material class interests and the knowledge one has. Smith proposes a *new materialism*, one where facts and texts rather than commodification produce alienation and objectification. With Marx, commodities and money mediate the relationships people have with themselves and others. That is, we relate and come to understand our self and others through money and products. Marx's theory was specific to industrialized capitalism—the economies of more technologically advanced societies may be different. Some of the important changes include shifts from manufacturing to "service" economies, increases in the use of credentials and in the amount and use of expert knowledge, advances in communication and transportation technologies, exponential increases in the use of advertising images and texts, and so on. In such economies, relationships and power are mediated more through texts and "facts" than commodities and money. Further, just as people misrecognized the reality in back of money and commodities, so today most people misrecognize the relations of power in back of texts and facts.

In Marx's materialism, "relations between people are mediated by (and appear as) relations between commodities and money" (Smith, 1990, p. 68), and in Smith's new materialism, "relations between individual knowers appear as facts and are mediated by relations between facts" (p. 68). Texts and the facticity that text produces are the primary medium through which power is exercised in a society such as the United States.

Texts and Facts

Though the idea of text is gaining usage and popularity, it, like culture, is one of the more difficult words to define. Winfried Nöth (1985/1995) in his *Handbook of Semiotics* says that given that textuality is defined by the researcher, "It is not surprising that semioticians of the text have been unable to agree on a definition and on criteria of their object of research" (p. 331). Smith, however, gives us a broad, clear, and useful definition of *text* that includes three elements: the actual written words or symbols, the physical medium through which words and symbols are expressed, and the materiality of the text—the actual practices of writing and reading.

Smith is specifically concerned with texts that are officially or organizationally written and read. She gives us the example of two different texts that came out of an incident in 1968 involving police and street people in Berkeley, California. One text came in the form of a letter to an underground newspaper and was written by someone who was marginally involved in the altercation. His text was "written from the standpoint of an actual experience" (Smith, 1990, p. 63) and contained specific references to people, places, times, and events. It was embedded in and expressed actual life experiences as they happened. This was a personal account of a personal experience that reflexively situated the writer in the event.

The other text was the official incident report that came from the mayor's office. The standpoint of this second text is organizational. Rather than an account of a personal experience, it is written from the point of view of anonymous police officers who are portrayed as trained professionals and organizational representatives. In addition, the official report embedded the text within "sequences of organizational action extending before and after them" (Smith, 1990, p. 64) using reports from police, courts, and probation officers. In other words, the official text brought in many elements that exist outside of the actual situation and experience. In the end, every element of the actual experience was given meaning through these extra-local concepts rather than the experience itself.

The obliteration of the historical and specific sources is part of the process of creating facts (Smith, 1990, p. 66). The **facticity** of a statement is thus not a property of the statement itself. A statement simply proposes a state of affairs like "the earth is flat." For a statement to become fact, there must be a corresponding set of practices that provide its plausibility base, a group of people, beliefs, and practices that give substance to the statement. Facticity, then, "is essentially a property of an institutional order mediated by texts" (p. 79). Facts and texts are organizational achievements, not independent truths of the world. These, then, are the texts and facts in which Smith is interested: the ones that are written and read as part of organizational method and relations of power. They create an objective reality whose existence is dependent upon specific institutionalized practices.

Concepts and Theory: Lived Experience and Knowing

Smith argues that the distinction between abstract knowledge (or text) and lived experience holds for all people, whether male, female, black, white, Chicano, or anyone else. However, women's experience and knowledge are specifically important. Generally speaking, there are a few reasons why this would be accurate. First, knowledge of the oppressed is in some ways truer than that of the ruling. The ruling generally "believe their own press." For example, members of the ruling class generally believe the capitalist ideology that hard work results in upward social mobility. Research indicates, however, that gender, sexuality, race, ethnicity, and religion all play into the distribution of scarce resources. Members of an oppressed group may thus have more actual knowledge of how the system works. Because it crosscuts all other social categories, the oppressive system par excellence is gender. Thus, women's knowledge is uniquely suited to help us see an oppressive structure for what it is.

Another reason for privileging women's experience is that it is more grounded in the physicality of real life than is men's. We'll consider this again in our section on the fault line, but it bears mentioning here. While some of what Smith is saying about the difference between objective knowledge on one hand and subjective experience on the other is true about men, it is also true that women by and large take care of most of the details of life (such as cooking, cleaning, child rearing, and so on). These "details" are what specifically allow men to live a "man's life." Because women take care of the actualities, men are allowed to think that life is really about the abstract, general knowledge they construct and believe. Women thus typically provide a buffer between men and the actual demands of life. According to Smith, this difference means that women's knowledge is more materially real and grounded in the physical actions of the body. A woman's body is "the place of her sensory organization of immediate experience; the place where her coordinates of here and now, before and after, are organized around herself as center" (Smith, 1987, p. 82). And that center is where the basics of life are felt, managed, and known.

In the end, this is what Smith means when she talks about standpoint. Standpoint is nothing more and nothing less than the knowledge and perspective that is produced through actual experiences. Because of her emphasis on standpoint, Smith argues that her project is not an ideological representation or movement. Often when we think of feminism, we think of a social movement with a specific agenda and ideology. While liberation from oppression is certainly part of what Smith (1987) wants to attain, she doesn't offer us "an ideological position that represents women's oppression as having a determinate character and takes up the analysis of social forms with a view to discovering in them the lineaments of what the ideologist already supposes that she knows" (pp. 106–107). Whether it comes from social science or feminism, Smith is concerned about knowledge that objectifies, that starts from a position outside the everyday world of lived experience.

Smith gives us an example of walking her dog. When walking her dog, she needs to be careful that he doesn't "do his business" in places that are inappropriate. Smith points out that her behavior in this situation would generally be understood in terms of norms. From the normative perspective, she would simply be seen as conforming to the social norms of walking a dog. However, Smith (1987) contends that the idea of norm "provides for the surface properties of my behavior, what I can be seen to be doing" (p. 155). In other words, the normative approach can only give us a surface or simplistic understanding of what is going on. What is ignored in seeing the norm is "an account of the constitutive work that is going on" (p. 155). In this case, *constitutive work* refers to the efforts Smith must put forth in conforming to the norm. And in the process of conforming, there are any number of contingencies that include the kind of neighborhood, the type of neighbors, the kind of leash, the breed of dog, the weather, her subjective states, and so on. All of the contingencies require practical reasoning that in turn produces a specific kind of reaction to the norm. The issue for Smith is that the normative account ignores the actual experiences of the person: how, when, and why the individual conforms to, negotiates, or ignores the demands made by the norm.

Disregarding the site of constitutive work is how "the very intellectual successes of the women's movement have created their own contradictions" (Smith, 1992, p. 88). The contradictions arise, according to Smith, as feminism becomes its own theory, a theory that is seen to exist apart from the lived experiences of the women it attempts to describe. For Smith, resistance and revolution do not—indeed, cannot—begin in theory or even sociology. Such a beginning would simply replace the ruling ideas with another set of ruling ideas. In order to create a sociology of women, or to bring about any real social change, it is imperative to begin and continue in the situated perspectives of the people in whom we are interested.

Thus, Smith's intent is to open up the space of actual experience as the site of research. This is exactly what Smith means by the title of her 1987 book, *The Everyday World as Problematic.* Most social research creates problems that are guided by the literature, the researcher's career, or by the availability of funds. According to Smith, this practice results in a body of knowledge that more often than not only references itself or the relations of ruling that fund it. In Smith's work, it is the everyday world of women that is problematized. It's the actual experience of women that sets the problems and questions of research and provides the answers and theory. "Inquiry does not begin within the conceptual organization or relevances of the sociological discourse, but in actual experience as embedded in the particular historical forms of social relations that determine that experience" (Smith, 1987, p. 49).

Another way to put this issue is that most social research assumes a reciprocity of perspectives. One of the things that ethnomethodology (see Chapter 4) has taught us about the organization of social order at the micro level is that we all assume that our way of seeing things corresponds fairly closely to the way other people see things. More specifically, we assume that if another person were to walk in our shoes, they would experience the world just like we do. This is an assumption that allows us to carry on with our daily lives. It lets us act as if we share a common world, even though we may not and we can never know for sure. According to Smith, social science usually works in this way too, but she wants us to problematize that assumption in sociology. She wants us to ask, "What is it like to be that person in that body in those circumstances?"

Sociology and the Relations of Ruling

Smith (1990) talks about the practices, knowledge, and social relations that are associated with power as relations of ruling. Specifically, *relations of ruling* include "what the business world calls *management*, it includes the professions, it includes government and the activities of those who are selecting, training, and indoctrinating those who will be its governors" (p. 14, emphasis original). In technologically advanced societies that are bureaucratically organized, ruling and governing take place specifically through abstract concepts and symbols, or text. As Michel Foucault explained, knowledge is power; it is the currency that dominates our age. Authority and control are exercised in contemporary society through different forms of knowledge—specifically, knowledge that objectifies its subjects.

The social sciences in particular are quite good at this. They turn people into populations that can be reduced to numbers, measured, and thus controlled. Through abstract concepts and generalized theories, the social sciences empty the person of individual thoughts and feelings and reduce him or her to concepts and ideas that can be applied to all people grouped together within a specific social type. The social sciences thus create a textual reality, a reality that exists in "the literature" outside of the lived experience of people.

Much of this literature is related to data that are generated by the state, through such instruments as the U.S. Census or the FBI's Uniform Crime Reporting (UCR) Program. These data are accepted without question as the authoritative representation of reality because they are seen as *hard data*—data that correspond to the assumptions of science. These data are then used to "test" theories and hypotheses that are generated, more often than not, either from previous work or by academics seeking to establish their names in the literature. Even case histories that purport to represent the life of a specific individual are rendered as documents that substantiate established theoretical understandings.

Thus, most of the data, theory, and findings of social science are generated by a state driven by political concerns, by academics circumscribed by the discipline of their fields, by professors motivated to create a vita (résumé) of distinction, or by professionals seeking to establish their practice. All of this creates "textual surfaces of objective knowledge in public contexts" that are "to be read factually. . . . as evidences of a reality 'in back of' the text" (Smith, 1990, pp. 191, 107). Therefore, a sociology that is oriented toward abstract theory and data analysis results in a sociology that "is a systematically developed consciousness of society and social relations. . . . [that] claims objectivity not on the basis of its capacity to speak truthfully, but in terms of its specific capacity to exclude the presence and experience of particular subjectivities" (Smith, 1987, p. 2).

These concepts, theories, numbers, practices, and professions become *relations of ruling* as they are used by the individual to understand and control her own subjectivity, as she understands herself to be a subject of the discourses of sociology, psychology, economics, and so on. We do this when we see ourselves in the sociological articles or self-help books we read, in the written histories or newspapers of society, or in business journals or reports. With or without awareness of it, we mold ourselves to the picture of reality presented in the "textual surfaces of objective knowledge."

Smith points out that this process of molding becomes explicit for those people wanting to become sociologists, psychologists, or business leaders. Disciplines socialize students into accepted theories and methods. In the end, these are specific guidelines that determine exactly what constitutes sociological knowledge. For example, most of the professors you've had are either tenured or on a tenure track. Whether an instructor has tenure or not is generally the chief distinction between assistant and associate professors. And when a sociology professor comes up for tenure and promotion, one of the most important questions asked about his or her work is whether or not it qualifies as sociology. Not everything we do is necessarily sociology—it has to conform to specific methodologies, assumptions, concepts, and so on to qualify as sociology.

There is something reasonable about this work of exclusion. If I wrote an article with nothing but math concepts in it, it probably shouldn't be considered sociology. Otherwise there wouldn't be any differences among any of the academic disciplines. However, Smith's point is that there is more going on than simple definitions.

Definitions of methods and theory are used by the powerful to exclude the powerless. What counts as sociology and the criteria used to make the distinctions are therefore reflections of the relations of ruling. Sociology and all the social sciences have historically been masculinist enterprises, which means that what constitutes sociology is defined from the perspective of ruling men. The questions that are deemed important and the methods and theories that are used have all been established by men: "How sociology is thought—its methods, conceptual schemes, and theories—has been based on and built up within the male social universe" (Smith, 1990, p. 13).

Let me give you an example to bring this home, one that has to do with race, but the illustration still holds. In the latter part of the 1990s, two colleagues and I were untenured in our department. One of those colleagues is black. All three of us were worried about tenure and promotion—there was quite a bit of contradictory information circulating about how we could get tenure. So we had a meeting with the man who was department head at the time. Each of us had specific concerns. My black colleague's concern was race. As a result of some of the things the department head said, I asked him point blank: "Will the articles that [my black colleague] has published count for tenure and promotion or not?" The head answered that he wasn't sure because the articles were published in black journals and may not therefore "count as sociology."

The Fault Line of Gender

Smith argues that since the motivations, questions, and data come out of the concerns of those that govern and not the actual experiences of those living under the relations of ruling, masculinist knowledge is by default objective and objectifying—from beginning to end, it stands outside of the actual experience of those other than the ruling. Smith's sociology is thus not specifically concerned with what usually passes as prejudice or sexism that is expressed through negative stereotypes and discrimination. Rather, "We are talking about the consequences of women's exclusion from a full share in the making of what becomes treated as our culture" (Smith, 1987, p. 20).

One of those consequences is the experience of a **fault line** for those women training as social scientists. The idea of a fault line comes from geology and there refers to the intersection between a geologic fault (a fracture in the earth's crust) and the earth's surface. Many fault lines are dramatically visible. If you've not seen one, use an Internet search engine to find an image of a fault line. Smith's analogy is quite striking. She is arguing that the fault line for women is conceptual; it occurs between the kind of knowledge that is generally produced in society, specifically through the social sciences, and the knowledge that women produce as a result of their daily experiences. There is a decisive break between the two.

We generally think there are some differences between objective culture or knowledge and the lives that people live. But because the current relations of ruling produce masculinist knowledge, men do not sense a disjuncture between what they live and what they know of the world. Part of the reason for this is that many of the activities of men match up with or correspond to abstract, objectifying knowledge.

A male sociologist "works in the medium he studies" (Smith, 1990, p. 17). But even for men, there is still a clear distinction between objective knowledge, "the governing mode of our kind of society" (p. 17), and daily life. Thus, while there may be a correspondence for men, there is also a place "where things smell, where the irrelevant birds fly away in front of the window, where he has indigestion, where he dies" (p. 17). In other words, Smith is arguing that even for men there is a break between objective forms of knowledge and daily life as it is subjectively experienced. The difference is that generally men don't sense the disjunction. But why don't men sense or experience it?

The reason, Smith informs us, is that women have traditionally negotiated that break for men. Let's think about the usual distinction between boss and secretary. Generally speaking, the secretary is there to do the leg work, to take care of the mundane details through which an organization functions, and to keep the boss free from intrusions from the outside world by screening all calls and letters. Think also about the traditional division of labor in the home. Men go to work while women take care of the "small details" of running a household: grocery shopping, cooking, cleaning, and taking care of the kids. Both of these examples picture the mediation role that Smith tells us women play—women intervene between men and the actual lived world, and they take care of the actualities that make real life possible. In doing so, they shelter men from the "bifurcation of consciousness" that women experience (Smith, 1987, p. 82).

Standpoint and Text-Mediated Power

Bringing all this together, we end up with a rather new way of doing sociology, one that focuses on the experience of women as it is mediated through various texts, particularly those produced through the relations of ruling. I've diagrammed my take on Smith's ideas in Figure 16.1. As with any such model, especially one constructed to reflect a critical perspective, it is a simplification. But in some ways I think that a simplification is exactly what Smith is after. Her argument entails elements from existentialism, phenomenology, symbolic interaction, ethnomethodology, and Marxian theory. The argument is thus not simplistic. It is quite complex and nuanced and it can and will inspire intricate and subtle thought and research. But her point is rather straightforward—social research and theory need to be grounded in the actual lived experiences of people, particularly women.

The first thing I'd like for you to notice about Figure 16.1 is the central position of both actual lived experience and text. We've talked about the issue of lived experience, and I will come back to it in a minute, but let's start by noticing texts. As I've already noted, sociology and the social disciplines in general have experienced what has been called a linguistic turn. A good deal of this sea change can be credited generally to the effects of poststructuralism and postmodernism. We can understand the linguistic turn as a shift toward the importance of text, primarily written words, though other kinds of cultural artifacts such as film are read as texts through semiotic analysis. In this perspective, culture and cultural readings are fundamentally

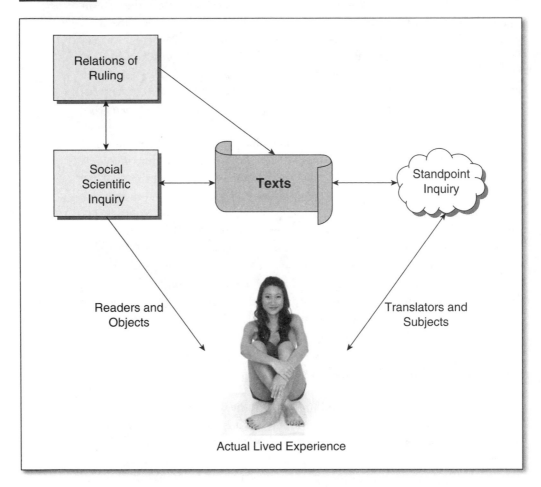

Figure 16.1   Smith's Standpoint Inquiry

Actual Lived Experience

important. The radical thread in this linguistic turn is that readings of texts are themselves seen as texts, which means that since humans are defined through meaning, all we have are texts.

In keeping with the linguistic turn, Smith (1992) acknowledges the importance of text, but she adds to it the ontology of lived experience. For her, text forms "the bridge between the actual and discursive. It is a material object that brings into actual contexts of reading a fixed form of meaning" (p. 92). The uniqueness of what Smith is arguing in light of the linguistic turn is that there is something other than text. Text isn't everything: There are embodied people who live their lives in actual situations that have real consequences.

When we become aware of the texts that surround our lived reality, they form the bridge that Smith is talking about. There are two ways through which these texts can influence us. First, we may become directly aware of them, generally through higher education but also through the media. At this point, the discursive text directly enters the everyday life of people. This kind of text is generally authoritative; it claims to be the voice of true knowledge gained through scientific or organizational inquiry. However, as Smith points out, social scientific research is based outside of actual lived experience. Its position outside is in fact what makes this knowledge appear legitimate, at least in a culture dominated by scientific discourse. It is this appearance that prompts us to privilege the objective voice above our own. But there is more to these texts, as you can see from the left side of Figure 16.1.

The relations of ruling have a reciprocal relationship with social scientific inquiry, as noted by the double-headed arrow. We believe that legitimate research produces the only real knowledge; government finances, directs, and thus defines the kinds of research that are seen as legitimate. Social scientific inquiry, then, produces the kinds of data and knowledge that reinforce and legitimate the ruling. The single-headed arrow from relations of ruling to texts implies the top-down control of knowledge that Marx spoke of: The ruling ideas come from the ruling people, in this case men. The arrow between scientific inquiry and texts, however, is two-headed. This means that the questions and theories that social scientific research uses come from the literature rather than the real lives of people. It also implies that social science is in a dialogue with itself, between its texts and its inquiry.

The second way we can become aware of these texts is through social scientific inquiry itself. Have you ever answered the phone and found that someone wanted you to respond to a survey? Or have you ever been stopped in a mall and "asked a few questions" by someone with a clipboard? Have you ever filled out a census survey? Through all these ways and many others, we are exposed to objectifying texts by social scientific inquiry.

Notice that the arrow coming from social scientific inquiry has only one head, going toward the actual world of women, and notice that the arrow has two nouns: "readers" and "objects." This one-way arrow implies that social scientific research produces readers and objects. The readers are the researchers. They are trained to read or impose their text onto the actual world. They see the lived experience of women through the texts and methods of scientific research. They come to real, actual, embodied life with a preexisting script, one that has the potential to blind them to the actualities of women. Further, when the questions and methods of science are used to understand women, women are made into objects, passive recipients of social sciences' categories and facts.

The right side of the model depicts Smith's approach. There are two important things to notice. First, there are no relations of ruling controlling standpoint inquiry. Part of this is obvious. As I've mentioned, Smith says that this way of seeing things is applicable to all types of people, but it is particularly salient for women. The reason for its importance for women is that the relations of ruling are masculine in a society such as ours. Men control most of the power and wealth and thus control most of the knowledge that is produced. And while there is a difference between objective knowledge on the one hand and the lived experience of men on the other, women mitigate that discrepancy.

But this issue of ruling isn't quite that clear-cut for Smith. Relations of ruling are obviously associated with men. However, there is a not-so-obvious part as well. The work of women, including feminists, can fall prey to the same problem that produces social scientific inquiry. This can happen when women reify the ideas, ideology, or findings of feminist research. Any time research begins outside of the lived experience of embodied people, it assumes an objective perspective and in the end creates abstract knowledge. This is how women's movements "have created their own contradictions" (Smith, 1992, p. 88). It's possible, then, for women's knowledge to take on the same guise as men's. In Smith's approach, there are no relations of ruling, whether coming from men or women. Standpoint inquiry must continually begin and end in the lived experiences.

The other thing I'd like to call your attention to is that all the arrows associated with standpoint inquiry are double-headed. Rather than producing readers and objects, standpoint inquiry creates space for translators and subjects. In standpoint, the lives of women aren't simply read; they aren't textually determined. A researcher using standpoint inquiry is situated in a never-ending dialogue with the actual and textual. There is a constant moving back and forth among the voice of the subject, the voice of authoritative text, and the interpretations of the researcher. Smith (1992) sees this back-and-forth interplay as a dialectic: "The project locates itself in a dialectic between actual people located just as we are and social relations, in which we participate and to which we contribute, that have come to take on an existence and a power over [sic] against us" (pp. 94–95).

Notice that the dialectic is between actual experience and social relations. Smith is arguing that in advanced bureaucratic societies, our relationships with other people are by and large produced and understood through text. For example, you have a social relationship with the person teaching this class. What is that relationship? To state the obvious, the relationship is professor–student. Where is that relationship produced? You might be tempted to say that it is produced between you and your professor, but you would be wrong, at least from Smith's point of view. The relationship is practiced between you and your professor, but it is produced in the university documents that spell out exactly what qualifies as a professor and a student (remember, you had to apply for admittance) and how professors and students are supposed to act.

This textuality of relationships is a fact of almost every single relationship you have. Of course, the relations become individualized, but even your relationship with your parents (How many books on parenting do you think are available?) and with the person you're dating (How many articles and books have been written about dating? How many dating-related surveys have you seen in popular magazines?) are all controlled and defined through text. However, as we've already seen, Smith argues that even in the midst of all this text, there is a reality of actual, lived experience. Smith is explicitly interested in the dialectic that occurs between abstract, objectifying texts on the one hand, and the lived actualities of women on the other.

We thus come to the core of Smith's project. Smith (2005) has termed this project *institutional ethnography*. The "ethnography" portion of the term is meant to convey its dependence upon lived experience. Smith's project, then, is one that emphasizes inquiry rather than abstract theory. But, again, remember that Smith isn't necessarily arguing against abstractions and generalizations. Smith herself uses abstractions. Notice this quote from Smith (1987) concerning the fault line: "This inquiry into the implications of a sociology for women begins from the discovery of a point of rupture in my/our experience as woman/women within the social forms of consciousness" (p. 49). In it she uses both abstractions and particulars: my/our, woman/women. To say anything about women—which is a universal term—is to already assume and use a theoretical abstraction. Thus, Smith uses abstract concepts, so she isn't saying that in and of themselves they are problematic— the issue is what we do with them. Her concern is for when abstractions are reduced to "a purely discursive function" (Smith, 1992, p. 89). This happens when concepts are reified or when inquiry begins in text: "To begin with the categories is to begin in discourse" (p. 90).

There are, I think, two ways that Smith uses and approaches abstractions. First, in standpoint inquiry, concepts are never taken as if they represented a static reality. Lived experience is an ongoing, interactive process in which feelings, ideas, and behaviors emerge and constantly change. Thus, the concepts that come out of standpoint inquiry are held lightly and are allowed to transform through the never-ending quest to find out "how it works."

The second and perhaps more important way that Smith approaches theoretical concepts is as part of the discursive text that constitutes the mode through which relations of ruling are established and managed. As we've seen, "The objectification of knowledge is a general feature of contemporary relations of ruling" (Smith, 1990, p. 67). A significant principle of standpoint inquiry is to reveal how texts are put together with practices at the level of lived experience. "Making these processes visible also makes visible how we participate in and incorporate them into our own practices" (Smith, 1992, p. 90) and how we involve ourselves in creating forms of consciousness "that are properties of organization or discourse rather than of individual subjects" (Smith, 1987, p. 3).

It's at this point that Smith's use of the word *institutional* is relevant. It signals that this approach is vitally concerned with exploring the influences of institutionalized power relations on the lived experiences of their subjects. Institutional ethnography is like ethnomethodology and symbolic interactionism in that it focuses on how the practical actions of people in actual situations produce a meaningful social order. But neither of these approaches gives theoretical place to society's ruling institutions, as Smith's method does. In that, it is more like a contemporary Marxian account of power and text. Thus, institutional ethnography examines the dialectical interplay between the relations of ruling as expressed in and mediated through texts, and the actual experiences of people as they negotiate and implement those texts.

Smith uses the analogy of a map to help us see what she is getting at. Maps assist us to negotiate space. If I'm in a strange city, I can consult a map and have a fair idea of how to proceed. Maps, however, aren't the city and they aren't our experience. Smith (1992) wants sociology to function like a map—a map that gives an account of the person walking and finding her or his way (lived experience) through the objective structures of the city (text). This kind of sociology "would tie people's sites of experience and action into accounts of social organization and relations which have that ordinarily reliable kind of faithfulness to 'how it works'" (p. 94).

Specifically, Smith is interested in finding out just how the relations of ruling pervade the lives of women. These relations, as we've seen, come through texts and researchers. But in most cases, the relations of ruling are misrecognized by women. They are rendered invisible by the normalcy of their legitimacy. Part of what these maps can do, then, is make visible the relations of ruling and how they impact the lived experiences of women.

Smith is also interested in how actual women incorporate, respond to, see, and understand the texts that are written from a feminist or standpoint perspective. This is an important issue. Looking at Figure 16.1, we might get the impression that standpoint inquiry automatically and always produces translators and subjects. Another way to put this is that it appears as if standpoint inquiry is a static thing, as if, once done, the inquiry stands as the standpoint forever. This is certainly not what Smith is arguing. Notice again that double-headed arrow between standpoint and texts. Once standpoint inquiry is expressed in text, there is the danger that it will be taken as reality and become discursive. Smith's is thus an ongoing and ever-changing project that takes seriously the objectifying influence of text.

> For me, then, the standpoint of women locates a place to begin inquiry before things have shifted upwards into the transcendent subject. Once you've gone up there, settled into text-mediated discourse, irremediably stuck on the reading side of the textual surface, you can't peek around it to find the other side where you're actually *doing* your reading. You can reflect back, but you're already committed to a standpoint other than that of actual people's experience. (Smith, 1992, p. 60, emphasis original)

Summary

- Smith argues that in contemporary society, power is exercised through text. Smith defines text using three factors: the actual words or symbols, the physical medium, and the materiality of the text. It is the last of the three with which Smith is most concerned, the actual practices of writing and reading. Most, if not all, of the texts produced by science, social science, and organizations achieve their facticity by eliminating any reference to specific subjectivities, individuals, or experiences.

- These texts are gendered in the sense that men by and large constitute the ruling group in society. Men work and live in these texts and thus accept them as taken-for-granted expressions of the way things are. Women's experience and consciousness, on the other hand, are bifurcated: They experience themselves within the text, as the ruling discourse of the age, but they also experience a significant part of their lives outside of the text. And it is in this part of women's lives where the contingencies of actual life are met, thus giving these experiences a firmer reality base than the abstract ruling texts of men. Further, men are enabled to take objective ruling texts as true because women provide the majority of the labor that undergirds the entire order.

- The bifurcated consciousness becomes particularly problematic for those women trained in such disciplines as business, sociology, psychiatry, psychology, and political science. In these professions, women are trained to write and read ruling texts, ignoring the lived experiences of women at the fault line.

- Smith proposes a theoretical method of investigation (standpoint inquiry or institutional ethnography) that gives priority to the lived experiences of women. In this scheme, texts are not discounted or done away with, but they are put into the context of the embodied, actual experiences of women. Smith thus opens up a site of research that exists in the dialectic interplay between text and women's experience.

BUILDING YOUR THEORY TOOLBOX

Learning More—Primary Sources

- See the following works by Dorothy E. Smith:
  - *The Everyday World as Problematic: A Feminist Sociology*, Northeastern University Press, 1987.
  - *The Conceptual Practices of Power: A Feminist Sociology of Knowledge*, Northeastern University Press, 1990.
  - *Institutional Ethnography: A Sociology for People*, AltaMira Press, 2005.

Learning More—Secondary Sources

- *Feminist Theory: From Margin to Center*, by bell hooks, South End Press, 2nd edition, 2000.
- *Gender Inequality: Feminist Theories and Politics*, by Judith Lorber, Roxbury Publishing, 3rd edition, 2005.

Check It Out

- Explore feminism: http://www.amazoncastle.com/feminism/ecocult.shtml

Seeing the World

- Write a 250-word synopsis of the theoretical perspective of standpoint theory.
- After reading and understanding this chapter, you should be able to define the following terms theoretically and explain their theoretical importance to standpoint theory: *practices of power, new materialism, texts, facticity, standpoint, constitutive work, relations of ruling, fault line, institutional ethnography*

(Continued)

(Continued)

- After reading and understanding this chapter, you should be able to answer the following questions (remember to answer them *theoretically*):

  o Explain how standpoint is more method than theory. How does some feminist work actually defeat standpoint?

  o How are the relations of ruling expressed through social science?

  o What is the new materialism? How does it affect what people accept as true or factual?

  o Explain the differences between the general sociological approach and Smith's.

  o How does the fault line perpetuate gender inequality?

  o Describe Smith's institutional ethnography. How is it dialectical? What do you think the benefits of institutional ethnography would be?

Engaging the World

- As a student, how do you see yourself being socialized to the relations of ruling? If you are a woman, do you see bifurcated consciousness in your life? As a sociologist, how will you avoid being trapped and controlled by the relations of ruling?

- In general, what implications do you see of objectified knowledge for the way people view and experience themselves? What are the implications if society were to do away with objective knowledge about social things?

Weaving the Threads

- Compare and contrast Foucault's and Smith's ideas about how power is mediated.

- Compare and contrast Smith's idea of the fault line and Chafetz's theory of male micro-resource power.

CHAPTER 17

Embodying Sex:

Judith Butler

(1956–)

S ociology is in the habit of exposing what exists beneath the surface of something. For example, when most people buy something, all they see is the thing they bought. If we ask them what it is and why they bought it, they'd probably say something like "It's a jacket and I needed it." But a sociologist would say, no, look deeper. If you look beneath the surface of that jacket, you'll see exploitation and alienation, and the reason you "need it" is because of commodity fetish. Look further, a postmodern sociologist would say, and you'll see simulacrum and hyperreality. As sociology students you're probably somewhat accustomed to this sociological move; and you're probably used to people looking at you a little odd when you try to explain social things.

Judith Butler is going to ask us to do what sociologists always ask: Look beneath the surface. What she asks us to look beneath is the body. That's not new for us; Bourdieu did the same thing in Chapter 8. You thought you liked meat and potatoes just because it was good. No, Bourdieu tells us; our tastes are insidious revealers of class. Like the postmodernist, Butler is going to ask us to take the next step and look deeper. The body isn't simply classed, it's sexed: The body materializes normative heterosexuality much the same way as it materializes class.

As we go through Butler's theory please keep in mind that there are fundamental differences between what we usually think of as socialization and Butler's idea of materialization. Gordon Marshall's (1998) *A Dictionary of Sociology* defines socialization as "the process by which we learn to become members of society, both by internalizing the norms and values of society, and also by learning to perform our social roles" (p. 624). Socialization seems to presume a preexisting person. Think of it this way: For me to internalize something, an internal must already exist with reference to an external, that is, a body; and, for me to learn anything, I must already exist. For example, it makes no sense if I say that yesterday my son who won't be born for another 5 years learned his multiplication tables.

Butler's notion of materialization is much more profound than the idea of socialization. Butler argues that the body, that which is the exterior, is socially created. *The body materializes or brings into physical existence society.* It isn't simply the case, then, that we simply internalize society's norms, values, and beliefs. The very external (the body) that internalization presumes is itself a social construction. Further, the individual doesn't "learn" society; he or she comes into existence through society. Our subjective self is historically and socially specific. We saw a bit of this with Foucault, and Butler builds on his argument.

THEORIST'S DIGEST

Brief Biography

Judith Butler was born in Cleveland, Ohio, in 1956. She became interested in philosophy at an early age and received her PhD in it from Yale in 1984. At Yale, Butler was influenced by Maurice Natanson, a student of Alfred Schutz. Natanson was significant in exposing Butler to phenomenology. The 1990 publication of *Gender Trouble* brought Butler international acclaim. Other of her important works include *Bodies That Matter: On the Discursive Limits of* Sex (1993), *Undoing Gender* (2004), and *Giving an Account of Oneself* (2005). She is currently the Maxine Elliot Professor of Rhetoric and Comparative Literature at the University of California, Berkeley.

Central Sociological Questions

In the preface to her book *Bodies That Matter: On the Discursive Limits of "Sex,"* Butler (1993) gives us the abiding curiosity that drives her thoughts: "What are the constraints by which bodies are materialized as 'sexed,' and how are we to understand the 'matter' of sex, and of bodies more generally, as the repeated and violent circumscription and violent circumscription of cultural intelligibility? Which bodies come to matter—and why?" (pp. xi–xii). Obviously, Butler is interested in how bodies are socially constructed, specifically how they become sexed, but there's more. Implicit in Butler's curiosity are deeper issues. Butler wants to know what the connection is between subjectivity—the way people think, feel, act, and relate toward the self— and the body. How is it that the body forms the basis of self, subjectivity, and other? How is it that without the body, "there would be no 'I,' no 'we'"? (p. xi). Further, Butler wants to know what bodies, what possibilities, are excluded through the construction of a socially intelligible body. This question goes deeper than simple oppositions, because oppositions are part and parcel of how things are defined. Butler wants to know what kinds of bodies are denied and unidentified. How does the unknown haunt the known? What physical loss do we sense but are unable to articulate? What "specter of its own impossibility" haunts our body?

Simply Stated

The human body is usually seen as simply biological; or in sociology it is typically seen as either a social object or something that can be used to express the self. Butler, however, shows that the body is in fact materialized, brought into existence. Humans inscribe everything with meaning, and that inscription molds, shapes, and changes the thing, including the body. The primary requirement of a social body is that it be sexed. Thus, bodies are carved by the norm of heterosexuality and called into existence through the practices of this cultural norm. In this culture, all sexualities other than heterosexuality act as subversions that overthrow the norm at its base; these acts of subversion open up possibilities.

Key Ideas

Arche-writing, hegemonic norm of heterosexuality, discursive function, iterability, performity, doer and the deed, presentist conceit, repression, melancholia, materialization, subversion, queer theory

Concepts and Theory: What's the Matter With Bodies?

For quite some time, sociology's approach to gender has been to grant a kind of independent existence to the body and sex. This approach is reflective of how social thinkers in general have thought about the body, if they thought about it at all. For example, George Herbert Mead (1934) gives us a warning about putting too much attention on the body: "It may be necessary again to utter a warning against the easy assumption ... that the body of the individual as a perceptual object provides a center to which experiences may be attached" (p. 357). This warning from Mead is particularly important for us to see because of all the classic or original thinkers in sociology, he would be the most likely to consider the body of consequence. Yet here he warns against giving too much significance to the body. Talcott Parsons was one of the first to explicitly include the physical body in theory, but for him the body was simply a biological organism—he made a distinction between organic and psychological systems in the hierarchy of control.

When social thinkers did begin to think about the body as perhaps something more than biology, it was as a social object, a thing that can take on symbolic meanings. Thus, Chris Shilling (1993), in one of the first sociological books dedicated to the body, says, "Growing numbers of people are increasingly concerned with the health, shape, and appearance of their own bodies as expressions of individual identity" (p. 1). Notice how Shilling talks about the body: It's a thing or social object with which we are increasingly concerned. This same approach to the body is seen in Seymour Fisher's (1973) book *Body Consciousness:* "My major intent in this book is to consider the strategies that people use in learning how to make sense of their own bodies" (p. ix). Again, the body is something separate from the actual person. It's a thing that we can decorate, be concerned about, or make sense of.

Pierre Bourdieu was one of the first theorists to clearly see that the body isn't simply an organism or a social object or even a vehicle for expression. Bourdieu argued that the body is classed through habitus. In Bourdieu's scheme, our bodies become enculturated—they are socialized into class-based tastes and dispositions. Class is thus structured and replicated in our bodies. The body is where class is located.

Butler takes Bourdieu's approach to the body an additional step. She tells us that the distinction between sex and gender is inaccurate. I'm sure you remember from any course on gender, even your introduction to sociology course, that your instructor said that sex and gender are different. The story goes that sex refers to the biological plumbing (the body) and gender to the socially constructed roles that are built around bodily sex differences. The reason for this division is to show that gender is a cultural entity, something that has been socially created to control and make distinctions between the sexes (the already existing body). It's a kind of ploy where sociology says, "Sure, there is biology in the form of sex, but it doesn't really matter. What matters is gender." In response, Butler says no, sex matters fundamentally.

Inscribing the Body

Butler argues that it isn't simply *the practices* associated with sex that are regulated; sex itself is controlled—it isn't just what we do, it's what we are. Butler means sex as we usually mean it when we say sex and gender—sex as the biological condition of the body. However, Butler (1993) argues that we mistakenly think that sex comes only from biology:

> The category of "sex" is, from the start, normative. . . . In this sense, then, "sex" not only functions as a norm, but is part of a regulatory practice that produces the bodies it governs, that is, whose regulatory force is made clear as a kind of productive power, the power to produce—demarcate, circulate, differentiate—the bodies it controls. (p. 1)

Using a poststructuralist idea of writing called arche-writing, Butler is arguing that bodies are inscribed. *Arche-writing is* a form of violent etching, engraving, or carving. As an analogy, we can think of the way young lovers used to carve their initials on trees. Everything humans do is like that—we carve a significance, meaning, reality upon the face of an otherwise smooth and meaningless surface. Butler is arguing that sex is just such an engraving, as if the body is a formless mass of senseless cells that society sculpts into what we call sex. The etching is violent because it forcibly denies other possibilities.

Notice that from the very beginning, sex is normative. Let's be very clear about something here. When we are talking about sex, we are not talking about "having sex." It isn't the activity that interests us here. You are a sex—a principal part of your very existence as a human is sex. And that sex is normative. What we mean by this is that sexed bodies are the result of social control. It's important to see that Butler isn't just talking about sexual behaviors or identities. Behaviors and identities are things that are about the body, but are not the body itself. It's not that things having to do with the body aren't important; they are. The way you relate to your body is crucial. You can tattoo it or not; you can condition it or not; you can abuse it through drugs and alcohol or not. In fact, the body is part of the reflexive project of the self in late modernity, according to Anthony Giddens. That's possibly one of the reasons why we are so concerned with it in our daily lives.

Butler (1993) is telling us that bodies matter intrinsically, in and of themselves—what they are and how they exist; their materiality. They matter because they are not simply biological organisms. Inside and out, the body is a social production—sex "is a regulatory ideal whose materialization is compelled, and this materialization takes place (or fails to take place) through certain highly regulated practices" (p. 1). Sex is what qualifies a body *as a body*. Try to imagine a human body without sex, and you probably come up blank. Sex is one of the essentials that qualify our bodies as specifically human—according to Butler (1993), sex is "that which qualifies a body for life within the domain of cultural intelligibility" (p. 2). We can't make sense of our bodies apart from sex.

Butler argues that the way the body is sexed is through psychodynamic processes surrounding the **hegemonic norm of heterosexuality**. That's a mouthful, so let's break it down. Let's take the easy part first: the hegemonic norm of heterosexuality. Hegemony means having superior influence or authority. Thus, what Butler is saying is that the superior authority over sex is heterosexual: two body types, male and female, that are mutually and exclusively attracted to one another. The key word in that definition is *exclusively*. Of course, it is biologically necessary for the males and females of our species to come together sexually. But it is not necessary for dimorphic (two bodies) sexual attraction to be exclusive, as Foucault demonstrated in his histories of sexuality. For example, in Greek society it was normal for men to be sexually active with boys, yet the Greeks replicated the species just fine.

The psychodynamic process is a bit more difficult to understand. Anytime we are talking about psychodynamic theory, we are alluding to or basing our ideas upon Sigmund Freud (we came across his theory in Chapter 7). Freud argued that people develop an ego through psychosexual stages and the resolution of the

Oedipus complex. For Freud, there are three parts to a person's inner being: the id, ego, and superego. The ego mediates the demands of the id and superego. Though there are important differences, the ego generally corresponds to what sociologists call the self.

People aren't born with either an ego or superego; at birth there is only the id, and it is the seat of our passions and desires. The important thing about the id is that it is the source of all our psychic energy, also known as the libido. It is our basic motivation in the world and corresponds to instinctual energy—the closest thing to instincts that humans have. The id pushes us to gratify our basic needs; among the most fundamental of these is sexual gratification. But the id bumps up against problems in its search for gratification. All its needs can't always be gratified immediately. This is obviously true for animals as well; the chief difference is that the basis of human gratification is other people and society. Thus, as the id meets resistance from its human environment when it cannot satisfy all of its urges, its energy kind of splits in two different directions: the ego and superego.

According to Freud, one of the most important steps in the development of the child is the Oedipus complex and its resolution. This stage occurs between the ages of 3 and 5. At the beginning of this phase, the child is fundamentally attached to the mother, most notably through breast-feeding and nurturing. This primary attachment occurs through the id and its libido energy, which means it is primarily sensual and emotional rather than intellectual. In order to successfully develop psychically, both boys and girls need to resolve this attachment issue. One of the challenges at this stage, especially for boys, is to detach from the mother and attach to the same-sex parent (for girls, this means reattaching to the mother), yet at the same time deny that sensual-emotional attachment. Resolution is achieved when the child identifies with the parent of the same sex and simultaneously represses its sexual instincts.

Remember, when babies are born they are nothing but a ball of desire. All of these desires are felt similarly and without distinction about when, why, how, or with whom the desires are met. Part of our development, then, is the channeling of these desires into their "proper" paths. A fair portion of this libido attachment that the child has to his or her mother is sexual. Freud didn't necessarily mean sexual in the way you or I might understand it. It's much more basic and primitive—part of the child's general instinctual drives. We can think of it like hunger for food. We have a fundamental instinct to eat. But what, when, and how we eat is culturally programmed. Psychodynamic theory sees sex in the same way. Sex doesn't magically appear at puberty; it's been there all along. It is a primary form of physical, sensual attachment to others. And, as with food, the child's desires must be channeled to "appropriate" objects of sensual attachment.

Of course, sex and food are different things. Sex is far more important for the psyche. With food there isn't a psychic perception of loss, just a sense of bodily hunger if we don't eat. But with sex there is a sense of psychic loss. Desires for the mother must be suppressed by the child in order to attach successfully to others. This idea of suppression parallels the poststructuralist notion of difference (*différance*)—significance and meaning are created by suppression. Using a mundane example, for a guitar to be a guitar all the particular meanings of "violin" have to be suppressed, held back. In the case we're talking of here, in sex we are called upon to suppress general sensual attachment in favor of a socially defined one. Within the hegemonic norm of heterosexuality, this means that the boy needs to shift his sexual attachment to other women and the girl needs to transfer it to men. *But the suppressed desires still exist in the id or the unconscious.* It's the job of the superego and ego to keep these passions in check by denying them.

Thus, Butler draws on Freud but she gives him a Foucauldian twist. Foucault argued that all knowledge is historically specific and is best understood in terms of discourse. What this means is that Freud's understanding of the Oedipus complex is specific to this time—it isn't an essential stage that humans universally have to work through. And, more importantly, it has a *discursive function.* Here discursive has the sense of analytical reasoning or logic. According to Butler, the cultural logic behind the embodied sex of this age is heterosexism. Freud's theory occurs within a "prevailing truth-regime of 'sex'" (Butler, 1993, p. 233). *The proper or appropriate heterosexual objects of sexual desire occur only within and simply because of this truth-regime.*

Performity—Declaring a Reality

Our bodies are thus inscribed, sculpted, and brought into existence by a culturally specific sex. Sex isn't mere biology. In fact, there isn't anything that is simply biology for humans; we inscribe everything. That's how things become intelligible (and thus possible) for us. In this truth-regime of sex, our possibilities are heterosexual. Our heterosexism is inscribed upon our bodies during early childhood. Through the practices of psychodynamic processes, certain options are closed off (*différance*), the body becomes intelligible and possible, and the power of hegemonic heterosexuality is reflexively applied by the individual.

However, heterosexuality isn't a once-and-for-all accomplishment. The desires of the id are always present. That's why we need the superego. The superego is formed as the voice of society or the parent, most notably the father in Freud's scheme. It protects the ego from the unconscious and overwhelming demands of the id—some possibilities are held off in favor of others. Thus, our homosexual desires are continually repressed so that heterosexuality can be continuously inscribed upon our bodies.

Here Butler uses another idea from poststructuralism: *iterability.* We are most familiar with this word in a different form. We may say something like, "To reiterate, let me state . . ." Reiterate obviously means to say again. But "iterate" doesn't mean to say the first time. If you look up both *reiterate* and *iterate* in an exhaustive dictionary, you will find that they both mean to repeat. And that's the poststructuralist's point. In order to be intelligible, all words, all text, must be in principle repeatable.

Let's imagine that you have a word that is only going to be said once in all of time. You say that word. However, if that word cannot be understood, then it isn't a word at all, just sound. But if the word is understood by others, then even if it is never said aloud again, it must in principle be possible for the word to be repeated.

The word's very **intelligibility** demands that it be repeatable. In fact, when you say the word and others hear it and understand it, that word is already being repeated in their minds. Every iteration is thus a reiteration, every statement is a restatement, and every text is a text of a text.

To get at this idea for the sexed body, Butler uses the term **performity**: a word, phrase, or action that brings something into existence. A clear example of performity is the phrase "I now pronounce you" in a wedding ceremony; the phrase itself brings something into existence at the moment of its pronouncement. To understand performity a little better, let's talk about Erving Goffman's notion of impression management. Goffman argued that we perform or display gender for others. We construct a front through our use of appearance, manner, and setting that communicates to others the kind of gendered self we are claiming. Once effectively claimed by the self, other people impute the gendered self to the person. They act in a particular way toward the social category that has been claimed, and they expect the individual to live up to the self that has been presented. This self, then, is a dramatic enactment; it's something that we produce that allows interactions to take place. The effect of this self upon the individual comes primarily from other people: Others form righteously imputed expectations that the individual must live up to. When performances and expectations are repeated over time, the individual becomes attached to his or her "face."

Goffman's notion of performance thus gives a great deal of latitude to the performer. Butler doesn't see it like that. Individuals *must perform* or, better, iterate/reiterate sex. As I mentioned earlier, to be a body means to be sexed. Butler is talking about something that is much more fundamental than Goffman's gender display. She's talking about *existing as a body*. Other people don't simply understand us as a gender; they see us as a material being, as a person with a body. Our most important method of being embodied isn't what or how we eat, it isn't how we dress or decorate the body, it isn't our health level. According to Butler, we are principally embodied in and through sex. In particular, we are embodied through the performity of sex.

We need to take this one step further. Goffman claimed that others form righteous expectations, that these expectations are attributed to us, and that we then become attached to the sacred-self implied in the expectations. Butler argues that performity does more than that: It constitutes the effect it names. Butler (1993) gives the illustration of a judge. When a judge makes a ruling, he or she cites the law. If the judge didn't cite the law, whatever he or she said would not be binding. The power of the judge therefore lies in the citation (iteration/reiteration) of the law. It's the citation that "gives the performative its binding or conferring power" (p. 225). Notice also that something comes into existence through citation. When the judge passes judgment citing the law, the judgment or punishment then exists. Think also of the wedding pronouncement or the act of accepting academic credentials in a graduation ceremony. These declarations are acts of performity: They simultaneously cite an authority and create a state of being. In Butler's scheme, then, heterosexual performity simultaneously cites the norm of hegemonic heterosexuality (thus giving it legitimacy) and produces heterosexual bodies (thus giving it existence). Performity thus has ontological power—it creates the reality in which we live.

The Doer and the Deed

I must modify something I just stated. I said, "we are principally embodied in and through sex." According to Butler, that's not quite true. The problem with the statement is it makes it seem like there is a subject ("we") that exists prior to the practices of the body ("are embodied"). To critique this assumption, Butler plays off of Friedrich Nietzsche's idea of the *doer and the deed.* Most of us feel, talk, and act as if there is a doer behind every deed. In other words, a person acts and exists outside of the practice. In this way, he or she expresses agency—agents act. Nietzsche (1887/1968) turned this idea around when he said, "there is no 'being' behind doing, effecting, becoming; 'the doer' is merely a fiction added to the deed— the deed is everything" (p. 481). In other words, the idea of agency is wrong-headed. The notion that there is an independent person that preexists and is the source of action is not a reflection of the way things actually work. There isn't really a you behind your actions—the doing creates the doer.

The idea that there is a you in back of your actions is, according to Butler (1993), a "*presentist conceit,* that is, the belief that there is a one who arrives in the world, in discourse, without a history, that this one makes oneself in and through the magic of the name, that language expresses a 'will' or a 'choice' rather than a complex and constitutive history of discourse and power" (p. 228, emphasis added). Here's an illustration. Let's say you are African American. If you had been alive in 1840, it would have been impossible for there to be an African American "you" in back of your actions. African Americans couldn't and didn't exist back then. The only way there can be an American "you" in back of your actions today is that history has socially and culturally produced African Americans. The perception of an African American "you" in back of your actions is, as Nietzsche says, a fiction. It's a conceit that sees the present as somehow less historical than all other time periods that have existed up to this point.

Whatever your subjective sense of you, whether African American or heterosexual, it is historically specific. Most of "you," with all your thoughts and feelings, actually existed prior to your birth. You might be an American, black, white, male, female, a student, a short-order cook, a homeowner, a Visa card user, a licensed driver, an alcoholic, and so on, but most of the meanings and relationships that each of these elements involves existed before you were born. Each identity and subject exists apart from you. You depend *upon them for your intelligibility and viability,* not the other way around. It's thus impossible for "you" to be in back of your actions. Further, what produces a sense of you are your actions: "This repetition is not performed *by* a subject; this repetition is what enables a subject and constitutes the temporal condition for the subject" (Butler, 1993, p. 95, emphasis original).

I've pictured this idea in Figure 17.1. There you will see a comparison between presentist conceit and performity. The first set of images, presentist conceit, shows how many people in contemporary societies see themselves. This view of self is

Figure 17.1   Presentist Conceit

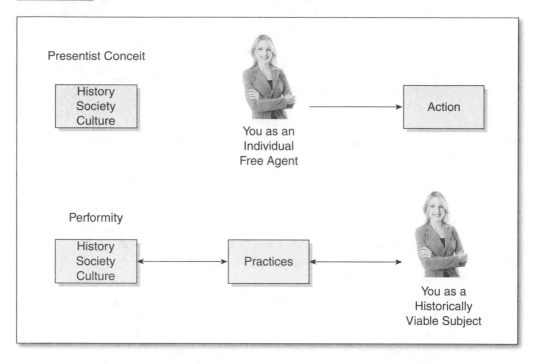

powered by the idea of the individual as a free agent, an idea that gained currency as Protestantism, nation-states, and capitalism took hold. As you can see, the individual is aware of history, society, and culture but these are bracketed off and the person is seen as independent of them. Once that is done, we are able to claim the individual as a free agent that acts. Note that this way of looking at things makes the idea of the acting individual the effect of a historically specific ideology.

Butler claims, however, that such a move gives a false sense of self. Society and culture do historically preexist the individual and his or her behaviors. In fact, the only behaviors that are intelligible are those cultural practices that are historically specific. The performity of these practices reiterates society on the one hand and produces the person as a knowing and knowable subject on the other.

One of the things we may not like about the performity model is that it seems to suggest that we're simply robots carrying out the demands of society. But this isn't the case. Notice that all the arrows in this part of the figure are double-headed. This implies that all these sites mutually constitute one another. In other words, under the idea of performity, the individual can influence his or her world. Behaviors, feelings, and ideas don't directly originate with the individual; they are specific to time and place. However, the person is the site through which culture and society are enacted, and every action is in some way particular to the individual. More importantly, as we'll see, the individual may intentionally subvert the practices that cite society. Whether incidental or intentional, the person's actions influence, constitute, and change history, society, and culture.

The main point here is that performity creates the subject, not the other way around. When we act in a way that can be understood by people, we are citing, iterating, and reiterating the textual scripts that have been handed to us. Our intelligibility as embodied persons begins as hegemonic heterosexuality is inscribed upon our bodies through psychodynamic processes, and it continues nonstop through our performative citation of hegemonic heterosexuality.

This citation isn't done by an independent subject that somehow transcends all history; the person's subjectivity, the ability to know and be known, is created through the naming effect of performity. "Sex is, thus, not simply what one has, or a static description of what one is: it will be one of the norms by which the 'one' becomes viable at all, that which qualifies a body for life within the domain of cultural intelligibility" (Butler, 1993, p. 4).

Concepts and Theory: Haunting, Subversion, and Queer Politics

But what about homosexuality? If sex constitutes the body as a meaningful body, and if sex is produced under the hegemony of heterosexuality, then how and where does homosexuality fit in? In order to begin to answer this question, we have to revisit psychodynamic theory for a moment.

As I mentioned earlier, based on Freud, humans begin with only the primitive energy of the id. The id is motivated by the libido, which is psychic power that comes from primary biological urges, particularly sexual energy. These urges come in contact with the human world and thus have to be controlled. Control happens first through the superego. The superego is the voice of society within the individual. It represents the moral restrictions and demands of the external world. The ego comes to exist as a mediator between the id and superego. The ego is oriented toward the internal world of the individual and seeks to satisfy the urges of the id within the framework given by the superego. An important way the ego mediates the relationship between the id and superego is through ego defense mechanisms, most notably repression. *Repression* serves to keep the ego unaware of the aggressive urges or painful memories associated with the libido.

According to Butler, this behavior of the ego does two important things. First, it serves to create boundaries between the individual and society and between the individual and his or her instinctual drives. These boundaries represent a crucial step in psychodynamic development—it is because of these boundaries that the individual can become self-aware, reflexive, and experience individual subjectivities. Remember that babies and infants are motivated only by their instinctual drives. At that stage of development, we are nothing but a series of never-ending desires. During this phase, we also see very little difference between ourselves and the world around us. In this sense, we feel ourselves to be a natural part of the environment, with a continuous and unbroken interplay between us and our world.

This condition is very similar to how we think most animals relate to the world, in a nonconscious flow of ongoing stimuli and experience. A prowling leopard, for example, is unaware of itself as a being separate from its natural environment. It instinctually responds to smells and sounds without having to think of itself within the situation. For the leopard, there isn't an awareness of separateness, only of continuous experience. In other words, the leopard doesn't have a self. If the leopard eats, it simply eats. If it has sex, it simply has sex. It isn't aware of itself eating—the awareness of self is a separate consciousness apart from the act of eating. The leopard cannot be "embarrassed" if it belches or makes a mess while eating. People, on the other hand, can become embarrassed, because we are aware of ourselves performing the action.

In order to be self-aware, psychodynamic theory argues that humans must first create a boundary between themselves and everything else. This happens principally through the formation of the ego. Through repression, the ego is structurally separated from the body's biological drives (the id) and from the moral demands of society (the superego). By definition, the desires of the id are not aware of themselves. The id is pure desire, just like the drives of the leopard. The demands of the superego initially come from the parent and subsequently society. Again, by definition there is no self-awareness present in the superego; it's the voice of the parent that speaks.

The person becomes self-aware when he or she individually negotiates the demands of the id and superego. A woman "finds" herself in the decision to act; her "voice" comes out of the contradictory demands of the id and superego. Interestingly, you and your subjectivity are formed as society denies your fundamental drives and desires, and since society is always politically and culturally constructed, the subjectivity that forms in response is always historically specific and fundamentally political.

In this separateness, there is a sense in which the ego becomes a substitute for the drives of the id. Let's use the eating example again. When my dog Gypsy eats, she is completely engrossed in what she is doing. She is utterly there, in the moment, caught up in her own behaviors. It's a different story when I eat. I'm generally aware of how I'm holding my fork; whether or not my mouth is closed while chewing; if I'm eating too fast, too loud, or too much. I'm not completely there in the behavior of eating; rather, a large part of me is watching the behavior and judging its appropriateness. In this sense, my ego, my self-awareness, takes the place of the object of my desire, in this case food. This is the second important effect of ego defense mechanisms, the substitution of the ego for the desire: "The turn from the object to the ego produces the ego, which substitutes for the object lost" (Butler, 1997, p. 168).

These effects are important, but the significant thing here for Butler is how this reflexive turn occurs. Notice what happens to the impulses of the id in psychodynamic theory. They don't go away; they are repressed. There is, then, a sense of loss in the formation of ego. The id, which operates according to the pleasure principle, desires something but can't have it or can't gratify the impulse immediately. The ego develops as the person tries to reasonably satisfy the desires to some degree (the reality principle). As the moral voice of authority (the superego) develops, the ego feels the demands of instinct and of society. In order to negotiate these contrary demands, the ego develops defense mechanisms. While there are several ego defense mechanisms, the most salient here is repression. The individual suppresses or pushes out of his or her consciousness the fundamental yet unsatisfied demands of the id. Therefore, the ego is principally formed and experienced through control and loss.

In Butler's scheme, this loss is experienced as melancholia. The "substitution of ego for object does not quite work. The ego is a poor substitute for the lost object, and its failure to substitute in a way that satisfies (that is, to overcome its status as a substitution), leads to the ambivalence that distinguishes melancholia" (Butler, 1997, p. 169). The problem with this kind of loss is that it is at once constitutive yet unspeakable. In other words, our self (ego) is created or constituted through loss; however, this loss not only occurs before it could be articulated, during early childhood, but the loss is also repressed and thus part of the unconscious—the loss creates the ego, and at the same time the ego denies the loss.

But because of the nature of loss, it haunts us. There is a sense of loss, but just what this loss is never fully appears. What we are left with is an ambivalent kind of sadness or melancholy. According to Butler (1997), this "melancholy is precisely what interiorizes the psyche" (p. 170) and permeates "the body with a pain that culminates in the projection of a surface, that is, a sexed morphology" (1993, p. 65). Both the self and the body are inscribed and circumscribed through loss. But what is this fundamental loss?

As we've seen, Butler argues that the body and ego are formed under historical conditions. For us, these conditions are set by the hegemonic norm of heterosexuality. The loss, then, is the refusal of the possibility of sexual or sensual connections between members of the same "sex." Remember that the **materialization** of the body, the body's ability to exist as a physical body, is normative. Biological sex is regulated socially. That's the underlying reflexive idea behind the title of Butler's 1993 book, *Bodies That Matter: On the Discursive Limits of "Sex."* Clearly, bodies matter in the sense that they are important, but more significantly, bodies are matter: They have material substance to them. Yet the material is socially regulated and created. The physical nature of the body is only intelligible to us under the dominion of a historically, culturally, and politically specific understanding of heterosexuality. Thus, these bodies we have are conditioned and given material through performity, the inscribing and citing of heterosexuality. This performity of the hegemonic norm, along with the oedipal law, constitutes the modality of the materialization of the body—the method or channel through which the body becomes a body.

Further, the ego or our subjective sense of self is formed under these same conditions. By its very nature, the ego is denial. It is formed in order to control and refuse the impulses of the id. The single most important energy coming from the libido is sexual. In this era, our claim to a "biological" sex is the basic way we understand our body. It's more fundamental than race or weight or any other "physical" characteristic. And the single most important denial or loss that occurs under the hegemonic norm of heterosexuality is, by definition, the lost possibility of homosexuality.

Butler argues that this loss haunts us; but, more importantly, this loss is also by definition underdefined or unspecified. I don't mean that we don't know what homosexuality is; we do have some sense of it. But the idea we have can't be its full declaration. First, the definition we have is politically created to be used in the production of a specific heterosexuality. Second, and more importantly, the definition we have exists under conditions of suppression. Think about it this way: Psychotherapy usually takes years and years because ego defense mechanisms prevent the person from bringing to his or her conscious mind the desires and pains associated with the id and the effects of working out stages of development. You've probably seen psychiatrists in movies use dream analysis, hypnotherapy, or free association. These techniques are used to get at the hidden secrets of the unconscious, because the individual can't directly access them. The same thing is true with Butler's concept of homosexuality. That loss we've all experienced is hidden in the deep reaches of the psyche.

Butler isn't saying that we should all go to therapy for our loss. But she is saying that "homosexuality" has a special kind of existence for us under the hegemonic norm of heterosexuality. It haunts each of us; it is the specter of loss that we sense but can't quite reach. Because of this effect, homosexuality is a particularly easy and important site for subversion and rearticulation. In other words, Butler is arguing that homosexuality lends itself particularly well to being used as a site that facilitates social change. It's an exceptionally sensitive point in the social psyche, a point that effortlessly yields itself to pressure and rebellion.

Before moving on, we need to consider the notion of subversion. It's an important idea, especially in feminism. *Merriam-Webster's* (2002) tells us that subversion comes from the Latin *subvertere,* which is formed from *sub,* meaning down or under, and *vertere,* meaning to turn. **Subversion**, then, means "to overturn or overthrow from or as if from a foundation." The latter part of the definition is important because subversion implies changing or overturning something from the inside at its core. Thus, acts of subversion are those that affirm and challenge at the same time.

For example, I was watching a film for class the other day. It was a film about women's bodies as the site for political struggle. In one segment, the film showed a photo shoot with three "overweight women." The women were dressed up, playful, and acting sexy. The photographer, herself a large woman, said that the intent of the pictures was to "show the beauty of all women . . . that large women can be sexy too." Notice that the images of these women will do two things. On the one hand, they will affirm that images of women are to be objects of gaze, and on the other hand, they will subvert those same images by not conforming to the assumptions of body type that go along with women and sexiness today.

The centrality of sex to the creation of the human body, along with the domination of heterosexuality in society, means that homosexual displays are politically powerful forms of subversion. Recall the distinction I made earlier between performance and performity—acting straight isn't a performance; it's performity. Performance presumes an already existing subject; performity creates the subject. The practices of heterosexuals in everyday life are not a performance; heterosexual practices create, cite, and regulate the sex and subjectivity they display. It's not performance; it's production. When you act straight, you are citing the discourse that dominates and creates human bodies. You are bringing your body under dominion; you are inscribing it with the political discourse of the day; and you are creating your body, but creating it in the image of society's power—the hegemonic norm of heterosexuality.

However, there is a way in which acting "gay" is more performance than performity. It's performity in the sense that there isn't a preexisting subject, but it is performance with reference to an open field. Rather than citing a hegemonic norm, homosexual cues are like referencing a dictionary that is always being rewritten. There is no authority, there are no relations of power, and there is no social norm for homosexuality to cite. Homosexuality is repressed in us (which is why, Butler might argue, so many people react strongly to it). Since there isn't a norm of homosexuality, acting gay cannot be a citation or inscription of the ruling discourse— homosexuality is an open field wherein the practices are not foreclosed. Thus, the performance of homosexuality does not cite an authority, nor does it inscribe the body in the same way heterosexuality does. To act gay or "queer" subverts authority and leaves the body undefined and open to possibilities.

To repeat the question we began this section with, what becomes of homosexuality? In Butler's scheme, homosexual practices become actions of subversion that can facilitate change. More than most other practices, they challenge hegemonic rule, especially gender oppression and patriarchy. In this scheme, femininity and masculinity are not choices, "but the forcible citation of a norm, one whose complex historicity is indissociable from relations of discipline, regulation, punishment" (Butler, 1993, p. 232). Choice, then, lies in the undisclosed field, in the

> theatricality of gender . . . the very signification that is "queer" . . . This kind of citation will emerge as *theatrical* to the extent that it *mimes and renders hyperbolic* the discursive convention that it also *reverses.* The hyperbolic gesture is crucial to the exposure of the homophobic "law" that can no longer control the terms of its own abjecting strategies. (p. 232, emphasis original)

Drag in particular is a powerful political and social statement. The performance of drag, a male wearing female clothing, challenges the "truth-regime" of sex that there is correspondence between the inside and outside, that there is actually a sexed person (the doer) in back of the sexed practices (the deeds). Drag "produces a contradictory formation of gender in which no fixed 'truth' can be established" (Butler, 1993, p. 234). Keeping in mind that a "vast number of drag performers [are] straight . . . drag thus allegorizes *heterosexual melancholy,* the melancholy by which a masculine gender is formed from the refusal to grieve the masculine as a possibility of love" (p. 235, emphasis original).

We're now in a place to consider **queer theory**. Gay and lesbian studies focuses on the same kinds of issues that traditional gender studies focuses on: the unequal distribution of scarce resources by specific group identities, how those identities are claimed and managed, and how they form the basis of prejudice and discrimination. Queer theory, on the other hand, sees homosexuality and heterosexuality as mutually constructed, as part of the same process of body sexing. Thus, being gay is just as "normal" as being straight; one exists only in the presence of the other. Analysis shifts from political oppression to the ways in which the categories of homosexuality and heterosexuality are used in culture and practice. And queer politics changes from the struggle for gay rights to subversive activities aimed at challenging the hegemonic norm of heterosexuality.

Queer, then, is a specific kind of deconstruction that exposes the hidden work and inconsistencies inherent within the sexual text of our bodies. In this sense, we can define queer as subversive behaviors or theories that bring into question the assumed natural relations among the body, sex, gender, and self. Remember our discussion of subversion. Queer acts are supremely subversive, which is why drag is so powerful. Drag appears to conform to the stereotypical, even blatant cultural expectations about women and sex. However, these stereotypes are powerfully overturned because the person presenting them is male.

Further, because many drag queens are heterosexual men, the representations of sex and sexuality may be doubly subverted. Drag affirms that "the images of women = sex objects," but it subverts the first element by putting men in the place of women. So, we now have something like "images of women performed by men = sex objects." But that may not be all there is to its subversion, because there is a cultural assumption in back of men acting like women: They must be gay. So, underneath the first subversion is an assumption that makes it intelligible: A gay man may act like a female sex object in order to attract other gay men. The second subversion comes when this assumption is overturned because it is a heterosexual man in drag. Our statement then reads something like "the images of women performed by men who desire women = sex objects."

If you are having trouble making sense out of that statement, then you're experiencing the intent of queer. Every set of cultural discourses, ideas, or images is based on assumptions about exclusion. For example, in contemporary Western society, masculinity is fundamentally formed by denying femininity. Subversion, especially queer, overturns those assumptions and renders them meaningless. Specifically, the notion of queer challenges society's sex regime by disrupting identity formation. Rather than performity, or even performance as I used the idea above, queer explicitly disturbs and dislocates both sex and gender identity formation. That's why queer isn't restricted to gay and lesbian studies. Queer theory is interested in all sites of disarticulation, such as cross-dressing, gender-corrective surgery, and hermaphroditism—anywhere the assumptions of sex, gender, and desire are challenged.

> If the term "queer" is to be a site of collective contestation, the point of departure for a set of historical reflections and futural imaginings, it will have to remain that which is, in the present, never fully owned, but always and only redeployed, twisted, queered from a prior usage and in the direction of urgent and expanding political purposes. (Butler, 1993, p. 228)

Summary

- Butler argues that both sex and gender are normative and expressions of power. The body is particularly significant in this regard because its creation sets the parameters of the person and his or her subjectivity. Like all things human, the body must conform to normative expectations in order to be intelligible. The body is primarily understood as sexed, and in this age it only becomes understandable when it conforms to the hegemonic norm of heterosexuality. This hegemonic norm is principally created through repression and performity.

- In this age, we understand and generate the body's sex nature through the eyes of Freudian theory, especially the oedipal law. In forming the ego, certain physical impulses and options that are presented by the id and libido are repressed in order to conform to normative expectations. Initially, both boys and girls are sensually attached to their mothers. However, in order to mature psychically, both must resolve certain issues revolving around identification and desire. For boys, this is referred to as the Oedipus complex, and for girls, the Electra complex (though Freud used Oedipus for both). In both cases, the child must resolve desire toward the parent of the opposite sex and rivalry and hostility toward the parent of its own sex. Both of these elements have to be successfully resolved. The important point in Butler's theory is that both boys and girls have to attach to the parent of the same sex without doing so with sexual (libidinal) energy. This detach/reattach process is somewhat more problematic for boys than for girls, which may be one reason why heterosexual men have a more difficult time with homosexuality. Thus, the oedipal law simultaneously leads us toward heterosexuality but at the same time leaves us haunted by the loss of homosexual possibilities.

- The ego is formed out of this dilemma of attaching and detaching with the same sex. In order to meet the demands of the superego, the desires of the id must be repressed. Through repression, the ego forms the psychic boundaries between the id, superego, and other. More importantly, the individual becomes self-aware and produces subjectivity through the process of repression under the hegemonic norm of heterosexuality: The person becomes individually aware of the demands of the id and superego and substitutes the ego for the needs of the id and requirements of the superego. Since the superego demands are historically and culturally specific, this process points to the importance of political ideologies in the formation of individual subjectivities. In this case, our self-awareness is produced in the context of the hegemonic norm of heterosexuality. More generally, this process means that there isn't a preexisting subject in back of the body and its behaviors.

- The body and the ego are continually formed through performity. Performity refers to behaviors that cite hegemonic norms. In other words, the body becomes understandable as a body when its actions conform to the hegemonic norm of heterosexuality. Performity also implies that people bring their own bodies and subjectivities under the dominion of the existing hegemonic norm.

- But subversion is possible. Subversion occurs when hegemonic ideas or images are overturned from within. Generally, this happens as one or more of the elements that make up the image or idea are inverted while holding the rest stable. Thus, subversion simultaneously affirms and denies. The notion of queer is a particularly powerful form of subversion in that it disrupts the contemporary Western assumptions about sex and gender, about the inner person and the sexual cues he or she gives.

TAKING THE PERSPECTIVE

Judith Butler draws on a number of theorists and philosophers to form her work, most specifically poststructuralism, Sigmund Freud, and Friedrich Nietzsche. To begin our consideration of Butler's perspective, we want to focus on the ideas of possibility and intelligibility, from Foucault. The word *intelligibility* means that something is capable of being understood or grasped. And, for humans, for something to be possible, it must be understood; thus, intelligibility sets the parameters for possibility. Further, Foucault tells us that things are only intelligible and possible within a historic, cultural context.

Foucault argues that the limits of our language, knowledge, and discourse set the boundaries for what is possible and impossible for us to know, think, and feel. This isn't simply a matter of translation. For example, we may know that the translation of the Greek word *aphrodisiakos* is "sexual," but the translated word only calls to our minds the meanings in our language at this time, which, as Foucault demonstrated, doesn't convey the meanings that would have occurred to the minds of Greeks living before the Common Era. These limits of possible and impossible thought are themselves the implementation or practice of power. Thus, for Foucault, knowledge isn't primarily something that is used by the powerful; rather, knowledge itself is power and it is exercised on the elite and common alike.

We need to remind ourselves of something else here as well: The knowledge, discourse, and language of any age are not an account of what actually exists. We can see this obviously in social knowledge. At one time, American society as a whole "knew" that people of color such as blacks, Indians, Chinese, and Irish are inferior. In America, we also used to "know" that homosexuality is a disease and that women are rationally inferior to men. But the historic specificity of knowledge isn't limited to social relations. Up until the time of Copernicus, we "knew" that the earth was the center of the universe. And, if we think back to the early 1800s, we see that doctors "knew" that all disease is created by an imbalance of bodily fluids or "humors": black bile, yellow bile, phlegm, and blood. In order to heal, then, doctors would try to balance out the humors, which is why doctors would purge or bleed their patients. But we "know better" now, right? Both science and society have progressed, right? Maybe, but how do we know that our knowledge has *progressed?*

Also remember the basic point of poststructuralism: Everything is inextricably textual. We continually write our version of the world upon the world. For example, right now I'm looking out my home office window. I see a small forest of trees and I see those trees as mine.

They are on my property, and only I have the right to cut them, sell them, or leave them wild. However, my ownership of those trees exists only because of our cultural and legal structures of "private property." Those trees are mine only because "it is written" in legal documents that we as a society collectively accept as true and because we inscribe the meaning of private property upon the trees when we look at them. In this way, culture is utterly reflexive. The only way to ever think that we are not simply writing reality is to have a solid center—something that exists apart from our texts. But poststructuralism shows us the impossibility of that as well: Centers are by definition outside the text and thus not a center at all, and centers historically come and go.

Poststructuralism also argues that the space of possibility and meaning is opened up through difference (*différance*). If every meaning is possible, then meaningfulness is impossible. Meaning, therefore, comes through holding off some possibilities in favor of others. It's in the process of deferring that meaning is possible. Let's use an obvious example from the subject of this chapter. Masculinity has meaning only insofar as feminine possibilities are deferred. We must foreclose or deny certain possibilities (a boy can't act like a girl) in order to open other possibilities—those behaviors that are not-girl are the "boy" behaviors available or possible for a young male.

Bringing all this together, our knowledge—in Butler's case, our bodies—is a function of the historical period and culture in which we live. Thus bodies are formed by opening up some possibilities and closing off others, and social differences are produced through specific institutional, organizational, and individual practices. Knowledge thus forms the historical condition of possibility and is the true power of any age. By definition, then, when we "know" something, we reflexively bring our thoughts, feelings, and actions under the power of that knowledge and discourse, those possibilities.

From Freud, Butler takes the idea of psychodynamic processes and intrapsychic structures. But this really needs to be read in the context of poststructuralism. Remember Foucault's notion of truth-games? Language and discourse refer only to themselves, not some external reality. Language is its own center. When people claim to have the truth, it's a move of power, an attempt to silence all other voices. Thus, Freud didn't "discover" something universally true about people. But his theory is a truth-game, one that came out of the episteme of the time and has been used to create a discourse around heterosexuality. A note of caution here: This isn't the same as legitimation. Legitimation justifies a reality; truth-games and discourses bring it into existence. This is one of the most difficult things to understand, but also one of the most important. We tend to view the knowledge that sociology, psychology, psychiatry, medicine, history, and the like as factual; explanations about the way things are. These explanations may at times be wrong, but that's all they are, wrong, as if some other than linguistic reality exists. But what poststructuralism and other contemporary theories tell us is that these explanations fully create the things they discover (for an example, research repressed memories and satanic rituals). Butler's debt to Nietzsche is principally for the idea of the doer and the deed, which in the main, gives "body" to the ideas of discourse and truth-games.

BUILDING YOUR THEORY TOOLBOX

Learning More—Primary Sources

See the following works by Judith Butler:

- *Bodies That Matter: On the Discursive Limits of "Sex,"* Routledge, 1993.
- *The Psychic Life of Power: Theories in Subjection,* Stanford University Press, 1997.
- *Undoing Gender,* Routledge, 2004.
- *The Judith Butler Reader,* edited by Sara Salih, Blackwell, 2004.

Learning More—Secondary Sources

- *Judith Butler: Essential Guides for Literary Studies,* by Sara Salih, Routledge, 2002.
- *Butler Matters: Judith Butler's Impact on Feminist and Queer Studies,* edited by Margaret Sonser Breen and Warren J. Blumenfeld, Ashgate, 2005.

Check It Out

- Judith Butler on YouTube: http://www.youtube.com/watch?v=Q50nQUGiI3s
- *Freud: A Very Short Introduction,* by Anthony Storr, Oxford University Press, 2001.
- *Nietzsche: A Very Short Introduction,* by Michael Tanner, Oxford University Press, 2001.
- *A Genealogy of Queer Theory,* by William B. Turner, Temple University Press, 2000.
- *Queer Theory,* edited by Iain Morland and Annabelle Willox, Palgrave Macmillan, 2005.

Seeing the World

- Write a 250-word synopsis of the theoretical perspective that Butler uses.
- After reading and understanding this chapter, you should be able to define the following terms theoretically and explain their theoretical importance to Butler's theory of sexing the body: *arche-writing, hegemonic norm of heterosexuality, discursive function, iterability, performity, doer and the deed, presentist conceit, repression, melancholia, materialization, queer theory*
- After reading and understanding this chapter, you should be able to answer the following questions (remember to answer them *theoretically*):
  - How are intelligibility and possibility related to sex? How do these issues set the boundaries for the body?
  - What is the hegemonic norm of heterosexuality, and how is it inscribed upon the body through psychodynamic processes?
  - What is performity and how is it related to the hegemonic norm of heterosexuality and the sexing of the body?

o   What is the idea of the "doer and the deed"? How is it related to one's subjective experience?

o   How are haunting, melancholia, and the ego related? How is the loss of homosexuality unspecified?

o   In what ways is "queer" a kind of deconstruction? Specifically, how does queer subvert sexuality and gender? Can you think of other issues or identities that can be "queered"?

Weaving the Threads

- Bring Smith's and Butler's theories together to form a synthesized theory of gender construction. How are the body and consciousness involved in gender inequality? Consider Smith's and Butler's ideas of subversion with Chafetz's notion of social change. Use these three approaches to form a theory concerning gender social change.

- What implications do you see?

Glossary

Account-able: Account-able (accounts, accounting) is a theoretical idea in ethnomethodology. The term implies that the basic requirement of all social settings is that they be recognizable or accountable as whatever social setting they are supposed to be. Members visibly and knowingly work at making their scenes accountable; this work, in turn, organizes the situation and renders it meaningful and real.

Black nihilism: Black nihilism is a theoretical concept from the work of Cornel West. Nihilism in general refers to the idea that human life and existence are meaningless and useless. West uses the idea to describe the African American experience as the result of market saturation. Up until the 1950s, blacks were not considered a viable or large market for capitalism. Since the era of civil rights, however, African Americans have been increasingly targeted: Blacks have been inundated with new commodities and enticed by values of consumerism. Consumerism along with upward mobility for some blacks has weakened the civic and religious community base that has traditionally been the source of strength and validation for blacks living under American Apartheid. For West, the main problem is that true equality and justice still do not exist for African Americans: the black life is still one of oppression, yet it is experienced under the shroud of consumerism and the belief that owning more and more commodities is the source of happiness. The loss of community coupled with consumerism and continued oppression has contributed to a growing sense of meaninglessness and loss of purpose for African Americans.

Civil society: The first idea of civil society emerged during the birth of modernity. It refers to the sphere between citizens and the state and initially included capitalism, voluntary or moderate religion, and education. Together, these provided both structural and cultural bases for democracy. The culture of civil society is particularly important, as it provides the moral, ethical force of democracy. However, because of changes associated with organized capitalism, the civil sphere must change, according to.

Colonization of the lifeworld: Colonization of the lifeworld is a theoretical concept used by Jürgen Habermas to describe the process through which the everyday life of people is taken over by economic and political structures. By definition the lifeworld is the primary place of intimate communication and social connections. These functions of the lifeworld are overshadowed by the values of money and power that come from the economic and political realms, which in turn reduce true communication and sociability. Lifeworld colonization tends to increase as social structures become more complex and bureaucratized and when the state creates a climate of entitlement.

Consumer society: Consumer society is a theoretical idea from the work of Jean Baudrillard. Goods and services have always been consumed; it's a basic fact of economic existence. However, in postmodernity consumption itself drives the economy rather than basic needs and production. Pure consumption has no natural limits— that is, consumption for consumption's sake cannot be satisfied and produces a never-ending demand for new and different commodities. Further, consumption becomes a primary, if not *the* primary, way people define themselves and experience life.

Critical theory: Critical theory is a theoretical, philosophical perspective that refers to schools of thought in literary criticism and social theory. In social theory, this critical standpoint began with the Frankfurt School (Frankfurt Institute for Social Research). Max Horkheimer, director of the institute from 1930 to 1958, was the first to coin the term. Generally speaking, critical theory in the social disciplines assumes that all knowledge that is not critically and reflexively assessed is based in material relations of power. The purpose and outcome of this kind of knowledge— whether produced in some form of science, politics, or popular culture—is always ideological: it produces false consciousness and oppression. Critical theory, on the other hand, intends to be critical and reflexive and is aimed at uncovering the political underpinnings of taken-for-granted, hegemonic culture and how it is used to suppress other ways of knowing and oppress various class and status groups (such as race, gender, and sexual preference). True critical theory has the additional quality of resulting in emancipatory practices or praxis.

Critical theory (Jürgen Habermas): For Habermas, civil society is a social network of voluntary associations, organizations (especially mass media), and social movements; its purpose is to inform and actualize the public sphere. To function properly, the civil society must be free from control by the state, economy, and religion; and it must exist within a liberal culture that values equality and freedom.

Cultural capital: Cultural capital is a theoretical concept used in Randall Collins' theory of interaction ritual chains and Pierre Bourdieu's theory of class replication. *For Collins,* cultural capital is defined as the amount of cultural goods— such as knowledge and symbols—that a person has at his or her disposal to engage others in interaction rituals. The more cultural capital is held in common, the more likely people are to interact with one another. But because it is a capital, people are also looking for a return on their investment—they hope to take more culture away than what they brought in to the interaction. Collins conceptualizes three types of cultural capital: generalized (group specific), particularized (specific to relationships between individuals), and reputational (what is known about the individual). *For Bourdieu,* there are three kinds of cultural capital: objective (material goods that vary with class), institutionalized (official recognition of knowledge and skills), and embodied (the result of class-based socialization (habitus). Generally, the concept refers to the social skills, linguistic styles, and tastes that one accrues through education and distance from necessity (a measure of how far removed someone is from basic sustenance living). As the levels of education and distance from necessity increase, language, taste, and social skills tend to become more complex and abstract.

Dialectic: Dialectic is a theoretical concept that describes the intrinsic dynamic relations within a phenomenon, such as the economy. The term is generally, though not exclusively, used in conflict or critical perspectives. The idea of dialecticism came to sociology through Karl Marx; and Marx, for his part, got the idea from the philosopher Georg Wilhelm Hegel. A dialectic contains different elements that are naturally antagonistic or in tension to one another—this antagonism is what energizes and brings change. Dialectics are cyclical in nature, with each new cycle bringing a different and generally unpredictable resolve. The resolve, or new set of social relations, contains its own antagonistic elements and the cycle continues.

Discourse: Discourse is a theoretical concept that is widely used but is most specifically associated with the work of Michel Foucault. A discourse is an institutionalized way of thinking and speaking. It sets the limits of what can be spoken and, more importantly, how something may be spoken of. In setting these limites, discourses deliniate the actors of a field, their relationships one to another, and their subjectivities. Discourses are thus an exercise of power.

Dramaturgy: Dramaturgy is a theoretical perspective that is most closely associated with the work of Erving Goffman. Dramaturgy uses the analogy of the stage to analyze and understand what people do in social encounters. People are conceived of as actors, sometimes working as teams, who work to convey specific self-impressions to an audience (others present). This work is referred to as impression management. Emphasis is placed on the continual production of a social self, which places moral imperatives on the interaction order.

Emotional energy: Emotional energy is a theoretical idea that originated with Émile Durkheim and is used by Randall Collins in his theory of interaction rituals. It is defined as the level of motivational energy an individual feels after leaving an interaction. Emotional energy is specifically linked to the level of collective emotion formed in a ritual, and it predicts the likelihood of further ritual performance and the individual's initial involvement within the ritual.

Episteme: Episteme is a theoretical concept from Michel Foucault's theory of knowledge and power. Episteme refers to the fundamental notions of truth and validity that underlie knowledge. It's the hidden order of knowledge. Epistemes organize and are a necessary precondition for thought; epistemes set the boundaries of what is possible and knowable. One important implication of this concept is that an episteme will maintain the order produced by a knowledge system even in the face of contradictory events or findings. Epistemes are historically specific and change through rupture rather than linear progress.

Ethnomethodology: Ethnomethodology is a theoretical perspective in sociology that began with the work of Harold Garfinkel. Ethnomethodology is the study of the everyday methods that ordinary people use to make sense of, organize, and act in the situations in which they find themselves. The central question of the perspective is that of social order. Some sociological perspectives explain social order by referring to cultural and social structures that impinge on the situation. Ethnomethodology, on the other hand, explains social order as a local achievement. As people in the situation act in such a way as to give to themselves and observers the impression of such-and-such a social order, they in fact produce such an organization. In other words, the main idea of ethnomethodology is that the methods people use to organize a situation are identical to the methods used to render the situation accountable.

Exploitation: Exploitation is a central concept in Marx's theory of capitalism. It is the measurable difference between what a worker gets paid and the worth of the product produced—it is the source of capitalist profit. Exploitation also has the characteristic of giving workers leverage over capitalists. The dependency of capitalists upon exploitation for profit is what gives labor the power to negotiate and strike.

Facticity: Facticity is a theoretical concept found in a number of different social constructivist approaches. Facticity refers to the quality of being a fact. Implicit in this concept is the idea that facts are produced; they don't intrinsically exist as facts. Events, objects, and phenomena in general become facts under certain knowledge systems.

False consciousness: Generally, false consciousness refers to the inability of people to think past their own oppression and it implies a denial of human nature. For Marx, false consciousness comes about through capitalism and is the incapability to see human nature as defined by creative production. Rather than linking false consciousness to capitalism, the Frankfurt School of critical theory sees it produced from the Enlightenment's emphasis on rationality and reason. In either case, false consciousness is insidious in that it blinds us to its very existence. In place of true human awareness, people believe ideologies, any set of cultural practices that undergird and legitimate relations of power and prevent workers from bringing about social change.

Fault line: Fault line is a theoretical concept specific to Dorothy Smith's feminist theory. Smith argues that a gap exists between official knowledge—especially knowledge generated through the social sciences—and the experience of women. This fault line is particularly important for understanding how men are able to not see the differences between objective, public knowledge and the reality of day-to-day existence: women traditionally negotiate or obscure the disjunction for men through their caring for the daily administration of the household, including meeting the sustenance and comfort needs of both men and children.

Field: The field is a theoretical concept from Pierre Bourdieu's constructivist structuralism approach. The concept functions to orient the researcher to an arena of study. Field denotes a set of objective positions and relations that are tied together by the rules of the game and by the distribution of four fundamental powers or capitals: economic, cultural (informal social skills, habits, linguistic styles, and tastes), social (networks), and symbolic (the use of symbols to recognize and thus legitimate the other powers). People and positions are hierarchically distributed in the field through the overall volume of capital they possess. Symbolic and cultural capitals are specifically important: cultural capital is important in forming habitus and thus the replication of the field, and symbolic capital is important because it gives legitimacy and meaning to the empirical field.

Frames: The idea of frames is a theoretical concept in Goffman's analysis of how people experience reality. The analogy is to a film strip and its frames or to the frame of a picture on the wall. In both cases the frame delineates certain features as important by excluding all others. Frames, then, tell people what to pay attention to and thus how to organize their subjective involvement. There are two primary frames: natural and social. These are perceived as solid and factual. These frames may be keyed and thus given different meanings. Keying generally makes a primary frame seem less real. The five keys are make-believe, contests, ceremonies, technical redoings, and regroupings.

Frankfurt School: The Frankfurt School is both an actual school and school of thought (its most usual connotation today). The school began in Frankfurt, Germany, in the 1920s and has included such thinkers as Theodor Adorno, Max Horkheimer, Herbert Marcuse, Walter Benjamin, Herbert Marcuse, Eric Fromm, and, most recently, Jürgen Habermas. In general, the founding members sought to update Karl Marx's theory of material consciousness by returning to Marx's Hegelian roots and synthesizing elements from Max Weber and Sigmund Freud. Of Marx's work, the *Economic and Philosophic Manuscripts of 1844* and *The German Ideology* were key texts. *See critical theory.*

Free-floating signifiers: The idea of free-floating signifiers comes from the postmodern writings of Fredric Jameson. In traditional and modern societies, signifiers, or signs, are set and understood within a social or linguistic structure, what is sometimes referred to as a signification chain. In postmodernity, however, the chain or context of signs has been disrupted by machines of reproduction, or mass media. This break in the signification chain indicates that each sign stands alone, or in relatively loose association with fragmented groups of other signs. Signs, then, become free-floating signifiers. *See simulacrum.*

Front: The theoretical idea of a front comes from Erving Goffman's dramaturgy. Front refers to the totality of identity cues offered by an individual in a social encounter. These cues come from the setting, manner, and appearance.

Generalized other: The generalized other is a theoretical concept used in symbolic interactionism that refers to sets of perspectives and attitudes indicative of a specific group or social type with which the individual can role-take. In the formation of the self, the generalized other represents the last stage in which the child can place herself in a collective role from which to view her own behaviors. It is the time when the self is fully formed as the person takes all of society inside.

Governmentality: Governmentality is a theoretical term from Michel Foucault's theory of knowledge and power. The term refers to a specific kind of institutionalized power. In Foucault's scheme, modernity is unique because of the manner through which states control populations. Generally speaking, in previous ages power and control were exercised upon the individual from without. Governments would actively and directly control the person, when domination was necessary or desired. In contrast, modern states exercise power from within the individual. Governmentality, then, captures the process through which the person participates in his or her own domination—control is exercised within the person by the person. *See panopticon, discourse, and power.*

Habitus: A central theoretical term from Pierre Bourdieu's theory of class replication. Habitus refers to the cultural capital an individual possesses as a result of his or her class position. Habitus is embodied; that is, it works through the body at a nonconscious level. Cultural capital and thus class position are expressed unthinkingly. On the one hand, this embodied expression structures class; on the other hand, habitus works creatively as it is possible to make intuitive leaps. Habitus varies by cultural capital and is expressed in linguistic markets.

Hegemonic norm of heterosexuality: The hegemonic norm of heterosexuality is a theoretical idea from Judith Butler's feminist theory. The idea simply says that heterosexuality—exclusive attraction to members of the opposite sex—is governed by social norms. The power of this term in Butler's hands is that she sees that this norm truly is about sex and not just gender. In other words, Butler is arguing that normative scripts of sexuality are materialized in the body. Thus, being heterosexual is the result of social, normative pressures that produce heterosexual bodies.

Hyperreality: Hyperreality is a theoretical concept from the work of Jean Baudrillard and refers to the preference in postmodern societies for simulated experiences rather than real ones. In Baudrillard's scheme, the real has been stripped of all meaning, authenticity, and subjective experience through the proliferation of simulacrum. People thus seek emotional experiences in images of reality that have been exaggerated to the grotesque and fantastic (breast implants and video games are good examples). *See simulacrum.*

Ideal speech communities: The concept of ideal speech communities comes from the work of Jürgen Habermas. Ideal speech refers to communicative acts or interactions where every member is granted full participation and is free from any type of coercion. Each member is responsible to express their opinions, keeping their speech free from ideology and objective standings (such as educational credentials).

The goal of ideal speech is consensus. Habermas argues that reasoned consensus—and thus emancipation—is possible because of the inherent assumptions of communication. The act of communication assumes that communication, inter-subjectivity, and validity are all possible. The latter implies the possibility of universal norms or morals; and the fact that validity claims can be criticized implies that they are in some sense active and accountable to reason.

Indexical expressions: The idea of indexical expressions comes from ethnomethodology and conceptualizes the notion that the meaning of all conversation is dependent upon a context that is assumed to be shared by all interactants. Talk, then, indexes contexts in order to be sensible and taken for granted.

Institutionalization: Institutionalization is a theoretical process through which social and cultural elements become patterned. In Berger and Luckmann's theory, institutionalization is the result of habitualized behaviors and reciprocal typifications.

Intelligibility: Intelligibility is a theoretical concept most closely associated with the feminist work of Judith Butler. The word itself simply means that something is understandable. However, the concept takes on social and political significance because intelligibility is based on commonly accepted ways of knowing and knowledge. Rather than pure information, knowledge here is seen as a product of institutional practices and relations of power. Intelligibility, then, sets the limits for what a person may feel, think, and be, these parameters being set by hegemonic (or authoritative) culture and institutionalized power. *See hegemonic norm of heterosexuality.*

Interaction: Interaction is a central theoretical idea in symbolic interactionism. Interaction is the intertwining of individual human actions. In symbolic interaction, the interaction is the true acting unit in society. According to this view, interaction is not simply the means of expressing social structure or the individual's personality traits; rather, the interaction is the premier social domain and is thus the chief factor through which social structures and individual personalities are created and sustained. Interaction occurs through a three-part process through which meaning, society, and self emerge: the presentation of a cue, the initial response to the cue, and the response to the response. However, the end point of the process generally becomes itself an initial cue for further interaction, staring the process over again.

Joint action: Joint action is a theoretical term from Blumer's symbolic interactionism that describes the process through which various individual and discrete actions and interactions are brought together to form a meaningful whole. This joining is accomplished symbolically by both individuals and groups and constitutes a significant portion of what is meant by "society." The insight of this concept is that at every point of interaction or joint action there is uncertainty. The implication is that society is emergent.

Legitimation: Legitimation is a theoretical concept that describes the effects that specific stories, histories, and myths have in granting ethical, moral, or legal status or authorization to social power and relations. Legitimation is particularly important in the social construction of reality. According to Berger and Luckmann's theory, there are three levels of legitimation (self-evident, theoretical, and symbolic universes) each more powerful than the previous.

Life politics: Life politics is a theoretical idea from Anthony Giddens' theory of modernity. Life politics is an outgrowth of emancipatory politics. Emancipatory politics is concerned with liberating individuals and groups from the constraints that adversely affect their lives—people are thus liberated to make choices. Life politics is the politics of choice and lifestyle. Life politics is concerned with issues that flow from the practices of self-actualization within the dialectic of the local/global, where self-realization affects global strategies. Life politics is dependent upon the individual creating and maintaining inner authenticity.

Lifeworld: The lifeworld is a theoretical concept that came into sociology through the work of Alfred Schutz. The lifeworld refers to the world as it is experienced immediately by each person. It is a cultural world filled with meaning and is made up of the sets of assumptions, beliefs, and meanings against which an individual judges and interprets everyday experiences.

Linguistic market: Linguistic market is a theoretical concept from Pierre Bourdieu's theory of class replication. The idea emphasizes the importance of language and social skills in reproducing class. Every time a person speaks with another there is a linguistic market within which each person has different skill levels and knowledge. These differing levels lead to distinct rewards in the market that in turn announce one's class position. The power of the market is that people tend to sanction themselves because they intuitively understand how their culture and language skills will play out in any given market.

Materialization: Materialization is a theoretical idea used in Judith Butler's theory of sex and gender. The term refers to the process through which hegemonic norms of sex and sexuality are scripted within the body. With materiality, Butler moves beyond the idea that gender is a social construction that is built on distinct male and female bodies. That approach ultimately restricts the possibilities of change and choice. In Butler's scheme, the sexed body itself is socially constructed. When sex is materialized, it produces a feminism that opens up difference, subversion, choice, and change.

Modalities of structuration: Modalities of structuration is a concept used in Anthony Giddens' structuration. Modalities of structuration are the paths through which structure is expressed in social encounters. There are three modalities (interpretive schemes, facilities, and norms) that are linked on the one hand to structures (signification, domination, and legitimation) and on the other to social practices (communication, power, and sanctions). These modalities are socially and culturally specific. *See structuration theory.*

Ontological security/insecurity: Ontological security is a theoretical concept from Anthony Giddens' structuration theory. Ontology refers to the way things exist and specifically implies that human existence is different than all other forms of existence because of meaning. Meaning is not a necessary or intrinsic feature of any event or object. This characteristic of meaning implies that human reality is unstable. This intrinsic instability creates an unconscious need for ontological security—a sense of trust in the taken-for-grantedness of the human world. This need motivates humans to routinize and regionalize their practices.

Panopticon: Panopticon is a theoretical concept from Michel Foucault's theory of knowledge and power. The panopticon was an architectural design for a prison that allowed for the unobserved observation of prisoners. The idea behind the panopticon is that if prisoners thought they were being watched, even if they weren't, the prisoners themselves would exercise control over their own behaviors. Foucault sees this physical prison as a metaphor for the way control and power are exercised in modernity. He specifically has in mind the self-administered control that comes through the knowledge produced by the social and behavioral sciences as well as medical science.

Performity: Performity is a theoretical concept from Judith Butler's feminist theory. Performity refers to performances, practices, or actions that bring something into existence. An example of performity is the moment in an academic graduation when the qualifications for graduation are announced fulfilled and then accepted by the presiding officer. It is at that precise moment that the student graduates—the fact came into existence through performity. The important performity for Butler occurs through the gendered and sexed practices that cite the hegemonic norm of heterosexuality.

Phenomenology: Phenomenology is a school of philosophy developed by Edmund Husserl that argues that consciousness is the only experience or phenomenon of which humans can be certain. It seeks, then, to discover the natural and primary processes of consciousness apart from the influence of culture or society. Husserl hoped to create "a descriptive account of the essential structures of the directly given"; that is, the immediate experience of the world apart from preexisting values or beliefs. Social phenomenology, on the other hand, argues that nothing is directly given to humans; we experience everything through stocks of language, typifications, and so on. Social phenomenology, then, seeks to explain the phenomena of the social world as they are presented to us. This approach is distinct from most sociology in that phenomenologists reduce phenomena to the simplest terms possible. For example, a structural sociologist will study racial inequality and its effects. Race is simply a given in this kind of approach. A phenomenological approach will take race itself as the most basic problem to explain: how is it that race can be experienced as a given, as something that can be taken for granted, as an intersubjective reality? How does "race" present itself to us in just such a way as to appear real, taken for granted, and intersubjective?

Postdemocratic age: This idea comes from the work of Cornel West. The notion of a postdemocratic age is based on a definition of democracy as a community of involved citizens actively engaged in open and critical dialogue, under the condition of the freedom of ideas and information, and oriented toward achieving justice, equity, compassion, and acceptance of diverse others. West argues that the American postdemocratic age has come about principally through the work of the Christian right amplified by the fear generated by 9/11. Three dogmas are associated with this fundamentalist movement, all of which contribute to postdemocracy: free-market fundamentalism, aggressive militarism, and escalating authoritarianism.

Poststructuralism: Poststructuralism is a theoretical perspective. However, poststructuralism doesn't refer to a clear body of knowledge that is universally accepted by its adherents. It is, rather, a loose amalgamation of ideas that in general define an approach. Overall, poststructuralism is defined in opposition to structuralism, an attempt to discover and explain the unobserved foundations for empirical phenomena. Implicit within such goals is the belief that a metalanguage (like science or mathematics) can be created that will adequately and objectively express the characteristics of such a structure. It is the criticism of this belief that forms the core of poststructuralism. Poststructuralism assumes that all languages are based on values, most of which are political in nature. Thus, a "pure science" of any social structure is impossible. Rather than language being able to represent an independent reality, language is inherently self-referential, creating a world of oppressive power relations. Additionally, poststructuralism is characterized by several denials: poststructuralism rejects the belief in essentializing ideas that conceptualize the social world or a portion of it as a universal totality—rather, the social world is fragmented and historically specific (general theories are thus impossible and oppressive); poststructuralism denies the possibility of knowing an independent or objective reality—rather, the human world and knowledge are utterly textual; poststructuralism discards the idea that texts or language have any true meaning—rather, texts are built around différance and carry a surplus of meaning (humanity is thus left with nothing but interpretation and interpretations of interpretation); and, poststructuralism rejects the idea of universal human nature developed out of the Enlightenment—rather, the meaning of the human subject is historically specific and is an effect of discourse, with the discourses of an age producing the possible bodies and subjectivities of the person.

Power: Power is a theoretical concept found in many social and sociological theories. The short definition of power is the ability to get others to do what you want. Yet, in terms of how it works and where it resides, power is one of our most difficult and controversial terms. For Anthony Giddens, power is part of every interaction and is defined in terms of autonomy and dependence. The greater our level of autonomy and the greater others' level of dependence, the greater will be our power in an encounter. Thinking of power in this way makes it an outcome rather than a resource that is possessed. It also makes power part of face-to-face encounters rather than part of an obdurate structure or linked to group politics. In structuration theory, power is one of the results that comes from the use of allocative and authoritative resources. For Peter Blau, power is the result of unequal exchange relations. Power refers to the other individual's or group's ability to recurrently impose its will on self. There are four conditions of power in Blau's exchange scheme: the power of Actor A over Actor B is contingent upon (1) B having limited needs; (2) B having few or no alternatives; (3) B unable or unwilling to use force; and, (4) B continuing to value the good or service that A controls. Michel Foucault sees power in two ways; both are hidden rather than overt. Most importantly, power is exercised through knowledge. The knowledge that any person holds at any given time is the result of historically specific institutional arrangements and practices. For Foucault, knowledge isn't simply held; it is applied to every aspect of the person's life by the individual. Thus, knowledge exercises control over people's bodies, minds, and subjectivities. The second way Foucault uses the notion of power is in daily encounters with others. In every social encounter people's actions influence other actions; these practices enact the social discourse or knowledge and serve to guide and reinforce one another.

Pragmatism: Pragmatism is a school of philosophy that argues that the only values, meanings, and truths that humans hold on to are the ones that have practical benefits. These values, meanings, and truths shift and change in response to different concrete experiences. Pragmatism forms the base for many American social theories, most specifically symbolic interactionism.

Problem of reification: Reification is a concept that captures the idea that concepts and ideas may be treated as objectively real things. In social science generally, reification can be seen as a methodological problem because of the tendency to ascribe causation to ideas, as in gender causing inequality. In critical theory, reification is taken further and refers to the process through which human beings become dominated by things and become more thing-like themselves.

Public sphere: The public sphere is a theoretical construct from the critical work of Jürgen Habermas. The public sphere is an imaginary community or virtual space where a democratic public "gathers" for dialogue. With the idea of the public sphere Habermas is arguing that true democratic process demands an active, public dialogue that takes place outside the influence of government or the economy. To function properly, the public sphere demands unrestricted access to information and equal participation of all members.

Queer theory: Queer theory is a critical, theoretical perspective as well as a method for unpacking (or deconstructing) the commonly accepted naturalness of sex, sexuality, desire, and gender. As with any deconstruction, the gap between the ideal and its expression is exploited in order to show the inconsistencies and political discourses through which sex, gender, and desire are constructed and made to seem natural and stable.

Rituals: In Randall Collins' theory of interaction rituals, rituals are patterned sequences of behavior that tend to re-create high levels of co-presence, bounded interactions, common emotional mood, and common focus of attention. For Collins, rituals not only function to reinvigorate a group's moral and sacred base, as in Durkheim, rituals also are the key social mechanism through which macro-level social phenomena are produced. According to Collins, macro-level phenomena are created through the simple building up of interactions through time and space. Ritual performance provides the links that allow interactions to be built up: emotional energy and cultural capital.

Role-taking: Role taking is a theoretical concept in symbolic interactionism that describes the process through which an individual places herself in the role of the other person in order to see her self from that position. Role-taking is the chief mechanism through which the self is produced and interactions are successfully carried out.

Self: The self is a theoretical idea that describes various features of the individual. According to symbolic interactionist theory, the self is a social object, a perspective, a conversation, and a story. In interactionist theory, the self is seen as arising from diverse role-taking experiences. The self is thus a social object in that it is formed through definitions given by others, especially the generalized other, and is a central meaningful feature in interactions. The self is a perspective in the sense that it is the place from which we view our own behaviors, thoughts, and feelings. It is an internal conversation through which we arrive at the meaning and evaluation we will give to our own behaviors, thoughts, and feelings. This conversation is ongoing and produces a story we tell ourselves and others about who we are (the meaning of this particular social object). The self is initially created through successive stages of role-taking and the internalization of language. The self continually emerges, is given meaning, and furnished with stability or flexibility through patterns of interactions with distinct groups and generalized others.

Simulacrum: Simulacrum is a theoretical concept that is most closely associated with the postmodern work of Jean Baudrillard. The word itself simply refers to a representation or simulation. For example, a statue of Karl Marx has a similar appearance to and thus represents or simulates Marx. Baudrillard argues that in postmodernity most cultural images and signs do not have an actual reference and thus don't represent or simulate anything. Further, simulacra in postmodernity are simply images of images that never existed in the first place. The Disney Pirates of the Caribbean is a good example. Pirates certainly existed, but never in the form presented at the Disney ride: the ride is an idealized version of the fantasy of pirates given life in such novels as *Peter Pan*. So, the ride is an image of an image that doesn't truly represent. But the slide of simulacrum doesn't end there: Disney produced a movie based on the ride. The movie is thus an image of an image of an image, which never referred to anything real in the first place.

Social exchange: According to Peter Blau, exchange refers to those voluntary social actions in which people engage that are dependent upon some present or future reward from others. The concept of exchange does not encompass all behavior.

It particularly does not address those choices and preferences influenced by personality preferences, social position and experience, coercion, morals, or irrational emotions. Social exchange is distinct from economic exchange in that social exchanges lack specificity and social meaning, they build trust over long periods of time, and social benefits are less detachable from the source of the benefits.

Social objects: The idea of social objects is a theoretical concept in symbolic interactionist theory. Social objects are anything in an interaction that we call attention to, attach legitimate lines of behavior to, and name.

Standpoint: Standpoint is a theoretical idea that is most prominent in the feminist work of Dorothy E. Smith. Standpoint argues that what one knows is directly linked to her or his social position or class. Inherent within this idea is the notion that being outside the ruling group yields a particularly powerful and critical standpoint. Smith is particularly interested in validating and exploring the standpoint of women living under a patriarchic system.

Structuration theory: Structuration theory is the theoretical perspective developed by Anthony Giddens. The perspective is more an analytical framework—or ontological scheme—than a complete theory. Structuration tells the theorist researcher what kinds of things exist socially and what to pay attention to. Structuration denies the existence of structure and free-agency (seen as a false dualism) and argues that these generally reified concepts form an active duality: two parts of the same thing. In order to act, social actors must use known rules and resources. Giddens conceptualizes rules (normative rules and codes of signification) and resources (authoritative resources and allocative resources) as structural elements, which means that actors constitute or enact structure through their agency. Giddens applies this concept to the issue of time-space distanciation. Thus, in structuration, local interactions are linked with distant others through the use of known rules and resources. This way of seeing things avoids the reification of agency or structure, places the structuring (patterning) elements within the observable interaction, and encourages a historical sociology. The latter is important for Giddens as he explains the ways through which modern society stretches out time and space, or links local interactions with distant ones, and allows him to explicate some of the unique features of modernity.

Subversion: Subversion is a critical concept closely associated with the work of Judith Butler. Subversion is based on the insight that there is a gap between the norms regulating sexuality and the actual enactment. The gap creates the conceptual and cultural space to critique the claim that sex and sexuality make to naturalness. Intentionally acting outside the norms highlights this gap which in turn subverts the claims. Subversion deconstructs sex and sexuality.

Symbolic capital: Symbolic capital is a theoretical concept from Pierre Bourdieu's theory of class replication and refers to socially legitimated symbolic power of definition. Bourdieu argues that social groups and status positions exist empirically and symbolically; but it is the symbolic that gives groups and positions meaning and legitimacy. This power of definition is thus an important factor in creating the social world. Symbolic capital varies by social credentials, which generally come through education and political office.

Symbolic exchange: Symbolic exchange is an idea from Jean Baudrillard's theory of postmodernism that he uses as a comparison point for the pure sign-value of post-modern culture. In more traditional societies, when communication was closely tied to human interaction in social groups, symbols carried meaning. The symbols that people used arose from and represented real-life concerns and experiences. In contrast, much of postmodern culture has been created for or trivialized by mass media and advertising. These signs, rather than symbols, do not and cannot represent any kind of real social existence. Thus, cultural signs in postmodernity carry no meaning, are free-floating (released from all social context and linguistic structure), and are simply used by mass media and people in endless fields of play. *See simulacrum and hyperreality.*

Symbolic violence: Symbolic violence is a theoretical concept from Pierre Bourdieu's theory of class replication that refers to the self-sanctioning that occurs in linguistic markets.

Time-space distanciation: Time-space distanciation is a theoretical concept from Anthony Giddens' structuration approach. This concept reformulates the problem of social order by focusing on the stretching out of time and space rather than the patterning of behaviors. Generally speaking, concentrating on how behaviors are patterned has resulted in an emphasis on either structure or agency. Giddens sees this distinction as a false dualism; and focusing on time-space distanciation avoids this issue. Specifically, time-space distanciation refers to the process through which local social interactions are linked to distant ones either through time (as in future or past interactions) or geographic space (as in an interaction in New York City with one in Los Angeles), thus ordering society. *See structuration theory.*

World-systems theory: World-systems theory is a critical theoretical perspective that is most closely associated with Immanuel Wallerstein. The perspective employs three unique concepts: globality (conceptualizing the world as linked through a single system), historicity (history defined in terms of structural cycles rather than events or people), and unidisciplinarity (denial of multiple disciplines, such as sociology and political science, with knowledge and research conceptualized holistically). Wallerstein conceptualizes two world-systems: world-empires and world-economies. In world-empires connections among countries are created through military dominance and tribute; in world-economies nations are linked through the capitalistic division of labor, accumulation, and exploitation. Each world-system is characterized by a core country with periphery dependent countries and by dialectical cycles that create the conditions for the system's demise.

References

Addams, J. (2002). *Democracy and social ethics.* Chicago: University of Chicago Press. (Original work published 1902)

Alexander, J., & Smith, P. (2001). The strong program in cultural theory: Elements of a structural hermeneutics. In Jonathan H. Turner (Ed.), *Handbook of sociological theory.* New York: Kluwer Academic/Plenum Publishers.

Alexander, J. C. (1985). Introduction. In J. C. Alexander (Ed.), *Neofunctionalism.* Beverly Hills, CA: Sage.

Allan, K., & Turner, J. H. (2000). A formalization of postmodern theory. *Sociological Perspectives, 43*(3), 363–385.

Al Qaeda training manual. Retrieved October 27, 2004, from http://www.usdoj.gov/ag/trainingmanual.htm

Alway, J. (1995). *Critical theory and political possibilities: Conceptions of emancipatory politics in the works of Horkheimer, Adorno, Marcuse, and Habermas.* Westport, CT: Greenwood Press.

Anderson, P. (1998). *The origins of postmodernity.* London: Verso.

Bandura, A. (1977). *Social learning theory.* New York: General Learning Press.

Baudrillard, J. (1975). *The mirror of production* (M. Poster, Trans.). St. Louis, MO: Telos Press. (Original work published 1973)

Baudrillard, J. (1981). *For a critique of the political economy of the sign.* St. Louis, MO: Telos Press. (Original work published 1972)

Baudrillard, J. (1987). When Bataille attacked the metaphysical principle of economy. *Canadian Journal of Political and Social Theory, 11,* 57–62.

Baudrillard, J. (1990). *Seduction.* New York: St. Martin's Press.

Baudrillard, J. (1993a). *Baudrillard live: Selected interviews* (M. Gane, Ed.). New York: Routledge.

Baudrillard, J. (1993b). *Symbolic exchange and death* (I. H. Grant, Trans.). Newbury Park, CA: Sage. (Original work published 1976)

Baudrillard, J. (1994). *Simulacra and simulation* (S. F. Blaser, Trans.). Ann Arbor: The University of Michigan Press. (Original work published 1981)

Baudrillard, J. (1995). *The Gulf War did not take place* (P. Patton, Trans.). Bloomington: Indiana University Press.

Baudrillard, J. (1998). *The consumer society: Myths and structures* (C. Turner, Trans.). London: Sage. (Original work published 1970)

Bauman, Z. (1992). *Imitations of postmodernity.* New York: Routledge.

Benford, R. D., & Snow, D. A. (2000). Framing processes and social movements: An overview and assessment. *Annual Review of Sociology, 26,* 611–639.

Bentham, J. (1996). *An introduction to the principles of morals and legislation* (J. H. Burns & H. L. A. Hart, Eds.). New York: Oxford University Press. (Original work published 1789)

Bernauer, J. W., & Mahon, M. (1994). The ethics of Michel Foucault. In G. Gutting (Ed.), *The Cambridge companion to Foucault.* Cambridge, UK: Cambridge University Press.

Bernstein, J. M. (1991). Introduction. In T. Adorno, *Culture industry*. London: Routledge.

Blau, P. M. (1968). Social exchange. In David L. Sills (Ed.), *International encyclopedia of the social sciences*. New York: Macmillan.

Blau, P. M. (1994). *Structural contexts of opportunities*. Chicago: University of Chicago Press.

Blau, P. M. (2002). Macrostructural theory. In Jonathan H. Turner (Ed.), *Handbook of sociological theory*. New York: Kluwer Academic/Plenum.

Blau, P. M. (2003). *Exchange and power in social life*. New Brunswick, NJ: Transaction.

Blau, P. M., & Meyer, M. W. (1987). *Bureaucracy in modern society* (3rd ed.). New York: McGraw-Hill.

Blumer, H. (1969). *Symbolic interactionism: Perspective and method*. Berkeley: University of California Press.

Blumer, H. (1990). *Industrialization as an agent of social change: A critical analysis*. Chicago: Aldine.

Bourdieu, P. (1984). *Distinction: A social critique of the judgment of taste* (R. Nice, Trans.). Cambridge, MA: Harvard University Press. (Original work published 1979)

Bourdieu, P. (1985). The genesis of the concepts of *habitus* and of *field*. *Sociocriticism, 2,* 11–29.

Bourdieu, P. (1989). Social space and symbolic power. *Sociological Theory, 7*(1), 14–25.

Bourdieu, P. (1990). *The logic of practice* (R. Nice, Trans.). Stanford, CA: Stanford University Press. (Original work published 1980)

Bourdieu, P. (1991). *Language and symbolic power* (J. B. Thompson, Ed.; G. Raymond & M. Adamson, Trans.). Cambridge, MA: Harvard University Press.

Bourdieu, P. (1993). *Outline of a theory of practice* (R. Nice, Trans.). Cambridge, UK: Cambridge University Press. (Original work published 1972)

Bourdieu, P., & Wacquant, L. J. D. (1992). *An invitation to reflexive sociology*. Chicago: University of Chicago Press.

Boyne, R. (1990). *Foucault and Derrida: The other side of reason*. London: Routledge.

Braithwaite, R. B. (1953). *Scientific explanation: A study of the function of theory, probability and law in science. Based upon the Tarner lectures, 1946*. Cambridge, UK: Cambridge University Press.

Braudel, F. (1981–1984). *Civilization and capitalism, 15th to 18 century, 3 vols*. New York: Harper & Row.

Business and Professional Women's Foundation. (2004). *101 facts on the status of women*. Retrieved May 9, 2005, from http://www.bpwusa.org/files/public/101FactsOct07.pdf

Butler, J. (1993). *Bodies that matter: On the discursive limits of "sex."* New York: Routledge.

Butler, J. (1997). *The psychic life of power: Theories in subjection*. Stanford, CA: Stanford University Press.

Calhoun, C. (2003). Pierre Bourdieu. In G. Ritzer (Ed.), *The Blackwell companion to major contemporary social theorists*. Malden, MA: Blackwell.

Cassirer, E. (1944). *An essay on man*. New Haven, CT: Yale University Press.

Castells, M. (2000a). *The end of millennium* (2nd ed.). Malden, MA: Blackwell.

Castells, M. (2000b). *The rise of the network society* (2nd ed.). Malden, MA: Blackwell.

Castells, M. (2004). *The power of identity* (2nd ed.). Malden, MA: Blackwell.

Chafetz, J. S. (1990). *Gender equity: An integrated theory of stability and change*. Newbury Park, CA: Sage.

Charon, J. M. (2001). *Symbolic interactionism: An introduction, an interpretation, an integration* (7th ed.). Upper Saddle River, NJ: Prentice Hall.

Chodorow, N. (1978). *The reproduction of mothering: Psychoanalysis and the sociology of gender*. Berkeley: University of California Press.

Cohen, A., Baumohl, B., Buia, C., Roston, E., Ressner, J., & Thompson, M. (2001, January 8). This time it's different. *Time, 157*(1), 18–22.

Coleman, J. S. (1990). *Foundations of social theory.* Cambridge, MA: Harvard University Press.

Collins, P. H. (2000). *Black feminist thought: Knowledge, consciousness, and the politics of empowerment* (2nd ed.). New York: Routledge.

Collins, R. (1975). *Conflict sociology.* New York: Academic Press.

Collins, R. (1986). Is 1980s sociology in the doldrums? *American Journal of Sociology, 91,* 1336–1355.

Collins, R. (1987). Interaction ritual chains, power and property: The micro-macro connection as an empirically based theoretical problem. In J. C. Alexander, B. Giesen, R. Münch, & N. J. Smelser (Eds.), *The micro-macro link.* Berkeley: University of California Press.

Collins, R. (1988). *Theoretical sociology.* San Diego, CA: Harcourt Brace Jovanovich.

Collins, R. (1993). Emotional energy as the common denominator of rational action. *Rationality and Society, 5,* 203–230.

Collins, R. (2004). *Interaction ritual chains.* Princeton, NJ: Princeton University Press.

Condon, W. S., & Ogston, W. D. (1971). Speech and body motion synchrony of the speaker-hearer. In D. D. Horton & J. J. Jenkins (Eds.), *Perception of language.* Columbus, OH: Merrill.

Cook, K. (1978). Power, equity and commitment in exchange networks. *American Journal of Sociology, 43,* 712–739.

Cooley, C. H. (1998). *On self and social organization* (H. Schubert, Ed.). Chicago: University of Chicago Press.

Coser, L. A. (1977). *Masters of sociological thought: Ideas in historical and social context.* Prospect Heights, IL: Waveland Press.

Dahrendorf, R. (1959). *Class and class conflict in industrial society.* Stanford, CA: Stanford University Press. (Original work published 1957)

Danto, A. C. (1990). The hyper-intellectual. *New Republic, 203*(11–12), 44–48.

Davidson, A. I. (1994). Ethics as ascetics: Foucault, the history of ethics, and ancient thought. In G. Gutting (Ed.), *The Cambridge companion to Foucault.* Cambridge, UK: Cambridge University Press.

Davis, A. (2007). *Angela Y. Davis commencement speech.* Retrieved November 12, 2009, from http://74.125.155.132/u/grinnell?q=cache:bbiBuZPCT2EJ:www.grinnell.edu/car/confops/commencement/archive/2007/davis/+angela+davis&cd=5&hl=en&ct=clnk&gl=us&ie=UTF-8

Derksen, L. (2010). Micro/macro translations: The production of new social structures in the case of DNA profiling. *Sociological Inquiry, 80*(2).

Derrida, J. (1978). *Writing and difference* (A. Bass, Trans.). Chicago: University of Chicago Press. (Original work published 1967)

Dicker, R., & Piepmeier, A. (2006). Catching a wave: Reclaiming feminism for the 21st century. In L. Heywood (Ed.), *The women's movement today: An encyclopedia of third-wave feminism.* Westport, CT: Greenwood Press.

Drake, J. (1997). Review essay: Third Wave feminisms. *Feminist Studies, 23*(1), 97–108.

Dreyfus, H. L., & Rabinow, P. (1982). *Michel Foucault: Beyond structuralism and hermeneutics.* Brighton, UK: Harvester Press.

Du Bois, W. E. B. (1996a). The souls of black folk. In E. J. Sundquist (Ed.), *The Oxford W. E. B. Du Bois reader.* New York: Oxford. (Original work published 1903)

Du Bois, W. E. B. (1996b). Darkwater. In E. J. Sundquist (Ed.), *The Oxford W. E. B. Du Bois reader.* New York: Oxford. (Original work published 1920)

Durkheim, É. (1938). *The rules of sociological method* (G. E. G. Catlin, Ed.; S. A. Solovay & J. H. Mueller, Trans.). Glencoe, IL: The Free Press. (Original work published 1895)

Durkheim, É. (1984). *The division of labor in society* (W. D. Halls, Trans.). New York: The Free Press. (Original work published 1893)

Durkheim, É. (1995). *The elementary forms of the religious life* (K. E. Fields, Trans.). New York: The Free Press. (Original work published 1912)

Ellis, D. P. (1971). The Hobbesian problem of order: A critical appraisal of the normative solution. *American Sociological Review, 36,* 692–703.

Emerson, R. (1972). Exchange theory part I: A psychological basis for social exchange; Exchange theory Part II: Exchange relationships and network structures. In J. Berger, M. Zelditch, & B. Anderson (Eds.), *Sociological theories in progress.* New York: Houghton Mifflin.

Engels, F. (1978). The origin of the family, private property, and the state. In R. C. Tucker (Ed.), *The Marx-Engels reader.* New York: Norton. (Original work published 1884)

Erlewine, M. (1999). Foreword. In M. Erlewine, V. Bogdanov, C. Woodstra, C. Doda, & S. T. Erlewine (Eds.), *All music guide to the blues: The experts' guide to the BEST BLUES recordings.* San Francisco: Backbeat.

Fanon, F. (1967). *Black skins, white masks* (C. L. Markmann, Trans.). New York: Grove Press. (Original work published 1952)

Fanon, F. (2004). *The wretched of the earth* (R. Philcox, Trans.). New York: Grove Press. (Original work published 1961)

Fausto-Sterling, A. (1993, March–April). The five sexes: Why male and female are not enough. *The Sciences, 33*(2).

Fine, G. A., & Manning, P. (2003). Erving Goffman. In G. Ritzer (Ed.), *The Blackwell companion to major contemporary social theorists.* (pp. 34–62). Oxford, UK: Blackwell.

Fisher, S. (1973). *Body consciousness.* London: Calder & Boyars.

Flash mob. (n.d.). *Wikipedia, the free encyclopedia.* Retrieved June 8, 2005, from http://en.wikipedia.org/wiki/Flash_mob

Florence, M. (1994). Foucault, Michel, 1926–. In G. Gutting (Ed.), *The Cambridge companion to Foucault.* Cambridge, UK: Cambridge University Press.

Flyvbjerg, B. (2001). *Making social science matter: Why social inquiry fails and how it can succeed again.* Cambridge, UK: Cambridge University Press.

Foucault, M. (1982). The subject and power. In H. L. Dreyfus & P. Rabinow, *Michel Foucault: Beyond structuralism and hermeneutics.* Brighton, UK: Harvester Press.

Foucault, M. (1984). Nietzsche, genealogy, history. In P. Rabinow (Ed.), *The Foucault reader.* New York: Pantheon.

Foucault, M. (1988). *The history of sexuality, volume 3: The care of the self* (R. Hurley, Trans.). New York: Vintage. (Original work published 1984)

Foucault, M. (1990a). *The history of sexuality, volume I: An introduction* (R. Hurley, Trans.). New York: Vintage. (Original work published 1976)

Foucault, M. (1990b). *The history of sexuality, volume 2: The use of pleasure* (R. Hurley, Trans.). New York: Vintage. (Original work published 1984)

Foucault, M. (1994a). *The birth of the clinic: An archaeology of medical perception* (A. M. Sheridan Smith, Trans.). New York: Vintage Books. (Original work published 1963)

Foucault, M. (1994b). *The order of things: An archaeology of the human sciences.* New York: Vintage. (Original work published 1966)

Foucault, M. (1995). *Discipline and punish: The birth of the prison* (A. Sheridan, Trans.). New York: Vintage. (Original work published 1975)

Foucault, M. (1997). A preface to transgression. In D. F. Bouchard (Ed.), *Language, countermemory, practice: Selected essays and interviews* (D. F. Bouchard & S. Simon, Trans.). New York: Cornell University Press.

Fromm, E. (1955). *The sane society.* New York: Henry Holt.

Garfinkel, H. (1967). *Studies in ethnomethodology.* Cambridge, UK: Polity Press.

Garfinkel, H. (1974). On the origins of the term "ethnomethodology." In R. Turner (Ed.), *Ethnomethodology: Selected readings.* Harmondsworth, UK: Penguin Education.

Garfinkel, H. (1996). Ethnomethodology's program. *Social Psychology Quarterly, 59,* 5–21.

Gergen, K. J. (1991). *Saturated self: Dilemmas of identity in contemporary life.* New York: Basic Books.

Giddens, A. (1986). *The constitution of society.* Berkeley: University of California Press.

Giddens, A. (1990). *The consequences of modernity.* Stanford, CA: Stanford University Press.

Giddens, A. (1991). *Modernity and self-identity: Self and society in the late modern age.* Stanford, CA: Stanford University Press.

Giddens, A. (1992). *The transformation of intimacy: Sexuality, love and eroticism in modern societies.* Stanford, CA: Stanford University Press.

Global Exchange. (1998). *Wages and living expenses for Nike workers in Indonesia, September 1998.* Retrieved December 22, 2004, from http://www.globalexchange.org/campaigns/sweatshops/nike/IndonesiaWages.html.pf

Goffman, E. (1959). *The presentation of self in everyday life.* Garden City, NY: Anchor.

Goffman, E. (1961). *Asylums: Essays on the social situation of mental patients and other inmates.* Garden City, NY: Anchor Books.

Goffman, E. (1963a). *Stigma.* New York: Touchstone.

Goffman, E. (1963b). *Behavior in public places.* New York: The Free Press.

Goffman, E. (1967). *Interaction ritual.* New York: Pantheon.

Goffman, E. (1974). *Frame analysis.* New York: Harper & Row.

Goffman, E. (1977). The arrangement between the sexes. *Theory and Society, 4,* 301–331.

Goffman, E. (1981). *Forms of talk.* Philadelphia: University of Pennsylvania Press.

Goffman, E. (1983). The interaction order. *American Sociological Review, 48,* 1–17.

Gramsci, A. (1971). *Selections from the prison notebooks.* London: Lawrence & Heinemann. (Original work published 1928)

Habermas, J. (1984). *The theory of communicative action, vol. 1: Reason and the rationalization of society* (T. McCarthy, Trans.). Boston: Beacon. (Original work published 1981)

Habermas, J. (1987). *The theory of communicative action, vol. 2: Lifeworld and system: A critique of functionalist reason* (T. McCarthy, Trans.). Boston: Beacon. (Original work published 1981)

Hall, S. (1996). The question of cultural identity. In S. Hall, D. Held, D. Hubert, & K. Thompson (Eds.), *Modernity: An introduction to modern societies.* Malden, MA: Blackwell.

Handel, M. J. (2002). *Sociology of organizations: Classic, contemporary and critical readings.* Thousand Oaks, CA: Sage.

Herdt, G. (Ed.) (1996). *Third sex, third gender: Beyond sexual dimorphism in culture and history.* Boston: Zone Books.

Heritage, J. (1984). *Garfinkel and ethnomethodology.* Cambridge, UK: Polity Press.

Homans, G. C. (1950). *Human group.* New York: Harcourt Brace Jovanovich.

Homans, G. C. (1958). Social behavior as exchange. *The American Journal of Sociology, 63*(5), 597–606.

Homans, G. C. (1961). *Social behavior: Its elementary forms.* New York: Harcourt, Brace & World.

Homans, G. C. (1964). Bringing men back in. *American sociological review, 29*(5), 809–818.

Homans, G. C. (1987). Behaviourism and after. In A. Giddens & J. Turner (Eds.), *Social theory today.* Stanford, CA: Stanford University Press.

hooks, b. (1989). *Talking back: Thinking feminist, thinking black.* Boston: South End Press.

Horkheimer, M. (2004). *Eclipse of reason.* London: Continuum.

Horkheimer, M., & Adorno, T. W. (1972). *Dialectic of enlightenment.* New York: Herder & Herde.

Income, Poverty, and Health Insurance Coverage in the United States (2008). Retrieved November 12, 2009, from http://www.census.gov/prod/2009pubs/p60-236.pdf

Jameson, F. (1984). Postmodernism, or the cultural logic of late capitalism. *New Left Review, 146,* 53–92.

Johnson, A. G. (2000). *The Blackwell dictionary of sociology: A user's guide to sociological language* (2nd ed.). Malden, MA: Blackwell.

Kagan, H. L. (2008, March). Why did my patient develop a taste for paper? *Discover.*

Kanter, R. M. (1977). *Men and women of the corporation.* New York: Basic Books.

Kellner, D. (1989). *Jean Baudrillard: From Marxism to postmodernism and beyond.* Stanford, CA: Stanford University Press.

Kellner, D. (2003). Jean Baudrillard. In G. Ritzer (Ed.), *The Blackwell companion to major contemporary social theorists.* Malden, MA: Blackwell.

Keynes, J. M. (1936). *The general theory of employment, interest and money.* New York: Harcourt, Brace.

Kozol, J. (1991). *Savage inequalities: Children in America's schools.* New York: Crown.

Kuhn, M. H. (1964a). Major trends in symbolic interaction theory in the past twenty-five years. *Sociological Quarterly, 5,* 61–84.

Kuhn, M. H. (1964b). The reference group reconsidered. *Sociological Quarterly, 5,* 5–24.

Lakatos, I. (1970). Falsification and the methodology of scientific research programmes. In I. Lakatos & A. Musgrave (Eds.), *Criticism and the growth of knowledge.* Cambridge, UK: Cambridge University Press.

Legal Information Institute. *White collar crime: An overview.* Retrieved June 30, 2005, from http://www.law.cornell.edu/topics/white_collar.html

Lemert, C. (1990). The uses of French structuralisms in sociology. In G. Ritzer (Ed.), *Frontiers of social theory: The new syntheses.* New York: Columbia University Press.

Lemert, C. (1997). Goffman. In C. Lemert & A. Branaman (Eds.), *The Goffman reader* (pp. ix–xliii). Malden, MA: Blackwell.

Lemert, C. (2005). *Social things: An introduction to the sociological life* (3rd ed.). Lanham, MD: Rowman & Littlefield.

Lengermann, P. M., & Niegrugge-Brantley, J. (1988). *The women founders: Sociology and social theory 1930–1930.* Boston: McGraw-Hill.

Lévi-Strauss, C. (1963). *Structural anthropology.* New York: Basic Books.

Lidz, V. (2000). *Talcott Parsons.* In G. Ritzer (Ed.), *The Blackwell Companion to Major Social Theorists.* Malden, MA: Blackwell

Lilley, S. J., & Platt, G. M. (1994). Correspondents' images of Martin Luther King, Jr: An interpretive theory of movement leadership. In T. R. Sarbin & J. I. Kitsuse (Eds.), *Constructing the social.* Thousand Oaks, CA: Sage.

Lipset, S. M. (1962). Harriet Martineau's America. In H. Martineau, *Society in America.* New Brunswick, NJ: Transaction Publishers.

Lorber, J. (2005). *Breaking the bowls: Degendering and feminist change.* London: W. W. Norton.

Lukács, G. (1971). *History and class consciousness: Studies in Marxist dialectics* (R. Livingstone, Trans.). London: Merlin Press. (Original work published 1923)

Lyman, S. M., & Vidich, A. J. (2000). *Selected works of Herbert Blumer: A public philosophy for mass society.* Urbana: University of Illinois Press.

Lynch, M. (1997). *Scientific practice and ordinary action: Ethnomethodology and social studies of science.* Cambridge, UK: Cambridge University Press.

Macionis, J. J. (2005). *Sociology* (10th ed.). Upper Saddle River, NJ: Prentice Hall.

Mahar, C., Harker, R., & Wilkes, C. (1990). The basic theoretical position. In R. Harker, C. Mahar, & C. Wilkes (Eds.), *An introduction to the work of Pierre Bourdieu.* London: Macmillan.

Marshall, G. (Ed.). (1998). *A dictionary of sociology* (2nd ed.). New York: Oxford University Press.

Martin, E. (2007). *Jeff Foxworthy's passionate, show-stopping speech at the CMT awards.* Retrieved September 3, 2009, from http://www.freerepublic.com/focus/f-news/1821089/posts

Martineau, H. (2003). *How to observe morals and manners.* New Brunswick, NJ: Transaction Press. (Original work published 1838)

Martineau, H. (2005). *Society in America* (S. M. Lipset, Ed.). New Brunswick, NJ: Transaction Publishers. (Original work published 1837)

Marx, K. (1978a). Economic and philosophic manuscripts of 1844. In R. C. Tucker (Ed.), *The Marx-Engels reader.* New York: W.W. Norton. (Original work published 1844)

Marx, K. (1978b). Manifest of the Communist Party. In R. C. Tucker (Ed.), *The Marx-Engels reader.* New York: W. W. Norton. (Original work published 1848)

Marx, K. (1978c). The German ideology. In R. C. Tucker (Ed.), *The Marx-Engels reader.* New York: W.W. Norton. (Original work published 1832)

Marx, K. (1995). Economic and philosophic manuscripts of 1844. In E. Fromm (Trans.), *Marx's concept of man.* New York: Continuum. (Original work published 1932)

Marx, K., & Engels, F. (1978). Manifesto of the Communist Party. In R. C. Tucker (Ed.), *The Marx-Engels reader.* New York: Norton. (Original work published 1848)

McCready, S. (Ed.). (2001). *The discovery of time.* Naperville, IL: Sourcebooks.

McGrew, A. (1996). A global society? In S. Hall, D. Held, D. Hubert, & K. Thompson (Eds.), *Modernity: An introduction to modern societies.* Malden, MA: Blackwell.

Mead, G. H. (1934). *Mind, self, and society: From the standpoint of a social behaviorist* (C. W. Morris, Ed.). Chicago: University of Chicago Press.

Mehan, H., & Wood, H. (1975). *The reality of ethnomethodology.* New York: Wiley.

Menand, L. (2001). *The metaphysical club: A story of ideas in America.* New York: Farrar, Straus & Giroux.

Merriam-Webster. (2002). *Webster's Third New International Dictionary, Unabridged.* Retrieved November 12, 2009, from http://unabridged.merriam-webster.com

Milgram, S. (1974). *Obedience to authority: An experimental view.* New York: Harper & Row.

Mills, C. W. (1956). *The power elite.* New York: Oxford University Press.

Morris, C. W. (1962). Introduction: George H. Mead as social psychologist and social philosopher. In C. W. Morris (Ed.), *Mind, self, and society from the standpoint of a social behaviorist.* Chicago: University of Chicago Press.

National Academy of Sciences. (1995). *National science education standards.* Retrieved August 20, 2004, from http://www.nap.edu/readingroom/books/nses/html/ action.html

National Urban League. (2009). *State of black America.* Retrieved November 12, 2009, from http://www.nul.org/newsroom/publications/soba

Nietzsche, F. (1968). On the geneology of morals. In W. Kaufmann (Ed. & Trans.), *Basic writings of Nietzsche.* New York: The Modern Library. (Original work published 1887)

Nöth, W. (1995). *Handbook of semiotics.* Bloomington: Indiana University Press. (Original work published 1985)

Outhwaite, W. (2003). Jürgen Habermas. In G. Ritzer (Ed.), *The Blackwell companion to major contemporary social theorists.* Malden, MA: Blackwell.

Parsons, T. (1949). *The structure of social action: A study in social theory with special reference to a group of recent European writers* (2nd ed.). New York: The Free Press.

Parsons, T. (1951). *The social system.* Glencoe, IL: Free Press.

Parsons, T. (1961). Culture and the social system. In T. Parsons (Ed.), *Theories of society: Foundations of modern sociological theory* (pp. 963–993). New York: The Free Press.

Parsons, T. (1966). *Societies: Evolutionary and comparative perspectives.* Englewood Cliffs, NJ: Prentice Hall.

Patterson, T. E. (2002): *The vanishing voter: Public involvement in an age of uncertainty.* New York: Alfred A. Knopf.

Pianin, E. (2001, July 10). Superfund cleanup effort shows results, study reports. *Washington Post,* p. A19.

Plato. (1993). *The last days of Socrates* (H. Tredennick & H. Tarrant, Trans.). London: Penguin.

Plummer, K. (1998). Herbert Blumer. In Rob Stones (Ed.), *Key sociological thinkers*. New York: New York University Press.

Pollner, M. (1991). Left of ethnomethodology: The rise and decline of radical reflexivity. *American Sociological Review, 56*, 370–380.

Popper, K. (1959). *The logic of scientific discovery*. New York: Basic Books.

Rabinow, P. (1984). Introduction. In P. Rabinow (Ed.), *The Foucault reader*. New York: Pantheon.

Rawls, A. (2003). Harold Garfinkel. In G. Ritzer (Ed.), *The Blackwell companion to major contemporary social theorists*. Malden, MA: Blackwell.

Ray, L. (1990). Introduction: The formation of a critical theory of society. In L. Ray (Ed.), *Critical sociology*. Hants, UK: Edward Elgar.

Redford, G., & Kinosian, J. (2008). Your brain on exercise: How breaking a sweat can make you smarter. *AARP: The Magazine, 51*(2A), 26.

Research working group on cyclical rhythms and secular trends. (1979, Spring). Cyclical rhythms and secular trends of the capitalists' world-economy: Some premises, hypotheses, and questions. *Review, 2*, 483–500.

Roy, W. G. (2001). *Making societies*. Thousand Oaks, CA: Pine Forge.

Sacks, H. (1995). *Lectures on conversation*. Malden, MA. Wiley-Blackwell.

Sanderson, S. K. (2005). Reforming theoretical work in sociology: A modest proposal. *Perspectives, 28*(2), 1–4.

Sassen, S. (2007). *A sociology of globalization*. New York: W. W. Norton & Company.

Saussure, F. de. (1986). *Course in general linguistics* (C. Bally, A. Sechehaye, & A. Riedlinger, Eds.; R. Harris, Trans.). Chicago: Open Court. (Original work published 1916)

Schutz, A. (1967). *The phenomenology of the social world* (G. Walsh & F. Lehnert, Trans.). Evanston, IL: Northwestern University Press.

Shilling, C. (1993). *The body and social theory*. Newbury Park, CA: Sage.

Simmel, G. (1950). *The sociology of Georg Simmel* (K. H. Wolff, Ed. & Trans.). Glencoe, IL: The Free Press.

Simmel, G. (1971). *Georg Simmel: On individuality and social forms* (D. N. Levine, Ed.). Chicago: University of Chicago Press.

Smith, A. (1937). *An inquiry into the nature and causes of the wealth of nations*. New York: The Modern Library. (Original work published 1776)

Smith, D. E. (1987). *The everyday world as problematic: A feminist sociology*. Boston: Northeastern University Press.

Smith, D. E. (1990). *The conceptual practices of power: A feminist sociology of knowledge*. Boston: Northeastern University Press.

Smith, D. E. (1992). Sociology from women's experience: A reaffirmation. *Sociological Theory, 11*, 1.

Smith, D. E. (2005). *Institutional ethnography: A sociology for people*. Lanham, MD: AltaMira Press.

Snow, D., & Anderson, L. (1993). *Down on their luck: A study of homeless street people*. Berkeley: University of California Press.

Spence, J., & Helmreich, R. (1978). *Masculinity and femininity*. Austin: University of Texas Press.

Statistical abstract of the United States. (2002). *The national data book*. Washington, DC: U.S. Department of Commerce.

Stiglitz, J. E. (2003). *Globalization and its discontents*. New York: Norton.

Stryker, S. (2003). *Symbolic interactionism*. Menlo Park, CA: Benjamin/Cummings.

Survivor show concept. (n.d.). Retrieved July 27, 2005, from http://www.cbs.com/primetime/survivor/show/concept.shtml

Sydmob. (n.d.). Retrieved June 8, 2005, from http://www.sydmob.com

Tocqueville, A. (1969). *Democracy in America* (J. P. Mayer, Ed.; G. Lawrence, Trans.). New York: Harper Perennial. (Original work published 1835)

Turner, J. (1991). *The structure of sociological theory* (5th ed.). Belmont, CA: Wadsworth.

Turner, J. H. (1988). *A theory of social interaction*. Stanford, CA: Stanford University Press.

Turner, J. H. (1993). *Classical sociological theory: A positivist's perspective*. Chicago: Nelson-Hall.

Turner, V. W. (1969). *The ritual process: Structure and anti-structure*. Chicago: Aldine.

Ulmer, J. T., & Wilson, M. S. (2003). The potential contributions of quantitative research to symbolic interactionism. *Symbolic Interaction, 26*(4), 531–552.

Urry, J. (2006). Society. In J. Scott (Ed.), *Sociology: The key concepts*. London: Routledge.

U.S. Census Bureau. (n.d.). *Historical income tables–people*. Retrieved June 27, 2005, from http://www.census.gov/hhes/www/income/histinc/incpertoc.html

U.S. Department of Justice. (2008). Prison statistics. Retrieved November 12, 2009, from http://www.ojp.usdoj.gov/bjs/prisons.htm

Veblen, T. (1899). *The theory of the leisure class: An economic study of institutions*. New York: Macmillan.

Vitousek, P., Ehrlich, P. R., Ehrlich, A. H., & Matson, P. (1986). Human appropriation of the products of photosynthesis. *BioScience, 34*(6).

Wacquant, L. J. D. (1992). Preface. In P. Bourdieu & L. J. D. Wacquant, *An invitation to reflexive sociology*. Chicago: University of Chicago Press.

Wallerstein, I. (1974). *The modern world—system I: Capitalist agriculture and the origins of the European world-economy in the sixteenth century*. New York: Academic Press.

Wallerstein, I. (1980). *The modern world—system II: Mercantilism and the consolidation of the European world-economy, 1600–1750*. New York: Academic Press.

Wallerstein, I. (1989). *The modern world—system III: The second era of great expansion of the capitalist world economy, 1730–1840*. New York: Academic Press.

Wallerstein, I. (1995). The end of what modernity? *Theory and Society, 24*, 471–488.

Wallerstein, I. (1999). *The end of the world as we know it: Social science for the twenty-first century*. Minneapolis: University of Minnesota Press.

Wallerstein, I. (2000). *The essential Wallerstein*. New York: The New Press.

Wallerstein, I. (2004). *World-systems analysis: An introduction*. Durham, NC: Duke University Press.

Weber, M. (1968). *Economy and society* (G. Roth, Trans., & C. Wittich, Eds.). New York: Bedminster. (Original work published 1922)

Weber, M. (1993). *The sociology of religion* (E. Fischoff, Trans.). Boston: Beacon Press. (Originally published 1922)

Weber, M. (2002). *The Protestant ethic and the spirit of capitalism* (S. Kalberg, Trans.). Los Angeles: Roxbury. (Original work published 1904–1905)

Webster's new universal unabridged dictionary (2nd ed.). (1983). New York: Simon & Schuster.

West, C. (1999). *The Cornel West reader*. New York: Basic Civitas.

West, C. (2000). Cornel West's opening remarks. Retrieved June 30, 2005, from http://www.essentialschools.org/lpt/ces_docs/87

West, C. (2001). *Race matters*. New York: Vintage. (Original work published 1993)

West, C. (2004). *Democracy matters: Winning the fight against imperialism*. New York: Penguin.

West, C., & Zimmerman, D. H. (1987). Doing gender. *Gender and Society, 1*, 125–151.

Wharton, A. S. (2004). *The sociology of gender: An introduction to theory and research*. Malden, MA: Blackwell.

Wiggershaus, R. (1995). *The Frankfurt School: Its history, theories, and political significance* (M. Robertson, Trans.). Cambridge: MIT Press. (Original work published 1986)

Williams, R. (1983). *Keywords: A vocabulary of culture and society* (Rev. ed.). New York: Oxford University Press.

Wilson, W. J. (1980). *The declining significance of race: Blacks and changing American institutions* (2nd ed.). Chicago: University of Chicago Press.

Wilson, W. J. (1996–1997). When work disappears. *Political science quarterly, 111*(4), 567–595.

Wilson, W. J. (1997). *When work disappears: The world of the new urban poor.* New York: Vintage.

Wright, E. O. (1978). *Class, crisis and the state.* London: New Left Books.

Zerubavel, E. (1993). *The fine line: Making distinctions in everyday life.* Chicago: University of Chicago Press.

Index

About the Author

Kenneth Allan received his PhD in sociology from the University of California, Riverside (1995), and is currently Associate Professor of Sociology at the University of North Carolina at Greensboro (UNCG). Before moving to UNCG, he directed the Teaching Assistant Development Program at the University of California, Riverside, and coedited *Training Teaching Assistants*, 2nd edition (1997), published by the American Sociological Association. In addition to teaching classical and contemporary theory at UNCG, Allan also regularly teaches graduate pedagogy courses and oversees the department's online iSchool program, which currently offers university-level courses to over 2,000 high school students per year. Allan's research areas include theory, culture, and the self. He has authored several other works in the area of theory, including *The Meaning of Culture: Moving the Postmodern Critique Forward, Explorations in Classical Sociological Theory: Seeing the Social World*, and *Contemporary Social and Sociological Theory: Visualizing Social Worlds*.